Against the Tide

This portrait of Harriet Keyserling by Susan Graber hangs in the Beaufort County Courthouse. Courtesy Beaufort County Clerk of Court.

AGAINST THE TIDE

One Woman's Political Struggle

Harriet Keyserling

Foreword by Richard W. Riley
New Preface by the Author

UNIVERSITY OF SOUTH CAROLINA PRESS

Cloth edition published by the University of South Carolina Press, 1998
Paperback edition published in Columbia, South Carolina, by the University of South Carolina Press, 2004

Publication of this paperback reprint was made possible in part by a grant from the Caroline McKissick Dial Fund, University Libraries, University of South Carolina.

Manufactured in the United States of America

08 07 06 05 04 5 4 3 2 1
Library of Congress Cataloging-in-Publication Data

Keyserling, Harriet, 1922–
Against the tide : one woman's political struggle / Harriet Keyserling ; foreword by Richard W. Riley ; new preface by the author.— Pbk. ed.
p. cm.
Includes index.
ISBN 1-57003-541-5 (alk. paper)
1. Keyserling, Harriet, 1922– 2. Women legislators—South Carolina—Biography. 3. Legislators—South Carolina—Biography. 4. South Carolina. General Assembly—Biography. 5. South Carolina—Politics and government—1951– I. Title.
F275.42.K49A3 2004
328'.092—dc22

2003024314

In loving memory of my parents,
Pauline and Isador Hirschfeld, and my brother, Lennie.

Contents

Illustrations

Illustrations

Foreword

The mid-1970s through the 1980s marked a very interesting transition for South Carolina and other Southern states. We were breaking loose from the "good ol' boy" control of state government and searching for direction into the "New South." I had the good fortune of being governor of South Carolina during that time and plunged headfirst into the deep water of change, of reform, of shifting emphasis from power politics to the power of ideas.

South Carolina was fortunate that Harriet Keyserling, a new kind of leader, came along during that era. She was willing to work hard to accomplish goals in which she believed. She was more given to quiet research, serious conversation, and careful organization—and less to the smoke-filled-room politics of much big talk and little listening.

It seems implausible that Harriet was elected to the South Carolina House when she was. She described herself as "a New York Jewish liberal" representing the small Southern town of Beaufort. Pat Conroy's novel *Beach Music* reflects many aspects of this charming community, which holds tightly to family ties and tradition and has deep feelings about its sensitive environment. So imagine the shock when Representative Keyserling walked onto the floor of the House to take her seat as the "Lady from Beaufort."

Against the Tide is not just the fascinating story of this strong, effective, and caring woman. It is the story of changing times in Southern politics. It is an "inside the ballpark" look at the players, issues, strategies, and frustrations of taking on the power structure and effecting change. One can read all the newspaper reports and political scientists' studies and not gain real insight into how decisions were made as the old order gave way to the new.

This was a time in South Carolina history when new approaches were examined to solve very old problems and when thoughtful leaders saw education as the only long-term answer. Harriet Keyserling was one of those responsible leaders willing to risk personal political security by fighting openly for public investment in improving schools and the lives of our children. She was a key member of the small group of legislators, called the Smurfs by the press, who felt that talk about education was not enough. (We had heard that rhetoric from politicians for years. Action was needed.) They believed that we must have high standards and accountability for our students and our schools; elevated teaching standards and professional recognition of teachers with competitive pay; early childhood education; and higher expectations for all our children, schools, parents, businesses, and communities. Everyone had to be involved and the improvements had to be financed. The Education Improvement Act, for which this small group fought through the briar patch of state government, was a comprehensive education reform package of more than sixty amendments to the 1985 appropriations bill; it was an exciting, uplifting movement for a better South Carolina.

Against the Tide contains Harriet Keyserling's thorough explanation of how "the tide" was turned in our state on the critical subject of education reform. No state legislature had a tougher fight than South Carolina. And, in the end, no lawmakers were held higher in the eyes of the people they represented. Harriet was no sunshine soldier in that fight. She was there, standing alongside other courageous public servants whom she credits in her book. I have never been more proud of my state than during that period. It was as if we were climbing out of the darkness and into the light. This record of how it all happened is invaluable.

Harriet Keyserling was also a recognized leader in protecting the environment. She was convinced that South Carolina had too long been the nuclear waste dumping ground of America. It was an honor to work with her to try to turn that tide, too. Her sensitive accounts of environmental issues, her tireless fight for the arts, and her commitment to improving the lives of children and women—all of these elements add up to an exciting account.

Harriet Keyserling gives us more here than factual occurrences. She describes the people and the unique groupings that developed in the legislature—the Crazy Caucus, the Fat and Uglies, the Young Turks. Her observations constitute an important reflection upon elected representatives and government work and how difficult it is to bring about a new direction.

Against the Tide is about Harriet Keyserling's role as an effective legislator and community leader, but it is also about the workings of state government: the hanging on of the "old guard" of Southern politics, the fresh air of change, and now the resurgence of "good ol' boy" politics, with old-line Democrats augmented by hard-line Republicans. The real struggle, as Harriet defines it, is to defend the public interest against the special interest.

As Harriet said in this very personal account, "There was so much to do and I wanted to do it all." She served us well and has done us a great favor by sharing with us this account of her public life.

Richard W. Riley

Preface

I knew that I was entering a minefield by writing *Against the Tide*. I also knew the effort was worth the risk because I had a message: Get Involved. From the moment we wake up in the morning until we go to bed at night, our lives are controlled in some way by government laws and regulations—local, state, or federal. If we care about the quality of our lives and the world we live in, we must take part in the effort to elect public officials who will support the laws we believe are needed for the world we want.

I did not know who would read my message. And I wasn't sure how to package this message to attract the audience I wanted—college students, women, and those inclined towards progressive politics but not yet involved. Because important issues drew me into politics, I concluded I should focus mainly on the issues to draw others in. I would add a very short personal history, a primer on the political process, and the political facts of life in South Carolina, as seen by me, an outsider. Daring to present an outsider's view of the South Carolina political process was the minefield I feared.

A few friends previewed the early chapters and told me I must write more than two pages about myself. The reader would want to know my background, my biases, my experiences, a few amusing stories. So, I took their advice and dropped my "private-person" persona.

Now that the book has been out for several years I know my audience. Some readers tell me they enjoyed the personal parts but haven't slogged through all the issues. They are intrigued that a liberal, middle-aged Jewish woman from New York could be elected to the South Carolina legislature and become a leader. Others tell me they are more interested in the issues. And a few cherished readers say they like it all.

I have had such interesting experiences and conversations with my readers—the college students whose classes I have spoken to, women whose leadership groups I've addressed, neighborhood book clubs, women legislators from many states around the country. I was amazed when a Hawaiian woman legislator told me that she read my book and passed her copy around to the other women in her legislature. One of them asked me for backup material and a copy of my bill mandating deposits on soft-drink and beer containers, a bill that I had worked on for years—unsuccessfully. Lo and behold, in 2002 Hawaii was the first state in sixteen years to succeed in passing such a "bottle bill" despite the powerful lobby against it. Did my material help? I don't know, but it's fun to imagine that some of my ideas and work may have helped that effort.

Usually one or two people will come up to me after I speak and tell me that I was inspirational and my personal struggles "motivated" them to do more politically. Their comments make me a little uncomfortable. I never liked "inspirational" or "motivational" speakers and always thought I wouldn't cross the street to hear one. However, to write a book with a message urging people to "Do Something" is an attempt to motivate or inspire, and the person who writes it can be labeled a motivator. I sheepishly admit now that to be "inspirational" is okay, at least when it's my cause.

I consider myself fortunate to have had so many different stages in my life—a stimulating childhood growing up in New York City; thirty years spent as a busy housewife, community volunteer and mother in the small town of Beaufort; and a twenty-year career in politics. The challenge of promoting my book opened a fourth stage—lecturer. Over the past three years I have spoken at nearly every college in South Carolina, to classes of students, at teachers' meetings, and to women's leadership groups. I have traveled the east coast, as far north as the Harvard Kennedy School of Politics, as far south as the University of Miami in Florida, and to places in between—Washington, D.C., North Carolina, Virginia, New York, Connecticut. What a learning experience that has been! Not only do I enjoy the lecturing, I also love being with so many people who like to talk politics as much as I do.

I have learned that a healthy majority of the people I meet with (and the national polls bear this out) really care about women's rights, protecting the environment, improving education, and putting the public interest before special interests in government. But it is sad to find that even in these special audiences, few think they are capable of doing anything that will make a difference.

There also seems to be a disconnect between what people say they want in the polls and how they vote. The gap may be a result of the discrepancies between politicians' campaign rhetoric and the policies they support once elected. Too many politicians these days, of both major parties, are packaged and marketed by handlers who study the polls and tailor the campaign to match the poll results; real positions are disguised with misleading labels and incomplete information. These politicians simply tell the people what they want to hear, having no intention of carrying out their platforms. It seems Machiavelli is alive and well in the modern world.

I keep asking myself why the public doesn't see through this deception. In defending himself against the charge of being a spoiler in the 2000 presidential election, Ralph Nader claimed there was no difference between Republicans and Democrats, so it didn't matter whether either Bush or Gore won. Many of the candidates, of both parties, sounded equally moderate in the images they presented of themselves. They all claimed concern for the environment and education. An observer who paid attention could see the masks peel off after the election. It is obvious now that Nader was wrong: the differences between the two parties are great now that campaign generalities have been replaced by the specifics of policies on the environment, reproductive rights, taxes, education, and judicial appointments. It is also obvious that the game of deception continues when you read the titles of the bills and policies advocated by the present Republican administration. Just as I fault the policies of George W. Bush, I also fault the Democrats for lacking the courage to speak out against them before the 2002 elections and for not presenting positive alternatives. Were they all, Republicans and Democrats, thinking more about the next election than the country's future?

I don't see enough discussion in the media about this gap between image and reality, between heart-warming themes and hard-line action. For instance, despite the Bush administration's constant labeling of themselves as "compassionate conservatives," recent editorials in the *New York Times,* aptly titled "The War against Women," and "The War on the Environment," spell out administration actions and policies that make the label "compassionate conservative" ludicrous. There is no compassion in its policies on women's health and reproductive choices, no conservatism in its rapacious environmental policies. The photo ops offer an illusion of caring for the working man. But the presidential pep talk to miners rescued from a mine collapse was soon followed by the weakening of safety regulations for mines in response to industry pressure; the president's praise of the troops in Iraq soon was followed by cuts in veterans' benefits and combat pay.

Recent legislation bears titles that proclaim exactly the opposite of what the bills actually promote: Clear Skies, Energy Security, Healthy Forests, No Child Left Behind. The Clear Skies Initiative actually weakens provisions of the Clean Air Act that require coal-burning power plants to install modern pollution controls when they build new plants or upgrade existing units. The administration also opposes regulations to reduce emissions of carbon dioxide in the air despite the president's campaign promise to reduce these emissions.

The president rejects concerns about global warming, going so far as to censor scientific studies from his own agencies. According to the *New York Times* (June 20, 2003), a recent report of the Environmental Protection Agency originally included a long section on the risks of climate change. The statement "Climate change has global consequences for human health and the environment" was replaced by some pablum about the complexities of the issues requiring further study. Gone also from the report was any mention that the 1990s are likely to have been the warmest decade in the last thousand years. The voices of industry—coal, oil, timber, automobiles—have far greater clout than the voices of environmental scientists. But with so much money being collected for the next election, why should we be surprised? Placing special interests and politics above science is not limited to the environment. Experts on the economy, health, and budget issues can testify to that.

The Energy Security Act calls for opening up the Arctic National Wildlife Refuge to oil drillers. Scientists argue that to open up the refuge will not decrease our dependency on Middle East oil. Rather than being the "quick fix" its advocates claim, it will take at least seven years to bring Arctic oil to the market and will supply less than 2% of the oil we consume each year. Only the oil producers will be more secure, not the country. Some scientists assert that an improvement of only three miles per gallon for automobiles would eliminate our need for all Persian Gulf oil. Yet the Republican Congress and administration oppose a measure to make SUVs and minivans conform to the same fuel economy standards as cars, standards that are achievable with current technology. Some Democrats, persuaded by automobile unions that jobs would be lost if such standards were adopted, gave the Republicans the votes they needed to defeat the fuel conservation bill. Despite the rhetoric about the need for energy conservation, billions are earmarked for incentives to produce more oil and gas energy, but only pennies for conservation and renewable energy sources.

Another dramatic example of the disparity between the titles of bills and reality is the Healthy Forests Initiative, which actually opens the door to unfettered commercial logging in our national forests. As Mary McGrory of the *Washington Post* (January 26, 2003) says, the administration "endorses clear-cutting to save our national forests from fiery death." The administration also proposes drilling for oil and gas and mining coal in our wonderful national forests. Efforts to save the forests were initiated, fought for, and won almost a hundred years ago by President Teddy Roosevelt, a Republican. Other presidents, Democrats and Republicans, expanded on his efforts by creating more national forests and parks as monuments. Even if a future president were to reverse Bush's policies, we can never replace those ancient majestic trees, once they are gone.

The environment and energy conservation have long been priorities for me. I am angry and saddened to see us lose ground that had been won only after years of struggle. In this administration, conservation and environmental policies are rarely weakened by changing laws in open legislative debate. Changes in administrative regulations are slipped quietly into appropriations bills which must be swallowed whole by Congress, even when it opposes some provisions in them. Nearly invisible executive orders go into effect without congressional approval—often on Friday afternoons when nobody is watching. Promises of support are irrelevant when funding cuts mean there are no funds to carry out the promises. Appointing to regulatory commissions individuals who have worked for the industries being regulated, or whose views contradict their agency's purpose, is another method of circumventing regulation. For example, three people who oppose all forms of contraception were appointed to the Food and Drug Administration's Advisory Committee for Reproductive Health Drugs, the committee that evaluates the safety and effectiveness of drugs used in obstetrics and gynecology and makes recommendations to the FDA commissioner.

President George Bush's promise to improve education by initiating a policy called No Child Left Behind is laudable. The legislation requires every school and student in the nation to meet a standard of proficiency by the year 2014. But last year the administration did not request sufficient funding for the states to cover all the programs in the bill. In this year of economic crisis, the federal funding gap is worse. States, which were given the mandate to achieve these goals, are billions of dollars in debt and cannot make up the difference. It is not enough to mandate higher standards; there must be remediation and adequate resources to carry them out. Although the president speaks passionately about closing the gap in achievement between affluent and low-income students, funding has been cut for such initiatives as after-school and early childhood programs that can close the achievement gap.

Just as education programs are being cut, so too are other programs to benefit children: school lunches for 2.4 million children, medical coverage for 13.6 million children, child-care benefits for 65,000 abused children according to the Center on Budget Policy and Priorities. So much for "leave no child behind." These cuts, and others in environmental protections and healthcare, are the end result of tax cutting to the tune of $1.4 trillion, with most going to the wealthiest. Why is there so little protest? Paul Krugman suggests in the *New York Times* that the Republican leadership, having wrapped itself in the flag and denounced its critics as unpatriotic, can get away with just about anything under cover of the war.

A Bush administration policy to expand coverage for prenatal care has a compassionate-sounding title, but it applies only to the unborn, from the moment of conception to birth. Once born they have no health insurance. Those who have been working to protect women's choices are concerned this is not really about children's health, but is an attempt to undermine the legal foundation of *Roe v. Wade* by elevating the status of the fertilized egg to that of a person with rights equal to, or possibly exceeding, those of the mother.

Which leads me to the ever-increasing attacks on women's reproductive rights. In its January 12, 2003, editorial, "The War against Women," the *New York Times* pulled no punches. "Running for the White House in the fall of 2000, George W. Bush did not talk about ending the right to abortion. To avoid scaring off moderate voters, he promoted a larger 'reverence for life' agenda that also included adoption and tougher drunken driving laws." The *Times* continues: "Voters were encouraged to believe that while Mr. Bush was anti-choice, he was not out to reverse Roe v. Wade. Yet two years into the Bush presidency, it is apparent that reversing or otherwise eviscerating the Supreme Court's momentous 1973 ruling that recognized a woman's fundamental right to make her own childbearing decisions is indeed Mr. Bush's mission. The lengthening string of anti-choice executive orders, regulations, legal briefs, legislative maneuvers and key appointments emanating from his administration suggests that undermining the reproductive freedom essential to women's health, privacy and equality is a major preoccupation of his administration—second only, perhaps, to the war on terrorism."

I am in the camp of those who want to keep *Roe v. Wade* in place, who feel it is important to allow women to make their own wrenching decisions on abortion. Administration policies are being driven by the religious right in the name of religion—their religion. The religious right is behind the roadblocks the administration has erected against family planning, contraception, and sex education—other than abstinence—in schools. These policies are aimed not only at the United States but at the third-world countries that most need these programs. The mind boggles at the thought of abstinence-only funds directed toward AIDS prevention in Africa, where women are men's property to do with what they will. No compassion there for the millions of women exposed to AIDS.

I worry about the threat to the separation of church and state required by the First Amendment. For that reason, I also worry about the policy of using public moneys to pay for vouchers for religious schools and to support faith-based charities, even to the length of using federal housing moneys to build church buildings. I can foresee the walls between church and state tumbling down.

Of course, as a progressive, I am not happy with the policies noted above. But it is more than policies that concerns me. It is the way the policies are being spun, the way they are being put into action. It is the deception in touting them as good for all Americans, when actually they are targeted to please the special interests that have financed the campaigns, be they the corporate sector, the extreme religious right, the energy industry. And it does not help that a compliant (or lazy) press does not fully examine or explain to the public the undercurrents, the hypocrisy, the rationalizing, the whole story.

David Broder of the *Washington Post* is an exception as he reports on a book about the political realities of today: *No Way to Pick a President: How Money and Hired Guns Have Debased American Elections* by Jules Witcover, a concerned veteran political reporter. According to Broder, Witcover says "the cost of a presidential candidacy—in time, money and privacy—has grown so great that many of the ablest politicians flee from the prospect of running." He says the gauntlet of primaries "has made it nearly impossible for the public to take a measured view of those who do run." And the entire campaign finance system, "with its incalculable costs and unworkable regulations has virtually forced anyone who wants to run for president to cheat one way or another." The whole political system has fallen increasingly under the sway of "hired gun" consultants who instill a campaign mentality of anything goes. "Whatever it takes to win is done, the only caveat being that one's tactics should not be so egregious that they backfire." And the news media, Broder quotes

Witcover, "that traditionally played watchdog, holding the candidates and their handlers to account for what they say and do, has been reduced to being either bystander or accomplice in the artful manipulation of politics by the hired guns" (November 24, 1999).

In *One Scandalous Story,* his book on the news media, Marvin Kalb explains why the media isn't doing the job it used to do. As the press competes with TV and the Internet, there is intense economic pressure in the news business, and there is no time for in-depth coverage. When huge corporations acquire newspapers and networks, only the bottom line counts. Fear of slippage in ratings and advertising results in infotainment and scandal being reported rather than hard news.

As for the state of our state, it may be too early to predict, but I assume that, with the new (and first-time) Republican control of both the legislative and executive branches, South Carolina's policies will not stray far from national policies. The drive to cut taxes, coupled with unrealistic budget practices, has resulted in shortfalls everywhere. Across the nation, states are desperate, struggling with their worst financial crisis since World War II, but are receiving less help from the federal government. As with federal budget cuts, state cuts in health programs and education will be borne by the weakest and poorest, the children, and the elderly.

In South Carolina everyone agrees education should take priority in the budget. Yet, education funding is being cut and cut and cut. Last year the Senate approved the House proposal for education funding, funding which, when adjusted for inflation, would be at its lowest level since the Education Finance Act was passed in 1977. This after years of successfully struggling to bring South Carolina out of the national education cellar. This at a time when higher and higher standards have been set. These budget cuts could mean fewer teachers, larger classes, and, in many districts, the end of remediation, summer school, early childhood education and after-school programs—all programs created to meet the higher standards. Most local districts can not absorb the costs of these programs without raising taxes, a politically difficult response. And the poorest counties are the least able to do that. The Senate Finance Committee proposed another alternative: increasing the cap on sales tax of automobiles, planes, and boats from $300 to $2,500 and removing sales tax exemptions on some items. Some committee members were part of past efforts to improve education, and they were fighting to keep the clock from turning back twenty-five years. Unfortunately, they lost.

Several bills I introduced or supported twenty years ago, unsuccessfully, and discussed in *Against the Tide* are still being introduced, year after year, still without success. These perennial issues seem sensible and uncomplicated, but there's always someone around to keep them from passing. One bill I introduced calls for shortening the legislative session. House Speaker David Wilkins has been pushing it for years, and perhaps this is the year it will pass, as a way to economize in this time of deficit. Another good idea that hasn't come to pass is zero-based budgeting, which would make every department analyze and prove the need for every program, old and new. I don't know a legislator or governor who publicly opposes this, but so far attempts to get it passed have staggered to a halt. Perhaps because it seems an impossible task for the Ways and Means Committee to accomplish.

Like the nation, the state has faced efforts to weaken environmental regulations. So far an active public has convinced the majority of legislators that our natural environment, which attracts tourists, industry, and new residents, must be protected.

One worrisome change is that the number of women in our legislature has decreased, while their number has increased in the U.S. Congress and many state legislatures. We now have the dubious distinction of being worst in the nation for electing women to public office. When I left the legislature in 1992, there were 20 women members; now there are only 16—not even 10%

of the 170 legislators. That is unfortunate for many reasons. The nonpartisan Institute for Women's Policy Research has awarded South Carolina a D– for women's lagging status in education, health, income, child care, and poverty. These are the issues that most women relate to and care about. We need more women in positions of power, sitting at the table making decisions about these very issues where so much needs to be done. We know that in Congress it is the women who lead these battles. We women who have served must work to bring more women into politics, as voters, as volunteers in campaigns, and as candidates. It is my personal mission, whenever I speak to women's groups, to implore them to get involved. It is one reason I wrote this book.

Do I miss being part of the action? You bet. I miss the camaraderie of my colleagues. And I miss the chance to publicly address the issues that have a direct impact on the things we should be protecting: liberty, justice, and equality. I do not miss the increasingly bitter partisanship which polarizes and paralyzes the democratic process.

I have tried in my preface to encapsulate some of the changes I see in the political landscape since I wrote *Against the Tide*. They all relate to the issues I discuss in this book. And now let me end as I began, with the urgent reminder that every issue acted on by our public officials affects our daily lives in some way. We must pay constant attention to what political parties and their candidates promise for the future. Even more important, we must pay attention to their actions.

October 2003

"My activism pays the rent on being alive and being here on the planet. If I weren't active politically, I would feel as if I were sitting back eating at the banquet without washing the dishes or preparing the food."

Alice Walker

Introduction

My entry into the South Carolina legislature twenty years ago, at the age of fifty-four, was a source of wonder to everyone—my New York family, my Beaufort friends, even myself. On that first day, December 12, 1976, when I walked up the wide marble staircase of the State House to the enormous hall of the house chambers and watched the chattering, back-slapping mob of strangers—114 men and 9 women—I felt I was entering an exclusive men's club where everyone had something in common—school, family, church, business—except me. The walls were covered by large portraits of men, only men, watching over us, safeguarding their legacy.

I didn't know anyone, and they didn't know me. I was intimidated by them, and I felt they were wary of me. All the men over forty looked alike and all the men under forty looked alike, and I assumed they all thought alike. The older men were gracious and courtly but oh so restrained. The younger men, on the whole, were more relaxed about us new women, perhaps because many of them were new there also. Although I would have trouble distinguishing them from each other for a while, they had no problem knowing who I was. I was easily pegged as a middle-aged Jewish woman with a New York accent. Their only problem was to differentiate between two other Jewish women legislators—Irene Rudnick and Sylvia Dreyfus—and me. To them we were interchangeable for years, although we looked nothing alike and came from different parts of the state.

It was months before I stopped thinking "What have I done? What am I doing here? How could I possibly have thought I could effect change and get things done in this environment?" The fact that what I wanted to get done were the priority items on the agenda of the League of Women Voters—education reform, day care, environmental and consumer protection, a mandatory deposit for bottles and cans, a waiting period for purchasing handguns—only confirmed their suspicions that I was a pesky outsider at best, a Yankee liberal at worst.

But once I got to know them, it turned out that not all the men thought alike, or even looked alike. Thus, my first lesson in the dangers of stereotyping. Our freshman class included an unusual number of thoughtful, progressive members who were just as interested in reform as I was. They say timing is everything in politics, and it turned out my timing was perfect. I was in the right place at the right time. About eight of us, later self-named "the Crazy Caucus" as a response to our natural opponents, "the Fat and Uglies," became a powerful force for change on issues which had resisted change in the past.

We complemented each other with individual skills and assets which made the whole group stronger. Most of our caucus were busy lawyers and experienced leaders. I was neither, but I did have tenacity, laced with a naïveté about state politics that allowed me to plunge in when others wouldn't. And I had the time needed to put that tenacity to its best, most productive use. But there was one thing that was most important of all: for eight years we had a governor, Dick Riley, who was on our side most of the time.

We were not a group forged by partisan politics, but by ideas and issues. We shared a similar agenda. We made waves by bucking the power structure. The media recognized us from the start, which gave us an identity in the public's eyes. It didn't take us long to realize that the only way to beat the establishment was to educate the public and stir up grassroots activists. For the battles we took on often pitted the public interest against special interests. We were open and honest with the press, and the press responded, which made our job of involving the public easier. And we did involve the public, thereby achieving successes in changing policy and enacting legislation and having an exciting time while it lasted. The issues we took on, and the people and politics involved in South Carolina during this period, prompted the writing of this book. The stories have all been reported in the press, but the public memory is so short, and often the connections between issues, and between the players, go unnoticed or are forgotten.

It is dispiriting to watch some of the policies we initiated and laws we passed weakened or undone years later by a legislature and governors frequently driven more by partisanship than by issues. They say everything—the stock market, morality, government—is cyclical and that the pendulum always swings back and forth. But in such a short time? I only hope that some of the progress we made is valued enough to narrow the span of the pendulum's arc as it swings backward. A look at South Carolina history makes one wonder if state leadership is just one small factor in change or if events are controlled more by the ebb and flow of vast tides caused by events more national and international in origin.

I am grateful that when I was ready to sail out of one period of my life into the world of public service, the political winds were blowing in the right direction. Most of us have a series of changes in our lives, with some more divergent than others. The chapters of my life seem now like a series of unrelated essays: the search for I did not know what in my younger days, a difficult but self-improving period as wife and mother of four in a land of strangers, and finally an exciting and satisfying eighteen-year career in politics. And still with a few years left to contemplate and continue public service in smaller ways.

CHAPTER 1

Family

I was born in New York City in 1922, attended public schools, and was graduated in 1943 from Barnard College, the women's college of Columbia University. I was an economics major with a particular interest in labor relations. I worked one year as assistant employment manager of the Eagle Pencil Company. My office was in the basement of a huge old factory on the lower East Side of New York, and because it was the only place in the building where smoking was permitted I spent a lot of time talking with both the union reps and the department foremen who came to smoke. I learned what life was like on thirty-five cents an hour for women and fifty-five cents for men. I saw firsthand the bleak outlook for those who came out of the tenements unskilled and uneducated. There was a certain irony in my position. While at Barnard, I had done an independent study course centered on the National Labor Relations Board, and I felt strongly that collective bargaining for unions was necessary. My view of life on the lower East Side of New York did nothing to diminish this conviction. Yet, there I was, part of management. At the start of my second year, at the age of twenty-two, I was offered the job of employment manager with a promise of raising my salary of twenty-five dollars a week. But I turned it down to marry Herbert Keyserling, a handsome young doctor from Beaufort, South Carolina.

My parents were great examples of the unlimited possibilities open to immigrants of their era, the late 1880s. My father, Isador Hirschfeld, was six years old when his family, headed by his mother, emigrated to America from Riga, Latvia. They were part of the mass migration to America of Jews leaving Russia and the Baltic countries to escape religious persecution and discrimination, which kept them from owning land, attending public schools, and joining most professions. Dad was the youngest of seventeen children, one of four sons and thirteen daughters. His father owned a shoe factory, but his mother ran the factory while her husband spent his time in religious study—as was the custom in that time and place. Dad's father died when he was five, and a year later his mother brought the whole family, except for one son who was already married, to New York, where most of them settled into a six-room apartment, with fire escape, on the lower East Side. The sisters worked, helped keep house, and married. (When later in life we lived in a penthouse, Dad would sleep on the terrace one night a year as a reminder of sleeping on that fire escape on hot summer nights.)

I know little about my paternal grandparents. In fact, the only grandparent I knew was my mother's father, who died when I was about six. Dad's mother and his many sisters doted on him, and they all worked so he could stay in school. There was a story, possibly apocryphal, that they warmed his bed for him on cold nights. He was the only child in his generation to go beyond high school. In the next generation, all my cousins went to college or beyond.

I have few memories of his brothers, one of whom moved to Tennessee and occasionally visited family in New York. I do remember Dad's many sisters who lived in or near New York City. The family was so large that eventually a Hirschfeld family organization was created, and we met two times a year. This was the best way to keep up with everyone, for there wasn't time enough to fit them all separately into our lives. In the summer we met in Far Rockaway, at the boarding house of one of the sisters, gatherings Dad documented with his sixteen-millimeter Bell and Howell moving picture camera. He would have the family march through the door, out of the house, and down the steps in single file; as my brother pointed out, the scene reminded him of the circus where the clowns kept unfolding themselves endlessly out of a little car.

Against tough odds, Dad became a prominent dentist. After finishing high school, he took equivalency exams and somehow bypassed college, graduating from New York College of Dentistry in 1902 at age nineteen, too young to get a license. So for a year he apprenticed himself to another dentist. He then set up a general practice in downtown

New York, growing a mustache to look older. He had considered going to medical school but chose dentistry after observing that his sister Mary's husband, a physician, worked such long hours and had little control of his life. He became a periodontist because one of his sisters had a periodontal problem. He took her to the one specialist he could find, and after watching him work and discussing her case with him, Dad decided this was what he wanted to do. He studied, he learned and became a teacher as well as a practitioner. He taught one of the first postgraduate courses in periodontology in this country at the New York University Post Graduate School of Dentistry. He was chief of the first periodontal clinic in an American hospital at the New York Nose, Throat, and Lung Hospital and served also at the New York Hospital for Joint Diseases and Presbyterian Hospital. He founded the Department of Periodontology at Columbia University Dental School.

In his late twenties, he decided to see the world before he became too tied down by his practice. He "leased" his practice to a dentist friend who was to forward him money as he traveled. When his lessee did not send the promised sum, Dad stopped in Chicago to earn traveling money as an extra, or "super," in the Chicago opera. He was able to do this because he had attended every opera he could in New York, either sitting high up in the peanut gallery or working as an unpaid extra, or spear carrier, just for the pleasure of being there. (Both Mother and Dad were opera devotees, but opera was the last art form I came to appreciate, possibly because there was no first-class live opera accessible to me in my adult years.) When Dad reached California there was still no money waiting for him. After "supering" in the opera there to earn money to travel home, he gave up his plan to see the world and returned east to resurrect his practice.

Years later he was able to travel extensively when invited by dentists in every part of the world who wanted to hear his theories about the treatment of gum diseases and see his unusual stereoscopic slides, which he introduced as a teaching tool in dentistry. In his classes at Columbia, every student would have a stereoscope and a set of slides which made the photographs three-dimensional. As one of his students told me, "You felt as if you were inside the mouth." Dad's photography was as outstanding as his research. Years later I met younger dentists who told me of the important impact of those slides on their understanding and diagnoses of periodontal diseases. His book *The Toothbrush: Its Use and Abuse* was also known for its unusual illustrations.

When Dad was first nominated for the presidency of the American Academy of Periodontia he was rejected because he was Jewish. But he was ultimately elected, finally breaking down the barriers to Jews in that field. Ironically, periodontics later became a predominantly Jewish field.

A few personal memories stay with me. Every morning Dad walked from the Nineties on the West Side down to his office on Fifth Avenue and Fifty-seventh street. He walked briskly through Central Park, swinging his cane with a silver inlaid handle. His office on the twentieth floor had a view of Central Park in which he gloried every day. And in the spring and summer, he would walk over to the Central Park Lake, rent a rowboat, and eat his lunch parked under a large tree. He always took with him a ham and cheese on rye and a chocolate milkshake. When he had visitors from other countries who came to watch him work, and there were many of them, he would take them to lunch in the rowboat, too. My memory of lunches with Dad was different. When I came up from South Carolina for visits we took a ritual trip to the Sixth Avenue Delicatessen, now Wolfe's, and had the most wonderful hot pastrami sandwiches. Dad was a regular there, and the waiters hovered over him affectionately.

Dad had a rotten memory for names. I remember on one visit to Beaufort we took him to an oyster roast and introduced him to friends; one was Mr. Snow and the other Mr. White. As we were leaving, he said with a satisfied smile to Mr. White, our host, "I am known for forgetting names. But I haven't forgotten yours, Mr. Snow."

Dad was a compulsive punster, as was my brother. And there was great competition at the dinner table between the two, while neither Mother nor I had any skill in that sort of wordplay. Our part was to groan when the pun was unduly labored.

He loved his work and loved his patients, who, in later years, were the rich and famous. Yet he always found time for, and never raised the fees of, his longtime patients who could not afford his going rate—which was still lower than others at his professional level. Between his teaching, practice, research, and writing he was away from home a lot. I have a few memories of ice skating or sailing boats in the park with him, or typing some of his first book, but those memories were reinforced more by photos in the album than by their frequency. Actually, I think he would have done less writing and research and more rowing in the park if my mother hadn't pressed him onward. She felt his knowledge would benefit more people if printed in a book and research papers. The dental profession benefited, but his family lost out.

My mother, Pauline Steinberg Hirschfeld, was six years old when she came to America from Kovna, Lithuania. She was next to the youngest of six girls and three boys. I never knew her mother, whose name was Mary Evins. Her father was called Red Mike, and we assume it was his genes that gave our two sons their wonderful red hair. When I knew Grandpa he was old and had a white beard. Like my father's father he studied more than he worked. The family had a small farm and general store near Elizabeth, New Jersey. There was little conversation about the past and the older generations of our family when I was growing up, which makes me feel deprived in this time, when there are so many aids to tracing family lineage and taping oral histories. I have not even snippets of memory, and certainly no papers to start me off. And family members older than I, who might have stored some memories, are gone.

I first realized this loss in the 1970s, when I read an eloquent op-ed piece in the *New York Times* which touched me so deeply I cut it out and still have it filed away. It was written by an author who expressed regret that she knew nothing about her great-grandparents because, as new immigrants, the family talked about the future and America, never about the past and Europe. As both my parents were born when their parents were well on in years, and were themselves married relatively late in life for those times, I knew nothing about my grandparents, much less my great-grandparents. And I am sad about this void.

Mother, as Dad, was the only member of her family in her generation to be a college graduate. She went to public school, then transferred to a convent school, then on to a New Jersey Normal School to prepare her for teaching. Not satisfied with that, in 1904 she insisted on going to Barnard College for a broader education, which her father thought unnecessary and unaffordable. So she paid her own way the first two years by delivering the milk from her sister's dairy farm in New Jersey every morning at four A.M. before taking the ferry, then the trolley to commute to Barnard. She even found time for extracurricular activities. She belonged to the mandolin club and was captain of the basketball team, despite being only 5'2". After two years, her father relented and helped pay her tuition. She loved Barnard, was an active alumna, and served as her class treasurer until she died, in her seventies.

Mother's sisters lived nearby and saw each other often: one was married to a dairyman, another to a meat packer, a third to a businessman, a fourth to a printer. A fifth sister lived near Boston, married to a manufacturer of wonderful girl's smocked dresses made of Liberty lawn cotton. Both I and my daughters were proud wearers of these lovely dresses. One sister, Aunt Tillie, lived with us for a while after her husband died.

Mother wanted to teach biology or mathematics, but the only job she could find was teaching shorthand at Erasmus High School in Brooklyn. She bought a shorthand book and learned the night before what she would teach the following day. After a few years she took a leave of absence to travel. She and a friend canoed from New York to the Chesapeake Bay down the Inland Waterway, the first women to do this. In their bloomers and middy blouses they made quite a stir, and the press gave them full coverage, calling them the "bloomer girls." They had one frightening adventure, when swamped by a storm. They were picked up by the crew of a barge, then had to fight off the rescuers, who tried to push themselves on them. But Mother stuck with canoes. The publicity from her trip generated a job offer from the Old Town Canoe Company to sell canoes in Venice. She took a canoe over there, but Venice wasn't interested. So she went to Rome, where her knowledge of shorthand, added to her degree from Barnard, made her a valuable commodity. When offered a job by the International Agricultural Society, she set the terms. She would work four days if she could travel the other three. They accepted, and she spent a year in Italy, seeing it all.

She came back to New York to teach, this time at Horace Mann. She and my father met at a canoe club, and when she was thirty-two they married. They honeymooned in the Adirondacks, canoeing. My brother reports that they used to canoe across the Hudson River over to New Jersey on Sundays, taking us little babies with them. I don't know if the love of canoeing is in the genes, but it is curious that, skipping a generation, my daughter Beth and her husband also met at a canoe club, in Charleston.

I had one older brother, Lennie, handsome and bright, thoughtful and gentle. I idolized him, and he was good to me. We were casual friends growing up and grew closer with age. He gave my father great joy by following him in his profession, becoming his partner, and perpetuating his wonderful reputation. Lennie loved his work and enjoyed his patients just as my father did, but learned from his own childhood experience to spend more time with his family than his father did with him.

In his teens Lennie developed a serious strep infection in his leg, but thanks to a colleague of Dad's who was working on the new sulfa drugs, the doctors were able to save his leg and his life. He was sent to Florida for a year to recuperate. When he returned he transferred from his public school, Townsend Harris, to Lincoln School, where he had exciting and challenging friends who continued to be an important part of his life after graduating. As I was at a large public high school of seven thousand girls, it is not surprising that I envied him this school experience. . . . My parents may have realized this, because they had me apply to Lincoln School, but there were no empty slots at the time.

I had an enormous number of cousins but only spent time with a few of them. Because my mother and father were so much younger than their siblings, I was much younger than my first cousins, most of them a generation away. Cousins on my father's side we saw at family meetings. Many lived in other boroughs of New York or other states, and we didn't have a car, so there was not much visiting back and forth. My mother's family lived in New Jersey when I was young. When I was a teenager, our aunts and uncles started moving into the city, some nearby, and I had the chance to know them better. The Aronsons, Aunt Minnie and Uncle Will, who had been a silk manufacturer in Patterson, New Jersey, became a neighbor on our block, and their son Lee visited us often. He was an artist, a hunter, and a gun collector, a cowboy-like figure who seemed exotic to me. His sister, Cecile Starr, was a talented artist who spent more time making life pleasant for her husband Harry, who directed a foundation, than painting. Another cousin, Jerry Hirschfeld, left New York to become a success in Hollywood in the film industry.

On my mother's side I had one favorite cousin, Rita Hershey, also an artist, whose husband was in theater and also represented musicians. They lived in Greenwich Village, exciting enough in those days, and to top it off, I often went with them to the Village Vanguard where Don represented or was friends of some of the musicians, such as Pete Seeger. There were other first and second cousins who were more traditional—lawyers, accountants, meat packers, and dentists whom I rarely saw. But when I left New York at the age of twenty-two the links I had with even close cousins were weakened. My trips to New York were rushed or filled up by my immediate family. We didn't correspond. After my children were grown, I reconnected with some, for dinner or lunch, once every few years, but there was no depth to our relationships. Some moved out of the city. Lennie kept up with them and their children and reported their vital statistics—marriages, births, deaths—to me.

My cousin Rita told me later that mother doted on Lennie, and she felt I was not given enough attention, especially after Lennie's illness. I don't believe I consciously resented this, but I often wonder if I didn't subconsciously seek the attention of my high achieving parents by becoming an underachiever. I was a poor student. In the fifth grade I was called into the principal's office and scolded for doing mediocre work when my IQ was "so high." I studied piano with a fine teacher, played competently, but refused to memorize or perform. At Julia Richman High School, with its 7,000 girls, I was one of 175 selected for a special "country school" for the gifted, but I managed to maintain my mediocre record. It was only in college that I finally woke up and graduated with honors.

Recently I thought of another explanation for my poor academic record. As a mother of two dyslexic children not recognized as such in their time, I could very well have been dyslexic myself. I was a very slow reader, avoiding anything less exciting than Nancy Drew and Sherlock Holmes for my recreational reading. Just as my dyslexic son Billy bloomed at Brandeis and graduated with high honors by finding many courses which did not require a lot of reading, I had majored in economics and mathematics, taking biology, statistics, and music, thereby also avoiding a great deal of reading. Though we both chalked up good records, we lost out by depriving ourselves of the marvelous literature and history courses available to us at both these schools. It wasn't just the content we missed, but the discipline to keep reading, hard as it was. The less I read, the slower I became. The practical consequences of this became painfully evident when I began reading legislative bills, full of new vocabulary and hidden loopholes. Luckily, my allies filled in the gaps for me.

While I was growing up nobody talked about the importance of self-esteem and self-confidence, but looking back I had all the signs of having little of either, due either to my poor school performance or the emotional fallout from my parents' greater attention to my brother. If I had recognized this earlier I might have sought some kind of help, but as it turned out, I just worked my way through this weakness as life moved on. However, I still protest, feeling almost a fraud when people praise me for doing something exceptional. I was lucky, I say, although luck often had little to do with it. When I began reading about women's issues, I recognized the symptoms of my lack of confidence and self-esteem as quite normal for women of my generation. And they leaped out at me when I jumped into that most competitive arena of a man's world, politics.

So many people, in books and TV ads, attribute their success in life to a parent saying "You can do anything, be anything you want to be." I don't have such a memory, and I am almost ashamed to admit that I set very few goals to do anything, beyond getting married. I have forgotten most of my childhood, I suppose because I daydreamed it away, or possibly I blocked it out. Interestingly, my brother, who had an encyclopedic mind, and who, I thought, had wonderful times in his youth, told me he remembers almost nothing about his early years, either.

I do remember spending a lot of time pining for attention from boys who were not interested in me—and avoiding the attention of boys who were. My rebellion against my parents came in other forms than being a nonachiever in school. Dad felt so strongly that sweets caused tooth decay and periodontal disease that he never allowed candy or desserts in our home except when company came. I occasionally stole pennies (only pennies) out of any available pocketbook in the house and went down to the little stationery store on the corner, where they had pinball machines and sold penny candy. I bought the candy and hung out with friends, none of whom my parents would have approved of, playing the machines. My parents didn't smoke. I shudder to think of it now, but the superintendent's daughter and I used to find cigarette butts in the courtyard of our apartment building and smoke them—when I was twelve years old. Pretty tame rebellion compared to drugs and alcohol and guns of today, but rebellion just the same. I don't even know if my parents knew about these underground activities; I don't remember family discussions about them. I imagine most children have some sort of secret lives, but often, my psychotherapist daughter tells me, they talk to someone about their thoughts and dreams. I don't remember doing that. Which may have made it easier for me when I came to Beaufort to keep my thoughts to myself when necessary.

Of course I remember a few happy, generalized highlights of living in the city: playing ball with the boys and ice-skating in Central Park (I was a tomboy), going to Damrosch's children's concerts and the nearby Museum of Natural History, and dancing at the Glen Island Casino to the music of Tommy Dorsey at what seems now to have been a very early age.

When I was very young I went to summer camp. The first camp was owned by friends of my mother's, and we learned music and dancing à la Isadora Duncan, grew vegetables, and probably ate health foods. From there I went to a real camp, where I loved the sports and was a pretty good swimmer and diver. When I was fourteen my parents sent me to Scandinavia with a group. The original plan was to go to Germany for the 1936 Olympics, but because of Hitler we were rerouted to Norway, Denmark, and Sweden. I remember more details of that summer than most, though looking back I was pretty young to be sent on such a trip. I remember the fjords, watching the King of Sweden playing tennis, the Tivoli Gardens, and having a mad crush on a handsome Norwegian "man" who must have been twenty and with whom I corresponded for a while.

Correspondence was an important part of my life. I was always rushing to meet the postman, to give or to receive. When I went away during the summers, there were always some neighborhood kids I talked into corresponding with me. When I went to Penn State College for a year, I had a heavy correspondence with a boyfriend back home. When I returned to Barnard, the letters came from the friends I made at Penn State, both male and female. Letters were very important to me. When my husband-to-be was overseas, the letters flowed in and out for two years. Perhaps I could say things in writing that I couldn't say in person. (In my political life, I found my most comfortable form of communication, especially when angry, was by letter.) Or perhaps I needed to stay connected with people I had learned to be comfortable with. I still have bundles of letters saved from those days. And I still have the memory of being teased for waiting so impatiently for the incoming mail. When I was ensconced in Beaufort with little chance of actually getting together with my faraway friends, and as we all got busy with families and jobs, the letter writing ended. Except for one Israeli friend who was in the foreign service, with whom I corresponded for thirty years as he moved from country to country. Other than this unusual correspondence, phone calls became my connection with others, especially immediate family.

Some summers, my parents rented houses in Connecticut, then various towns in Cape Cod, with Dad commuting part of the time, as is the custom with New York working fathers. I learned to sail, improved my tennis, dug for clams, went to summer theater, dated.

We managed to lead a very comfortable, but not extravagant, life. We had no car, no second home, and we went to public schools until Lennie made the change because of illness. Mother was very frugal. We did live in a penthouse for a while, but it was in a modest neighborhood. My parents loved the outdoors, and the penthouse was the equivalent of a country house. We probably spent more time outside than in, when the weather permitted. Mother had a large garden; we ate, gave parties, played ping pong, and slept outside when the weather turned hot. Any luxuries we had later came not from my father's practice but from his friendship with Hazel and Ben Graham, an economist who turned out to be a Wall Street whiz. Ben taught business and economics at Columbia University and at some point in his career decided to put his knowledge into action. He and his partner Jerry Newman started up the Graham-Newman Company, which bought up small, emerging businesses. One move led to another, which led to their buying the Government Employees Insurance Company, which became a giant in the insurance industry. Ben wrote several books on investment strategies which were cited as classics then and are still quoted extensively. Dad invested just a little in Graham-Newman, and that one investment provided the cushion for "extras" without his having to raise his professional rates, as the younger dentists were doing, especially for his older and less affluent patients. One of Dad's sisters, Aunt Bea, worked in his office, and she kept prodding him, as his reputation grew and he climbed to the top of his profession, to raise his fees, but he resisted. He loved his practice, not the money, and didn't want to change its flavor. When I first married, Dad gave me a little of his stock in Ben's company, and as it grew I in turn was able to supplement my husband's low fees to his patients, as well as set some aside for our children's education and travel.

It wasn't until I hit college that I became interested in politics and causes. My father was an old-time, but inactive, socialist, as were many other Eastern European Jews of that time. There were some discussions about presidential and gubernatorial races around the dining room table on Sundays when he was home (after listening to *The Eternal Light,* a radio show of Jewish stories, culture and values followed by the Mormon Tabernacle choir on the radio). Dad was not an organization man, and not a political activist. The only organizations other than professional that I remember hearing about were the Masons for Dad, and Hadassah for Mother. My brother and his friends, on the other hand, flirted with left-wing groups, but I was more like Dad. I never felt comfortable with dogma or blind loyalty to any group. I was only interested in a particular problem or issue with which I could personally have a hand in helping. I was leery of just talk, which I felt was usually one-sided, in order to excite or incite; I went for personal action. I was and am a moderate pragmatist, wanting to hear both sides of the argument before I take a stand. I distrusted rhetoric then, and I don't like sound bites now. And layered on top of that was a personal fear of, and resistance to, being swept away by passion of any sort, personal or political. This, of course, has its downside in life. When I came to the legislature, I finally become passionate about issues—cautiously passionate, after carefully looking at both sides of the issue—and I discovered how much I had missed by all that self-restraint.

Dad and Mother had great sympathy for those who had to struggle in life, and were generous to those who needed help. Though never wealthy, they found many ways to help young artists and musicians. They sold tickets to build audiences for their concerts and found customers for their art. I remember my mother pushing tickets for a concert by young Isaac Stern at the Needle Trades School in downtown Manhattan. I remember that concert especially because it was the first time I realized how exquisite violin music could be. There were, of course, many other ingenues who never made it to the top, who faded out of our lives.

To help a struggling opera singer my mother engaged her to give me vocal lessons. She wanted me to sing soprano, but I wanted to be a contralto, so the lessons didn't last long. I still don't like to sing, and get the hiccups when trying to join a group having a good time singing old songs. If I had stuck with those voice lessons I might have at least learned to breathe.

We have several paintings in our home by artists celebrated enough now to be featured in coffee-table books, paintings which my father was given in lieu of dental fees or pieces he bought to encourage artists onward. We have followed in his footsteps; I have enjoyed finding young artists, and some pieces have been given to my husband by "GPs" (grateful patients).

There was always someone living in our home—a widowed aunt, a maiden cousin. The cousin, Ethel Green, was a redhead with fiery temperament to match. She gave piano lessons, and I was one of her pupils. The lessons were torturous, with Ethel pulling at my hair when dissatisfied with me. She gave up and suggested I go to the Diller-Quayle School. Between the two I did learn more about harmonics than most. Then there was Adele Marcus, a struggling pianist, later a star teacher at Juilliard, who lived with us for awhile. She also gave me lessons (which were very pleasant) until she realized I would not be a serious musician, at which point she suggested I learn to sight-read, hoping that would keep me playing. She found a handsome young college student who came to our house to sight-read four-handed piano music with me, in place of my lessons with her. She was right. That kept me playing. In Beaufort I found satisfaction and pleasure from playing four-hands with friends and duets with my flutist daughter, until the legislature consumed all my free time.

When she was living with us, Adele took on Byron Janis, a talented youngster from Pittsburgh whose parents scraped together enough money to send him to New York for lessons. She arranged for him to live with her friends and practice at our house. He did so for several years, even after being taken under Vladimir Horowitz's wing. Byron moved into our apartment when I moved out my first year in college. At that time he was working on a Prokofiev piano concerto, and he would warn Mother of his practice time so she could do her shopping and escape the loud discordant sounds. One personal memory I have of Byron was when I visited New York with my two-year-old daughter. Judy sat on his lap and banged away on the piano and I said, "Maybe she will grow up to be a pianist." Byron said, "I wouldn't encourage her to be a professional musician. It's a tough life." (Judy did not become a musician, but she has worked with performing artists most of her professional life, managing musicians and more recently as marketing and public-relations director for the Washington Ballet.) After my parents died I brought our piano to Beaufort, replacing most of its insides, which had been worn out by the pounding it had sustained over the years.

I remember also the refugees from Hitler's Europe who flowed through our house in the late 1930s and 1940s, mostly dentists who were looking for direction, jobs, and financial help, but also musicians and artists. None were related by blood, but all were treated as family. My father was part of a group which gathered supplies for Israel to sustain her in her infancy. And dental equipment and funds to start up a dental school. And equipment and drugs for dental care during Israel's war for independence. Dentists from all over came to organize aid at his office every Saturday morning during that period, but it wasn't until much later I found out what those meetings were about.

Despite my early rebellions against my parents, there is no doubt that their interest in the arts, these experiences they brought into my life, and their concern for those who needed help propelled me into promoting the arts in Beaufort and South Carolina, into raising money for Israel, and finally into political action. I am so grateful to them for that.

Like my father, I was not religious, but I went to Sunday School at the Free Synagogue, the most reform my parents could find, and was then confirmed at Rodeph Sholom, a neighborhood temple across the street from where we lived. During college I spent some time at the Ethical Culture Society, which I didn't realize then was a religion unto itself because so many of those who attended were Jewish. The ethics bit appealed to me more than the Bible stories I had learned in Sunday School. It was there I learned about work camps. I spent two great summers at camps run jointly by Harvard's American Friends Service Committee and the International Students Service, whose patron saint was Eleanor Roosevelt. This was during World War II, when manpower in America was short. We took the place of the men who went to war. It was my introduction to public service, and I loved it.

The first of these camps was in Grafton, New Hampshire, where we built a dam for the farmers who needed more water. We worked for ten weeks, supervised by an engineer. I remember the locals who sat on the bank of the river and watched with amusement as we girls and boys swung our pickaxes, carried boulders, and turned cement mixers. Although we resented their watching rather than working, we joined them at Sunday night baked-bean church suppers, an experience few of us had had before. We played the piano and sang songs with them. We were students from many colleges and several countries. It was very satisfying that, when we were not able to finish the dam in our allotted ten weeks, the spectators who had sat on the banks took over and finished our work. Many years later I went by to see it and could hardly believe we youngsters had helped create that beautiful lake. My children's favorite home movies are of mother swinging the pickaxe and turning that cement mixer.

The following year I went to a camp in Connecticut where we were supposed to take the place of farmworkers. It soon became obvious that we city kids were not physically up to the job. Our productivity was poor. Between the blisters from hoeing and the backaches from planting and weeding, we failed. So we were shifted over to work at groundskeeping for neighboring estates. The goal was to replace people who could then work more efficiently than we did on the farms. I don't know whether that happened. I do know that my feeling of satisfaction from this service was considerably less than from building a dam. But it gave me a new insight into the work and wages of farm labor.

Two years later, in 1944, I married Herbert Keyserling, the son of old family friends. Herbert used to visit us when I was a little girl, but I hadn't seen him for years, until we became reacquainted in 1942, when he came to New York to work in a hospital while waiting for the Navy to call him to duty. He looked us up, and that was the beginning of our grown-up relationship. After he joined the Navy, he was stationed at the tent city that is now Camp LeJeune Marine base in North Carolina. We visited back and forth. One of my work-camp friends, Joan Bleuthenthal, had a home in Wrightsville Beach, and her family knew Herbert's family. (All Carolina Jews were connected in some way.) They made me feel welcome with their wonderful Southern hospitality. Although this was for a rather short period, and weekend visits were brief, when Herbert went overseas there were long letters daily from both directions. Herbert was a Navy doctor, a battalion surgeon stationed with the Marines. He landed on Guadalcanal with them and was in the field during combat, taking care of the wounded. He was awarded the Silver Star, an unusual medal for physicians, who are rarely in combat. I learned a lot more about Herbert through the mail than during a relatively short courtship.

When we talked of marriage, we didn't talk about where we would live after his Navy stint. When that time came, after his hospitalization for "combat fatigue" and malaria, there was little room for discussion. It was to be Beaufort, South Carolina, his hometown, where his family doctor, Bill Ryan, offered to help him get started in general practice.

CHAPTER 2

The Keyserlings

Herbert's father, William, came to Beaufort from Lithuania in 1888, at the age of nineteen, with little English and no family. In Lithuania, the large family eked out a living and were often terrorized by the Russians, who, at times and without warning, would attack Jewish neighborhoods, looting and plundering and assaulting innocent and helpless Jews. William was educated in parochial school, then a "gymnasium," and had the equivalent of what is a junior-college education here, judging from the subjects taught. He lived in fear of being drafted and kept forever in the army. Somehow, William became friendly with the son of a prominent family in his city and was engaged as a tutor for the boy, who was having trouble in school. It developed that his student had other troubles. He was suspected of some complicity in a scandal which was thought to be anti-Czarist in nature, and there was the possibility of disgrace to his family. William proposed a plan to have the blame placed on him in exchange for assistance in getting out of the country. A friendly farmer was found to hide William in his wagon beneath his wares. The scheme was for the farmer, as he neared the border of the state, to challenge the border guard to a horse race for a small wager. The guard, very proud of his horse, readily accepted the challenge, and away they galloped. As soon as they were out of sight, William crept out of the wagon and took off across the border. The details of his progress to freedom and travel to America are not known.

Upon arriving in New York he looked up relatives but did not like what he found. Someone suggested he go to Walterboro, South Carolina, to visit an uncle, which he did. From there he decided to move forty miles south to Beaufort, which was on the coast and was more cosmopolitan, with its port and thriving mercantile business. It was also an agricultural community. He had always wanted to be a farmer, just a dream in Lithuania, where Jews couldn't own land. By finding Beaufort, he achieved his dream, ending up as president of a large farming and mercantile business which covered the county. On his arrival in Beaufort, where he knew no one, he apprenticed himself to a retired sea captain as a machinist, learned about cotton ginning and found a job with Macdonald-Wilkins, a cotton and mercantile business. Several years later he brought his mother, four brothers, and a deceased sister's children from Russia. Eventually, his brothers operated, then bought, the commissary stores of Macdonald-Wilkins, which were scattered through the county. They lived in the communities where the stores were—Dale, Seabrook, Sams Point, and Beaufort. All but one brother married, and between them they produced fourteen children, mostly boys, for the next generation.

At the age of thirty-eight William imported a wife, Jennie, from New York. Jennie was a friend of my mother's. I have been asked if the families knew each other before coming to America, but I don't know, and there is no one left to ask. We do know they both belonged to a discussion group called the Davidson Club, which may have been the equivalent of a great books club. Or possibly they discussed politics and world problems. After Jennie left for South Carolina, she and Mother kept in touch through letters and visits, and we have many bundles of letters between them. Many summers Jennie and her children escaped the heat of Beaufort and came North to visit family and friends. Jennie's brother was the obstetrician who delivered me and, twenty-two years later, delivered my first child. Our family visited Beaufort once, when I was ten, in 1932. I remember how disappointed I was that Herbert wasn't there. He was off taking a math course at Annapolis, Maryland, to help gain admission to the U.S. Naval Academy. We have wonderful home movies of our family's visit, with so many Keyserlings parading up and down steps, in and out of the large family home, now the Two Suns Inn, on The Bay. And of me, repeatedly sliding off the back of a pony on Lady's Island. Viewing these old movies was a favorite recreation for my children when growing up. Now they seem pretty primitive, shown on a wrinkled screen with no sound, compared to the video recordings which document my grandchildren's lives.

William and his family first lived on St. Helena Island, which was connected to Beaufort, also on an island, only by an informal ferry service. There were no bridges, no causeways. The island population was about ninety-nine percent African American. There were no public schools. Several families hired a teacher to teach the few white children. William's oldest son, Leon, was educated this way during his first few school years. The family moved to Beaufort when the fourth child was ready for school. William's mother, who spoke only Russian and Yiddish, had moved to Beaufort earlier so she would have more than family with whom she could talk. At that time there were about twenty-five Eastern European Jewish families in Beaufort, most of them foreign-born.

Once the family settled on the mainland, Herbert's mother became active in many civic activities. She taught Sunday School, which was a part of the synagogue that was built in 1906. She was a founder of the Beth Israel Synagogue sisterhood in 1928, and took part in statewide Jewish activities. At that time, most of the Jews of South Carolina knew each other and visited back and forth. She also was a member of the Clover Club, a book club in Beaufort, which is still going strong in 1997, with many of the present members daughters and granddaughters of the founders. She participated in the Chattaqua Society, which brought theater and music to Beaufort. William spent a great deal of his time traveling to his far-flung farms, by ferry, company boat, and country roads, leaving early in the morning and coming home late in the evening. Jennie's health was not good, and she was hospitalized several times, in Charleston and New York. She died of cancer when Herbert was nineteen, during his first year of medical school. She was not very happy in the later years when she was ill and missed her New York family.

William, on the other hand, had a long and productive life. Over the years he started the first farmer's cooperative in South Carolina. He initiated a private welfare system when the deep poverty of Beaufort County was too much to ignore, served on the board of Penn School, was elected to the Beaufort City Council, and served as mayor pro tem. He spoke out against the Ku Klux Klan. He spoke up for racial justice and was an energetic fund-raiser for the state of Israel. He vigorously made his views known in letters to the editor, no matter how controversial the subject. In one such letter to the *Beaufort Gazette,* he castigated an Episcopal minister, R. Maynard Marshall, for heading the local chapter of the Klan.

William died at the age of eighty-two of a heart attack in 1950, while making a speech at a national United Jewish Appeal meeting in New York. The *New York Herald Tribune* reported that "in his final address he spoke of his own advancing years and of the increasing insight that brought to him in seeing the need for charity and helping one's fellowmen." Another news account said that Mr. Keyserling, "with almost prophetic insight," was urging younger leaders to take the place of those who could not serve much longer. According to the *New York Times,* his last words were "We must save lives." Frederick Warburg, general chairman of UJA said "He died as he had lived, devotedly serving the cause of humanity and of his fellow Jews. He will be sorely missed by those who took deep inspiration in his untiring activities in behalf of needy and homeless Jews overseas, whose struggles and problems he took to his great heart and sought constantly to alleviate." As a memorial to this remarkable man, Herbert and I took over his task of selling Israel bonds, then collecting funds for the UJA in Beaufort, and have continued to do so to this day.

William and Jennie's children were as different from each other as my four children are. Leon was an intellectual giant, who was obviously not handicapped by his early education on St. Helena Island. He loved to claim that he was admitted to Columbia College in New York only because his high school principal was so proud that a Beaufort boy was applying there that he pegged up all his grades. True or not, he entered Columbia with extraordinarily high entrance exam scores, was an outstanding student there, graduated from Harvard Law School, and went back to Columbia to teach; then he moved on to Washington, where he held exciting and challenging jobs in government, culminating in his appointment as chairman of President Truman's Council of Economic Advisers. On his way up, he was special assistant to Senator Robert Wagner, for whom he drafted almost all of the economic and social legislation which pulled the country out of the Great Depression. Ironically, he was never truly recognized by his beloved Beaufort or South Carolina, which, because of its deep poverty, benefited from his legislation more than any other part of the country. And when he came for visits he was always bemused to hear criticism of "those liberals in Washington," because he knew that the bankers, the farmers, the poor of Beaufort had all been rescued by New Deal legislation. However, his abilities and skill were recognized by some South Carolina politicians. James F. Byrnes, a former governor of South Carolina, Supreme Court justice, and a longtime family friend, started his career in Beaufort as a court stenographer and was Leon's friend in Washington.

There were two daughters born after Leon, then Herbert. Beth, the oldest, also went to New York to college, married an economist, and lived in Washington, where she worked in a relatively undemanding job, although she was capable of much more. Rosalyn, a beautiful but happy-go-lucky student at South Carolina, married a New York physician and died of leukemia at the age of thirty-four. Over the years I have met countless men who knew her in college and spoke wistfully of her charm and beauty.

Herbert was the youngest, and from the stories I've heard, he was the most mischievous and lovable. With his many cousins and friends, he played sports and pranks, enjoyed the small-town life, worked in his father's stores, swam in the Beaufort River, and drove the family car at the age of twelve. I often marveled at Herbert's memory of things that happened to him and others almost from the time of birth. I finally realized that these stories were told over and over at the Sunday dinners of the families of William and his four brothers, and were preserved thus forever, as is the case in so many Southern families. Such story-telling has been the bedrock foundation for many Southern writers. Unlike my growing up days, he was surrounded by his cousins, whom he saw all the time, at school, on Sundays, at play. I must admit I found this closeness a little smothering when I came to Beaufort, but I came to appreciate the benefits of this extended family as the years went by. In our children's generation there were many fewer cousins their age, and most left for college and moved to other cities. But they still enjoy reunions in Beaufort and telling the childhood stories, in the good old small-town Southern tradition.

Herbert wanted to be a naval officer; his mother wanted him to be a doctor. She won. He went to the College of Charleston, then on to the Medical College of South Carolina in Charleston. After his internship he joined the Navy, then while waiting to be called, he came to New York to work in a hospital. That is when we became reacquainted as adults. When, three years later, we told my parents we were going to be married, Mother was happy to hear the news but worried, thinking of Herbert's mother's last years. Would I be happy in Beaufort? She suggested that Herbert might want to go to dental school and join my father's practice in New York, but the suggestion didn't take.

CHAPTER 3

Beaufort

I found Beaufort in 1944 very small, conservative, and one-dimensional. The town had a population of under thirty-five hundred, half white, half black, each completely separate from the other. I gradually found companions and friends. Old friends of Herbert's parents were gracious and kind. There were others with whom I worked and played, or visited when our children played together. I envied the Southern women for their easy charm and grace and social skills and wished I could be more like them in that respect. For the most part, our friends were divided into separate compartments: bridge, golf, cultural activities, synagogue, the medical and military communities. The women of the Jewish community were very friendly and always there to help. Lucille Greenly, Evelyn Neidich, Celia Lipson, Rose Mark had children our children's age: we taught Sunday School, put on community suppers at the synagogue, and were like family, appreciated and comforting at times of trouble. Then there were friends like Biz Campbell, Madelaine Pollitzer, Gladys Butler, the first Yankee World War II brides brought home by Beaufort men. We had that common bond, and I believe we brought a more direct and energetic approach, probably considered aggressive at the time, to projects we undertook. Madelaine brought dance classes and a pony club to Beaufort, Biz her managerial skill and a successful business. I enjoyed them all, but our day-to-day lives were different from each other's. They, like many other of my new friends and acquaintances, did not share my political interest or concerns. So I was always on the lookout for kindred spirits to fill that void.

Beaufort then was a far cry from the cosmopolitan, prosperous Beaufort of today. Most people were poor; even the houses on the historic Old Point were run down. The owners did not have the money to paint their houses regularly (as my husband describes it, they were too poor to paint and too proud to whitewash) or to keep beautiful gardens as they do today. In fact, many people who lived on the Point were ordinary working people. This has changed with the many newcomers who have come to Beaufort from wealthy communities around the country, bringing their wealth and upkeep standards with them.

Herbert and I lived in a very small house, less than 1,000 square feet, in a little development of similar houses about ten blocks away from Bay Street. There was no other housing available just after World War II, and most of our neighbors were people Herbert grew up with—the Thomases, the Foxes, the Pollitzers—a few professionals, others businessmen. On the other side of town was the Point, where the old and beautiful and large homes of the pre–Civil War plantation owners were many summer homes to which plantation owners came to escape the heat and the malaria-carrying mosquitoes. The streets were lined with great oak trees, and many sat facing the river, with their great columns and porches. The Point was just south of Bay Street, the commercial street of Beaufort, and as its name implies, it was surrounded by the Beaufort River. The older houses around town were still occupied by the families who built them years before. Eventually, when someone died or moved away, we of Floyd Heights, who were outgrowing our houses as we had children, found larger homes. My one imperative when it was time to move was that we live on the water.

What I needed most was someone with whom I could freely express my opinions about such controversial subjects as politics, race relations, and state's rights. For many years, in conversation with most people, I would stay away from these topics. It wasn't just that I didn't want to tell people I felt differently than they. It just seemed pointless to do so. Certainly I would not change their views, and they would not change mine. So why create barriers to friendship when I needed friends? On the pragmatic side, with Herbert starting out in medical practice I felt it my duty to help him build a practice, not alienate everyone. He had been gone from Beaufort a long time, starting with college at the age of fifteen, then medical school, then the Navy, and had lost touch with most of his high school friends. He had no time to cultivate new ones. So it was up to me to build those necessary bridges in the community.

I don't remember at what point I felt the impact of being of a minority religion, or how long it took to adjust to this. I grew up on the upper West Side of Manhattan, where about ninety percent of the people, I assumed, were Jewish, including all my neighborhood friends, my schoolmates, and some teachers. (That ratio changed at Barnard.) I never thought about this until, in my new Beaufort life, the ratio was reversed. Several incidents cropped up to remind me. I was invited by Helen Christensen to join the Clover Club, the literary club Herbert's mother had belonged to. I was pleased to be asked, and I accepted. I was somewhat surprised to find I was not only the youngest member, but twenty years younger than the second youngest. Meetings were every Monday afternoon at four. I was naturally the only member with small children, so I was the only one who had the problem of getting early supper for the children, as well as late afternoon energy depletion. I found the papers we read very interesting and the women charming, but when I discovered I was pregnant with twins, I thought it best to resign. I was horrified to learn later that Helen Christensen had met resistance to my nomination for membership because I was Jewish but had fought and won. She was mortified when I resigned, probably the first (and last) ever resignation.

Another example of prejudice cropped up when a new country club was started. One Jewish family were members, the Scheins, who were friends of the club founders. When our name was proposed, we were blackballed; fear was expressed that our admission would open the floodgates. (The same argument was used at the Clover Club.) However, several members came to us and said they wanted to resubmit our name, if we didn't mind. Angus Fordham, who grew up with Herbert, said he wanted to fight such prejudice. After a family discussion with Herbert's father, we agreed. Angus won, we were invited in, and we became not-very-active members. A few other Jewish families eventually followed. Although personally hurt when we learned of these incidents, upon later reflection we found Beaufort compared favorably to other communities, especially in the North. Support for such discrimination turned out to be thin and was quickly reversed by the majority.

In fact, South Carolina, as compared to other colonies and states, had a long history of hospitality to Jews, who first arrived in the seventeenth century. According to an editorial in the *State* on May 28, 1997, by Belinda and Richard Gergel, who have researched the history of Jews in South Carolina, "From the earliest days of the Carolina colony, religious dissenters were invited to settle here, free from persecution and oppression. The colony's first constitution, written by the most eminent political philosopher of his time, John Locke, guaranteed religious freedom to any group of seven or more persons, including 'Jews—and other dissenters.'" This document, called the "Fundamental Constitutions" was the first instance where religious freedom was made a constitutional right. By 1755, according to the Gergels, the colony's reputation for religious tolerance had become so well established that London merchant Joseph Salvador, one of the world's preeminent Jewish businessmen, purchased 100,000 acres of land in the upcountry of South Carolina, which was called "Jews Land." Twenty years later, this area elected Joseph Salvador's nephew Francis to South Carolina's First Provincial Congress, the first Jew in the modern world to hold elective office. This history of unusual acceptance and tolerance must be one reason why Charleston, in the early 1800s, held the largest Jewish community of any city in the United States.

In the 1950s and 1960s a tension developed for the Jews of the South when their consciences, and sometimes their rabbis, told them to side with blacks in their struggle to gain civil rights. But for many Jews taking such a public position conflicted with their desire to melt into society. A recent lecture on Jews in the South by Professor David Goldfield of the University of North Carolina, given at the South Carolina Jewish Historical Society, clarified for me the unease I experienced in my early days in Beaufort. In the South, he said, the importance of "place"—race, religion, family—accentuates the difference between Jew and Christian. The South is ambivalent about Jews because they love their own and hate outsiders.

Yet Southern Jews are both. Many Jews felt the need to adopt the Southern code on race in order to be accepted, yet this conflicted with their own knowledge of the pain caused by discrimination and oppression. The relationship between Jews and blacks was just as complicated. Goldfield described these Southern relationships as triangular, with the three sides being the blacks, the whites, and the Jews. He described Jewish tolerance of racial oppression in the South as a "dance for acceptance." And said such acceptance of oppression tortured the Jewish soul. And that Southern writers and Jews share a sense of loneliness. Jews, he said, are the quintessential outsiders, and they preserve themselves by invisibility. It was hard to be a Jew in the South during those times, especially a Northern Jew.

I opted for preservation by invisibility. Religious differences, added to political differences, intensified my feeling of being in a land of strangers and were yet another barrier to opening myself up. Add all that to my natural condition of lack of self-confidence, stir it up, and you have turmoil. With no one to talk it out. Herbert had his own problems of adjusting to the new life, setting up a practice, dealing with his own insecurities. In addition, he was rarely home, but that was a given in his job in those days. He was a general practitioner with no partners. The hospital had no emergency room doctors. There were only four other physicians in town. There were no specialists. Herbert delivered babies, performed emergency surgery, set broken bones, gave anesthesia, and was forever being called to the emergency room. For many years he worked twelve to sixteen hours a day, seven days a week. That didn't leave much time for family, though sometimes he would take one or two of us with him to make house calls out in the country as a way of spending time with us. This followed the pattern of his father, the farmer, who was not home much either, but took Herbert with him to make the rounds of the farms.

I finally found the friend I was searching for when Ann Christensen Head moved back to Beaufort, three years after I arrived. Ann's grandparents were Neils and Abbie Holmes Christenen. Abbie came to

Beaufort in 1864 with her parents as part of a contingent of New England volunteers sent to rehabilitate the Union-occupied shipping center at Port Royal. The town was deserted except for the remaining Union soldiers and former slaves. Abbie's mother, a schoolteacher, is believed to have been one of the first Northern educators of African-American children under government auspices in the old South.

Abbie met and married Neils Christensen, a graduate of the University of Copenhagen, who left Denmark to make his fortune in America. Pressured by an uncle in New York, young Neils joined the Union forces in the Civil War. He was severely wounded and was subsequently appointed director of the federal cemetery in Beaufort. Abbie was a free thinker. She was a strict vegetarian, a Norman Thomas socialist, and a personal friend of temperance leader Carry Nation. She believed in and promoted the concept of social security twenty-five years before Franklin Roosevelt set the program in motion. She was an ardent advocate of women's rights and reportedly was the first to use the term *Afro-American.* She also had a strong interest in education and was a follower of Maria Montessori. In 1917 she started a Montessori school, which Herbert attended with Ann as kindergartners. The building still stands, not as a school, but as a beautiful home on the Old Point.

Ann's father was a businessman and, for a short time, state senator. She was sent off to Boston to school at an extraordinarily early age and graduated from Antioch College, a liberated Southerner. After a short marriage she came back to Beaufort with a young daughter to write novels. When she wasn't writing, and I wasn't taking care of children, we had serious Scrabble games where the point wasn't to win but to see how great a combined score we could get, creating as many seven-letter words as possible, playing more as a team than against each other. We talked easily about those subjects I avoided with others: integration, racism, Southern politics. I also learned a lot about the people of Beaufort from her. When she married Stan Morse, a physician, there were less free hours to while away together and fewer opportunities to talk, as Stan was not the free spirit Ann was. Tragically, Ann died suddenly of an cerebral aneurysm when she was fifty-two. Her death was a great loss for me. Her daughter Nancy, now the age of her mother when she died and a lot like her, has recently bought a vacation house on Fripp Island, and we have taken up the friendship where I left off with Ann so long ago.

From time to time Herbert and I found friends who were stationed at Parris Island, Navy doctors and dentists from New York and other cities. We did not usually meet them until they had been here a while, and most had only two-year stints, so the friendships were short, but important for both of us. For me, they were a link with my New York past. From time to time, one of them comes through Beaufort. and it is fun to talk about the past life which was so different from what it is now, for all of us.

I gained another friend when Elizabeth Siceloff drove her car into mine and came to our house to discuss her insurance. Her husband was the director of Penn Center on St. Helena Island, one of the oldest and most historically significant African-American cultural and educational institutions in North America. Originally called Penn School, it was one of the first schools for freed slaves in the South, founded in 1862 by two white women from Philadelphia, Laura Towne and Ellen Murray. Penn was established during the war as part of the "Port Royal Experiment," focusing on teaching self-sufficiency during the transition from slavery to freedom. According to a history written by Penn Center, "The emancipation of thousands of slaves, and the geographic and economic isolation of nineteenth-century St. Helena Island, presented the people of this and surrounding islands with a host of challenges and difficulties. Funded by an association of Philadelphia churches, missionaries came to aid in the social and economic education of over 10,000 African-Americans who had been slaves."

By the turn of the century, Penn Normal, Industrial and Agricultural School developed into a source of outstanding industrial training, following the model of the Tuskegee and Hampton Institutes. In the early 1900s the leadership of the school was turned over to Rosa Cooley and Grace House, who became friends of William and Jennie Keyserling. Herbert remembers visiting the school with his father when he made the rounds of the carpentry and masonry shops to check up on Penn's progress.

In 1948, when Beaufort County finally brought public schools to St. Helena Island, Penn changed its name to Penn Community Services, focusing on community self-reliance and economic development. Projects included organizing cooperatives for farmers, helping landowners hold on to their property in the face of rising taxes and development pressures, providing early childhood education, bringing public drinking water to the islands, and advocating better housing and health care for low-income residents. During the 1950s and early 1960s, Dr. Martin Luther King, Andrew Young, and others used Penn Center as a meeting place for strategy planning sessions. It was one of only a few places in the South where whites and blacks could meet together in a social setting.

It was in the early 1950s when I met the Siceloffs, when integration battles were being fought and Penn Center was a part of the fight. Elizabeth and Courtney Siceloff were Southern Methodists who became Quakers when they were young and met at a Quaker camp in Scandinavia. They were bright, interesting, and idealistic. Most of white Beaufort hated Penn and treated the Siceloffs, including their young children, like lepers. But there were some who, if they had occasion to know them, appreciated their quiet sincerity and eventually their efforts to move justice forward. I was in that group. They became my good friends, one of my first steps toward coming out of my closet and openly acknowledging that I differed with Beaufort on maintaining the status quo against any integration. Now, thirty years later, it is no longer radical to be associated with Penn, and the Keyserling connection with Penn is acceptable rather than suspect. My father-in-law, William, was the first white Beaufortonian to serve on the board of directors in the early 1900s, Herbert served on the board during the '50s, and Billy helped raise three million dollars to restore its deteriorating historic buildings. I also served on the board, helping to bring state funds to Penn and expertise from the University of South Carolina. Our family connection with Penn Center and St. Helena Island was a most important factor in my political life. The people of St. Helena Island carried me to the top in every election.

Penn Center is now considered an exotic attraction which most of Beaufort not only accepts but is proud of, thanks to its history and new visibility as one of only three black institutions in the country designated as historic landmark districts, its partnership with South Carolina's flagship university, and its popularity for tours by local, state, and national organizations of all kinds. The Gullah culture it promotes and protects receives national media attention and attracts tourists from all over. It is not just the times that have changed but Beaufort itself. Beaufort has become sophisticated and cosmopolitan as newcomers from around the country are attracted to its natural beauty and cultural riches. When Penn is criticized now, it is not for promoting integration but for showing symptoms of separatism.

In my early friendship with the Siceloffs, though I was not as convinced as they as to the best way to change the rules in moving towards integration, I knew they had to be changed—for the sake of the country as well as the sake of justice. I was in that group of Southerners who at the time wanted to make change but had fears about integrating the schools completely, immediately. Wouldn't it be better, I wondered, to start with the first grade and each year add a grade? I recognized the problems with doing it that way, but we might have avoided other problems, such as massive private school openings and resegregation. I still haven't reached a conclusion.

I had hoped that it wouldn't be too long for Beaufortonians of good will to realize that change was necessary. But I had an experience which jolted me back to reality. We were playing bridge with friends the night Governor Folsom of Alabama defied the federal troops who had come to protect students trying to integrate the University of Alabama. I inched my toe into unknown waters and said it was hard for me to believe that a governor would physically challenge federal law enforcement troops. I really expected everyone to agree with me. But they didn't. In fact, they were in total support of Governor Folsom. Having stayed away from such subjects over the years, I was jolted by the intensity of feeling, even among the brightest of our friends, and realized how far apart I still was from them.

How relative politics are in place and time. In New York I was a moderate, feeling apart from friends who were radical in their thinking. But in Beaufort I was no doubt considered radical by those who came to know I did not believe in the absoluteness of states' rights, for being friends of the Siceloffs, for thinking integration was necessary.

It was in the early 1960s that we decided to send our oldest daughter Judy to boarding school up North. One of her close friends got married at fifteen, and another pregnant, and we wanted her to know another life before she too got on a track she couldn't get off. Added to those tensions, it was the time of school integration, when passions were high and open racism escalating. We hoped that if she had a peer group with a wider range of views on race relations than her Beaufort peer group, we could reduce those tensions which exist when parents' views differ from the views of their teenager's friends. The Cambridge School of Weston, in Massachusetts, was a progressive coeducational school recommended to me by Ann Head, who had been a student there many years before. Interestingly enough, the speaker at Judy's graduation was Clifford Durr of Birmingham, father of a member of the graduating class, who expressed very eloquently his reasons for sending his daughter to the Cambridge School, the very same reasons I had for sending Judy. I sat there nodding in agreement.

Although we were unsure we were doing the right thing at the time, Judy assured us later that she had a fine educational experience and urged us to send the other three up there when they were ready, which we did. So our nest was empty earlier than usual. Three of the four children stayed in the Northeast for college; the boys graduated from Brandeis, Beth from Boston University. But they eventually found their way back to South Carolina to live. Judy, who graduated from Sweet Briar College in Virginia, is still in the Washington, D.C., area.

Because of Herbert's killer schedule and enormous pressures, most of the responsibility of running the house and raising the children was left in my untutored hands. I learned a lot by trial and error, with some of that error caused by my own insecurities. I also took on the bookkeeping problems of Herbert's office. He didn't like to talk about money to his patients because he knew just how poor many of them were, and there were many months when his assistants didn't have time to send out bills. It was all they could do to keep up with the flow of people in and out of the office. This became a critical problem when Medicare and Medicaid papers started flooding the office. So I developed a billing and bookkeeping system and helped fill in the gaps until they got caught up and the problem became manageable. But I did this at home and never worked at the office. I also took care of all the family finances and bookkeeping, and that I still do. I soon began to develop and enjoy some new skills. I learned to make my own clothes, I canned pickles and tomatoes. But I consciously decided not to learn anything about fixing lamps or household appliances, for fear these duties would be ceded over to me also. I took up painting but gave it up because I couldn't paint what I wanted to hang on my walls. My favorite period was impressionism, but I could only create literal likenesses. I played four-handed piano, pretty good tennis, and became a professional volunteer—the PTA, hospital auxiliary, mental health, Sunday school, United Jewish Appeal. I helped revive and was president of the Community Concert Series for years, and I took my turn as president of the Beaufort Little Theater and the Beaufort Dance Theater. I helped develop an art collection for Beaufort and started a foreign film series with a young friend, Tim Belk, who taught at the University of South Carolina campus at Beaufort. There weren't a lot of people in Beaufort who even thought about coming to our films, but Tim required all his students to attend, thereby selling enough tickets to pay for the films. He recently reminded me that we started off with *Birth of a Nation* to give us a conservative look. But we soon veered off to *Knife in the Water*, *Jules and Jim*, and Fellini—everything both of us wanted to see—gradually losing our audience along the way. In 1997, with a greatly changed population, there is once again a foreign film series in Beaufort, and so far it is strong and healthy.

I worked especially hard to develop the arts because I wanted my children to have the same experiences I had when I was growing up. And because I knew how much pleasure and growth the arts contribute to both the individual and the community. The bonus benefits were that these activities proved to be a training ground for me in developing the organizational skills which came in handy when I later turned to politics, and that the volunteers who sold the tickets and helped me organize those cultural activities provided the core group of volunteers for my campaign.

We took few vacations as a family, which I regret now, wishing we'd had more of the shared experiences travel can bring. It seemed impossible to tear Herbert away from his practice. But I did understand that it was important for my psyche to get back to New York a few times a year to visit family and get my cultural fix. I managed to do that until I became a legislator, when it no longer seemed fair to leave home to pleasure myself in that way, when I was away at the legislature and meetings so much of the time. Also, it was not quite as necessary, since Beaufort and environs was beginning to have its own share of culture and a new, cosmopolitan aura.

My visits to New York always provided me with a special dividend—evenings with interesting people who were friends of my brother Lennie and his wife Phyllis. Lennie had always had a stimulating group of friends, cultivated during his school years then enlarged by devoted patients. Many were in the cultural world—musicians, artists, producers. Through their closest friends, *New York Times* journalists Sydney and Flora Lewis Gruson, others were added: journalists, actors, writers. When I came to New York, they always fit me into whatever was going on in their lives, so I had experiences far removed from my day-to-day, small-town life. I returned home with stories to tell—dinner at the home of Abe Rosenthal of the *New York Times;* sitting next to Beverly Sills and across the table from Barbara Walters; dinner at Leonard Bernstein's at Martha's Vineyard with a dazzling group, including Lillian Hellman and Marc Blitzstein; going backstage to chat with Celeste Holme; dinner at Lennie's with Chaim Herzog, president of Israel, as a guest. I was more a spectator than a participant. I never felt deprived that these brief encounters were not part of my regular life, because I never thought I belonged there in the first place. I was a housewife in a small Southern town, and my only connection with all those glamorous people was my daily reading of the *New York Times* and Lennie and Phyllis. But I did enjoy those escapes from reality. Later on, in a role reversal, I enjoyed bringing Lennie and Phyllis together with some of my prominent friends—Governor and Mrs. Riley, Pat Conroy, Liz Moynihan—and other interesting but lesser-known people I met during my political life.

Occasionally, I found ways to connect some of my New York friends to Beaufort and generate my own experiences with interesting and unusual people. I brought Byron Janis to perform in the concert series I ran, as well as opera singer (now actor) Jan Rubes, a friend of the family. When Sydney and Flora Lewis Gruson were visiting Mrs. Marshall Field at nearby Chelsea Plantation I was invited to dinner when Mrs. Field heard they were my friends. During the evening I mentioned that the Ku Klux Klan was having a rally the next evening, and Flora immediately said she would like to go. Mrs. Field said she didn't even want her car there, so I agreed to take Flora and another guest. It was just like in the movies—large, burning cross, hooded men, and nauseating invectives. Flora sent an article to the *New York Times.* That was my first and last KKK rally. In fact, I believe it was the last to be held in Beaufort.

When my children started leaving home, I had more time to entertain. I was still keeping my eye out for anyone new in town who would be potential friends. I had small dinner parties for newcomers who were more interested in politics and more liberal than most of my friends in Beaufort. They are what I suppose the term "The New South" represents. Most were a generation younger than I, closer to the age of my children. I introduced them to each other; I introduced them to anyone who came along with whom I thought they would have something in common. My motives were mixed. First, of course, I enjoyed their company. Second, I was a matchmaker at heart. But above all, I knew the loneliness of not having like-minded friends, and I wanted them to be happy, to stay in Beaufort.

My son Billy, who spent a year at USC–Beaufort, was a connecting link with the younger generation. One of my first young friends was his teacher, Tim Belk, with whom I ran the foreign film series. Then there was Bernie Schein and Pat Conroy, whom I first had met when, as a high school student, he came to Ann Head's to talk about poetry and writing. After graduating from the Citadel, Pat came back to Beaufort to teach. When the school superintendent fired him, some say for his teaching methods, others because he brought some black Daufuskie children to Beaufort and they stayed in his home on the Point, Herbert and I went to the school board meeting to support him (unsuccessfully).

While still teaching, Pat met and married Barbara, the widow of a Marine Corps pilot who was killed in action. At the time of his death she was pregnant, and Herbert was her doctor. It was his heartbreaking task to accompany a Marine Corps officer to the school where Barbara was teaching to tell her that her husband had been killed in action. Herbert felt close to Barbara, and she to him; when she and Pat were married, we had the wedding reception at our house, for neither of them had parents in Beaufort at the time. Because Barbara's two very young children sometimes made writing difficult for Pat in their small house, he wrote some of his book *The Water Is Wide* in our home. Pat writes in longhand, on a yellow legal pad, so when it came time to send off the manuscript to the publisher, I was one of many enlisted to type a chapter or two.

We came to know and enjoy other young people; some were new to the area, others were our friends' children who returned to Beaufort after college and graduate school, like John and Caroline Trask, Dale and Charles Friedman, George and Connie Trask, and Jimmy and Nancy Thomas. Sue and Scott Graber arrived in Beaufort about that time, and we became friends. Scott loved to talk politics, and Sue liked tennis. We played tennis and talked politics. Sue and Nancy were founding members of the League of Women Voters with me. When I ran for the legislature, they were the energetic workers who made my campaign hum. Scott had moved to Beaufort from Washington to work with a large law firm, left the firm to run a program at Penn Center to save "Black" family land on St. Helena Island, then opened his own office. Sue kept searching for her own identity and finally discovered painting in the early 1990s. She has become an accomplished and popular portrait painter, and it is her portrait of me which hangs in the Beaufort County Courthouse. I feel a strong kinship to her, as a fellow searcher who finally found the right niche, I at the age of fifty-two, she in her mid-forties.

Another friend, actually older than I but also drawn to the younger generation, was George McMillan, a complicated, professional liberal Southerner, a journalist who enjoyed being controversial and irascible and with whom I had a modified love-hate relationship (modified because both words are too strong for the up-and-down friendship we had) I introduced him to my friends because he was lively and challenging, and for the same reason I overlooked his faults. George often came to dinner, bringing out-of-town friends who were writers, journalists, and historians. George would always tell you the inside story about a lot of things; he was smart, gossipy, and often outrageous. He used to make quips about my "salon" or was it "soirees" he called them. Despite his sometimes snide comments about my food or my guests, he never refused an invitation and usually drew into his own circle those he met in our home. My friendship with George came to a halt when he was divorced, and he felt I didn't properly welcome his new, younger wife, Cecily. After he died, Cecily moved to Cambridge but kept their house at Coffin Point. She and I eventually became friends.

The Siceloffs, from Penn Center, were the only ones, other than George, who were close to my age, and the age differences grew when the circle was enlarged by Billy. One of the attractive things about Beaufort, then and now, is that there are few age barriers in friendships. At almost any large party (except in the retirement enclaves) you will see a good mix of generations. I think my friendships with these young people made it easier to adjust to the legislature, when I found most of the people I was drawn to there were again a generation younger than I. Just as at home, I seemed to have more in common with them than with legislators my own age.

My political life began in 1972. Billy, out of college, where he worked on political campaigns in the Boston area, came to South Carolina to run the McGovern campaign. He asked me to help, but I declined. I didn't like McGovern. I didn't like his foreign policy, and his domestic policies seemed too extreme and too nebulous for my pragmatic tastes. Although I would not work for him, I did agree to help register voters. I discovered how difficult it was for anyone with a 9-to-5 job to register. The county voter registration office was open for limited hours during the week, never during the lunch hour, never on weekends, and there were no volunteer registrars sitting at tables in public places as there are today.

After the 1972 election, Carol Tuynman Fader, the wife of a Navy doctor stationed at Parris Island, and I decided we had to find a way to open up the voter registration system and introduce a voter education program for future elections. Carol thought we needed a credible organization to back us up and suggested starting a NOW chapter. She obviously hadn't been in Beaufort long. I suggested that the League of Women Voters might be more acceptable. And that's what we did. I was asked to be the first president but turned it down because I had made plans for a long visit with my old friends the Siceloffs, who were then in Afghanistan with the Peace Corps.

I gained some interesting new friends as a result of a phone call from Flora Lewis. One day, in 1973, she called to tell me that she had given my name to a young man with whom she had just had lunch in Washington. He worked with Pat Moynihan at a high-level job in the Nixon White House, he loved to talk politics, he was a good tennis player, and he was coming to Parris Island, and she thought I might enjoy knowing him. His name was Dick Blumenthal, he was twenty-four years old and a college friend of her daughter. I waited for him to call me, but he didn't. I called Parris Island and was told he was a recruit. Recruits can't make many telephone calls. I contacted a base officer and was told we could arrange to visit him on visitor's day, which we did—several times. Recruit training isn't easy for anyone, but he was given an especially hard time because of the mail and messages he was receiving from the White House. I didn't have any children at home then, but I sent Tim Belk, my foreign films partner, and his friends to visit with Dick with the thought that might help keep his spirits up. I think it did.

After Dick graduated from boot camp he was assigned to Parris Island, and I invited him to live with us. I think that my having so many young friends made this easy for me and comfortable for him. He made good use of the tennis court in the front and the creek in the back. One day when he was on the tennis court and I was watching the news, Walter Cronkite announced that Dick Blumenthal had been appointed to head up VISTA, the youngest person to fill such a job. I rushed out to tell Dick, who was pretty upset, because he had not agreed to take the job. For weeks there were long phone calls coming from the White House, from all the people whose names we became so familiar with during the Watergate hearings, people I assumed were trying to persuade him to take the job . He didn't accept, and soon after he finished his tour, he joined the Marine Reserve and entered Yale Law School.

During this time, Dick told me an old friend from the White House, Checker Finn, was coming to see him, and they would stay in a motel. As we had empty bedrooms, I said I would be delighted to put him up for the weekend. He came, and we enjoyed having him. Later in the year we received a mimeographed group letter from Checker announcing he was leaving the White House and taking a trip around the world. He enclosed his itinerary, which included a stopover in Kathmandu, Nepal—the same week I was going to be there. I was going to Afghanistan to visit the Siceloffs, and Elizabeth and I had plans to travel in Nepal and India. I wrote Checker to tell him I'd look for him on a street corner; he suggested we set a time and place. He traveled through Nepal with us, negotiating money-changing and other chores for us. He decided to change his plans to take advantage of having a new friend in Kabul, and he came to Afghanistan and traveled into the hinterland with us. Two years later he wrote to say he was going to India with Pat Moynihan, would have an apartment of his own on the ambassador's compound, and I was invited to visit at any time. I was planning a trip with my oldest daughter Judy to go back to Afghanistan, and we of course accepted. It was fun to meet and spend a little time with Liz Moynihan, an open and charming woman. She hadn't been in India long and was not yet caught up in embassy life, so she had time for me. She included me in a luncheon she hosted for prominent Indian women and a shopping trip. I have lots of mementos from the trip: a dress I made from a sari, table linens, a little art, and embroidery. Years later, when Moynihan was in New York campaigning for senator, I introduced Lennie and Phyllis to them, my first step in the role reversal of my introducing my well-known friends to my New York family. Other such occasions followed: a wonderful family breakfast at the Governor's Mansion when Dick Riley was governor, and friendship with Pat Conroy that developed after they visited him in Italy in my place, a visit I never managed to make.

Checker came to be a leading authority on education, teaching at Vanderbilt, advising Lamar Alexander when he was governor of Tennessee, and continuing in that capacity when Alexander sought the presidency. He is very good about keeping in touch. When we in South Carolina were working on education reform, and Checker was working with Bill Bennett in the Department of Education, I brought him to Columbia to speak at a seminar I was organizing in connection with the Education Commission of the States and introduced him to Governor Riley. At that time they had many ideas in common, but now their philosophies seem far apart. Checker's parents moved to Hilton Head, and now they are our friends. We get regular reports on his and his wife's very busy lives and occasionally see Checker when we go to Washington. I have not heard from Dick Blumenthal in years. He is presently attorney general of Connecticut, and I am told will one day be governor. Just recently I have heard him, several times and on several subjects, being interviewed on National Public Radio, possibly a signal that he is moving up.

A most important person in my life was wonderful, wonderful Maybelle Mack, who ran my house, my children, and my kitchen for over twenty-five years. Maybelle made possible my volunteer work and allowed me to pursue my political life without feeling too guilty, for she kept the house clean and put food on the table. When she was very young, Maybelle had left her home on Warsaw Island to go to New York. She worked as a children's nurse in a three-generation household. The grandfather was a rabbi, the mother and father worked. There was also a cook, whom Maybelle watched carefully, and when the cook left, Maybelle was promoted. The family lived in the same neighborhood I lived in while growing up, and their lifestyle was similar to my family's. Maybelle made roast chicken, matzah balls, pot roast, and chopped chicken liver better than anyone I ever knew, including my mother. She came back to Beaufort to help her ailing mother, and I was lucky enough to get to her before anyone else. She fit right into our way of life.

Maybelle was cheerful, upbeat, patient, and smart. My children went to her with their problems. She just smiled at Herbert when he came home tired and cranky. When my friends called, they often mistook her for me because she adopted my telephone manner. Yet when she talked with her friends, I could barely understand her island patois. And she never complained when I had dinner parties, which meant more work. With Maybelle there to advise and cook, it became fun to have dinner parties. My guests always wandered into the kitchen to tell her how good dinner was, and they mourned with me when she became ill at much too young an age.

Maybelle was a heavy smoker, and one winter she started coughing and couldn't stop. She had lung cancer, in her early fifties. For some reason they didn't tell her she had cancer in the beginning, but we both knew. She underwent treatment, talked about coming back to work, but started losing weight and got weaker, not stronger, after the treatments. I would visit her in her pleasant home on Warsaw Island and listen to stories about the island from her and her family. It was an island where only blacks lived at the time. The islanders had formed an association to protect themselves from speculators picking up pieces of land at the tax sales. They created a fund and paid the overdue taxes until the owner could scrape together the money to pay the fund back. In the last few years, the value of waterfront land has risen so fast that some islanders sold their empty waterfront lots. This is the story of many areas in the Low Country, where the land and heritage of the black families, is being lost.

When Maybelle's son or sisters were not there, we talked about writing a cookbook together. I would write down her recipes and comments, which would eventually be in the book. But she didn't last long enough for that. I still have the recipes, but no one else seems to be able to duplicate the final product. At her funeral the family insisted that all six of us Keyserlings sit up on the platform behind the preacher and face the audience. It was the toughest emotional experience I can remember. We sat there facing the congregation and cried, seeing her young son Kenny in such a state of despair, as well as her daughter Corinne, who by then was married and had children and lived in Ohio with her soldier husband. Maybelle was a central figure for all of us and made possible so much of what I did in my life. I sometimes have pangs of guilt about how hard she worked and how little I paid for what

I received. I paid more than others and set up a personal retirement fund, but the pay was not nearly enough, and she never got to enjoy retirement.

My world was far different from the lifestyles of the next generation of women like me. Most do not have the luxury of having time to play and volunteer. I watch my daughter struggling to manage a job and care for her young children, feeling stymied because she can't be involved as she would like to be in her community. There are no Maybelles in her world, just a string of sitters and, fortunately, a helpful husband, enough to help her take care of the chores of life but allowing little time for self-exploration. Think of the toll this also takes on organizations such as the League of Women Voters and Planned Parenthood. In my day, it was the young women who were their foot soldiers. Thank goodness for young retirees who still have the interest and energy, but still there is no question that the pool of volunteers has shrunk.

CHAPTER 4

County Council: The First Step

When I returned from Afghanistan I volunteered to "observe" county government for the League of Women Voters. I was amazed, as only a city girl from New York would be, to discover how county government impacted our lives. Home Rule for South Carolina had just been enacted in 1975 as part of the 1972 constitutional reform led by Lieutenant Governor John West and Representative Dick Riley. Until that time, the county boards of supervisors wrote county budgets and the state Department of Education wrote county school budgets. But these budgets had to be approved by the legislative delegations and passed by the entire legislature. Legislative delegations made almost all appointments. The intent of Home Rule was to turn over these responsibilities to county government, and Beaufort County was one of the first counties to move, once given the authority. By the time I arrived, Beaufort County Council was setting taxes and was responsible for funding education, building roads, law enforcement, zoning, and more.

As I sat there week after week "observing" the nine councilmen, I thought how differently I would have voted on some issues, no doubt influenced by my life's experiences, as they were by theirs. One day there was prolonged discussion about funding a Christmas party for all county employees from road workers to office managers. I thought that if a woman were on the council she would suggest that a large turkey for each family would be more appreciated than what would have to be a sticky party, at best. That was a flippant thought. More importantly, I saw that the county council was not doing enough for education. Our schools were on shaky ground after integration, and public support was fading fast. Efforts to create decent jobs through economic development were foundering, and local government was not pushing hard enough for state help. The world was beginning to discover Beaufort, and our zoning and land-use plans had to be strengthened to provide a better balance of economic, social, and environmental factors. We also needed better day-care facilities. Would it make a difference to have a woman's voice and perspective on council to tackle these issues?

I mentioned my observations and question to George McMillan over dinner and said half-jokingly that I could probably do a better job than some of those council members. His response was "Well, why don't you run?" He talked me into it. I succumbed to his flattery. The word was out before I had a chance to retreat. With time to think, I conjured up so many reasons not to run—I was shy, I was afraid of speaking in public, I didn't know enough about government or the men who ran it. These are pretty typical reasons most women give for not running for office. They would rather work for candidates, stuffing envelopes and making phone calls, than be candidates. But it was too late for me to change my mind. The newspapers had the story, and there was no graceful way to retreat.

Although I was headlined as the first woman to run for county council, I did not consider that being a woman was an issue. I don't remember any public opposition to me as a woman, but there may have been backroom talk. In fact, I don't remember any openly negative campaigning on any issue. I really thought of myself as just another candidate qualified to handle the issues I was most interested in. However, I discovered during the campaign and after that others saw me first as a woman candidate. But that wasn't all bad. I got a little more press coverage, and a lot of women volunteered to help me.

I was one of seven candidates running for three at-large seats. As the only woman in the field, I stood out in the crowd. Watergate had soured people on politicians, and I think in that climate a woman who was a community worker and not a politician had an advantage. In the southern half of Beaufort County, Hilton Head, with its many newcomers from the North, promised strong support. I was one of them, with my Northern accent and Ivy League diploma. I also had name recognition from a column I wrote for the Hilton Head magazine on cultural happenings in Beaufort. And I often attended meetings of Hilton Head's branch of Planned Parenthood.

In the northern part of the county, many of Herbert's patients, white and black, knew his family or had worked for his father on farms across the county. They voted for me because my name was Keyserling. And as George McMillan so neatly put it in an article he wrote about me in *McCall's* (March 1980), "What had for years been a hard and lonely facet of her life, the fact that her husband was busy at the hospital almost every night, now turned to her advantage. He had delivered, or so it seemed, half the babies in Beaufort County, black and white. He had friends up every sand and shell road in the Low Country." Whenever Herbert had free time he would take me out to the country stores and churches to introduce me around. Herbert had delivered most of the younger generation of St. Helena Island, and his long hours and hard work paid off in political patronage. The St. Helena precincts swept me in.

And then there were the volunteers with whom I had worked for so many years. Add them all together and the sum was victory, which was especially sweet because I was the top vote-getter in both the primary and the general elections—and the first woman ever elected to Beaufort County Council. Once the door was opened, others walked in. Many women followed in future elections: Janet Sawyer, an ex-northerner was elected in 1982 and served as vice-chairman. Also elected that year was Hilton Head Republican Martha Baumberger, a midwesterner. In 1984 when the Republicans gained the majority on Council, she became the chairman when the Democrats supported her as the more moderate, and less partisan candidate seeking that post. In 1990 Beth Grace, a Beaufort Republican, was elected and she became vice-chair in 1992. In 1997 three of the eleven members were women, all very active.

After my election to county council, Arthur Horne, who was vice-chairman, was the natural choice to follow former chairman Colden Battey, who chose not to run for reelection. But Arthur discovered he had lung cancer and asked me, as top vote-getter, to run for the chairmanship. I said absolutely not. I didn't know enough about the operations of county government, had not enough self-confidence to control a group of men I hadn't worked with before, and the incumbents would resent my walking in and trying to take over. I wanted nothing more than to sit and watch for awhile. Fear of leadership and confrontations? Fear of failure? Probably both. Fortunately, he remained alive and healthy for quite a few years. Arthur was a retired marine, a fair and honest man who really cared about all the people of Beaufort. He was also skilled in finding solutions by mediating between warring parties. In other words, he was a deal-maker in the finer sense of the word.

I found that my presence did change the dynamics of the council in the beginning. I watched as the men around the table struggled with such problems as addressing the body, hesitating after saying "Gentlemen" and then adding "and Lady" Or "Mrs. Keyserling and gentlemen." Should they be their usual Southern gentlemanly selves and treat me as a lady or as a fellow colleague? Obviously, people were conscious, even self-conscious, about the presence of a woman where there had not been a woman before. I was a little annoyed with my colleagues' self-consciousness but equally bothered when I realized that when I took the floor I often sounded strident or combative, when I didn't feel that way at all. But then I read an article in a public management magazine that Jim Zumwalt, our talented county manager, gave me and found an explanation for everyone's behavior, theirs and mine. Its thesis was that when a woman moves from the traditional female role as we know it into the more aggressive man's world, with more decision-making and leadership responsibilities, in the beginning this is done with great awkwardness by the woman and will also cause disquiet, even discomfort in the men with whom she is working. For they also have to readjust their roles to her new one. And it all takes practice, doing, and time. My personality didn't help matters. Most people who enter politics are extroverted, hail-fellow-well-met, and aggressive, but I was far from that. I was shy, not great at small talk, and not even assertive, much less aggressive. I was slow to make decisions. Although I had accumulated a lot of generalized information, I was not good on details and always had to double check facts, figures, or names, good member of the League of Women Voters that I was, before venturing an opinion, as compared to most men, who would rather bluff it out than stay silent. Gradually, as we learned more about each other, and as I passed a few tests, the dynamics changed for the better.

There were occasions when I even tried to be one of the boys. When the county council and school board members decided to have a tug-of-war contest during the Beaufort Water Festival, there was much hoopla about the relative strength of members of each group and whether substitutes should be obtained for the undersized or weak. The two female school board members opted to get substitutes, but I announced that "after consulting with friends and advisors" I was going pull my own weight.

Although I had not discussed women's issues during the campaign, it turned out that this was central in many people's minds. When I was asked to pinch hit for Chairman Horne and speak at a local Rotary Club meeting, I really wanted to take that opportunity to educate my audience about the county budget; but no, I was assigned the topic "What is it like to be the first woman on county council?" When I was asked to write a book review for the Hilton Head newspaper, the book was on the women's movement—the first I'd ever read—*Between Myth and Morning: Women Awakening* by Elizabeth Janeway, a collection of essays which were variations on the theme of her previous book, *Man's World, Woman's Place* (It's a man's world and woman's place is in the home). Needless to say, it struck a chord in me as I wandered around a man's world. My first year in office I was asked by every women's club in Beaufort to speak on a variety of women's issues. How surprised I was when the Officers' Wives Club on the Parris Island asked me to talk about the Equal Rights Amendment, a subject I'm ashamed to say I knew not enough about. I went to the library and read up on the ERA.

At first I felt my image as a serious politician was diminished by this consignment to women's issues. Why didn't they ask me to talk about the important government issues the men on council were asked about? But after reading several more books to prepare myself for speeches, I finally woke up to the fact that the condition of women in South Carolina was at least as important as county government. I became grateful for the opportunity to educate the public about a topic no one else was addressing here. When the time came that I was given my choice of subjects, I usually found a way to tie women into the topic of the day.

In the aftermath of this reading and speaking, I learned a lot about myself that I had not understood before. My "weaknesses"—shyness, lack of confidence, fear of rejection or repudiation, dislike of confrontation—were typical for most women venturing out into the man's world, not mine alone. I learned from Carol Gilligan, a Harvard psychologist who wrote in her book *In a Different World* that there is an internal conflict between our feminine side and the competitive world of politics. As girls, we are brought up to be followers, not leaders, care-givers and not rivals, whereas in politics you risk making enemies, when you really want to be loved—or at least liked—risk being attacked when you want praise, and invite controversy when you are trained to be polite.

In retrospect, my woman's consciousness was first raised by going into politics. One small example: I had spoken to the Rotary Club several times in the past, but it was not until the year of my awakening that I wondered if a civic organization made up of business and professional leaders should not include the business and professional women of the community.

Like all converts, I was excited to realize I could be a positive force in educating others about the status of women in today's society. As I advanced politically, I not only championed women's issues but tried to expand the field of advocates and women candidates by initiating a network for South Carolina women in government at all levels and starting a women's caucus in the legislature. During my years in the legislature I saw firsthand the importance of having women in elective office. It's just plain undemocratic to have men making decisions about women's lives, women's bodies, women's work, and women's status as citizens, with little or no input from women colleagues—simply because there are so few women colleagues. Women bring different experiences, viewpoints, thought processes, and priorities to the table, and it is important that they be expressed, considered, and fought for in the governing of our cities, states, and country. More on this subject later.

After my election to county council in 1974, I formed a "kitchen cabinet," à la Golda Meir, to talk about issues and problems in my home. One vexing problem I wanted to address was the split between the northern and the southern halves of Beaufort County and the animosity of each side towards the other. I wanted to narrow the gap between us, and I hoped that by bringing together leaders from both communities around my dining room table we could dissect the problems and eventually improve the relationship. Six to eight of us met regularly: two friends came from Hilton Head, John Trask and Gen. George Forsyth from Beaufort, several women and businessmen, white and black. I would tell them about the issues the council was considering and ask for their opinions. Their input broadened my view. They would tell me about problems I had no inkling of, which I would ask to be put on the council agenda as new items. After I went to the legislature I continued to call on my "cabinet" for advice and input.

One half of Beaufort County, south of the Broad River, was dominated by Hilton Head, a resort and retirement community with wealthy retirees from many parts of the country. Most were newcomers, but there were also black native islanders, and the ratio between them has changed radically over the past thirty or forty years. At one time, over ninety percent of the islanders were black. Now, ninety percent are white. The newcomers wanted more control of their own destiny, which they saw as different from the rest of Beaufort County. Although they comprised less than a third of the county population, they paid more than half of the property taxes, and they wanted a greater say in the spending of those taxes. They wanted services that were at least as good as those available in Beaufort, the county seat. They wanted stronger zoning laws to prevent the sprawl, pollution, and destruction of natural resources they had seen firsthand in the cities they had left behind in the Northeast and Midwest. They even talked of seceding to rural Jasper County, which they would no doubt control. Eventually they gave up on county zoning and became the city of Hilton Head. As a municipality they could write their own zoning ordinances. They also would pay city taxes, but that was a small price for them in exchange for control of their land.

North of the Broad River the centers of population were the cities of Beaufort and Port Royal and St. Helena and Lady's Island. The people there were more likely to be natives or long-time residents. They felt Hilton Headers were a selfish elite who looked down on them as country bumpkins. There was some truth to both perceptions. But I personally was delighted to have the newcomers on Hilton Head Island, because they brought with them new ideas and more cultural activities. They were people who had been leaders in other communities, unaccustomed to having time on their hands. I felt we should tap their experience and spare time to help solve some of our problems.

The men from Hilton Head who came to my lunch meetings became quite active in politics later: Ben Racusin, a former CIA official and a relatively early settler, who is still trying to build bridges between the white newcomers and black natives, became the first mayor of Hilton Head. Bill Marscher, a Beaufort native who went off to MIT to be an engineer and worked in the Northeast until retirement at a very early age, became a leader on Hilton Head in confronting environmental and growth-management issues. We stayed connected throughout my stay in the legislature.

We didn't succeed in solving every immediate problem, but we did open up good lines of communication and found some common ground: both sides were concerned about education and expanding the tax base through better employment opportunities. Both sides wanted to protect our wonderful natural resources—our magnificent live oak trees draped with Spanish moss, our greenways and open spaces, our salt marshes and freshwater rivers, our beaches—which had drawn them, and kept us, here.

As I was leaving county council in 1976, the Hilton Head newspaper printed letters of complaint about the island's lack of county services. This really irked me. My skin was still thin. I wrote a letter to the editor in response:

"When I ran for County Council two years ago, one of my stated goals was to improve the relationship between the people of Hilton Head and the rest of the County. Since elected, I believe that County Council has made every effort, within the limits of our resources, to respond to the needs of Hilton Head.

"I am saddened to see a resurgence of discontent triggered by a few problem areas such as recreation and emergency medical care. I realize it is human nature to dwell on things that are wrong. I would like to put the focus back on the many things that are right, that are so much a part of your readers' lives that they go unnoticed, or that perhaps they do not realize are being performed by Beaufort County government. I hope the exercise of compiling the enclosed list of County services will prove to be mutually beneficial: in writing this list we in county government will be reminded of what needs to be done, in reading the list the people of Hilton Head will be reminded of how much has already been done. The perspective of all should be broadened."

The enclosed list of services brought to Hilton Head in the past two years included: a mini courthouse which housed a tax information service, a drivers licensing office, a voter registration service, probate services, and half the sheriff's deputies; a new elementary school; a new library; family court; and a speech and hearing clinic. Some of these projects were on the drawing boards before I came, others I initiated or helped push along. As I reviewed my correspondence file to freshen up my memories for this book, I was reminded how many Hilton Head Island residents wrote to me, as "their" legislator, to ask for help—for guidance with personal problems, or requests for votes on particular issues, or to praise or castigate me for my actions. Although my district did not include any part of southern Beaufort County, they either mistakenly thought I was their state representative or they had given up on their own. And I must say I enjoyed this perception of being connected to Hilton Head. As I wrote to one island correspondent who asked my opinion about plans brewing in Hilton Head to start its own school district because of the lack of public school support in northern Beaufort, "I love having Hilton Head as part of my community, I love its energy, its persistence. I love you and your friends for having done so much for education for the whole county at a time we lacked leadership on this side of the river. I love your Chamber of Commerce for making our Chamber look so bad when they opposed the school building program, for this eventually led to new leadership over here. Everyone knows that one never wants to see a rift with those one loves. Your money is nice, but to me it is not your biggest contribution to Beaufort County. So I hope you will think in terms of the whole—as I try to think about the state as a whole when I legislate. It is important for those who have the resources—whether they be brains, energy, passion, integrity or money—to spread them as far a they can go."

Over the years the tensions have eased and opinions have moderated, possibly because the populations have changed. Now we in Beaufort and the adjacent islands attract a great many wealthy retirees of our own, and now there are more working people living on Hilton Head to service the tourist trade and retirees. The distinctions have blurred a little. Leaders on both sides have joined to face the common enemies, poor public education and uncontrolled growth. Contrary to the accepted wisdom that senior citizens are selfish, Hilton Head, with its preponderance of wealthy retirees, voted overwhelmingly for a $120 million county school bond referendum in 1995. I was so proud of the men and women who led that battle.

Shortly before I took my place on county council, the county hired a very talented manager, Jim Zumwalt. While Arthur Horne taught me the value of compromise, Jim taught me about budgets, priorities, and the importance of always looking at the bigger picture. This fit my natural tendency to take the long view rather than the short-term fix, so we suited each other. Jim arranged a tour for new members of all county facilities, and we met with the managers of all county offices. We visited the Health Department, the jail, the workshops—even the garbage shredder. I was reminded of the importance of seeing with my own eyes and hearing with my own ears everything about which I had to make decisions. These vivid pictures were far more effective than reports. I had experienced this before. Although my sons had taken hundreds of wonderful photographs of Daufuskie Island when Pat Conroy taught there, and although Pat told me in his descriptive style much about Daufuskie, I didn't really get a feel for the island until I spent a day there. This confirmed what I had said in my campaign: a woman who is not confined to a nine-to-five job has something special to offer county council—her ability to dig deep and learn by hands-on experiences.

I also learned that even with my extra time it would be impossible to become an expert in everything and that I had better concentrate on areas I knew the most about, areas which had touched my life more than the male members, perhaps: the areas of education, day care, cultural affairs, and social services. When Arthur Horne was setting up committees, I asked to serve on the education committee, and he was kind enough not only to put me there, but he made me chairman.

He gave me some interesting assignments. First he asked me to make a recommendation for a project to be funded by a grant from the South Carolina Arts Commission's Art in Public Places program. Beaufort had received a grant the year before but had not moved on it. Jim Zumwalt told me of some ideas which had been tossed around, then came up with a daring suggestion which I jumped on enthusiastically—that we commission a bust of Robert Smalls, a former slave who came back to Beaufort after the war and was elected state senator, then was elected to Congress, where he gave strong support to the new concept of public education. This bust could be in front of Tabernacle Baptist Church, which was a key public place. It also was the church Robert Smalls had attended.

We invited Robbie Wright, a well-respected black school principal, to show council a slide show she had prepared on Small's fascinating life. (The part I liked best took place after the Civil War, when Smalls returned. When he heard that the house of his elderly mistress was up for tax sale, he paid the taxes, moved in, and took care of her until she died, without ever letting her know he owned the house.) Council endorsed the idea. We even went so far as to select Marian Etheridge, a woman sculptor! Beaufort was the first government body in South Carolina to honor a slave, much less a slave who had turned a ship over to the Union navy and joined them in battle. I received just one hate letter, but evidently there were others who were unhappy. One night someone sprayed blue paint on the Robert Smalls bust. There was no public outcry, either about commissioning the sculpture or the desecration. Robert Smalls is now prominently featured on the Beaufort tour guides' route. It pleases me to think how surprised tourists may be to see this former slave honored by a small Southern town. I hope they think the faded blue stain was caused by oxidation. When I recently listened to the ugly debate in the state legislature about erecting a monument to African Americans on the State House grounds, I wondered if Beaufort was just a more open town than the rest of South Carolina. Or is it that political partisanship has increased racism to that level in the past twenty years?

On the other hand, our liberality on this issue may have been the product of a black majority county council at that time, and a good argument for the importance of a truly representative government. It is strange what we do and do not remember. I did not remember council as having a black majority. Two of the black members were elected at large, in a county where sixty-seven percent of the population was white! It wasn't until I began searching my memory about what we did and who did what that I was suddenly reminded of the racial makeup of the council. This is a tribute to our chairman, Arthur Horne, who kept us moving in a harmonious and cooperative manner.

I do believe that many hard-headed businessmen often worry about soft-hearted women who will not understand that budgets must be balanced. But I found in working on my first county budget that long years of managing my household money and trying to get the most out of the family budget made me at least, if not more, careful about spending money than most men who work with other people's money in business or government. A national consumer agency (headed by a woman) lobbied successfully for stores to mark their prices by units of measurement, so buyers would know how much each ounce costs rather than judge volume by the size of deceptively boxed package. Well, I had been dividing ounces into dollars for years. This parsimonious trait was the center of my approach to the next assignment from my chairman.

I was asked to consider a county commitment of $300,000 to enlarge the University of South Carolina–Beaufort's library. USC–Beaufort is a two-year branch of the University of South Carolina, which provides services such as libraries and faculty to it. In going over reports on educational facilities, I was struck by the fact, pointed out to me by Jim Zumwalt, that Beaufort's Technical College of the Lowcountry (TCL) was also planning to build a $1.2–million-dollar library, with $700,000 of that coming from the county. And the Beaufort County Library projected a need for $500,000, also from the county. My housewife's instinct made me wonder if Beaufort County could afford the luxury of such triplication, especially when we had so many other pressing needs.

I called a meeting of local officials of TLC, USC, and the public library to see if one really GREAT library wouldn't be better than three. They were all pleasant but told me they couldn't make such decisions because they were part of state agencies. So I called a meeting of the state agencies, and much to my amazement all their presidents came, along with the director of the South Carolina Commission on Higher Education, which controls spending and programs of all public higher education. They all agreed it would be a good idea to study the possibilities of cooperation in library, curriculum, and student services. Then they said, when all the facts were in, that the decision should be made locally.

The county manager suggested I create a blue-ribbon committee to supervise such a study, which I did. I appointed as chairman a retired army general who had a great interest in libraries and computer technology, and I was able to enlist the dean of the library school at Chapel Hill, then president of the American Library Association, as our consultant. His very thorough report recommended that we create one central library for administration, purchasing, and record keeping, with three specialized branches. He argued that it made no sense for a town of fewer than ten thousand people to have three separate library systems. One library card would be honored by all branches, which would give citizens, for the first time, access to the college libraries. The committee chairman liked this recommendation, which made computer technology the linchpin. I loved it because it was a shining example of my pledge (and everyone else's running for office) to use taxpayers' dollars in the most productive way by reducing unnecessary duplication. The libraries and their institutions hated it, and they put up an unbeatable fight. They wanted their independence and their own libraries, period. This was my first lesson in turf protection. Because I hadn't worked in big business or with bureaucracies, I had naïvely jumped into the cauldron of territorial conflicts and entrenchment. This just might be another asset a woman brings to government, because she usually has fewer vested interests to manipulate her judgment and fewer qualms about plowing through barricades which she sees as irrelevant to the real question of efficiency and economy.

We finally worked out a compromise—we created a consortium, mandating regular consultations between librarians for purchasing books, periodicals, and reference materials, each with holdings to meet their specific missions. They would build a common card catalog of periodicals and reference books and install an interlibrary telephone. USC–Beaufort's and TLC's collections would reflect their courses and programs, and the public library would have fiction and children's books. This agreement was honored for quite a few years, because with the escalating costs of books and reduced state funding the economics of sharing made it attractive. But with population growth and most of the original players in the agreement gone, the meetings between librarians fell off, and all the libraries expanded. However, one card still serves at all three libraries. It was a good learning experience for me. In addition to feeling the bruising effects of turf protection, I learned about compromise and the value of blue-ribbon committees led by people with impressive credentials, lessons which were useful in my later, larger battles in the legislature. This experience also dispelled a myth I held about men. I thought that when men got together to discuss important matters, they were more open, more frank, more to the point, more efficient (you know, all those masculine traits) than women. I found instead that I had an unexpected problem of having to interpret what some men really meant when they spoke, as well as the problem of convincing them that I really did mean what I said. However, that may have really been a discovery about men in politics rather than men in general.

My gift to Beaufort County was a logo. It was accomplished with little opposition and seems to be permanent. A councilman suggested we have a logo for stationary and signage and proposed we commission an artist to design it, at a cost of five thousand dollars or so. I suggested instead that we have a contest (an echo from my PTA days?) with a prize of a hundred dollars to the winner. I was put in charge of the project. We advertised, and as luck would have it, a schoolgirl persuaded her father, a commercial artist who had just moved to Hilton Head from Atlanta, to enter the contest. He won, and so did we. The logo is a square (with rounded corners) with four pictures: a large house, a spreading oak tree, a shrimp boat, and a fish . . . all significant to Beaufort. The only objection was from a black activist who I believe prided himself in finding something to object to at each council meeting. (Often he had cause, but not this time.) He said the house evoked memories of a slave owner's home and the tree was a hanging tree for lynching. Fortunately, four of the five black members of council had the courage to not be intimidated by his far-fetched argument. The vote was eight to one.

A major disappointment was failing to strengthen our zoning and land-use planning. I proposed that council hire an expert with experience in communities which had experienced rapid growth, especially in coastal areas, but I lost. The resident planner, who may have taken this as criticism, had many friends on council. Too bad Arthur Horne hadn't given me the advice then which he gave me when I was on my way to the legislature: "Harriet, always count your votes before you call for the question." If I had, I might have worked harder, rather than dropping the ball on a crucial issue which gets more difficult to solve as each day passes.

Twenty years later, Beaufort County Council finally woke up to the fact that we have doubled in population, with another doubling to take place within a few years. Council created a citizen's committee, called Target 2010, to examine all facets of growth. I chaired the committee on land-use and growth management. We spent a year developing findings and recommendations. Another year passed after our report was issued, until council retained experts to draw up a plan. If this plan withstands the assaults of developers and large land holders, I fervently hope there will still be time to close the proverbial barn door before it is too late. If only we had started twenty years ago.

Those two years on council gave me a new sense of self. I no longer thought of myself as only my husband's wife or my children's mother. I was my own person, with a newfound sense of personal control and public power. It was exhilarating.

CHAPTER 5

Running for the Legislature

When Jim Moss, our representative to the legislature decided not to seek reelection, he urged me to run and offered to be my campaign chairman. After discussing it with my husband ("It's your turn to do your thing") and my political son ("What a great idea"), I announced my candidacy, again with fear and uncertainty. But not with quite as much stomach-lurching as the first time.

My two years on county council had helped me to find ways to compensate for the lack of confidence I felt in a man's world, so common to women based at home. Working on the county level was a good first step for me. We worked with problems I had some knowledge of, which seemed manageable and finite. My successes bolstered my self-image, though I usually attributed those successes to those who helped me rather than to my own skills. I also learned that when I simply had to remember facts and figures, I could. And when I had to make a speech, I could. This was fortunate, because making speeches turned out to be a necessary part of being an effective legislator.

In one of my forays to encourage women to become interested in seeking political office, I discussed my experience at a women's seminar at the Technical College of the Lowcountry: "Once over the hurdle of running for higher office, I can tell you from my personal experience of the advantages of running and serving first on the local level. Most of us—especially those who have not had careers—need to develop skills, build confidence, and discover that we can serve as well as men. If we work in small units, with people we know, who know us, we don't have to work so hard proving ourselves, as we would with large groups of strangers in the legislature. We can learn more easily how one level of government works, and sometimes doesn't work. We can begin to understand the politics of power, how to build a collection of IOU's judiciously—favors that can be called on as needed—how to build a coalition. And we can build credibility, to become known as the kind of person who can get things done. And we can break down the stereotype of women as emotional and unrealistic. Many of us have done this in volunteer work, but in politics you have to prove yourself in the man's world. It is sad but true that a man is assumed to be competent until he proves himself incompetent. But with a woman the opposite is assumed. If you build this record, then you are in a much better position to run for higher office, to face stiffer competition."

And stiffer competition there was when I announced for the legislature. Because I had been elected to county council as top vote-getter, and because I thought I had passed the novice's test, it didn't occur to me there would be much resistance to me as a candidate for the House. I was actually surprised to discover that I did not have the support of the white Democratic establishment. What I didn't understand then was that one's success in running for local office does not translate into an easy run for the state legislature—especially for women. It took me a while to figure out that, once again, this was a typical women's problem, not just mine alone.

There are many reasons that the number of women in local office is growing rapidly, the number of women in state legislatures moderately, and number of women in Congress is just inching upwards. First, there is less competition from men for local offices, which are not as prestigious and do not attract the politically ambitious. And men are more ambitious, probably because of those sex roles we have been assigned at birth. Boys are told they can be president when they grow up. Girls don't receive that message. When there is less competition in a political race, the party machine is more tolerant of women running. Until recently, the only legislative races women were encouraged to enter were throwaway races—where a candidate is needed but there is little chance of winning.

When there is less competition, there is more chance of success, and so women are more willing to try at the local level than to run for highly sought offices, where more ego, more self-confidence, and a greater drive is needed. Could it be that many of us women do not think we are as capable to run government, to make major decisions in the legislature, and so we don't even try?

The most powerful barriers can be psychological. As Madelaine Kunin, former governor of Vermont, pointed out in a speech to women legislators at a National Conference of State Legislatures meeting, "The precedent for women in leadership is not there. The portraits on the walls in every state house transmit the message that it is still the average white young man who is thought of as the most obvious candidate and for a woman to enter that arena you have to break precedent, go against usual expectations." And the higher you go, the harder it gets.

Then there is the matter of money. The cost of running a legislative race is much greater than a local race, an important factor for women who don't have independent incomes. Most women hate asking for money and are reluctant to run when they learn how much a campaign costs. They can't count on funds for the primary campaign from the party, which prefers to support sure winners. Recognizing this problem, women's organizations like Emily's List (Early Money Is Like Yeast) have recently sprung up to raise early money for pro-choice Democratic women candidates, but so far these efforts have been limited to helping congressional or statewide candidates. There is also a similar organization dedicated to helping Republican women.

It is harder for women to serve in the legislature, as their life patterns have to be altered, especially for those who live too far from the capital to commute. Women traditionally put their families first, where men's focus is generally on furthering their business or professional careers. I am sure most men want to further their careers in order to give their families more, but many are motivated by the pursuit of power and all that follows power. On the other hand, most women are more interested in issues than power—until they discover that they need power to further their issues. The public is more likely to be critical of a woman putting her career before family, if that is how it is perceived, especially in the more socially conservative Southern states. This may be why few of my women colleagues in the legislature had young families. This is changing.

Finally, most women were untrained in political strategy. When I was first elected to county council I searched for some organization to help me learn the political process, how to be effective, how to overcome my self-doubts. And I couldn't find one. I wrote to the National Women's Education Fund, which had sent me materials on campaign strategy, and I said, "You've helped me get elected, now can you help me be effective?" They said they had no follow-up program at that time. Now there are many groups—the political parties, the National Women's Political Caucus, the Center for the American Woman and Politics at Rutgers University—which offer help to women in developing skills and understanding the political process. They hold training sessions for new office-holders. And conferences to learn about issues and be inspired to action.

I won the Democratic primary for House seat 124 in 1976 despite the opposition of the town establishment and the party leaders. Our lieutenant governor, Brantley Harvey, was from Beaufort and had been a family friend for two generations. In fact, his father was urged to come to Beaufort to practice law by my father-in-law, William. I thought that he would at least be neutral in the party primary, since he was a friend and the sitting lieutenant governor. He may have been neutral, but one of his law partners ran the campaign of my opponent, George O'Kelley, whose campaign literature was on display at the Harvey office. Perhaps they thought I was still an outsider, or too liberal, or that I just couldn't win the general election. Perhaps my library consortium, and possibly the Robert Smalls bust, were seen as negatives—or was it my connection with the Siceloffs at Penn Center? Or did lawyers help lawyers? I never did ask, and so I never learned why they opposed me. But happily, my corps of volunteers, women and new Beaufort residents who came to retire, the African-American community and my husband's patients, provided a counterbalance.

My son Billy, who was living in Washington and running a South Carolina congressional campaign, proposed a strategy for me and organized my campaign. He told me I had to go door to door. That was very difficult for me, and I kept putting it off. I found a way to reduce the number of visits by printing up notes saying "I came to ask for your support. Sorry you were not home," and I left them when no one answered my knock at the door. And I never went back. But finally I found that if someone I knew from the neighborhood went with me, my discomfort was reduced. In fact, I enjoyed some of the visits and learned more about the way people in the community lived and thought. Sometimes I was disappointed at the level of indifference or lack of knowledge. Other times I was gratified by the interest and awareness I found. I even made some new friends.

Then there was the matter of money, which I hated asking for. Most of my acquaintances in business and the professions whom I asked to serve on my committee were very pleasant, but they declined. John Trask, Jr., was an exception; he agreed to be my treasurer. He helped raise money without my personal involvement, initially. Several retired men, military and civilian, offered to help around the campaign office. I welcomed their participation, not just for the extra volunteer hours but because it helped dissolve any image that this was an all-female campaign. The women with whom I had worked for so many years as volunteers were always available when I called on them. My family was wonderful. Herbert was totally supportive, willing to do anything we asked, including folding and stamping. My photographer son, Paul, took some great pictures. My psychotherapist daughter, Beth, kept my spirits up. My oldest daughter, Judy, who lived in Washington and couldn't do much except give me words of encouragement, had changed careers a few times. She strengthened me by saying that her mother was going to be her role model as a late bloomer at the age of fifty-two. My housekeeper of twenty-odd years, Maybelle, was an ardent campaigner on Warsaw and St. Helena Islands and exhorted her many friends and large family to go to the polls on election day. How could I lose?

I had good press and competent advertising. In reading over a pre-election interview with the local paper I am pleased to see now that my platform really turned out to be the base of most of my work in the legislature. I was for equalization of school financing, raising teacher's pay to the southeastern average, the ERA, judicial reform, stronger tidelands protection, containment of utility rates, strong controls for nuclear and hazardous wastes, public kindergartens, and clean, nonpolluting industries with jobs above minimum wage for Beaufort. Of course, these are boilerplate issues (except for the ERA), but I did stick with this agenda and made a difference in all but the industry jobs, the one area I felt shut out of by the local development board and county administration. I initially thought this was because I was a woman but later decided that it was just a closed shop. There was not the will or the vision to bring industry to Beaufort, and they didn't want anyone else's vision to get in their way.

In addition to a platform, I had several slogans: "Thirty years of public service! A full-time worker for Beaufort! If she wins . . . we all win!" My direct mail was written by others. A retired Marine Corps officer wrote to members of the Retired Officer's Association, as did a retired noncommissioned officer to his peers. An educator wrote to educators, a doctor to doctors, an art advocate to artists, a tennis player to tennis players. It all helped.

I won the primary by about two hundred votes, but the election was contested because my opponent's name and mine were somehow left off the ballots in one small precinct. Brantley Harvey's other partner, Colden Battey, represented my opponent before the County Executive Committee and asked for another election. Although I had been told I did not need a lawyer for this hearing, a member of the committee came out of the hearing room to where I was waiting and advised me to get one. I rushed out to find Jim Moss, who came to my rescue. The committee ruled in my favor, noting that if everyone in the precinct had voted for my opponent he still couldn't have won, because there were fewer than two hundred people in the precinct. Therefore, another election could not change the outcome. My opponent appealed to the state party, which sustained the decision in my favor—barely. The vote was eight to six. I went on to win the general election with a comfortable sixty percent of the vote. My friendship with Brantley and Colden was renewed, and they became my supporters. I made it easy for them by having no opposition for the next twelve years.

There were lessons learned from this campaign. As I went to neighborhood coffees, visited door-to-door, or walked down the street everyone was so cordial, so encouraging, so positive about my campaign that I was unrealistically optimistic. I naïvely took everyone at their word, not factoring in Southern good manners or people's reluctance to state their personal political preferences or take a chance on being negative to a candidate who just might win. When the tallies came in after the election, I found I had won only one white-majority precinct, the one encompassing the Old Point, our silk-stocking district. Even my polling was misleadingly optimistic. I was stunned, but I learned a lesson. I had to find some way to communicate to my constituents who I really was—what I was doing in Columbia and why, how I was voting and why.

Billy suggested I take the time to write a column in the local newspaper, if they would have me. The editor agreed, and at least once a month I discussed the issues of the moment, pro and con, in the *Beaufort Gazette*. The *Gazette* also invited the representative from Hilton Head and our senator to write columns. They wrote a few, then disappeared from print. It took time, but in the long run it probably saved me time. Many feel that it was this regular communication with the voters that kept me happily unopposed for twelve years and kept me in office when I was finally opposed. But above all, it was a great discipline for me. In order to write a column, I had to thoroughly examine the issue. Such in-depth knowledge of the important, or controversial, issues can be enormously helpful to a legislator on many fronts. In my last election I won all but one white precinct, and that one was Fripp Island, home of straight party-line Republicans, many of them newcomers who were detached from local politics.

What was it that pushed me to run despite my real and many fears? I had learned in those two years on county council that there had to be changes on the state level before we could improve the problems at home. Education across the state, not just in Beaufort, was dismal. South Carolina was at or near the bottom nationally in all the rankings by which public education was measured. Conversely, we were at the top of the list in illiteracy, school dropouts, infant mortality, teenage pregnancy, unemployment, and underemployment .

We had a very fragile environment, and precious, irreplaceable resources—marshes, rivers, beaches and forests—with few policies in place to protect them. We had a good ol' boy system which protected the status quo and vested interests at the expense of the public interest and open government. The oil embargo in 1973 highlighted our vulnerability with respect to energy dependence. We were an energy-wasting state with few energy sources other than nuclear plants, and we were doing nothing about alternatives. Energy costs were skyrocketing, with insufficient control by a Public Service Commission influenced by special interests, which Jim Moss, my predecessor, had been battling to change. Women were grossly underrepresented as lawmakers, board members, and state employees. There was so much to do, and I wanted to do it all.

CHAPTER 6

Cast of Characters

When I arrived at the legislature, Jim Edwards was governor, the first Republican since Reconstruction. He was elected in 1974 because the Democratic Party became deeply divided when the charismatic Charles (Pug) Ravenel, after winning the Democratic nomination, was declared ineligible to serve on the grounds that he had not lived in the state the five years mandated by the constitution. Pug came from a blue-collar family in Charleston, won a scholarship to Exeter, the prestigious northern prep school, provided by a Charleston newspaper to an outstanding newsboy, and a football scholarship to Harvard. He then worked in a Wall Street firm before coming home to Charleston. When he ran for governor, he challenged the good ol' boys and promised to be a reform governor. But he was stopped by the courts in a suit he believed was initiated by his primary opponent, William Jennings Bryan Dorn. Pug made the mistake, fatal to his political future, of not supporting Dorn who then became the Democratic candidate in the general election. As a result of this split in the Democratic party Edwards walked into the governorship. Although I understood Pug's anger, I personally was sorry that he reacted as he did, because this resulted in the state losing a strong, progressive leader who could otherwise have been elected to any number of offices further down the road.

Jim Edwards was an oral surgeon, a very genial man who understood the need to work pleasantly with the overwhelmingly white Democratic legislature. South Carolina Democrats, for the most part, were like the congressional Southern Democrats, a different breed from the "national" party. When I arrived in 1977, of 124 House members, there were only twelve Republicans and thirteen blacks. In my early years, partisanship did not control the agenda, as it does now. Republicans cosponsored Democrats' bills and vice versa. I remember working with Republicans on at least three bills in my first two years of office: with Moffatt Burriss on an energy conservation building code bill, with Ed Simpson in his eternal struggle to pass a bill requiring deposits for soft drink and beer containers, and with Joyce Hearn on my bill to prohibit open containers with alcohol drinks in automobiles.

There were certainly differences between legislators, but at that time they were based more on local constituencies than political party—rural versus urban, black versus white, Low Country versus Upstate. I found myself at odds with Governor Edwards on several issues. I was for kindergartens in all public schools, he was not. I was for the Coastal Zone Management Bill, and he vetoed it the first go-round. He did accept a compromise beach management bill the year I arrived. But our greatest differences were on energy conservation and nuclear waste policy. And those differences persisted long after he left the Governor's Office, because he was appointed by President Reagan to serve as secretary of energy, a department he pledged to shut down. He was a strong supporter of nuclear energy, "the cleanest, safest, cheapest form of energy," as he used to say, ignoring the untold costs of handling and disposing of the waste. For me, energy conservation was a driving issue, which I pursued in bills of many forms, losing some and winning some over the years. I believed in subsidies or tax incentives for solar and other renewable energy forms. He didn't. I worriedly watched the 1973 oil embargo increase our dependence on Middle East countries, which could affect public opinion and our foreign policy. I also was becoming an environmentalist, and renewable energy and recycling seemed the most sensible way to preserve our resources and save energy. But despite our differences on these issues, we had a cordial relationship, without the partisan acrimony which came later as the Republicans gained more power and saw the possibility of gaining control. After Jim Edwards left the Reagan administration, he came home to Charleston to become the president of the Medical University of South Carolina, aggressively building new buildings, new programs, and re-creating a medical center which attracts physicians and faculty from around the country.

One of the first calls I received the night of my election was from Nancy Stevenson, a House member from Charleston. She called to welcome me to the House and told me, "I'll be so happy to have someone I can walk up to and say, 'Let's go to dinner.'" She had heard about me from a mutual friend and knew we would be compatible. Finding someone to go to dinner was a social problem for women in legislatures, especially Southern ones. The men somehow just couldn't allow themselves to let us pay our way, so we hesitated to invite ourselves. Added to that was a fear that our presence might inhibit them or make them ill at ease.

Nancy's mother was from old-line Charleston society, and her father, William Backer, was a New York businessman. Nancy had lived in both cities. After her father died, her mother returned to Charleston. A graduate of Smith College, Nancy worked as a newspaper journalist for a short while, married a Scandinavian diplomat, and, like her mother, returned to Charleston when she divorced. She married a Charleston lawyer, raised children, and wrote mystery books. She tried to guide me. She suggested I stay in the hotel where most legislators stayed, the Wade Hampton, right across the street from the capitol, and I did. She insisted I come to the hotel lounge where all the legislators (and lobbyists) sat around in the evenings, drank, and talked about the day's actions, and I did. I drank very little and did not feel like one of the crowd, but I hung in there—and it paid off in building connections and alliances, if not friends.

When the hotel was sold I had to find another place to live for those two nights a week. I had a variety of "homes," all of them pleasant. I lived with two women law students in a small house next to the University of South Carolina campus. When the students who had invited me in graduated and moved out, and a succession of others moved in, I decided it was time to leave. I lived next in the master suite of the James F. Byrnes House museum, which was carefully cared for by Kay McCoy, a charming woman close to my children's age, who worked for the state and seemed happy to have my company. She loved politics, liked my stands on the issues, and was always waiting to hear at the end of the day what went on in the legislature. Two years after I moved in, the Byrnes House was rented to Strom Thurmond, who wanted a presence in Columbia. Kay had to move out and so did I. I stayed for a while in a hotel, but I really didn't like changing rooms and beds every week. One year I lived with Margaret Carter, a friend of Tunky Riley, a fine artist with a cheerful home and a wonderful art studio. Margaret's husband fortuitously worked in another city on Tuesdays and Wednesdays, which just fit my schedule, as those were the nights I stayed in Columbia. She also loved to hear of the day's happenings and plied me with wonderful biscuits and muffins for breakfast while she listened. Then the Whitney Hotel opened, with its comfortable suites: two bedrooms separated by a living room and a small kitchen. They attracted many legislators and offered us the luxury of keeping the same room every week. Senator Nell Smith and I decided to try it out, and we shared a suite there until we both left the legislature, after the 1992 session.

Nancy Stevenson decided to run for lieutenant governor in 1979 and won, the first woman to be elected to a statewide office. As a legislator and lieutenant governor she was a strong supporter of women and children, started an innovative consumer service with a toll-free number for all citizens to use, and supported the environmental issues which took center stage during that period. When we were working on the first educational reform bill she insisted we should not succumb to minimum standards but raise our sights. She turned out to be right. After her term was up she moved to Washington and opened an art gallery, came back for an ill-advised run for Congress, then disappeared from South Carolina again. I was sorry to lose a friend.

There was a small group of legislators to whom I was attracted from the start. They were bright, progressive, funny, and very energetic. They became the nucleus of what we came to call the Crazy Caucus. In the House there are all kinds of groups, and they were my group. We were all freshmen, except for Bob McFadden, who had been there for years, and Jean Toal, who came just one session ahead of us.

Jean Toal was another woman legislator who welcomed me enthusiastically and helped me, but in different ways than Nancy. She was a young lawyer with a steel trap of a mind who could always give me colorful background information on any ally or opponent, as well as historical analysis of most issues. She was a leader in finally passing

Home Rule in 1975. She became a coleader of our group, along with Bob Sheheen, her law-school classmate and close friend. She became the first woman to hold a leadership position in the House when she chaired the Rules Committee. This was a fitting honor, as there was no one better than she in her understanding and use of the rules. She probably could have won the chairmanship of the Judiciary Committee if she had fought for it. Jean and I were on the same side most of the time; the exceptions were the Living Will and abortion-related bills. Jean left the House in 1988 when she was elected to the state supreme court after a hotly contested battle, the first woman to be elected to the highest court. In running for reelection in 1995 (the legislature elects and reelects supreme court judges), she was strongly opposed by the Republican Party. As the majority party in the state, they wanted at last to elect one of their own to the court. Jean was a Democrat, but she was also a pro-life spokesperson when a legislator. She managed to peel off a few Republicans to join her coalition of Democrats by getting the endorsement of the Citizens for Life organization. With this show of strength, the other candidate, a judge who had allegedly been recruited by the Republicans, withdrew, and Jean was elected unanimously. Many believe she will be the next chief justice, one more reason for the Republicans to have tried to push her out before that seat opens up.

Bob Sheheen was a lawyer from Camden with a wonderful mind and tremendous energy. He commuted during the session, arriving earlier than most and reading every bill in the bill book which might come up for discussion that day, as compared to some of us who read some bills and others who barely looked at the calendar before the House came to order. He also was a master of the rules, which he played as if in a competitive sport. He never left the House chambers while we were in session; he never left his seat but concentrated totally on the bills before him and what was being said about them. He didn't even leave his seat to use the telephone. He was our very effective watchdog. He didn't go to the podium often, but when he did, there was silence and everyone listened. Even when he was chairman of Judiciary Committee, he knew the details of the appropriations bills better than most Ways and Means Committee members. He maintained his interest in the appropriations bill after he was elected Speaker of the House. He was elected speaker earlier in his career than most, by dint of his hard work, intelligence, and straightforwardness. He remained speaker until the Republicans took over in 1994.

Although Bob had been bipartisan in his appointments and friendships as speaker, he was made a victim of partisanship by his Republican friends. There were also some Democrats who faulted him for being too friendly with the Republicans, and some of the Black Caucus who felt he did not support them enough. He had supported Republican David Wilkins, his personal friend and tennis partner, for chairman of Judiciary Committee, with the understanding David would not direct reapportionment when it came up. He supported David for speaker pro tem with the understanding David would not oppose him for speaker. He was disappointed in both respects. Bipartisanship became a one-way street and was a bitter pill for Bob to swallow. I asked him in 1996 why, when so many moderates of both parties were leaving the House, he chose to stay. He answered, "Someone has to stay and watch and try to keep them honest." He is the only one left of our group. In the 1996 elections the Republicans tried their best to unseat him, but he survived easily in his Republican district.

Palmer Freeman was the man who drew me into the group, and it turned out to be a group which blew away my worries about finding dinner company. He was a young lawyer from Fort Mill, also in our freshman class. Palmer had an easy-going casual air, almost concealing his quick mind and seriousness about issues, most of which were my issues. Best of all, he treated me as a peer, not a woman old enough to be his mother. He knew of me because he grew up with my friend Tim Belk, the college professor with whom I ran the foreign film series. But our more recent connection was through his law partner, who sat on the Executive Committee of the state Democratic Party when they voted on my election appeal. His vote in my favor made the difference between my winning and losing. Palmer Freeman left the House in 1987 when he married a judge who did not live in the district he represented. He moved to Columbia, where she lived, and gave up his seat. He joined a law firm and spends some of his time lobbying for environmental and other good causes.

Palmer hung out with his seat mate, Bob McFadden, who was the chairman of his legislative delegation from York County. Bob was chairman of the Judiciary Committee and a longtime House member. He was a quiet, modest man, not the partying kind. He preferred a quiet dinner with a few members and staff of his Judiciary Committee. This included Palmer, who often invited me to come along. Jean Toal and Bob Sheheen, two of the most active members of Judiciary Committee, were often there. Also part of the group was Tommy Hughston, who was at the Citadel with Pat Conroy. He won me over when I asked, "How much of the *Lords of Discipline* was true?" and he answered, "Ninety-five percent." At that time Pat Conroy was the person most Citadel graduates despised. (That hatred intensified in the early 1990s when he took up the cause of admitting women to the Citadel.) Tommy left the House when the legislature elected him to the circuit court, surely to be a judge with a broader view than many of our other choices.

Malloy McEachin, a young lawyer from the Pee Dee area, was the most conservative of the group, especially on fiscal issues. But he was multifaceted. He was a strong environmentalist. He also gave good cover to those of us who supported early the removal of the Confederate battle flag from the top of the capitol dome. He made a wonderful and surprising (to me) case for removing it. He talked about his grandfather who had fought in the war and ended dramatically with a quotation from Robert E. Lee telling the people of the South the war is over, take down the flag. Malloy left in 1990 to go home to make a living for his wife and three children. He must have missed the legislature because he ran again in 1994, but his district had been changed by reapportionment, and he lost by a very small margin.

Ginger Crocker of Laurens came a year later, in a special election. She played a very specific role in our group. She had been a worker in Democratic Party politics since college and knew every connecting link between every political activist and elected official in the state. And she could count. She knew what votes we had on each issue and who could turn a legislator's vote around in a crunch. She also knew how to locate missing legislators when we needed them. She was not the party whip, but she was our whip. She rarely went to the podium, but she played an important role in her Labor, Commerce and Industry Committee and could tell us the good and bad about the complicated legislation coming out of that committee. She left the legislature in 1984 when appointed by Governor Riley to serve on the Worker's Compensation Commission. Before she left, she filed the first bill which would have had the effect of ensuring women the right to attend the Citadel. Sarah Manly tried again. As the whole country knows, much to our embarrassment, it was finally the courts, not the legislature, that put this plan into action.

Paul Cantrell was with us too short a time. He was lawyer from Charleston who replaced Nancy Stevenson and joined us in all our causes. He decided to run for the Senate, and one foggy night, when he was flying his own plane on the way home from a campaign function, he crashed while landing and was killed.

These legislators were the nucleus of the Crazy Caucus, and around us were many others who swirled in and out, depending on the issues. Between us we could count on thirty-five percent of the votes on most issues but had to be on our toes to win a majority on the controversial ones. The Black Caucus usually voted with us, until reapportionment, when everyone was on their own. (And the bruises didn't go away after that action was over.)

What were our issues? We were for reforming the way government works, including the House rules and filibusters, judicial selection, campaign reform, and ethics. We worked to improve education; we were environmentalists. We worked for tax reform, for removing the sales tax from food, for eliminating the hundreds of millions of dollars in tax exemptions for special interests. We supported the arts. We did not all agree on all those issues all the time. There were varying opinions on abortion rights and affirmative action, as well as taxes. If I were asked to pick one major pursuit which drove us, I would say it was defending the public interest against special interests. And that is why we were almost always opposed by another informal "caucus," the Fat and Uglies, who were the spokesmen for the special interests.

As important as the coalescence on issues was, an added bonus was that we also enjoyed each other's company. In addition to the ordinary, day-to-day interactions, there were special events. Some of us played tennis when we adjourned early. We were at all levels, but it was fun. Bob Sheheen was the best, but he rarely played with us. As a commuter and practicing lawyer, he went home to work if we adjourned early. But we forgave him because he cooked wonderful Lebanese dinners for us when the workdays were not too long and he could get back to Camden in time to set up for us. We attended each other's celebrations. One year, the entire caucus came to Beaufort for the annual Water Festival. Other years Bob invited us to the horse races in Camden. It was great fun. By the time I left the House, the others, except for Bob, were gone, and the fun had long since disappeared.

Our major opponents were the Fat and Uglies, sometimes joined by the Sol Blatt "old guard" and sometimes by Republicans. The Fat and Uglies were a group of young conservative representatives who were restive because of their lack of influence and were against anything the leadership was for. They felt locked out by the traditional seniority system which existed under the reign of Sol Blatt and his followers, whose place they yearned to take. They opposed the Crazy Caucus, whom they saw as the more likely successors to the old guard in power and leadership positions. They were Democrats and Republicans, blacks and whites. I never knew the extent and depth of their membership, but I knew who their leaders were, from time to time: David Hawkins, John Felder, Jack Rogers, George Gregory, and Ron Cobb, all Democrats. Hawkins and Felder later switched parties. Gregory was defeated. Rogers was indicted as part of Operation Lost Trust. Bob Kohn and Bill Cork were Republicans from the start.

David Hawkins owned a filling station in Roebuck, near Spartanburg. He was a colorful clown who led the group and was its spokesman. He was closely allied with Carroll Campbell and resigned to become his legislative aide when Campbell became governor. When we were trying to pass legislation to shorten the session, Hawkins, who opposed this, told Palmer Freeman, who sat across the aisle from him, "I can go home and pump gas in Roebuck or stay here and be treated like a King." He reveled in his Columbia life.

Robert Kohn, an early Republican, was an insurance agent from Charleston. He sometimes played the part of a clown. He sold vitamins to legislators, making his deliveries on Tuesdays. He was the first victim of Ron Cobb during the sting operation. He was pulled in first and in turn pulled others into the circle. The only legislation I connect with him are bills related to insurance. Like most of the other Fat and Uglies, his role was usually being against, rather than for, proposed legislation.

John Felder was the nephew of the powerful Senator Marion Gressette and a staunch defender of the status quo, the utilities, and the nuclear waste industry. When I was a freshman in the legislature I saw him as a populist and defender of "the little people" (his constituency was majority black) because of his silver tongue. He could sway an iron post, and he swayed me on many a vote. Until I broke through the spell of his oratory, to which I was admittedly susceptible, and came to understand more clearly the impact of demagoguery. We ended up being on the opposite sides of absolutely everything. His reactions to my name on a bill, or my presence at the podium were as predictable as the reflexes of Pavlov's dogs.

How to describe the group as a whole? *Southern Magazine* summed it up in an October 1986 article about this unusual group of men (and an occasional woman): "What truly holds this eclectic team together is their unapologetic lust for power and influence. What sets them apart from other politicians is a relentless self-parody in the gratification of that lust." The article continued: "What with Democratic moderates, the emerging Republican party, women and the new Black Caucus, state politics just wasn't the same. In 1978 they decided to form their own caucus, and the name was selected by Representative George Gregory, who said 'to look at us, you'd have to call us the Fat and Ugly Caucus.'"

According to the *State* (September 2, 1990), "It [the Fat and Ugly Caucus] billed itself as a social group whose primary function was to go to lunch each Thursday at the expense of that week's chosen lobbyist. Lobbyists say they had little choice but to pick up the tab for the 25 to 30 members, which could run as high as $600. . . . 'David (Hawkins) took care of everybody. David ran the thing. . . . He made sure there was always somebody there at night to take you out. It was a well-organized group.'

"That organization earned the group a reputation of pressuring lobbyists into granting monetary favors—a practice sources say may be at the heart of the federal probe of the sting called Operation Lost Trust. 'It reached a point where they started ganging up on votes, and if they decided a lobbyist wasn't doing right, they would take care of him,' said a veteran lobbyist who refused to be identified. . . .

"'Lobbyists who wouldn't take the caucus members out to lunch found that legislation they supported suddenly ran into trouble,' the lobbyist said. But David Hawkins, their leader, denied that."

It is also clear, with goals like theirs, why they were the core group investigated by the FBI in the vote-selling investigation called Lost Trust, which hit our state in 1990. Cindi Ross Scoppi writes in the *State* on September 2, 1990, "If all 17 current and former legislators known to have been questioned by the FBI in a federal vote-selling probe go to jail, it'll be like a big reunion of the House's now-defunct Fat and Ugly Caucus. . . . All five former and current legislators who have been indicted on charges of selling their votes were members of the caucus. Eleven of the 14 implicated lawmakers were members of the group. . . . One caucus member who no longer is in the House, and who insisted he not be identified, said some members of the group weren't as careful as they should have been in their dealings with lobbyists after founder David Hawkins left the House in 1987 to work for Governor Carroll Campbell. . . . Lobbyists say the caucus was disbanded when Rep. Bob Sheheen, D. Kershaw, became House speaker and wouldn't put up with it." Operation Lost Trust, otherwise known as "The Sting," decimated the ranks of the Fat and Uglies. It was actually self-destructive, with one of their own, Ron Cobb, a legislator turned lobbyist, choosing the victims, then bringing evidence on videotape to the FBI. Ron was in trouble with the law and agreed to finger other legislators. He first drew in a few of his friends, who in turn lured others into the trap. They were probably selected by Cobb because they had a reputation of being good buddies with many lobbyists. The perception was that he deliberately fingered more blacks and was reined in by the prosecutors when the racial makeup of victims became so unbalanced, according to the *State* (March 23, 1997).

I personally never felt that most of them "sold their votes." Most of the accused were already supporters, even sponsors, of the pari-mutuel bill before Ron Cobb entered the picture. Many believed they were being given the usual campaign contributions. But the videotapes used as evidence of giving and receiving certainly offered a display of the tawdry scene at the State House, where gifts, bribes, and campaign contributions were distributed casually by lobbyists, who mingled freely with legislators. The *State* (March 2, 1997) put it well: "Friendship and trust grew with the free lunches, dinners, weekend getaways and other gifts until there was, for some lawmakers, no clear line between social interaction and vote-selling." It was a climate that created a susceptibility to a corrupt political process. When the sting first came to light, I had a call from a friend at NBC who asked me what I knew about "Bubbagate." This one word aptly describes a very strong good ol' boy system full of little favors leading to larger favors. This in turn leads to an attitude by those in the system that giving and taking is a normal part of the political process. This good ol' boy relationship creates a climate that can produce decisions verging on small, maybe medium, corruption—although those involved would never see it as corruption. They called it cooperation, helping a friend.

It was bad government, but legal—until the Ethics Reform Act of 1991, passed in reaction to the public outcry about the sting, set strict limits and prohibitions against lobbyist contributions, entertainment, and gifts to legislators. Lost Trust has still not played itself out. It was resurrected in March 1997 by U.S. District Judge Falcon Hawkins, who, in a blistering, eighty-six-page ruling, dismissed indictments against five of the accused legislators who were appealing their sentences because of "egregious misconduct" of the prosecutor, Bart Cox. He said prosecutors had allowed witnesses to lie, failed to disclose evidence that might have helped the defendants, and lied to the courts. He was critical of the way the FBI and the prosecutor allowed Ron Cobb determine how the investigation would be run and then let him testify as he chose, selecting "victims" and writing the script. He further cited "inconsistencies in and omissions" from the record in the matter of Dick Greer, a close friend of Governor Campbell, and the retroactive capital-gains tax bill, which saved twenty-one people, many of them friends and supporters of the governor, eight million dollars. This bill was another part of Lost Trust, for which Representative Jack Rogers was found guilty and sent to jail. According to the *State,* Judge Hawkins said prosecutors didn't investigate the tax break fully, possibly because it came too close to persons in positions of power. Senate Democrats have followed up on Hawkins' statement by filing a bill to give them subpoena powers to investigate further. Republican leaders say that they are trying to "get Campbell." The Democrats deny this and say they are just trying to find out how the capital gains tax passed. Meanwhile, former prosecutor Bart Cox plans to appeal Judge Hawkins's ruling. There may be more scenes in this drama, which most had thought concluded years ago.

I had another theory about our legislature's susceptibility to the giving and taking of favors. South Carolina has one of the longest legislative sessions, as compared to other states our size. Georgia meets for about two months, South Carolina, five. North Carolina meets every other year, we meet every year. It is more and more difficult for wage earners to give the time necessary to serve in the legislature, especially where the pay is so low. Some come to think of the free meals and entertainment as something they deserve, something owed to them. And those looking for that got it—fancy nightclubs, free golf, trips to exciting places. The longer the legislature stayed in Columbia, the more of this they enjoyed. Year after year, I and others, after studying other states' schedules, filed bills to shorten our sessions, to study alternatives. The same people who fought ethics reform also fought off our efforts to shorten the session.

In a telling comparison to the ignominious end of the Fat and Uglies, the Crazy Caucus ranks were gradually depleted when many of our members left to become judges.

One of the first open battles between the Crazy Caucus and the Fat and Uglies was on reforming the Public Service Commission, a stronghold for the good ol' boys. Another was to limit filibusters, many of which were led by leaders of the Fat and Uglies, who seemed to serve the lobbyists at least as faithfully as their own constituents. Filibusters could stop bills the special interests wanted stopped. After all, the Fat and Uglies were wined and dined by lobbyists, and their campaign fundraisers were fattened by them. We, on the other hand, were usually working against special interest lobbyists, so collisions were inevitable. There was probably more personal heat generated between us and them over the filibuster than any other issue.

In the battles for speaker, speaker pro tem, and committee chairs, it was basically us against them. The winner was the group who could cajole enough other votes—they usually picked up most Republicans and we most of the Black Caucus—depending on the issue. The balance was tight. That's why Ginger Crocker's talent for counting and keeping track of votes was so important. And Bob Sheheen's power, derived from his extraordinarily hard work, and finally his position as speaker. And Jean's ability in molding compromise and dissecting issues complete with historical background, in committee and on the floor. Those were the days when people listened to those speaking at the podium, a civility which no longer exists in the House, I am told.

My contribution was in doing research, developing position papers, printing up persuasive materials, and working the floor to explain our position. My allies were masters of the House rules, which was one of our greatest weapons. I was not. When I was elected, my predecessor, Jim Moss, said to me, "The first thing you have to do is learn the rules. You can't win without that." Well, I tried, but gave up. I read them into my recorder and played the tapes while driving back and forth to Columbia. It didn't work. The rules are wordy and described procedures I did not yet understand. If I had waited a year or two, the tapes might have taken, but by then I had those allies who could take care of them for me. On technical issues I relied on the person who knew the most about whatever issue was up for debate. They relied on me when nuclear waste and cultural matters came up.

The Crazy Caucus was just one of many small groups in the House. Others were the Old Guard, who were mostly senior Ways and Means Committee members and entrenched committee chairmen who had served under Sol Blatt; the Black Caucus; the Republican Caucus; and the Democratic Caucus. There were others who drew together on specific issues: the Peedee tobacco farmers, the coastal tourism caucus, the rural caucus. There were some legisators who were in no group and had no special allegiance, and many of them were votes we could win when necessary.

As members of the Crazy Caucus peeled off and left the House, others were drawn in by Bob Sheheen when he became speaker. For me, when the tight circle dissolved in the middle 1980s, the group dynamics and élan which had been so supportive and bracing were gone. Fortunately, others arrived who became my friends and allies, and there were shifting alliances for each issue.

Crosby Lewis, Tim Rogers, and Jack Rogers were the leaders in helping to pass Governor Dick Riley's Education Improvement Act, otherwise known as the EIA. Crosby sat just behind me in the House and next to me in Ways and Means Committtee and became a great friend and support. He shored me up whenever my hopes flagged and kept telling me what a great job I was doing. Crosby had served in the House in the 1960s and had chaired a major committee, so he knew the ropes when he returned in 1983. I watched with dismay, then admiration as he bluffed and fought his way to win important points during the EIA confrontations. He was a trial lawyer who kept fighting ferociously when I, on the other hand, was ready to compromise. I understood that part of my positioning came from wanting to get along with everyone (a female trait?) and to protect my links with others whose support I might need for the next issue. When I chided him for an abrasive speech in committee he would remind me, "I didn't come to the legislature to be loved. I came to win what I believe in." He was right, and I was wrong. The lines had been drawn for me soon after I came to the legislature, on issues and between people, and giving in too much on a specific issue just to get along was a useless gesture, one that would not translate into support on the next issues.

McKinley Washington was the leader of the Black Caucus with whom I worked most closely. He was an ordained Presbyterian minister from the small town of Ravenel, near Charleston. He is now in the Senate, an articulate spokesman for education, minority rights, the environment, children, and women. He represents a long district stretching from Ravenel down into Beaufort. Unlike most nonresident senators, he amazingly attends meetings and special events in all the towns of his district. He is often a bridge between the white conservatives and the Black Caucus, a pragmatic leader who understands the limits of giving by both sides. I was sorry to see him leave the House, although he surely is an invaluable senator. He is still in the Senate.

Tim Rogers arrived in 1983. He was a young Columbia lawyer who fought for public and higher education in committee and on the floor. The University of South Carolina was in his backyard, and he was its staunchest defender. He also led the House Democrats as majority leader when many were fleeing the party. He was articulate, hardworking, and loved politics. He was an ardent defender of minority rights and civil liberties. He left in 1996, disheartened by the toll the redistricting lines drawn by Republicans and the Black Caucus had taken on moderate white Democrats. And by the fallout from the new, autocratic Republican majority. David Wilkins, the new speaker, removed him from the Ways and Means and Rules Committees and presided over the defunding of the Energy and Cultural Affairs Committees on which Tim had enjoyed serving. What was the point of sitting in the House and doing nothing, three days a week, when he had a family to support? He was willing to make sacrifices to serve when he was able to make a difference, but not if he was left powerless. My son Billy, who had been elected in my place, also left that year, for some of the same reasons.

As did Doug McTeer of Hampton, a hardworking straight arrow who commuted more than one hundred miles to be with his family and teach a computer course at a technical college on the nights he wasn't at his graduate classes at the university. Doug had chaired the Education Subcommittee on Ways and Means and was a fair and moderate presenter during appropriation bill discussions. He also was an effective spokesman for rural communities like the one he came from. He became chairman of the Rules Committee when Jean Toal left to become a judge. When the Republicans took over, he lost that chairmanship and his seat on Ways and Means; he was sent with Tim Rogers and other Democrats to Siberia, a weakened Medical, Military and Municipal Affairs Committee to which the speaker sent no important bills. What a waste of talent, when the supply of talent was increasingly limited.

Joe McElveen was the leader in the effort to control hazardous wastes. Joe was a lawyer from Sumter, where one of the largest hazardous wastes sites in the South was located—within a hundred feet or so from a lake which was a major water provider for the state. He did voluminous research, introduced bill after bill, fought battle after battle, making an inroad once in a while with the Department of Health and

Environmental Control (DHEC). He also served as a Democratic leader for several years. He was the prime target of the Republicans and the hazardous waste industries he tangled with, and in the 1996 election they finally accomplished their mission and removed him from the House.

Pete Pearce, a hotel owner and realtor from Myrtle Beach, came to the legislature in 1983. He was a great addition to our group, supporting our bills and issues with a calm and quiet manner. He was a strong advocate for beachfront management, looking at the issue from a long-term perspective rather than seeing only the immediate impact of such regulations on his own business and in his own district. He served on the South Carolina Coastal Council, a body which interpreted and administered the Beachfront Management Act, our state's answer to erosion and development threats to our coastal areas. He could always be counted on to support the arts, education, and women's issues, such as reproductive choice. To our dismay, he was targeted by the Republican Party and unexpectedly defeated by a young, pro-life conservative, Ken Corbett, who appeared out of nowhere in 1988. After I left the legislature and was coordinating a coalition to oppose national and state legislation threatening our environmental laws, Pete was a great help to me in his district, where he is well-respected. He seems happy to be out of politics.

Candy Waites was the first of several fine women legislators who increased the ranks of those trying to protect the environment, women, and children. Candy, who arrived in a special election in 1988, had served on Richland County Council for twelve years, including one term as chairman. She brought with her an understanding of politics, a concern for the problems of local government, and a passion to clean up the environment and state government. She was the lead sponsor of the ethics bill, the time for which had finally come following Lost Trust. In 1993 Candy was redistricted out of her seat when the lines were drawn to place her against an incumbent Republican in his Republican district. She chose not to run but to go back to school for a graduate degree in Public Adminstration—at about the same time her first grandchild arrived. She also is an adminstrator of women's leadership programs at Columbia College.

Jim Hodges of Lancaster was another progressive who chaired the House Judiciary Committee for a short time, then lost that position when the House changed hands and the Republicans took over in 1994. He then took on the unenviable position of minority leader. He was and is an effective spokeman in responding to the Republican leadership, speaking up against cuts in education, keeping the Barnwell nuclear waste dump open, the “Takings” bill (also called the Property Rights bill), and other items on the Republican agenda. At this writing, he has announced himself to be a Democratic candidate for governor and is seen as an articulate and credible candidate by those who watch politics.

Bob McLellan, a successful insurance executive in Seneca, was a fair, honest, and capable man who became chair of the Ways and Means Committee when the previous chairman, Tom Mangum, died suddenly. Although he was a close friend of Sol Blatt's, I always felt he was closer ideologically to us than to Blatt's group on most issues . . . possibly his spending his early years in an orphanage made him sensitive to problems of our society. He was very supportive of education and Governor Riley's reform efforts. To the great surprise and sorrow of everyone, he was defeated in his reelection bid of 1990 (chairmen of Ways and Means rarely get put out of office), and Billy Boan, also in insurance, a former schoolteacher and close friend of Bob Sheheen, became chairman of Ways and Means with the help of Speaker Sheheen. When the Republicans took over the House, Billy was dethroned and simultaneously lost his seat on the Budget and Control Board. He brooded, powerless and invisible, for a year, then switched parties. He's once again being quoted in the newspapers.

Alex Harvin was in my class. He was so very young, and twenty years later he still looks young. He came from a politically powerful family in the rural and predominantly black Clarendon and Williamsburg district. One year he was elected majority leader. When he was defeated in a subsequent election for this post, he managed to pick up the title “Majority Leader Emeritus,” which he still uses. Alex was with us in his heart, but he could be turned by factors beyond the issue at hand, usually related to his district. But for the most part, we could depend upon him for votes. He is still in the legislature, a real survivor.

Bill Campbell of Columbia was in the House when I arrived and was philosophically in tune with the Crazy Caucus, but he was a loner, not a part of any group. He was an early worrier about nuclear waste and the environment and helped when I started producing nuclear waste legislation. But what I remember most about him was the day he rushed up to me and said, "You've got to get up and speak against it. A woman has to do this." He was referring to Jean Toal's Human Life Amendment. I told him I didn't know the arguments and was not good at winging it. He managed to hold the bill up until the following week and asked the Planned Parenthood troops to rush over and bring literature to me. They did, I went home and studied, and the next week I was ready. We managed to stop the amendment. Bill left shortly after to become a family court judge.

Peden McLeod was a good ol' boy with ties to both the Old Guard and the Young Turks. Peden was from Walterboro, a neighbor of Beaufort, and he came from a family of politically active Democrats. He served in the House from 1973 to 1979, moved to the Senate, and left there in 1990 to become director of the Legislative Council, the office which puts ideas brought to them into bill form. Peden said he "carried the flag" for teacher pay equity, including increases with longevity. I remember, because I was surprised, that he was also supportive of choice on abortion and other social issues. I was surprised because on the outside he seemed like any other rural good ol' boy. He was also a senator I could go to for support on nuclear waste issues.

Jack Rogers of Bennetsville was the one member of the Fat and Uglies who became a close friend of mine. He was a lawyer, bright, quiet, with a courtly manner, who was the mastermind of the rules for the Fat and Uglies during debate on curbing filibusters. He used those same skills for our side when we were fighting for the Education Improvement Act. He served in the early 1970s, was defeated in 1976, but came back in 1981. After we of the Crazy Caucus lost the first attempt to limit filibusters, he indicated to me that we may have been right. But the next year he just couldn't break the tie and voted with the Fat and Uglies again. We became friends working together on Govenor Riley's EIA. He also was a steady supporter of women's rights, abortion rights, and all my bills to further the arts. He was concerned about the environment, except when related to the lobbyists for nuclear and other waste industries. He was an anomaly. Nell Smith and I often had dinner with him and enjoyed his company. As we worked together on issues of mutual interest, I didn't think of him as Fat and Ugly; in fact I thought he had detached from them. When he asked me to nominate him for speaker pro tem in 1986 after the present Speaker Pro Tem Sterling Anderson resigned his seat because of financial problems, I agreed to do so. I thought of him as a friend who had seen the light. I rarely saw him consorting with his old group. I was chagrined when I read recently in *Southern Magazine* that his election to speaker pro tem was felt to be a great victory for the Fat and Uglies! Jack was indicted as a player in the Lost Trust investigation and went to prison, bringing shame to his family and the legislature. Perhaps he just couldn't break away from the Fat and Ugly mentality of "beating the system." I visited Jack several times in the federal prison not far from Beaufort and found him uncomplaining. He worked in the library and gave reading classes for prisoners. He is home now, hoping to be readmitted to the bar and to practice law again. I hope some day he will achieve this.

John Talley was a young lawyer from Gaffney who was elected in 1983, threw himself into education reform, and was a leader in the EIA campaign. Unfortunately, in his reelection bid, a campaign was launched against him for supporting the increased penny sales tax, and he lost his seat after only one term, sacrificed, you might say, on the altar of the EIA. If he had been in office longer, he probably could have withstood that attack. Ironically, he was defeated by a woman, who became a member of the Fat and Uglies and was indicted during Lost Trust on drug charges.

Jim Mattos arrived in 1985, representing a Greenville district. He was a retired educator and coach who was a dependable ally for us on almost every issue—education, environment, women's rights. He was joined by some upstate women in the early 1990s, women I will describe later, and ended up defeated in 1994, as they did, after the districts were changed by reapportionment. Their defeat lessened the number of effective, progressive House members and confirmed my fears about the effects of the reapportionment plan.

This is a short, short history of some the House members I worked with during the heyday of the Crazy Caucus and after it finally disintegrated from attrition. And there were others who I hope will forgive me, or perhaps they will thank me, for not including them on this list of those with whom I worked closely and pleasantly. As the 1997 session gets started, only Bob Sheheen, Alex Harvin, and Jim Hodges are still in the House; the defection or defeat of the rest mirrors the changes in the United States Congress, where the middle-of-the-roaders are becoming an extinct breed.

There were also several senators I worked with on specific issues. In the early days, Alex Sanders, who left to become chief justice of the South Carolina Court of Appeals, was my partner on several nuclear waste bills. We held a news conference together, explaining bills we had filed jointly. Alex left the court when called by the College of Charleston to be its president. He is known for his droll wit and storytelling, as well as his intellect. He is known also as the South Carolinian who every year takes a month off to teach a course at Harvard Law School .

Phil Leventis of Sumter is another strong environmentalist who not only fights the hazardous waste threats near his home but is an advocate on all environmental bills. In 1996 he led the opposition against the "super" pig farms moving into the state, which were a pollution threat to our lakes and rivers. He was an important player in my becoming chair of the Energy Committee, a role in which he risked offending his fellow senators. More about this later.

John Land was the vice chair of the Cultural Affairs Committee, which I chaired, and was always supportive of my proposals. His wife, Marie, is very active in promoting the arts in their rural community of Manning, and I'm sure I benefited from her interest. John is a senior member of the Senate Finance Committee and listened kindly to my pleas for funding for various causes, such as the Spoleto Festival USA, when it ran into financial troubles. He also is an outspoken leader of the Senate Democrats, who are in 1997 the last bastion of Democratic strength in the state.

My best buddy and closest link to the Senate was Senator Nell Smith, with whom I shared a hotel suite my last four years in the House. Nell ran for the seat of her remarkable husband, Harris Paige Smith, when he died at a relatively young age of heart disease. Because of his poor health, for years Nell came to Columbia with him on the three days a week the legislature met. As she sat up in the balcony, watching and knitting, she learned about the issues and the senators and spent time with the Senate staff.

I knew about her from my son Billy, who talked her into running when her husband died, then ran her campaign. He felt we would be soul mates, and we were. We were in sync on almost every issue, even though our priorities for spending time and energy were not the same. And even though we had very different backgrounds and experiences. (Nell grew up in a small town on the Outer Banks of North Carolina and was a schoolteacher). We spent many, many evenings sharing our experiences at the end of each day, cheering each other up, and laughing at "those men" and at ourselves. Her decision not to run for another term was an influencing factor when I was deciding whether or not to run again.

Nell chaired the Children's Committee, and her bills were primarily related to the issues her committee studied and pushed, as well as education and health bills, all of which I supported when they came to the House. At that time I chaired the Cultural Affairs Committee, then the Energy Committee, and most of my bills were generated by those committees. If and when my bills arrived at the Senate, she kept me informed as to their progress and spoke up for them. The Comprehensive Health Education bill, otherwise known as the sex education bill, was an exception. It was a major interest to both of us. She filed her bill and I filed a companion bill in the House, and we worked and worked on those bills. Hers passed the Senate, then finally the House, after two torturous years of sparring with legislators and lobbyists representing the budding Christian Coalition. We ended up on the conference committee together, opposed by Mike Fair, the Greenville legislator who was the House spokesman for Morality. He was anti-choice as well as anti-sex-education—and seemed to us obsessive about all things sexual. One problem I had with those conference committee meetings was struggling to keep a straight face while being earnestly and persistently lectured to about the evils of what Nell and I thought were the most important parts of a bill. Our purpose was to remove South Carolina from the top position in the nation with respect to teenage pregnancy and venereal disease, but you would have thought from his remarks it was to encourage immorality. We finally got the bill passed, with the help of a strong coalition, led by Barbara Moxon, of many women's organizations, health-care providers, and educators. It was weakened by a few loopholes and amendments we had to swallow in return for the bill's passage. During this "morality" struggle I was delighted to receive a letter from E. C. Watson, executive assistant to the leader of the South Carolina Baptist Convention thanking me for my leadership on behalf of the passage of the Comprehensive Health Education Bill. He wrote, "Your concern for the wellbeing of our children and your understanding of the issues involved in this bill are appreciated by us all. Thank you, too, for your support for family-related issues which will help stabilize our state and nation." I thought "How about that, Mike Fair?"

I took on this issue because a new school board in Beaufort, one of the early religious right victories in the state, had removed sex education from our schools. I was determined to get it back in, by state law if necessary. A Mike Fair loophole sank that hope at the time, resulting in our school board's refusal to use the recommended text and insistence instead on using *Sex Respect,* a book pushed by the religious right which taught only abstinence. However, the furor we made, aided and abetted by two popular pediatricians in Beaufort who had to deal every day with the outcomes of teenage pregnancies, low-birth-weight babies, and venereal disease, led to a change in the school board and the return of sex education. One of the pediatricians, Chip Floyd, was so committed to the fight that he ran for the school board and won. Sad to say, in 1997 the chairman of the House Education Committee filed a bill to repeal our sex education act. It did not get out of committee in 1997 as it came up late in the year, but it has another year to pass, and who knows how it will fare in this legislature. The grassroots coalition formed to pass our bill better get on the stick.

There were many opportunities for House members to mix socially with each other and with the Senate. On our daily calendar were listed the invitations the legislature accepted from many, many lobbying and special interest groups at breakfasts, luncheons, and cocktail parties (called receptions) on the Tuesday and Wednesday nights we were in town. I usually went to find out what was going on in the Senate with bills I was interested in or to talk with members who were on House committees considering my bills. It was also a good opportunity just to chat with staff, lobbyists, and others I rarely talked with during the day.

Following the receptions many went their separate ways for dinner, often escorted by lobbyists who picked up their tabs. One significant and telling difference between the Crazy Caucus and other groups was that while we almost always paid our own way, many others rarely—and the Fat and Uglies never—did. There always seemed to be a lobbyist in the restaurant who would pick up tabs. In fact, if there had been Fat and Ugly bylaws, they would surely have declared that one of their goals was to get through a week in session without paying for a meal. That would be comic if it hadn't had a serious influence on those legislators during moments of truth when we voted on critical issues. This cronyism between legislators and lobbyists was made illegal by Candy Waites's ethics bill.

I have often said that I owed much to my friends in low places. First, the county manager who taught me how to navigate in the stormy seas of self-interest and parochialism. Then, in the House, there was Bud Ferillo, the director of the new House research department, which was created in 1975, two years before I arrived. He was a friend of Billy's; from the beginning, he took a great interest in my new career, not only because of friendship but because he realized he had a willing worker with concerns and goals for the state similar to his own. There was no subject I wanted information on that he didn't find for me. There was no time he didn't fill me up with useful advice if I asked for it. He worked for the speaker of the House and had an interesting kind of power. He hired the research directors for each standing committee and often had a hand in the appointments the speaker made to all standing, study, and national committees. I really appreciated Rex Carter, my first speaker, and his successor Ramon Schwartz, for being so responsive to my requests for committee appointments. Perhaps they thought I would be serious about my responsibilities, but more likely they acted on Bud's recommendation. One's career can be shaped by

the committees she serves on, and I was grateful to them all for giving me such free reign. Now I look back in wonder at their benevolence, for there were times I refused to vote their way on issues important to them. Today, that would land me in isolation. But then there was more civility and an acceptance of the fact that those who wanted to vote their principles over expediency should not be punished for that.

Liz Crum was the research director of the Judiciary Committee. She was helpful in translating legalese into layman's language, especially when I joined the Judiciary Committee. She also was a great research resource as I developed legislation. Liz is now a prominent lawyer in the Columbia office of the McNair law firm. Bud now heads up a successful public-relations firm. Liz and Bud were not part of the Crazy Caucus because they were not legislators, but they were adjuncts when it came time to have a working dinner, or even a social outing. They often were part of Bob Sheheen's Lebanese dinners, which had the effect of strong bonding glue for all of us, legislators and staff.

Inez Moore was research director for the Medical, Military and Municipal Committee, and she kept me informed on the committee's issues under debate and often helped in finding information I needed for bills I was working on. She also was a good friend. She left government service, which she loved, for law school and became an authority on children and family issues. She married Sam Tenenbaum, a successful businessman who was a prominent Democratic Party activist and contributor with a deep interest in education, race relations, ethics and many other issues. Inez would have liked to run for the legislature, but she lived in an overwhelmingly Republican district. She ran for lieutenant governor in 1992 and almost made it. After many years of working on children's issues, in 1997 she has decided to explore a run for state superintendent of education.

CHAPTER 7

The Beaufort Delegation

Unlike most legislative delegations that met regularly while in session, the Beaufort delegation met rarely. We had an occasional delegation meeting during the interim, between sessions. Our senator, Jimmy Waddell, was a very senior senator. As the Senate is organized on the seniority system, he chaired several committees and was a dominant member of the Finance Committee, which he eventually chaired. He didn't have time to meet with us, unless there was a local emergency. Another difficulty was that the Senate and House kept different hours, which made scheduling a problem when we were in session.

Jimmy was powerfully connected. Fritz Hollings was his roommate at the Citadel; he was close to Governors West and McNair. He exuded power. Our constituents went first to him for help, which was fine with me, because he had secretaries and aides galore, while I had none. When I asked him to help with my bills in the Senate, he never refused, unless he strongly opposed them, which was rare. Though he did not aggressively push them, just a nod of the head by him was enough in the Senate. He and I agreed on most issues, though with different degrees of intensity. As chairman of the Fish, Game and Forestry Committee, he shepherded through the Coastal Zone Management Act, a major effort to save our beaches, and he became chairman of the South Carolina Coastal Council, which was created to administer it.

Though we did differ on some issues, such as nuclear waste, I remember only a few major run-ins with him. The first was in my second term. As our population zoomed upwards, the Beaufort School Board and the League of Women Voters were campaigning for a school building program. The board and the League pressed for a bond issue of twenty-five million dollars, giving slide shows all over the county to prove the disrepair of some of the schools, as well as the lack of space. The Beaufort Chamber of Commerce, led by their director, conservative retired army colonel Charlie Stockell, who some said would have liked to return America to colonial times, and a group called Voters for Accountable School Management, fronted by two retired generals, opposed it. They threatened to bring a lawsuit against the school board, arguing that "it's not new buildings that improve education," and "the need has been exaggerated." The chairwoman of the school board was Dot Gnann, an educator and former nun; by her side were all the board members, including Paul Siegmund, a retired colonel who had been commanding officer of the marine air station and father of two daughters who attended the public schools. The atmosphere was stormy. The Voters for Accountable School Management sued the school board over fuzzy charges of misuse of public funds, and a grand jury was convened to look into the situation. At some point, the school board was marched off to jail to be fingerprinted and have mug shots. Onlookers remember Paul Siegmund's wife, June, a very demure lady, pulling on her white gloves and walking by Paul's side to the jail.

For some reason, Beaufort was the only county where there were no limits or public referenda required to issue school bonds. Senator Waddell, bowing to the Voters for Accountable School Management, filed a local bill which limited the dollar amount of school bonds allowable without a referendum to seven percent of the county's assessed value. This would have produced for the school board only seven million of the twenty-five million dollars needed; it was also lower than the average state limit of twenty-five percent of assessed value. I suggested he change his bill to match the state average, or at the very least set a limit which would cover the needs defined by the school board and League of Women Voters. He refused.

I took Dot Gnann and the superintendent of schools to see Governor Riley; they asked for his help and invited him to visit the schools. He came, which gave them a lift. We all met again with Jimmy Waddell to urge him to reconsider. As this was a "local" bill, only members of the Beaufort delegation would vote on it. I counted my votes (thank you, Arthur Horne) and told Jimmy I thought I could stop his bill in the

House. There were three House members in our delegation—myself, Wilton Graves from Hilton Head, and Martin Sauls from Jasper County, who also represented a portion of Beaufort County—and I knew I could get at least one to vote with me. Maybe he thought so, too. He raised his limit to twelve percent, which covered the needs of the schools, and the taxpayers' group dropped their threat of a lawsuit fifteen minutes before the school board met to vote on the bond issue.

One casualty for me was the loss of a friend. I had nominated George Trask to fill a low-country slot on the State Commission on Higher Education, but when I heard that he was a leader in the lawsuit I withdrew his name. I felt that if he thought saving taxes (and our property taxes at that time were quite low) was more important than fixing leaking school buildings and replacing trailers, then his priorities on education were not mine. I explained my reasons to him, but I don't think he has ever forgiven me.

We continue to add new buildings in Beaufort County to replace the trailers that keep popping up as the schools continue to overflow. In 1995 we passed a referendum for a $120 million bond issue, and, as a sign of changing times, I'm glad to note that it was supported by the chambers of commerce of both Beaufort and Hilton Head; the committee which was set up to advocate for the bond issue was headed by a businessman. It is a commentary on the times that all efforts to raise taxes for education must be led by businessmen in order to succeed.

The infrequent delegation meetings were the entire delegation's problem, not just mine. We were as accountable as Jimmy in selecting roads to be paved, making local appointments, and funding local projects and more vulnerable than he when they weren't done. Actually, we usually deferred to his wishes on these matters when we eventually voted. I personally thought the county should be making the decisions about roads and appointments, but some legislative control was a holdover from the days before Home Rule. Jimmy, as he got busier and busier, also suggested ceding more of these powers to the county. We were together on that. The county has developed a schedule for paving and maintaining roads, and most of the appointments are now in its hands. The few that aren't have become political footballs and a constant source of irritation for the delegation.

Although many delegations met for lunch or dinner occasionally, we never did. I saw Jimmy socially only at the evening receptions, where we would chat for a few minutes. He had his own Columbia social life and I had mine, and they never crossed.

Wilton Graves, who represented Hilton Head, was also a veteran legislator. He was a farmer and motel owner long before the world knew about Hilton Head. He was a Democrat in an area where the Republican strength grew day by day. He was supported by a black community which was becoming edgy about the influx of wealthy white people gobbling up the land—their hunting grounds and pasture lands—and causing land values and taxes to skyrocket. They once were more than ninety percent of the population. Now they are less than ten percent. Wilton had a very narrow tightrope to walk. He was not articulate, and he did not communicate too well with his new constituents; his political strength lay in his senior position on the Ways and Means Committee and his close working relationship with the State Highway Department. Taxes and roads were major concerns of both new and old residents, and he managed to satisfy them until the ratio of Republicans to Democrats became untenable for him in 1983.

I never felt either Jimmy or Wilton was really comfortable with me. It might be that neither of them had worked with women as peers. Surely I wasn't too aggressive. In fact, I found myself being uncomfortably self-effacing and accommodating just to get along. A clue might be what one of them said during the first days, wagging a finger at me: "We don't tell." Perhaps they felt threatened by having a woman in a position of responsibility in their man's world. Or with a woman who wrote a column for the local newspaper on controversial issues, expressing opinions which sometimes didn't match theirs. But even with this slight discomfort, we basically got along, accommodating each other's political requests and needs.

In 1983 the voters replaced Wilton with Republican Bill Cork, a successful businessman, formerly from a small town in the upstate. His boyhood friend was one the leaders of the Fat and Uglies, so that became his crowd, and he was proud to be one of them, according to a story in the *Island Packet*. Our relationship deteriorated swiftly, probably because of their influence on him. Bill was overheard in the State

House elevator saying "We've got to get rid of her," and he tried to when finally someone ran against me. I spoke at a rally for Wilton when he tried to regain his seat two years later. Bill chose to sit with his Republican friends in the House chambers rather than with me (delegations usually sat together), and we barely communicated. In 1985 the *State* put me on the cover of their weekly magazine, and Howard Schneider wrote a very pleasant article about me. He went to several of my friends and enemies for comments. Bill Cork said I was too liberal for South Carolina. "The fact that she has moved to South Carolina from the Northern area may have had some effect on her thinking." He added that he thought my positions on issues like abortion and gun control weren't sincere or well-thought-out, but were "all part and parcel of her feeling that she should be a leader in the feminist movement." I am sure that Bill was echoing what most of the Fat and Uglies said and felt about me. I am not proud of that poor relationship and probably should have tried harder to improve it in some way. But the differences between us were so vast. But then again, there were issues we agreed on, such as abortion, the living will, seat belts, and sex education.

Jimmy also represented Hilton Head as their senator and had to walk the same tightrope Wilton did, as Hilton Head's population became a larger and more important segment of his district. There came a time when he worked more closely with Bill than with me, as Hilton Head's demands grew stronger and became more important to him politically. It was a difficult period, and possibly another reason we met so rarely.

The fourth member of our delegation was Martin Sauls, an undertaker from neighboring Jasper County who was elected the same year I was. He was young and pleasant and found his own niche for the few years he was there. He was replaced by Juanita White, a black representative also from the rural, poor, and predominantly black Jasper County. Her agenda was a little different from ours, but because I had a vocal black constituency I understood the problems she was trying to address and supported her efforts most of the time.

Our relationship cooled during the reapportionment battle of 1982. I was on the Judiciary Committee at the time, and she thought I should have consulted with her more in drawing our district lines and should have defended her plan. She credited me with more power than I had. And besides, I didn't think her plan was the best for Beaufort or the state. I felt that even if a few more black candidates would be elected, black voters would have less power, not more. I felt our county would be cut into pieces, and many in Beaufort would have no local representative. I felt a plan that clustered all the blacks into one district would leave them no political clout at all in the other districts. The coalition between moderate white Democrats and blacks would disappear, because moderate white Democrats would disappear. The Republicans were their friends only in reapportionment, under which they both gained. We would be resegregating ourselves. The districts surrounding the minority districts would become unnaturally white, with their representatives indifferent to the needs of the blacks to whom they did not have to answer. There would be a black party and a white party, with increased racism and balkanization. Juanita, on the other hand, felt I wanted to maintain the status quo to save my seat. The same arguments were raised all over the country, but on a personal level it was tough to live with; we were both pretty intense about our convictions. It was during this period that I received a number of reports that several members of the Black Caucus, including my good friend McKinley Washington, were urging the black community to admonish me, even field a candidate against me in the primary or general election that year because of my stand on reapportionment. I wrote McKinley. "I feel that reducing the percentage of black population in either of Beaufort's two house districts in order to boost the black population in Juanita's district, already 62% black when the military population is factored out, is wrong. Such a move would not significantly enhance Juanita's political base, but it would surely threaten the ability of Beaufort County to continue to send progressive legislators to Columbia. On more than one occasion you and other members of the Caucus have confirmed privately this opinion and offered to help. To have private assent but public abuse from members of the Caucus is disappointing and mystifying."

I continued by pointing out my positive record on issues important to him and the Caucus. I had nominated him for chairman of the

House Education Committee. I coauthored legislation to expand the powers of the Human Affairs Commission and changes in electing members of the Public Service Commission to protect the interests of consumers, I led the fight to remove the sales tax on food, to institute a circuit breaker to reduce property taxes for low-income people, and to limit the length of service on state boards and commissions in order to open the doors of government to women and blacks. "When I felt inclined to vote for the reinstatement of the death penalty, I recognized it had historically been applied unfairly to blacks in our state and I abstained from voting when the roll was called. In the interest of fairness, I've voted for all qualified black candidates elected by this legislature. In every major battle where fairness, justice and opportunity were issues, I've been there. In light of my record (which I have maintained in a district of 65% white/35% black) I can't believe that my disagreement with several individuals over reapportionment affecting my county merit calls for my replacement in public office. I regret the tension and discord that has accompanied House reapportionment. This has been a difficult time for all of us, but, to my mind, I think now is the time for understanding and unity, not hostility and division." Eventually we managed to put our differences aside, and when reapportionment raised its ugly head the next time, in 1992, I was no longer there.

There were many issues Juanita and I agreed on: public education; reforming the property tax by adding a circuit breaker to protect low-income people who were living on land whose value had escalated so high that they couldn't pay taxes; reproductive choice; day care; health issues. We did not spend much time together, however, because the Black Caucus activities filled her time, and the Crazy Caucus filled mine. There was a brief period when the Democratic Caucus leaders brought together some of the newer members for suppers to discuss issues, and Juanita and I joined them. Juanita was the first black to chair a standing committee, Medical, Military and Municipal Affairs. She was ousted in a stealthy and, some say, underhanded move by David Hawkins, leader of the Fat and Uglies, after one term.

Bill Cork was an asthmatic and died suddenly and tragically during the end of the 1989 session. His twenty-three-year-old daughter Holly, who was working for Congressman Arthur Ravenel at the time, decided to run for his seat. She ran on a platform of safeguarding the environment and choice for women. She won a hotly contested and very bitter race. When she came to the House we tiptoed around each other without ever talking about the chasm between her father and me. When the next session began, I asked if she would sit with me. She hesitantly agreed, and I'm so glad I asked and she accepted. We became very good friends. She was strongly opposed to the religious right and took them on without wavering, just as she took on the lobbyists who worked for industry on environmental matters. I admired her ability to cut right to the issue and state her position in a straightforward, articulate manner. She touched me by saying at meetings where we appeared together that I was her role model. She moved on to the Senate when Jimmy Waddell, tiring of the pressures of satisfying two disparate communities and refusing to switch to the Republican Party to assure himself reelection, opted for a position on the Tax Commission, a job he was well qualified to fill.

After I left the legislature my son Billy ran for the seat and was elected. He and Holly were friends, and when Holly moved to the Senate, he found a kindred spirit in her successor, Scott Richardson. Scott had been chairman of the Beaufort County Republican Party, but in the legislature he found himself further and further isolated from a Republican administration which had become dominated by the Christian Coalition on social issues and catered to the special interests on environmental issues. When the district was split up by reapportionment so that it included pieces of three other counties, the delegation grew. It now included a black senator from the Charleston area, McKinley Washington, and Doug McTeer from Hampton, creating a Democratic majority. Billy was elected chairman, but he later turned the chairmanship over to Holly, with the approval of the Democrats in the delegation. They seemed a lot more compatible than the delegation I had been a part of.

Neither Scott nor Holly supported David Beasley in his race for governor. Each had their separate reasons, but also they both opposed his keeping open the Barnwell nuclear waste site and withdrawing from the Southeastern compact which had protected our state from forever burying most of the low-level waste in the country. (More about this later.) Both Scott and Billy decided not to run for reelection in 1996 because of the frustration they had experienced during the autocratic management of the House their last year there. Holly was reelected after a bitter battle in which both the state and local Republican Party opposed her. Her opponent in the primary was supported, possibly recruited, by the Christian Coalition. Holly won the votes of the many Republicans on Hilton Head who supported her positions on choice and the environment. Many Democrats voted in the Republican primary, and their votes helped. In South Carolina one may vote in either the Republican or Democratic primary, as we do not register by party. The percentage of Democrats in Beaufort and Hilton Head has decreased to the point where there have been few local contests in the Democratic primaries in recent years. Holly had no opposition in the general election, other than a write-in campaign for her primary opponent.

In the summer following my first year in the legislature I received a call from the White House. I was told that President Carter was going to speak at the National Conference of State Legislatures in Charleston and that it had been suggested that I be one of the greeting party at the Charleston airport. I know it is unbelievable, but I said I wasn't sure that I could do that; I had entered the Beaufort Water Festival tennis tournament, and I would have to check on the schedule. My political friends were furious with me. When the White House called the next day I reluctantly said I would be delighted to be there and would drop out of the tournament if necessary. What I don't remember about this affair is whether or not I played in that tournament, and if I did, whether or not I won. Even more unbelievable than my response was their tolerance in giving me a second chance.

In October I was asked to join a small group of Jews from South Carolina who were early supporters of Carter to visit the White House and discuss our concerns about the shifting Carter administration policy on Israel. Others in the group were Senator Isadore Lourie of Columbia, Greenville mayor Max Heller, Charleston attorney Jerry Kaynard, and Columbia businessman Sam Tenenbaum. We met with Hamilton

Jordan, who assured us that the administration had no intention of abandoning Israel to its enemies in the Middle East. We told him we felt there had been "an extreme tilt towards the Arabs and the PLO," which at that time was committed to the destruction of Israel. Our visit was prompted by several administration moves, including the endorsement of a PLO presence at Geneva negotiations.

I expressed my opinion that "the issue is complicated by our country's economic dependency on Arab oil on the one hand and the moral question of Israel's existence on the other" and that the issue of oil seemed to be taking priority over the moral question, despite the fact that Carter promised during his campaign he would have the country do without oil rather than bow to Arab or PLO pressure. I wish I could say we turned the president around, but I didn't notice any great change in attitude or policy after our visit. I must admit it was a heady experience for me to be able to say my piece to the president's top aide. But who knows, perhaps we prevented further erosion at that time.

For some reason, there was a great deal of state and local coverage of this trip; my local editor suggested that I write an op-ed piece with my personal reactions. As a result, when a controversial story with a local connection would surface about Israel or the Arab countries, I was called on for comment or a response. I was pleased to have this unexpected forum to express my point of view on the issue. This led me to further "activism."

When I read in a bulletin from the Anti-Defamation League (I was an inactive member of its Southeastern advisory board) about a story in the *Atlanta Constitution* citing new activites of the Ku Klux Klan in Georgia, I wrote my U.S. senators, the governor and the Department of Justice asking for stronger surveillance of such terrorist activities. When I noticed some headlines in the *Hilton Head Packet* which I felt were misleadingly biased against Israel I picked up my pen and wrote a personal letter to the editor, protesting. When I read in the University of South Carolina campus paper about a series of lectures which I believed would stress only the Arab point of view on events in the Middle East, I wrote to a friend on the university board stating my concern, and asking if any antidote—or the other side— was being presented. I doubt that I would have made these efforts in my other life; but as a public figure, I believed others would pay more attention to my opinion. The public had gotten to know me through my columns and positions on many issues. I had built up some credibility. We all know about political perks; mine were a little different from most. One of my perks was the opportunity to be a voice for the concerns of the Jewish community.

In 1982 I went to the White House again, as a member of the Executive Committee of the National Conference of State Legislatures, to meet with President Reagan and his staff and tell them of our concerns about the impact of his "New Federalism" on state and local government. It was a rather formal affair, with the president being announced, as at a royal ball, as he strode in. I was surrounded by senate presidents and speakers of the house from many states and felt once again more like an observer than a participant. Before the meeting we were told that we would each have an opportunity to ask questions and make observations, and I prepared a statement. But it didn't work that way. We were briefed about administration policy, our committee chairman made a statement, and the meeting concluded. I passed on a similar invitation the following year.

CHAPTER 8

Past Reformers

There were, from time to time, little pockets of progressive legislators in South Carolina that appeared, then disappeared, in response to changing times. And there were progressive governors who were their partners. In trying to define the place of my group, the Crazy Caucus, in the history of more recent legislatures, I talked with major reformers of the recent past—including former governors Dick Riley, Bob McNair, and John West—as well as a student (and teacher) of South Carolina government, Dr. Fred Carter. The following short history reflects these conversations, more than my own personal knowledge, which is more anecdotal than solid. I asked them if the Crazy Caucus was different from them and if so, how. The answer from all was that we were the natural progression, that the changes wrought by these former progressive governors and legislators were the stepping stones for us. What successes we had were made possible in part because of those stepping stones. And in part because of societal changes, statewide and national. And because the people we represented were ready for change.

The governor of South Carolina was viewed historically as one of the weakest among chief executives of all the fifty states, according to Fred Carter, college professor, executive director of the Budget and Control Board, and contributor to the 1996 *Journal of Political Science,* from which some of my information came. Until the cabinet form of government was adopted in 1993, it was the legislature, not the governor, which controlled the budget process, made a majority of the appointments to the many boards and commissions which ran state agencies, and elected judges and university boards, functions performed by governors in many other states. Significantly, the state constitution limited the governor's power even further by allowing only one four-year term. These powers were given to the legislature in 1895 when "Pitchfork" Ben Tillman led the way to turn the 1866 Constitution into a legislative document, to take power away from county governments and turn it over to the legislature.

Legislators, on the other hand, had no such legal restriction and usually were able to remain in office for many years—because they controlled the counties through their budgets and appointments and the counties in turn controlled the political machines which kept the legislators in office. Legislative power was diminished, however, when Home Rule transferred substantial parts of their authority to county governments. It was further reduced when single-member districts cut through county lines. The battle between local government and the legislature is still going on in 1997, with the counties demanding the remaining appointment powers still in the legislature's control and more autonomy in setting fees and local taxes to meet county needs.

According to Dr. Carter, who cites Daniel J. Elazar in his article "American Federalism," there are three major types of American political culture: traditionalistic, individualistic, and moralistic: "The *individualistic* culture derives from the mid-Atlantic states and views politics and political processes as market commodities. Political value and resources are accepted or rejected according to their merit and viability. The individualistic culture places a high premium upon political options and policy choice. Of course, implicit in this reasoning is an informed and responsible electorate.

"The *moralistic* culture stems from a New England orientation and encompasses attitudes and opinions predicated upon a sense of civic responsibility or common good. . . . It ascribes 'higher value' reasoning to political participation. . . . Increased participation in the political process serves to spread this sense of civic responsibility and is most desirous.

"The *traditionalistic* culture is distinctly Southern. This culture involves a citizenry, generally depicted as undereducated and lacking in initiative, deferring to an elitist social hierarchy. Governmental structures are paternalistic, and enormous emphasis is placed on preserving the status quo. Political processes are not overtly competitive, in that the hierarchy, both social and political, is entrenched and well defined, with seniority being the definitive factor in determining political ascendency."

How well this describes the way things were in South Carolina, with the legislature as the entrenched bastion of power which kept the governor's powers to a minimum.

Before the Civil War, the governor was eligible for only one two-year term. In 1929 his term was extended to four years. The five-member Budget and Control Board, created in the 1950s, further diminished his power. Although the governor is designated as chair, his power is shared with two legislators (the chairmen of Senate Finance and House Ways and Means Committees) and two other statewide constitutional officers (state treasurer and comptroller general). In fact, the power is not equally shared, because the two legislators can often win their way with these constitutional officers, whose departments' purse strings they control. The Budget and Control Board has the added power of making all fiscal decisions during the six or seven months the legislature is not in session.

There are those who feel that the makeup of the board violates the spirit of the constitutional separation of powers between the legislature and the governor, but the court has upheld its legality on that and other counts. In 1938, Representative John Bolt Culbertson challenged Speaker Blatt and other legislators sitting on the university board as being dual office holders, but the action failed. In 1967, the court ruled that the inclusion of two legislators on the Budget and Control Board does not violate either the separation of powers nor the dual office-holding provisions of the state constitution. In 1977, the court ruled that inclusion of legislators on the board did not usurp the decision-making authority of the governor given to him by the state constitution.

I remember that in my early years in the House, we tried to find a way to reduce the board's power, which was then held by the Old Guard legislators. Despite those efforts, the board's power continued to expand, with new duties assigned to it because no one could agree on a better, or even another, place to send them as state government ballooned.

In 1980, when Dick Riley was governor, the people, by referendum, gave the governor the right to serve two terms, which gave him more control over appointments to state boards and commissions, many of which had staggered terms overlapping the governor's term of office. In 1992 Governor Campbell pushed, the legislature acted, and the people approved another constitutional amendment to create a cabinet form of government, with the department heads appointed by the governor, thereby creating a balance of power between the legislature and governor and a more direct accountability, closer to what most other states have.

According to Charles W. Dunn in the *Journal of Political Science* (1996), persons at the peak of the economic, political, and social structure play the primary roles in the decision-making process in a traditionalist culture such as South Carolina's. They are the elite to which society and political leaders defer in decision making. Such a hierarchical society has as its top priority preservation of existing economic, political, and social order. In other words, hold back change, and if you can't stop it, be sure it is done in a gradual and quiet way. The existence of a controlling elite discourages the rank-and-file citizens from participating in political decisions. The elite controls the political parties with respect to their own major issues of concern. Elected political leaders take their orders from society's elite, who by virtue of their power can restrict public policy options.

If I had read Elazar or V. O. Key on political cultures earlier, if I had known how built-in was the resistence to change, I might never have ventured into politics at all. Or at least I could have understood better the deep differences between my political philosophy and that of South Carolina's elite. Coming from New York, I was halfway between the individualistic culture of the Mid-Atlantic states and the moralistic culture of New England but nowhere near the traditionalist culture as described by Elazar. In South Carolina in the 1940s, the elite were the textile industry leaders and planters. But as other industries moved in and textile factories began to move out, and as South Carolina became a haven for tourists and retirees, the large land holdings of the planters began to be break up and power began to shift to business and other industries. Historian Leslie Dunbar wrote in 1964, as cited by William

DeSoto in an article titled "Interest Groups in South Carolina" (*Journal of Political Science*, vol. 24, 1996), "Southern governors were defacto executive directors of state Chambers of Commerce." In South Carolina at that time, the SC Chamber of Commerce was controlled by the textile and insurance industries. Other interest groups, such as educators, environmentalists, women, and blacks, began an uphill battle to combat this power and began to make headway with moderate governors Hollings, West, and Riley. But their headway has been slowed, as the influence of the state chamber of commerce has grown, supported by conservative Republican politicians and the political influence of industrialists and large business interests. The chamber's influence reflects the influence of its respective members, which in turn influences the thinking of the legislature and the Governor's Office.

To go back in history to the 1930s and 1940s, before these changes began to take place: in the all-powerful legislature, the two most powerful men were from the small, rural county of Barnwell: Sol Blatt, the Speaker of the House of Representatives for thirty-three years (1935–45, 1951–73), and Edgar Brown, president pro tempore of the Senate (1942–72). Although they came from the same small county and had relatively similar philosophies, it is said there was great rivalry, even enmity, between them. Brown held de jure power via the Senate rules, which honored the seniority system, and his positions as chairman of the Senate Finance Committee and member of the Budget and Control Board, which he effectively controlled. Blatt's de facto power was maintained by longevity and great political skill. His power was also extended by his power of appointment of the Ways and Means Committee members, thereby controlling election of the chairman whose vote on the Budget and Control Board he could then control.

Until the Supreme Court ruled in 1964 that there must be reapportionment, each county had one senator and at least one House member, no matter the size—far from the present mandate of one man, one vote. Because legislators were elected by counties and because a majority of the counties were rural, the rural areas controlled the votes in both chambers and continued to support the reelection of Blatt and Brown as their leaders. Even in large counties which contained cities, the legislative delegations were also influenced by their rural areas.

The goal of the rural leaders was to protect the status quo, a philosophy which fit well with the conservative political environment of South Carolina. Until World War II South Carolina was basically a rural state, but it began to change as the country changed from small towns to cities and shifted from agriculture to industry and tourism. There were new centers of population and a shifting economy. Jobs in textiles, our major industry, were beginning to shrink as foreign competition, technology, and product demand changed; other industries were needed to provide jobs.

But the rural legislators resisted adapting to these changes, for change threatened their political way of life. What's more, change was opposed by the textile elite. They opposed school integration and kindergarten, which would have upgraded the labor force and increased wages. They opposed reapportionment, which would give the burgeoning cities and the black population more representation. And they opposed Home Rule for local government, which would have fragmented their power.

In the 1950s our governors began to reach for change. On May 17, 1954, the U.S. Supreme Court, in the *Brown* v. *the Board of Education* decision, decreed that public schools should be integrated. The *Brown* cases included litigation from five states, among them South Carolina, in which black parents and students challenged the state-mandated segregation of schools. In an effort to preserve South Carolina's segregated schools, Governor James Byrnes pushed for a three-percent sale tax to "equalize" the schools and comply with the 1896 Supreme Court case of *Plessy* v. *Ferguson,* which held that state laws barring blacks from whites-only schools were constitutional as long as the segregated schools were equal.

In conversations, former governors John West and Bob McNair led me through the next twenty years of history. New progressive legislators came and went, depending on events taking place outside the state and the thrust of each new governor. The preoccupation of the Old Guard in the legislature was to maintain segregation. The first wave of Young Turks (whom I will call Young Turks I) arrived in 1954, the same year as the Supreme Court decision—among them were Earl Morris, Marshall Parker, Billy Goldberg, and John West. They countered the Old Guard on integration. Although they were not outspoken integrationists (how could they be and still get elected?) they recognized that the courts had spoken and the law must be obeyed. When questioned about integrating the schools during his first campaign for the Senate, West responded, "We have to obey the law." He squeaked through that campaign with a margin of only three votes.

A stream of bills was introduced during that session to defy the Supreme Court decision. One bill West cited provided that if a black student was admitted to any South Carolina college, that college and South Carolina State College (which had only black students at the time) would be closed. Only three members voted against this bill, West and two others. The two others were defeated in the next election. West escaped their fate because he wasn't up for reelection that year.

In 1955, George Bell Timmerman was governor and Fritz Hollings was lieutenant governor. Timmerman wanted to raise money to give teachers scholarships, and he asked West to persuade Edgar Brown (whose campaign West had managed) to support the scholarships because "the governor wanted it." Brown purportedly answered, "I've worked under eight governors, and most of them were nice fellows and I got along well with them; however, I have to run the state after they are gone, and that's what I'm doing . . . I just can't let them do anything that will affect the financial stability of the state." Brown won out. In another battle West, Hollings, and other Young Turks wanted to raise teachers' pay by twenty-five percent. But Edgar Brown again said no, the state could not afford it. He won again.

Hollings was elected governor in 1958, the youngest governor in the state's history. Many feel that his agenda set the stage and is still a part of the progressive movement to provide an improved public education, a new technical education, and jobs for all the people of South Carolina, rich and poor, rural and city, black and white. Brad Warthen, in reporting in the *State* (March 1997) on an event at which Senator Hollings was honored for his establishment of the technical school system in our state, eloquently made some interesting points. He told of Hollings traveling in Ohio in 1954, seeing a school up and running late in the evening, preparing students for specific jobs. He marveled that such an affluent state was doing so much to help its people, while

South Carolina fell further behind. He made the establishment of such special schools his main goal if elected governor. Warthen quoted Hollings as saying this wasn't easy to do, because the state chamber of commerce "fought us tooth and nail." South Carolina business "leaders" didn't want the government transforming their cheap workforce into one with marketable skills.

McNair, in introducing Hollings at this event, said World War II veterans, having seen what was going on in the rest of the country and the rest of the world, returned to make things happen at home. Warthen continued: "But Hollings got the job done. . . . It was a time when leaders of determination, undistracted by pointless partisanship, took on seemingly insurmountable problems and overcame them in the interests of all. . . . In a day when governors rely on slogans and party loyalty to pass their programs, such a thing as selling an idea on its merits to a skeptical audience seems as weird as an episode of 'The X-Files.' We just don't have people who do things like that any more—not in the nation and not in the state. It's in the state that it hurts the most." The article was headlined "Where are those who will lead South Carolina?" I quote at length because Warthen sums it up better than I can on what progressive leadership is, who they were and why they were a most important part of our state's history.

Hollings campaigned for office on the issue of bringing industry to the state. He created a committee to study the needs of the State Development Board and appointed to it several of the Young Turks: Rex Carter, Bob McNair, Barney Dusenbury, John West, Marshall Parker, and Billy Goldberg. West was chairman and McNair, vice-chairman. The study committee recommended that the State Development Board be expanded from five to fifteen members, so that successful members of the business community could be a part of this effort. Among those appointed by Hollings were business leaders Francis Hipp and Jim Self. The committee also recommended that the state move forward with technical education, and the move toward establishing such a system began, culminating in 1962 when the State Board for Technical and Comprehensive Education was created. Finally, the committee concluded that it was essential for South Carolina to have a balanced budget. In preparation for the industrial development effort, Hollings proposed a "scatter-gun" approach to taxes, a medley of taxes. In the ongoing struggle between the governor and the Old Guard legislators, Senator Marion Gressette's Committee to Maintain Segregated Schools proposed a sales tax instead, saying everyone should have to pay, including the poor. Hollings opposed the sales tax as too heavy a burden for the poor, and this time he won. His scatter-gun approach to taxes passed.

During the terms of Governor Donald Russell, who followed Hollings, and Governor McNair, another great change took place. The 1964 decision in *Baker* v. *Carr*, a U.S. Supreme Court case that originated in Tennessee, was the first to enunciate the "one man, one vote" doctrine. At the time, South Carolina's forty-six counties defined the electoral district lines for both houses of the general assembly. In the Senate, each county was entitled to one senator. In the House, representatives were apportioned to the counties based on population, with each county, regardless of size, having at least one representative. Two years later, South Carolina's constitutional method of apportioning the general assembly was invalidated as violating the one person, one vote principle. In response, the general assembly enacted a plan with fifty senators instead of forty-six. The South Carolina Supreme Court ruled this unconstitutional. Following the 1970 census, the general assembly enacted two alternative plans for the Senate, with a mixture of single-member and multimember districts, using county lines as boundaries. These were declared unconstitutional. It wasn't until 1984 that the Senate, with the help of the courts, finally arrived at the single-member districts mandated twenty years before. (This was a speedy reaction as compared to giving women the right to vote. Ratification by the U.S. Congress of the Nineteenth Amendment to the Constitution, giving women the vote, was in 1920, but it was not ratified by the South Carolina legislature until 1969. Although women could vote in South Carolina after 1920, they did not gain other rights related to the vote, such as serving on juries, until the state officially ratified the amendment—forty-nine years later.

Bob McNair, who was lieutenant governor when Governor Russell resigned in 1965 to become a United States Senator after two years in office, stepped in to fill the void and served until 1971. He met a bushelful of problems, which were all coming to a head at the time he took office. Hollings and Russell had set the tone for adjusting to the realities of the world around them. McNair, who as a legislative leader had worked with them, had the personality and skills to continue the progress as governor. He was the right man to make the moves that had to be made in those times of major educational, civil, and economic changes, and one reason for our relatively calm adjustments to the major changes we went through. He said he was helped by strong support from the business community in dealing with civil rights and social issues.

McNair's message when he took office was that he was going to work with the legislature. He told them, "We were going to communicate, cooperate, and coordinate." He immediately called a meeting of all agency heads, a very uncommon occurrence. While waiting for them to congregate, he overheard one prominent agency head telling another, "Hell, I don't know ten percent of the people in this room." He cited that as a theme for the meeting, saying that from now on they were going to work together. He established interagency councils of all related agencies, such as criminal justice and health and welfare, and ordered agencies within them to work with each other—this at a time when turf protection was rampant. He communicated regularly with the legislative leaders at breakfast meetings. McNair was a get-along person. He got along with the business community and with the legislature, though there were times, he said, when he was at odds with Speaker Blatt, an old and personal friend. He was a close friend of John Cauthen, the director of the powerful S.C. Textile Manufacturers' Association and was influenced, but also helped, by him. He got along with the black leadership, and worked closely with I. DeQuincy Newman and Matthew Perry, then leaders of the South Carolina NAACP. He probably achieved his goals through this ability to bring people together and build consensus.

One overriding goal was economic development, and, like Hollings before him, he saw racial peace and universal education as the key. His arguments with Blatt came when he insisted that the state must reinstitute the compulsory school attendance law if there was to be progress with economic development. He sought money from the Carnegie Foundation to start a pilot program for kindergartens, causing another war with Blatt. He activated a statewide food stamp program, because the counties were unable to help the indigent. These issues ignited the flames of the revolt that was beginning to stir against Blatt in the House. During his six years, McNair had to deal with the continuing progress of public school integration from separate but equal, to freedom of choice, to geographical assignment of students and busing. He had to deal with all of these politically incendiary issues, plus the liquor issue, while running for election for another term to follow his two years of filling in for Russell. At that time governors could not succeed themselves. He was the exception because his first two years were considered Russell's.

A citizen in Columbia brought suit challenging, as unconstitutional, the prohibition against serving alcohol in public places—on the grounds that drinks were in fact being served in restaurants only in Charleston and private clubs across the state. McNair was presented with a Supreme Court decision upholding the prohibition and confirming that the sale of alcohol in public places was illegal. He cracked down in all the places this was happening, saying, as he did with integration, that he had to enforce the law. He closed down all the bars in Charleston and in the country clubs around the state. Then he went about finding a way to change the law, coming up with the idea of "brown bagging," which he saw at the Greenbrier Hotel in Virginia, where customers "checked" their own alcohol, which was then brought to them when they wanted a drink. (John West further refined the system with a constitutional amendment to allow the sale of mini-bottles, an idea he adopted after seeing them served on airplanes.) After a stormy session, the legislature went along, with McNair agreeing to take the political heat as the leader on this issue. He appeared at a meeting of the state Baptists, who of course opposed legalization of drinking, and reminded them that although he was proud to be a Baptist, he was elected governor to represent not just Baptists but people of all persuasions, and he had to do what he considered best for all South Carolina. (Oh, for the good old days when leaders understood this tenet of democracy.)

Another problem for McNair was the student unrest against the adminstration at South Carolina State College, the black college in

Orangeburg. According to McNair, it was time to find new blood, including black representation on the State College Board, but this was unlikely to happen with the all-white board elected by the legislature. He somehow worked out an agreement with the legislative leadership: when a vacancy occurred, the legislature would not fill it. When they went out of session, McNair would appoint some strong leaders, black and white, who recognized the need for change. When the legislature came back, they would allow the appointments to go through. In the same way, McNair integrated other boards whose actions impacted heavily on blacks, such as welfare and corrections. If the legislature wouldn't appoint blacks then he would, and he was willing to take the heat for it. In the present political climate it is hard to imagine a legislature winking at the rules to allow the governor to make appointments that were politically unpopular. Today, they would more likely posture loudly against such actions to gain political points.

There was one blemish on McNair's solid record of progress and achievement—the Orangeburg incident, a violent and bloody racial disaster which happened on McNair's watch. Orangeburg is a conservative rural county, the home of South Carolina State and Claflin, both historically black colleges. The once-docile students protested in 1963 against segregated lunch counters and were met with fire hoses. They became less docile. A group of students, one of whom was an avid bowler, demanded that they be allowed to bowl in the town's only bowling alley, one of the last bastions of segregation there. Their request was based on the section of the 1964 Civil Rights Act regarding public accommodations. Some townspeople agreed with them, but the owner refused.

There has been a great deal of debate and disagreement about the causes of the riots and many what-ifs as to how they could have been avoided. Reporters Jack Nelson of the *Los Angeles Times* and Jack Bass of the *Charlotte Observer* wrote a book which came out within six months after the incident, and as there were not other written reports other than those in the daily press, it is their book, *The Orangeburg Massacre,* which is most often quoted. In this book, they describe the months of talk, debate, and attempted negotiations which culminated in violence on February 8, 1968. Three black students were killed and twenty-seven others wounded when police, nervously reacting to rumors and misinterpreting sights and sounds, fired into an unruly crowd. Most of those shot were hit from the rear or from the side—some in the back, some when they were on the ground. Although the melee was called a gun battle between the students and the law, most witnesses said no early sounds of gunfire came from the campuses, and no law enforcement officers were shot. One officer, who was struck in the head by a bannister from a burning building, was first thought to have been hit by a bullet, and the spreading rumor created the panic and anger which resulted in random shooting at the crowd. Governor McNair blamed the shooting on rioting instigated by a few "black power advocates"; United States Attorney General Ramsey Clark blamed overreaction by patrolmen. Some wondered why the law enforcement and National Guard were so panicked when there were as many of them as there were students. McNair asserted all involved had been through FBI riot training programs.

The public responded approvingly to the governor's law-and-order response and explanation, but there were critics—Ramsey Clark, the Christian Action Council (led by ministers), and the NAACP—who felt the action could have been avoided. Some said if the Justice Department had acted on the many appeals to either open up the bowling alley to all or close it down, or if McNair had used his powers to close it down or had come to the college himself during the week of unrest and used his considerable consensus-building skills rather than send law enforcement people from whom he got his information secondhand, the festering turmoil would have been avoided. Or if gas had been used instead of live ammunition. Or if the law enforcement officers' ammunition had been bird shot rather than buckshot.

Nelson and Bass's interpretation of the confusion was that McNair heard reports from law enforcement which were skewed and one-sided and media reports which were based on this skewed information. Students and adminstration felt they were the scapegoats and their reputations would be restored if their side of the story was heard. A group of sociology professors from the University of South Carolina offered to make an investigation of the entire matter, but they were not given the go-ahead. Others asked the governor to appoint a biracial blue-ribbon committee to investigate, but this was not done.

I talked with McNair while trying to understand and write about this unhappy time, and he explained that he did not go to Orangeburg because he was told not to by Pete Strom, director of the State Law Enforcement Division (SLED). He said that he met often and regularly in Columbia with white and black leaders, the mayor of Orangeburg, college officials, and the NAACP in an effort to open up the bowling alley to the students and move the National Guard out. He felt he could do more by meeting with small groups than with unmanageable crowds and recalls that they were on the verge of an agreement when the last riot erupted. The troops had been withdrawn from the scene, but when the fire department, called to come back a third time to put out new fires in the burning house, refused to come without police protection, the troops rushed back. McNair described the students' actions as a riot led by outside agitators that had to be quelled. As governor, he said, it was his responsibility to preserve civil peace and to support his law enforcement.

He felt the incident would have been avoided if Ramsey Clark had responded to his repeated requests over the months, as well as requests from Dan McLeod, the state attorney general, to take federal action to force the bowling alley to integrate, as the law required. As it was federal law that was in question, it required federal action. If Clark had followed through, the point of dispute would have been removed. But Clark did not send the necessary papers to file suit, and the trouble kept festering until the situation reached a point of no return. After the riot had taken place, McNair said, he did not respond to the calls for SLED to investigate, or that he appoint a blue-ribbon committee, because SLED was one of the players and would be investigating itself. And if he selected the members of a committee his credibility would also be an issue. He asked, instead, for the FBI to investigate, which it did, but Attorney General Clark did not make the report public.

Knowing how important communication and consensus building was in McNair's political career, as well as his real desire to act within the law and the constitution, I found his lack of personal participation during the siege surprising. Possibly his strengths were counterbalanced by too much dependence on his law enforcement people or an ambivalence about the students who were causing troubles such as South Carolina had not experienced before, as compared to other Southern states. The disaster seemed to me a result of sins of omission, not sins of commission. Whatever, it was a sad, but fortunately short-lived, aberration for South Carolina and for a governor who was a strong leader in furthering education and economic progress for all the people, white and black.

Alex Sanders was part of the second wave of Young Turks, who arrived in the House in 1965 when Bob McNair became governor. Alex served in the House, the Senate, the S.C. Court of Appeals and is presently president of the University of Charleston. He was still in the Senate when I came to the House, and I got to know him when we worked on nuclear waste issues together. Alex, who was first elected at the age of twenty-three, told me he was "an impetuous youth" who ran against the entrenched Old Guard to bring change—and for the excitement. He also ran because of his revulsion at the statement made by a politician that Thurgood Marshall should be shot. Along with him came other progressive legislators, some who had started out as House members, stayed several terms, moved to the Senate, and then left the scene for greener pastures, or just went home to make a living. They led the 1965 education reform effort, which included public kindergarten for all who wanted it and the reinstitution of compulsory school attendance, which had been rescinded during the early days of integration. Passage of these reforms, adamantly opposed by Speaker Sol Blatt and Senator Edgar Brown, was a victory for the governor and the Young Turks. Despite these conflicts, Governor McNair got along with Blatt and Brown. On some issues he was a bridge between the Young Turks and the Old Guard.

The second wave of Young Turks included also Joe Riley, Dick Riley, Butler Derrick, Isadore Lourie, Harris Paige Smith, Tom Smith, and Nick Zeigler. They were elected in the late 1960s and coalesced with those of the first Young Turks who were still there around a major cause—to return power from the legislature back to county and municipal government by strengthening the articles in the state constitution relating to home rule. Together they began this arduous process of constitutional revision, which encompassed judicial reform and reapportionment as well as home rule. A Constitutional Revision Committee, chaired by Lieutenant Governor West, worked on these revisions from 1966 to 1969. Dick Riley became the floor leader in the Senate for the bill that emerged from this committee.

The bill finally passed, and the constitution was amended by referendum in 1972. The Voting Rights Act of 1965 should be credited for passage of this amendment which brought such tremendous changes to the state, because it opened up the voting rolls to the blacks. The changes were finally ratified, after intense power struggles, by the legislature in 1975, with the vigorous help of Jean Toal, the first member of the Crazy Caucus to arrive at the House. By 1977, when others of us arrived (Alex Sanders called the Crazy Caucus the third wave of Young Turks) most of the previous Young Turks were gone. A few were still in the Senate: some left soon after of their own volition; and one by one, Senators Hyman Rubin, Heyward McDonald, and Isadore Lourie lost their seats to reapportionment. When Senator Rubin was defeated I wrote him. "They say voters get what they deserve, yet there are all those constituencies which you have helped for so long who will have a hard time finding another to champion their needs. My sympathies to you and to South Carolina."

Most of the second wave Young Turks fit their name. They were actually young—in their twenties and thirties. Some came from urban areas strengthened by growing industrialization. One way the Old Guard drew its power from rural counties was by sending kickback money to the rural areas. When the legislators from the cities arrived and studied the budgets, they realized their districts were getting short shrift, and new battles began to create a fairer balance of state aid to local governments. They are still going on. Heyward Belser of Columbia was a constant champion of legislative revision to redistribute kickback taxes in a more equitable manner. Equitable distribution of state funds was a part of the battle to come in the Education Finance Act, when I first arrived in the legislature.

The Young Turks figured out that if they were ever to accomplish their goals, they would have to unseat Speaker Sol Blatt, who ruled with an iron hand and who opposed such major policies as Home Rule and mandatory public education. The speaker kept tight control of the agenda and floor debate by his power of committee appointments and his control of the rules. The only solution, they concluded, was a coup.

They began to recruit candidates for the 1972 elections for the legislature and exacted a promise from those they helped to vote for Rex Carter, then speaker pro tem, for speaker. Rex was not quite one of them, but he was from a large urban county and sympathetic to their frustrations, and he promised to open up the system. After the 1972 election, which produced the first three blacks to be elected since Reconstruction, a head count showed that Blatt could be ousted. Rather than go down in defeat, when Blatt heard the news he agreed that if they let him continue for the first year of the session, he would then resign in 1973 and Rex could take over. In exchange for avoiding a floor fight, he would keep his perks—his office, his secretary, and his pages. Rex Carter became speaker on August 4, 1973, ending an era in South Carolina politics. And on the Senate side, Edgar Brown had just retired.

When Blatt resigned, an article by Jack Bass appeared in the *New York Times* which gives an interesting overview of that period:

"An era in South Carolina politics ended last week when 78–year old Solomon Blatt of Barnwell announced his retirement as Speaker of the House of Representatives after 33 years. He is believed to have held the longest tenure as Speaker in any state legislative body in the United States. . . . The Speaker is one of the most powerful officials in the state government. Running unopposed to succeed Mr. Blatt is the Speaker Pro Tem Rex L. Carter of Greenville, a progressive Democrat and supporter of Gov. John C. West, whose social program had often been opposed by Mr. Blatt.

"Last year Mr. Blatt's 84–year old Barnwell County colleague, Senator Edgar A. Brown, retired after a half century in the Legislature. It was Mr. Brown who lost a race for the U.S. Senate in 1954 to a write-in candidate, Strom Thurmond.

"And it was Mr. Thurmond in his successful 1946 campaign for Governor, when he was something of a New Deal Democrat, who described the two legislative leaders as the 'Barnwell Ring' when they opposed his candidacy. Mr. Brown, taking a different view, described the Barnwell Ring a few years ago as 'two old men who sometimes agree and sometimes disagree.'

"Fiscal conservatism was always a point of agreement. Mr. Blatt, in his address to the Legislature formally announcing his retirement, said the Depression had taught him that 'balanced budgets should always be a way of life in government and public affairs.' He said the Legislature should never forget that lesson.

"He recalled that the state budget was cut from $9 million to $6 million in 1933, his first year in the Legislature, and that school teachers were paid in script. The budget for next year exceeds $900 million. . . .

"In his farewell speech, Mr. Blatt choked back tears and spoke in a hoarse voice caused by a sore throat. 'I conclude a phase of my public service,' he said, 'with a full heart, with fond recollections, with love for my colleagues in the House and Senate, with deep satisfactions outweighing, I hope, the mistakes of which I have been guilty.'

"Mr. Blatt, who is Jewish and whose father had settled in Barnwell County as an immigrant peddler from Russia, noted the presence of black legislators and expressed pride in a state 'where no longer a man's religious views, political affiliations or the color of his skin in any ways prevent him from walking the road of life to a distance far beyond that which he expected in the years gone by.'

"It was before an all-white legislature in 1966 that Mr. Blatt, in one of his rare speeches on the floor, shed tears in an attack on a bill to restore the state's compulsory attendance law. The original law had been repealed almost a decade earlier as part of 'massive resistance' legislation aimed at thwarting school integration.

"'You may want a 16–year old so-and-so to sit by your granddaughter,' Mr. Blatt had shouted, 'but Sol Blatt will fight and die to prevent it from happening to his granddaughter.'

"When he was asked whether he would prefer 16–year old illiterates to walk the streets rather than to go to school, Mr. Blatt had answered, 'I'd rather have them in the streets. They can be avoided there.'

"Senator Brown once confided that the reason Mr. Blatt had made such an issue on the bill was because 'folks back home think he's too much for the Negroes.' . . .

"The Legislature re-enacted a compulsory school attendance law in 1967.

"Although he will formally step down as Speaker July 31, Mr. Blatt said he planned to remain in the House and to seek re-election next year. He vowed he would not 'roll over and play dead.'"

Sol Blatt was still there when I arrived. He was a remarkable man whom I never got to know. He usually sat quietly in his seat and rarely spoke. When I began to question our policies on the Barnwell low-level nuclear waste dump in Barnwell, I ended any possibility of being his friend. This was one subject which brought him to the podium. There were also occasions for him to take the floor to make the speech, in a quavering voice, which I was told he gave often in the past. "I love America and South Carolina, the most wonderful place in the world, where the son of a Jewish immigrant peddler can rise to one of the highest positions in the state." Though there were times he used courtroom dramatics, that was one speech he really meant, and no one doubted it.

When I came to the House there were four Jewish House members and three Jewish senators in a legislature of 170 members—a large number considering that Jews made up less than one-half of one percent of the population. Now there is only one Jewish legislator, and he comes from a small town. This, I believe, is the result of reapportionment, which has reduced the number of white Democrats representing cities. Most politically active Jews live in the cities, as all three Jewish senators did, and all have been Democrats. The disappearance of Jewish members from the legislature could be reversed if new reapportionment plans return to more compact districts, as ordered by the Supreme Court in 1996—or, I suppose, if more Jews became Republicans. For cities now are represented (with rare exceptions) by white Republicans and black Democrats. For the same reason I was happy to be in a position to speak up for the Jewish viewpoint and be heard, I am sad that our numbers have so decreased, and with them, that particular voice.

The opposition to change by the rural legislators became almost irrelevant in the face of the United States Supreme Court's decision in 1964 mandating one man, one vote, and the 1965 Voting Rights Act, which brought an infusion of black voters into the political process. These mandates probably did as much to lessen the autocratic power of the rural counties' legislators than even Home Rule or the economic and demographic changes which brought into office the Young Turks. The Voting Rights Act brought the first black legislators since 1902 to the House in 1970—James L. Felder, Herbert Fielding, and I. S. Leevy-Johnson. The 1974 single-member districts for the legislature brought the number of black legislators from zero in 1968 up to thirty in 1995. Reapportionment of county and city governments and the Voting Rights Act brought the number of black local elected officials from 11 in 1968 to 255 in 1992.

Alex Sanders raised the question of why South Carolina, during the early days of integration, never had a Lester Maddox or a George Wallace as governor. Several avowed segregationists had run, such as Maurice Bessinger and Albert Watson. Bessinger didn't come close to being elected, but Watson did. In 1970, when Watson was making a stump speech at Lamar, some of his followers were so inflamed by his rhetoric they turned over a school bus to protest integration, but the people of South Carolina reacted with horror, not approval. Watson, who had turned Republican, was supported by Nixon and Thurmond in his race against John West. Two black candidates were recruited to run against West in the Democratic primary. They lost. Albert Watson also lost, but barely, with slightly less than fifty percent of the vote. This election was a preview of later campaigns in which partisan candidates exploited the race question and divided the people.

When other states' governors were resisting the enforcement of federal rulings striking down "separate but equal," South Carolina governors Hollings, West, and McNair were counseling acceptance of the law and seeking peaceful solutions to these drastic changes. There was little violent Klan activity, as compared to the other Southern states. "Is it that in South Carolina," Alex asked, "we have a higher moral sense, or is it just our good manners?" This provocative question should include another choice to consider, the strong leadership of a few businessmen who worked to avoid the rancor and violence which pervaded Alabama, Arkansas, and Mississippi during those days of turmoil. As businessmen, they understood the importance to the state in dealing with integration "with class and style," as my friend Senator Nell Smith described it. These businessmen, under the leadership of Bob

Davis, president of the R. L. Bryan publishing company, and John Cauthen, director of the SC Textile Manufacturers' Association and friend of the politically powerful, met regularly (but quietly) with leading elected officials and college presidents to plan for peaceful integration in the colleges, persuading even such powerful segregationists as Senator Gressette of the rightness of their strategy. This was a good example of the "elite" leading state government. This time they understood that their interests coincided with the best interests of the state, and we should be grateful for that. And Alex was right in that the people's good manners and sense of morality and pride made it easier for elected officials to follow the leaders down this tortuous path.

Jack Bass, journalist and observer of race relations in the changing South, had another theory. He wrote in *The Orangeburg Massacre*, "Historically, an aristocratic racism had dominated the white South Carolina social and political structure—a racism in which Negroes were looked upon as children rather than as a lower class of being and in which lower-class whites were also looked down upon. It contrasted with the democratic racism that prevailed in the Deep South in which all whites shared a sense of equality because they were white.

"Degrees of the two varieties of southern racism were found in all southern states, but the system of aristocratic racism, which gave more value to an orderly society, prevailed in South Carolina. The state, whose percentage of Negroes in the population was second only to Mississippi's, generally had responded to the assault on segregation with legal resistance through the reprisals, in contrast to the violence that frequently rocked the Deep South. . . .

"South Carolina had been one of the original thirteen colonies, and its lowcountry planters and wealthy men of commerce in Charleston had attempted to develop an aristocratic society. A certain amount of the aristocrat's sense of noblesse oblige remains to this day. In race relations, it developed as paternalism. . . . There evolved from this aristocratic racism a white social structure which seemed to value stability almost as highly as segregation."

James McBride Dabbs writes in *Who Speaks for the South?* that after the Supreme Court desegregation decision in 1954, South Carolina's leaders correctly rejected the extremism of Arkansas, Mississippi, and especially Alabama. "They saw both its futility as regards integration and its danger as regards the economic future of the state. . . . It is true, there has been, and there is, mean legal and economic infighting in South Carolina; but violence itself, even the suggestion of violence, is quickly condemned."

Bud Ferillo, my prop at the legislature and now a public relations consultant with a great love of history and politics, feels that South Carolina avoided the violence of other Southern states because the black leadership was satisfied with quiet progress. They demonstrated in the cities of Charleston and Columbia, where the business community had a stake in keeping order, understanding that disorder and violence was a threat to the economy. They did not march in the less controllable rural areas. The civility may have been a function of the smallness of the state, where everyone was so close. The Klan was not publicly active, nor were citizens' groups, which met among themselves but did not counter the demonstrations of the NAACP.

South Carolina fought integration every step of the way in the courts and in the legislature. But in 1962, when Harvey Gantt applied to Clemson, the first black to integrate a South Carolina college, the leaders were ready. Governor Hollings, who was at the end of his term, said the law must be observed. He said in an address to the legislature: "As we meet, South Carolina is running out of courts. If and when every legal remedy has been exhausted, this General Assembly must make clear South Carolina's choice, a government of laws rather than a government of men. As determined as we are, we of today must realize the lesson of one hundred years ago, and move on for the good of South Carolina and our United States. This should be done with dignity. It must be done with law and order." What a contrast to Governor Wallace, who was elected in Alabama by his promise to "stand in the schoolhouse door and fight." Hollings and Dr. Robert Edwards, president of Clemson, met Gantt as he walked towards the admissions office, shook his hand, and led him into the building. The newspaper reporters who were gathered waiting for action, were surprised by the peaceful accommodation to change, as compared to the riots which took place when James Meredith was admitted to the University of Mississippi. Gantt's admission took place after the Democratic primary of 1962, when Donald Russell was opposed by segregationist "Red" Bethea and by the establishment's choice, Lieutenant Governor Burnet Maybank. Donald Russell won. He followed his inauguration with an integrated barbecue luncheon at the Governor's Mansion, obviously a signal that his adminstration was ready for change.

Alex Sanders and I ruminated over the question of whether this good record was deteriorating as a result of partisan politics and agreed that it was. My opinion was that the Republicans have played up the volatile issues of reapportionment, integration, and civil rights as weapons to defeat Democrats and to become the majority party. Now that they have won, what now? Who will mend the ripped fabric of our society? Will settling the problem of the Confederate flag flying on the capitol dome be the answer? It may be one answer, and I am glad Governor Beasley stepped out to do that, but it may be one of the more cosmetic solutions to heal the deep racial problems in our state. It should be noted that once again, the business interests—the "elite"—led this latest effort at removing the flag as a means of improving race relations and our state's image. Here again, their self-interests merged with the public interest.

In 1974, in response to the Supreme Court one man, one vote ruling, the House also sent a number of plans to the Justice Department for reapportioning House districts. Instead of single-member districts, they called for numbered seats within the larger counties. House leaders argued that three black members had been elected in majority white districts and that more would follow, that single-member districts would limit the vision of legislators to the concerns of only their own constituency, instead of the state as a whole. Despite their arguments, the Justice Department would accept only a plan with single-member districts. Although the intentions and theory of single-member districts fit the description of democracy, there were what came to be known as "unintended consequences of single-member districts"—increasing balkanization and polarization in the state. District lines became Maginot lines between political parties and between races.

In 1972, in one of several moves to open up the legislative process, Representative Joe Riley, the same Joe Riley who has been mayor of Charleston these many years, offered a bill to create a House research department. Until this department was created, legislators' only source of information was the Legislative Council, which provided legislative history and analysis. But for background on the issues, legislators had to depend on lobbyists and industry representatives, who of course did not even-handedly give both sides of the issue. Riley's bill failed, but funds were put into the 1974–75 appropriations bill for research personnel. This was a major reform, among other reforms led by Speaker Rex Carter, who was inspired by the National Conference of State Legislatures and the state of Florida, which had already begun its institutional reforms. Carter convinced the House of the need for professional research staffing, a computerized bill-tracking system, prefiling, and streamlining the House rules. He inaugurated an orientation briefing for new House members and fought for the construction of modern office facilities. The year I arrived, House members had no offices. We could only work at our desks in the House chambers—and they were very small desks relative to the amount of paper we handled. There was no privacy to meet with constituents, lobbyists, or each other. No telephones at the desk. No filing space. No bookcases. By the second year, the offices were built, and what a difference that made.

The Young Turks were supported by Speaker Carter in their efforts toward changing the way public service commissioners are elected. Following the 1973 oil embargo, oil shortages caused prices to spiral dangerously, impacting heavily on consumers' electric bills. The Public Service Commission (PSC) had been created to regulate rates, and with the advent of oil shortages, regulation became crucial for consumers. It became obvious that our system needed to be changed. The Public Service Commission was run by seven commissioners who were elected by the legislature for four-year terms and were always reelected. The commission had little research staff, and the information on which they based their decision came from the utilities. The legislators who elected them had close ties to the utilities' lobbyists; the public had little input or resources to contest PSC decisions. Many lawyer-legislators were on retainer to the utilities, electric and telephone, which were regulated by the PSC. South Carolina was one of only two states to elect their commissioners in this way. The second generation of Young Turks laid the groundwork for changing this. In 1974, when John West was governor, they created a Commission on Consumer Affairs to operate the Consumer Protection Code and the Department of Consumer Affairs, which has oversight of utility rate requests. And they began talking about merit selection of PSC commissioners, which became the first major reform battle taken on by Governor Dick Riley and the Crazy Caucus, as opposed to the Old Guard and the Fat and Uglies.

The Young Turks also started the process of opening up the system which was continued by Speakers Carter and Schwartz. However, these speakers made little effort to unseat and replace the Old Guard committee chairmen, whose first loyalty remained with Sol Blatt. This was especially true of Ways and Means Committee chairmen. His friend Tom Mangum, who was chairman when I arrived, was an expert in keeping bills locked up in his desk drawer, never to see a place on the agenda. When Mangum suddenly died, Bob McLellan became chairman, and the grip of the Old Guard on Ways and Means was loosened.

In reflecting on the Crazy Caucus with Crosby Lewis, who was one of the original Young Turks and who returned in 1983 to work for education reform, Crosby told me how the Crazy Caucus affected other new legislators who arrived with him in 1983. He said his "classmates" were a serious group of activists who readily accepted the reasons the Crazy Caucus was pressing to control filibusters. His class of about twenty-four new members, almost to a person, gave us the votes we needed to control filibusters, which made it possible to continue the agenda set by the Young Turks—to equalize education financing, improve judicial reform, and control nuclear and hazardous wastes.

As I considered the work of the several waves of Young Turks, I saw a similar thread running through our experiences: we all had governors who were of the same mind as we on the issues that mattered most. Even though governors were relatively weak, their support could make the difference. In our case, Governor Riley had the same big picture of a dream, although the small frames may have differed with ours at times. We also were aided by national events and the federal courts. Jack Bass, in his *Unlikely Heroes,* wrote about the native Southern judges on the United States Fifth Circuit Court of Appeals, whose rulings effectuated great changes in the South. "They battled to make the role of law work during a period of social upheaval. . . . Fifth Circuit judges issued landmark decisions that struck down barriers of discrimination in voting, jury selection and employment. . . . The resultant reapportionment cases restructured state legislatures, Congressional districts, and local governments. The changes released the urbanizing South from political dominance by rural minorities and accelerated the forces of modernization that transformed a region characterized by Franklin Roosevelt as 'the nation's number one economic problem' into the expanding Sunbelt of the 1980's."

These rulings and the changes they brought in reapportionment, the Voting Rights Act, and the Civil Rights Acts brought more people into the political process, bringing the political process closer to democracy. This in turn increased the opportunities for those who wanted to run for office, who were ready to challenge the status quo, to be elected and institute reforms. In South Carolina, these were the Young Turks.

Alex Sanders gleefully pointed out that a respected caucus led by a Catholic, a Jew, and an Arab in the South Carolina legislature was a unique alliance indeed. Crediting intelligence and hard work, he called the Crazy Caucus the most productive of the Young Turks. But I would say, if we did indeed accomplish more, that it was timing and the work of predecessors that gave us an advantage. We were at the right place at the right time. But now I watch with pain our successors, legislators and governors, weakening or dismantling some of the work we did. And I am saddened that a group of moderate House members, including my son, dropped out of the legislature in 1996 because of frustration with the partisanship and mean-spiritedness which exists in a system just as closed and controlled now by the Republican leadership as it was by Sol Blatt and the Old Guard. They were in the right place at the wrong time. I wonder what it will take for the next generation Young Turks to come along.

CHAPTER 9

The First Year

House members sit on just one standing committee. Before each session we are asked to fill out a form listing the committees we would like to serve on. That first year I chose the Education Committee. I was advised that I would have a good chance to be appointed to it if I agreed to join the insurrection and vote for Nick Theodore to replace the current chairman, Gene Stoddard. Nick was a Young Turk, a close friend of Rex Carter and Dick Riley. His challenge was encouraged by the speaker, who wanted to have more influence on education issues. I agreed. Nick won, an exception to the norm of reelecting sitting chairmen, and was a strong leader for the short time he was there. He soon left for the Senate, then became lieutenant governor.

Nick put me on the subcommittee working on the Education Finance bill, a measure to equalize education funding by pumping state funds into local districts according to need, so that pupils in every public school would have an equal chance, regardless of the city or county in which they lived. The bill set minimum standards, required accountability for money spent, and mandated local participation. Because of its complexity, committee members were assigned separate sections to present and defend on the floor. The chairman asked me to take on accountability and public participation, probably because I focused on them during committee discussions—no doubt influenced by my county council experiences and League of Women Voters focus. This was my maiden speech on the floor, just two months into the session, with hands shaking:

"Everyone who ran for public office this year knows that there are certain things the people of South Carolina want very much—they want to improve public education, they want accountability in all areas of government, and they want more control of their own fate.

"The education finance bill is the vehicle to do this. Because it mandates citizen involvement in every school, through school councils made up of parents, teachers, students, all elected by their peers, and citizens appointed by principals, it will reestablish public confidence in our schools. I strongly believe that the people will agree to spend more on education IF they have the opportunity to be involved on the grassroots level, IF they can help set priorities on using their resources, IF they can be shown that the added money is producing better schools and IF they are regularly given information about what is happening in their schools."

Sound familiar? That bill passed almost twenty years ago, and yet we are now looking at the same problems, and politicians are making similar speeches. On the other hand, we probably would be even further behind other states who were moving forward if we had not passed this and other bills which built on it.

When, a year later, Nick left the House and ran for the Senate, Gene Stoddard tried again for the chairmanship. I nominated McKinley Washington, a fine legislator from Charleston, who would have been the first black committee chairman since Reconstruction. Chris Pracht nominated me for vice-chair. We both lost handily. Gene took me off several study committees Nick had appointed me to and assigned me to oblivion.

Bob McFadden, chairman of Judiciary Committee, suggested that I request to be moved to his committee when there was an opening—which happened every time a judgeship opened. The speaker agreed, and I became the first non-lawyer to serve on Judiciary, happy to be where most of my friends were.

As I searched my memory about my first two years I thought of myself as sitting back quietly and watching and learning. But as I look over my files I am amazed at the number of bills I became involved with, naïvely jumping in without knowing much about the process, the people, or the traditions I was challenging. But if I had known how wide and how deep the opposition was I might not have jumped. I spoke up against the blue laws (thereby opposing small merchants and large church groups); for the bottle bill (opposed by supermarkets, bottlers, and the formidable beer lobby); for the ERA (opposed by a healthy majority of the men). I joined the new consumer caucus, whose targets were the utilities and financial institutions. (I was even elected second vice president.) I know I turned off the conservatives and Fat and Ugly types with my positions on all the above, but I also caught the attention of like-minded legislators, the press, and my constituents, which is, after all, the name of the game in politics. Weighing the pros and cons, I believe there was a net gain in the long run, and isn't that what women do best? Keep long-term, rather than short-term, goals in their sights?

I found a major difference between county council and the legislature was the conduct of meetings. The rules and procedures of the House are complicated, and when they are challenged there is such intensity, such a competitive roil, as compared to the easygoing, courteous handling of county council under Arthur Horne. I watched these happenings on the floor of the House with various reactions—amusement, surprise, exasperation, and impatience. I felt like a spectator, not a participant. And even though in time I was seen as an insider, I never felt like one. Whenever I made speeches or wrote my newspaper columns I had a problem with the pronouns "we" and "they": My inclination was to say "we" when I meant the public and "they" for the legislature. That is not to say I wasn't proud to be a part of the legislature—I was. But I never lost that inner sense of being more an observer and a judge, rather than an insider and defender, of the institution—even after sixteen years.

I was more comfortable in committees, where from the start I took an active role. Maybe because it was easier for me to interact with smaller groups, or perhaps it was a continuation of my lack of self-confidence which inhibited me from speaking out or even asking questions in a large group lest I show my ignorance. Or perhaps the informality of committees was less threatening for me than the intimidating combative and competitive action on the House floor. Or even because in these smaller groups it was easier to see that I actually knew more than most about the subjects on the agenda. Because I did my homework.

There were skills I lacked that most businessmen brought to the legislature with them: how to dictate letters, how to use a secretary, how to file, how to delegate duties when my time turned out to be not as limitless as I thought. House members did not have secretaries in Columbia, but a secretarial pool was set up shortly after I arrived. One of the great prizes of being a committee chairman is to have a secretary. I didn't realize that until later, when I became chair of the Cultural Affairs Committee. What a luxury it was to have a staff—a secretary and a committee director to do all those things I had done on my own—setting up meetings, doing research, watching the bill calendars of both houses, contacting allies, and much more. Heaven.

I did have a succession of one-day-a-week secretaries at home, whom I paid out of my own pocket. They were a great help in filing (and finding) as the file cabinets started filling up with letters, clippings, speeches. I never did learn to dictate. I was a fast but sloppy typist, so I typed out rough drafts, and the secretarial pool learned how to decode my typing errors to an amazing degree. One day I had misplaced both my hands one key to the right of where they should have been on the typewriter. The lines came out as if in secret code, but the secretary diagnosed the problem and decoded the paragraph. This lack of skills may seem minor, but when that mail starts flowing in—the invitations and requests and demands—it is a major, not minor, handicap. My greatest shortcoming was in public speaking. I never did learn to give a formal speech without notes, much to my shame. I wrote my own speeches and worked hard to make them concise and to the point. Because I enjoyed turning a good phrase, and using just the right words, and because I wanted my message to flow so it would be easily followed, I wrote everything down and then was afraid to put my notes aside, for fear I would leave out one of those important words or phrases I had labored to find. I worried that when I looked up at the audience I might see someone or something that would cause me to lose my train of thought. Or that I'd ramble on and lose my audience. So I read my speeches for many years. Luckily, in the process of writing, which usually involved three drafts, the material was partially in my memory, so I could look up at my audience more than I looked down at the script. Oh, how I envied my son Billy, who never used notes, never lacked for the right word, never took his eyes off the audience, and could unhesitatingly ad lib to any audience reaction. My mother was right when she had urged me to take public speaking! Just in case I wanted to teach. Why didn't I listen to her? Because I didn't want to be a teacher and why else would I need to take such a course.

The number of issues we had to keep up with was overwhelming at first, and the bills introduced and discussed and voted on came fast and furious. But I gradually learned enough about the other members of the House to know how the key people worked, where they stood, and where they came from (in their heads). I learned how to get information quickly on bills before we voted—from staff who hovered around when their committee bills were up for debate, from other legislators, or even from lobbyists. And if I didn't have time for this, I learned whom to follow on specific issues when the green and red lights went on during the voting, especially when I wasn't sure what we were voting on—when the question became convoluted by a series of motions to kill, to table, to kill the tabling motion, to return to committee. I learned that if I was for a bill, I should follow the lights of the sponsor, and if I was against I did the opposite—most of the time. I also learned later that if I were the sponsor I had better know exactly what every motion meant, because others would be following my red or green light.

I came to the legislature with several ideas I wanted to put into law. I learned in general how to proceed with this at a workshop for freshmen, put on by the research staff and legislative leaders, a new attempt to open up the system by Speaker Carter. An added bonus of the workshop was the chance to learn more about the other freshman. We organized into a Freshman Caucus and elected officers. Although I often refer to our class as the best ever, the passage of time showed up some blemishes. We elected Ron Cobb, a Greenville businessman, to be our president, the same Ron Cobb who became the central figure in the sting operation six years later when seventeen legislators were questioned and five found guilty of selling their votes. Involved in personal disasters not related to the legislature itself but possibly the result of having legislative stature were Sterling Anderson, speaker pro tem for a short time, who was indicted for illegal financial business schemes, and Chris Pracht, a pleasant and eager twenty-two-year-old who sadly got caught up in drug problems.

During my first year several social issues came before the House, often reruns for the second or third or fourth time: the "blue laws," the Equal Rights Amendment, the death penalty, prayer in the schools, kindergarten regulation, living wills. They all had varying degrees of religious content, or at least the debates on them did. This was interesting to me, as a low-country legislator, where we did not see religion as the dominant factor in as many issues as the upstate Bible Belt folks did. But as a Jew, intrusion of religion into public policy and of the state into religion set off alarms in my head, and I paid close attention to the debates, did my own research, and wrote columns about all of them for my constituents. I wanted them to understand all sides of the issue and my votes on these sensitive matters.

The blue laws bill under consideration would have moderated an existing law by baby steps. On reading the pages of existing laws it seemed almost surreal to me that a law which was originally based on a genuine ideal had been so distorted by expediency, economics, and politics. I spoke up.

"Are we talking about a religious issue, or a sociological goal of a day of rest for everyone, or are we talking about economics? I've been lobbied twice on the blue laws recently—I received a letter from a minister who wants to do away with the Blue Laws altogether, because his Sabbath is not Sunday, and by a downtown merchant who wants to keep the Blue Laws intact. This demonstrates how irrational the blue laws have become."

Here are some sections of the blue laws that were in the Code in 1976. Section 53–1: "No public sports or pastimes, such as bearbaiting, bullbaiting, football playing, horse racing . . . or other games such as hunting, shooting or fishing shall be used on Sunday by any person whatsoever. [You can imagine how enforceable that was!]. . . . Any person offending shall be subject to a fine not to exceed fifty dollars or imprisonment. . . . The provisions of this section shall not apply to the holding of nationally recognized golf tournaments sponsored by nonprofit organizations held at any time other than hours of regular church worship"(!). Many other exceptions follow, including "operation of motion picture theatres is illegal, except in certain counties."

Section 53–2 stated that it shall be unlawful for any person to engage in worldly work, labor, or business on the first day of the week, to sell any goods, wares, or merchandise, or to employ others to engage in work. But again, there were exceptions. In Charleston, any person who believed because of his religion that the seventh day of the week ought to be observed as the Sabbath and does not work on his Sabbath is exempt. Also exempt are radio and television stations, the publication and sale of newspapers, books, and magazines, motor fuels, transportation, restaurants, and emergency food which can be sold at open-air markets and grocery stores which do not employ more than three persons. Also exempt are the sale of drugs, cosmetics, soft drinks, confections, novelties, souvenirs, and fish bait. Prohibited is the sale of clothing and cloth (except bathing suits), cameras (but not film, batteries, and flashbulbs), and sporting goods (except when sold on the premises of sporting events). And so forth.

Obviously, compromise, expediency, and politics had corrupted the intent of the blue laws. The exceptions and exemptions resulted in unequal treatment under the law for most citizens, and they made a mockery of moral arguments. They also violated the constitutional separation of church and state.

"If it is legislated that people should not work on the Sabbath for moral reasons," I asked, "then how about all those people we have exempted from the Blue Laws—the waiters and cooks, the filling station and grocery store operators, the transportation and radio and newspaper people and so on and so forth. What about their morality, their souls? If it is morally wrong to work on Sunday, then why should three people be permitted to work in a grocery store, or salesmen be permitted to sell sporting goods in certain special places? "

Weren't we really talking about economics rather than religion? The only lobbying I saw around the State House was done by the retail merchants who didn't want their competitors, the large chain stores. open on Sunday. They were no longer blue laws as invented by the Puritans. They were GREEN laws written by businessmen. Fundamentally it was an argument between some merchants who find Sunday profitable and wanted to remain open, and some who didn't and resented the competitive pressure to open anyway. Is that a problem the state government should be settling by legislative restrictions—and exceptions?

Another problem with the blue laws was enforcement. They were not, and could not, be enforced everywhere—and they were applied unevenly around the state. Wasn't it immoral to be writing laws which we knew would not be enforced?

The bill to moderate the blue laws was killed by the protectors of religion with little debate, by a parliamentary maneuver that year. But in 1985, we passed legislation to permit all stores to open up and sell anything, except alcoholic drinks, after 1:30 P.M. on Sunday. Several years later we allowed counties which collected over $900,000 in accommodations taxes to let their citizens vote on opening stores even before 1:30, counties where tourists might want to shop all day Sunday. Only three counties qualified. Following this there were further local option votes permitting the serving of liquor in restaurants, then selling beer and wine in convenience stores. Both restaurants and stores opting to sell were taxed very large fees, which went to the state treasury. (It's okay to sin as long as you pay?) In 1996 a bill was passed to require a local option vote in all other counties on whether restrictions should be taken off sales before 1:30. The question on the ballot as written by the legislature was so confusing, with a "yes" meaning "no" and a "no" meaning "yes," that it was voted down in all counties except Beaufort, possibly because the newspapers provided a good educational campaign here. The South Carolina Merchants Association is requesting another vote, with a committee of experts to put the ballot question in layman's language. This whole brouhaha is undoubtedly a consequence of the upsurge of fundamentalism in the legislature.

Another bill killed in 1977 was an effort to regulate day-care centers in a comprehensive way. The problem was that the church-run centers insisted on being exempt from state health and safety standards. My hometown paper, the *Beaufort Gazette,* commented: "To our way of thinking these contradictory positions just don't wash. We should not expect the state to back the sanctity of the church where 'blue laws' are concerned on one hand, while on the other declaring the state must stay out of religion-oriented matters. At base, that is trying to have our moral cake and eat it, too."

Sylvia Dreyfus from Greenville took on the bill allowing prayer in the school. She put up a valiant fight against the bill, researching other states' actions and distributing information to the members. She didn't get very far, despite the fact that everyone knew the courts would find the bill unconstitutional. Palmer Freeman tried to get the bill sent to Judiciary Committee for further study (i.e., kill it) before the debate heated up but was unsuccessful. When Sylvia was at the podium she pointed out that the issue was not prayer but setting aside time for prayer in tax-supported public schools. She asked, "Which prayer shall be used? Who decides this?" She pointed out that the South Carolina attorney general believed the bill to be unconstitutional. She reminded those who supported the bill of the contradiction when they opposed the state meddling with church-run day care centers. After she spoke, a black woman legislator who supported prayer in schools asked her about her religious preference. Sylvia, a Jew, replied that she would be happy to say but didn't feel it to be relevant. She was then asked, "Do you feel intimidated by our morning prayer here?" Sylvia replied, "I have often been asked to pray in a way not acceptable to me. That tends to estrange instead of to unify." I voted with her, along with twenty others (of 124). Bothered by the interchange, I exchanged notes with the other legislator. I wrote her, "I find it difficult to comprehend how an intelligent member of two minorities could turn a deaf ear to the expression of concern of another minority. We were not just talking about religion; we were deciding whether the Constitutions of South Carolina and the United States should prevail over emotion. The U.S. Constitution is what has preserved the very existence of all minority groups and if its integrity is endangered, then so is the integrity of every minority it protects." I quoted a speaker on her side, who said at the podium he "was sick and tired of having minorities keeping the majority from doing what it wants." She responded critically to my letter, and somehow the letters found their way into the newspapers. But the flap was soon buried by more important news. Sylvia, whose district included Bob Jones University, the seat of religious conservatism, was not reelected for a second term.

The bill to reinstate the death penalty, after the U.S. Supreme

Court ruled that we could, was a very different experience. It was opposed by the Black Caucus, those who were moved by religious principles, and the civil libertarians, who were concerned about unequal treatment. I was impressed by the diversity of those with religious convictions; in the group were some of the most conservative on other issues, who probably would have had a much harder time taking this stance in the political climate of today. This included my seat mate and member of the Beaufort Legislative Delegation, Wilton Graves, who stood solemnly at the front of the House with about twenty others, black and white hands clasped in solidarity against the death penalty. In this case I found religious expression very moving, because it was detached from any mundane considerations—no self-interest, no economic interests—just their commitment to the sanctity of life.

The Black Caucus formed the leading opposition to reinstituting the death sentence. They filibustered for days, often long into the night. I will never forget the mellifluous voice of Representative (and Reverend) B. J. Gordon as he held forth with true stories, allegories, and pleas. One day he brought an electric chair into the House, along with a movie showing the dead bodies of those who had been electrocuted. The caucus and the civil libertarians argued that justice was uneven in South Carolina, that only the black and the poor would be given the death penalty. Members of the Judiciary Committee took their concerns to heart and made every effort to protect against this.

Jean Toal, Bob Sheheen, and I had many discussions about the need for, versus the dangers of, this bill. We agreed on most of the points made by the opposition during the debate. But in the end, Jean voted against the death penalty because of deep religious conviction, Bob voted for it because he felt the bill had many safeguards against uneven justice, and I simply couldn't vote. At first I was leaning against it, but when I saw the movie showing the row of corpses the effect on me was the opposite of what was intended. I thought, instead, of the Nazi concentration camps and that I would put to death those responsible for death camps. But I wasn't as convinced as Bob about equal justice for all and was bothered because there was no way to reverse a mistake. I abstained.

The debate concerning living wills was introduced many times by

Senator Hyman Rubin, who endured the experience of watching his elderly, comatose mother being kept alive for seven years, even being shot full of penicillin when she coughed. The experience was a nightmare, emotionally and financially, for the family. The bill was filibustered or killed every year because of pressures against living will legislation from the Catholic Diocese in Charleston and the Bob Jones contingent from Greenville. Jean Toal, following the lead of the diocese, was an eloquent opponent; Bob Woods, a black minister from Charleston, took the podium to filibuster, citing the dangers of children plotting to kill off their grandmothers for their money. He called it "pulling the plug on grandma." Some upstate Bible Belt members joined in. Every year, the supporters of the bill gave up on waiting for an opportunity to vote and moved on to other issues.

When Hyman Rubin lost his election after his district lines were changed by reapportionment, I decided to introduce the bill again. By this time the filibusters were under control, and we had a chance. We gained a strong advocate, Bob Sheheen, who, although a devout Catholic, suffered through, with the family of a client, a hopelessly prolonged illness. He saw the toll it took on everyone. He researched the writings of popes through the years and found some who declared it was not right to prolong life artificially in some circumstances, when there was no hope of recovery. I believe Bob's support of the bill finally convinced Jean to pull back on her opposition. We lined up many people and organizations to vocally support the bill—doctors, ministers, the elderly—and when the vote came we won handily. My reward was my first political cartoon, by my favorite cartoonist, Robert Ariail, in the *State*. Bob Woods was at the podium, and there I was, pulling the plug of his microphone.

My experiences in that first term with those who unflaggingly fought issues on the basis simply of their religious tenets, issues which had other serious social and economic implications and religious tenets which were based on their interpretation of religion, not mine, sensitized me to the resurgence of fundamentalists onto the political scene. At that time we had the votes, but now they have the votes and therefore the political power to foist their religious beliefs on everyone else, and that frightens me. In addition to those bills I described there was more to follow. Sex education and teenage pregnancy prevention was a major battle several years later, and although we won two-thirds of the battle at the time, there is continuing pressure to do away with the legislation we passed. On the national level, the assault by the Christian Coalition and its followers on the National Endowment for the Arts and the National Endowment for the Humanities goes on and on and on, a real threat to all government support of the arts, including significant grants to arts education programs, which over eighty percent of the population wants. And the promotion by the coalition of school vouchers, creating government support of religious schools, is accelerating with U.S. congressmen and senators swinging in that direction, frightened by the prospect of Christian Coalition opposition in their next election.

I hasten to say it is not just Christian fundamentalists who scare me. Jewish fundamentalists in Israel frighten me in the same way, as do Moslem fundamentalists. I remember the day in a small village in Afghanistan when my friend Elizabeth Siceloff and I were sitting in a car, waiting for her husband, who had gone off to buy something in the market. A group of men approached our car and started shaking their fists because our dresses had short sleeves and our arms were bare. I think they would have beaten us up if they could have gotten us out of that car. Because of that and other experiences there, I have followed the news of the latest resurgence of religious extremism in Afghanistan with extra interest. In the name of religion, women may no longer leave their homes to work, not even nurses or teachers, may not go to school, may be stoned to death for veering from religious law. Theocracy is far from democracy, and I shudder to think of it creeping into American life.

My first year was so much better than I had expected when I arrived that first day. I had found friends, was learning about the process, and had begun to sort out my strengths and weaknesses in fitting into the system. I gained a little confidence. As soon as the session ended, I began to put some of my ideas into legislation and have them ready for the first day of filing for the next session.

The legislature meets from January to the first Thursday in June, after which we return for a few days to consider vetoes to end the session. But between June and January there was as much to do as I had time to do it. The businessmen and lawyer legislators went back home to make a living; I used the time for reading and research, attending local meetings and functions, talking with constituents about their concerns. I wrote my columns and was invited to speak by many groups. I also attended regional and national meetings related to my legislative work. Despite the annual criticisms in the newspapers about legislators wasting taxpayer's money by attending conferences at glitzy resorts at taxpayers' expense, I truly believe these meetings and the links forged there helped me become a more effective legislator.

CHAPTER 10

My First Bills

Before my first session I asked a veteran legislator to educate me on the strategy and pitfalls of trying to get bills passed. He said, "Watch carefully as someone else's bill works its way through the House—something noncontroversial and much needed." I picked one that fit that model—introduced by freshman Chris Pracht, who was disturbed by reports from doctors in his community of accidents involving pedacycles, which were resulting in serious injuries and death. A pedacycle is a very heavy bicycle, with at least one brake horsepower. It is started by jumping on a pedal and accelerated by turning the handles on the handlebar, just like a motorcycle. It can go twenty miles an hour.

Chris checked laws in other states and discovered that more than forty states regulate pedacycles in the same way they regulate motorcycles. But in South Carolina, anyone of any age could drive a pedacycle anywhere; for instance, a ten-year-old may drive one on I-95, at night. So Chris introduced a bill to classify pedacycles as motorcycles, subject to the same rules, requiring the operator to have a driver's license (and therefore to be at least fifteen years old and have passed a driver's test) and requiring the pedacycle to be registered, licensed, and insured.

The bill was quickly approved in our Education Committee after Chris handed out letters from the State Highway Department endorsing the idea. There were few questions and little discussion. Here was a good sample of a noncontroversial bill. Everyone is for safety. Well, it didn't work out that way. There was a spate of arguments against the bill when it got to the floor: people are being licensed to death; those whose driver's licenses have been suspended for drunken driving will not have a way to go to work, will not be able to support their families, and will go on welfare; low-income people who ride pedacycles to work because they can't afford cars are not able to pay for insurance (although liability insurance is only forty-five dollars, and, at 150 miles per gallon, that much is saved on gas money); the mentally retarded depend on pedacycles; thirteen-year-old newspaper boys will be deprived of a livelihood (whatever did they do before the days of pedacycles?).

Each time a new argument was mounted, there would be a huddle of people working on compromises. Amendments flowed: exempting drunk drivers, lowering the age of drivers to thirteen, eliminating licensing provisions. Finally a bill was passed. The original thrust of the bill, which classified the pedacycle as a motorcycle and regulated it as such, had vanished. Instead, the end result was a stripped-down bill saying only that no one under the age of fourteen could drive a pedacycle on public roads.

Despite such an intimidating lesson, I introduced several bills before the second year of the session opened to get at the head of the line as the committees began to consider new bills. Not that my head start made a difference. None of them passed that year. I knew that it was better to start off in the first year of the two-year session, as it often takes two years for any meaty bill to pass. I also knew that bills which do not pass by the end of the second year are dead. The process has to start all over again for those who have the fortitude to try again. I knew this, but I just couldn't wait. Those bills had been in my head so long I wanted to get started.

The first was the "contracts written in layman's language bill," an effort to mandate that language used in consumer credit and lease contracts be written in a clear and coherent manner using words with common and everyday meaning. This was inspired by my thinking, as I struggled through reading an insurance policy, "there ought to be a law." (This is how a lot of legislation starts.) I have always had a mental block about reading contracts. The print is so small, the vocabulary is so unfamiliar that my mind becomes numb and stops working when I try to read insurance contracts, loan agreements, rental leases. I consider myself an average person—therefore I assumed most people have as much trouble as I do. Why not help them, now that I was in a position to write laws? I read in the *New York Times* that a few states were passing such bills, so I asked the Legislative Council to find a good model and draft it up for me.

I worked with a lobbyist and representatives of the credit industry, as well as the director of the Department of Consumer Affairs. The industry people opposed any mandate, with a suggestion that I take the voluntary approach. I said no. My bill somehow passed the House, but it died in the Senate. The following year I started all over again, and this time agreed to "recommend" that the industry carry out this policy voluntarily rather than mandate it. The bill provided for the Council of Advisors on Consumer Credit, an association of businessmen, to look into devising contracts "written in common, everyday" language. The Department of Consumer Affairs was to review proposed contracts, then recommend and draft revisions. Both organizations would undertake educational activities within the industry and would report back their progress to the general assembly in a year. The bill passed. For several years I received from the finance industry representative copies of contracts which had been revised to fit the intent of my bill. I really could read them. I cite this bill not as a great public policy change but as a lesson learned by a freshman that you have to recognize the power of the business lobby and work with them when possible—and that three-quarters of a loaf can be better than nothing.

My next bill stemmed from my frustration while on county council about appointments we made to local boards and commissions, on which members often had served for twenty to forty years. I learned then what can happen to people who serve on boards for many years. They come on with enthusiasm and new ideas, but as the years roll by, many of them lose some of that enthusiasm. Attendance slacks off a bit, they become defensive about policies they have enacted, and they become resistant to change, even when change is necessary because times have changed. But they want to stay on—for status or just to be part of the action.

And I learned how very difficult it was to vote against longtime incumbents, friends who had done a good job and ask for "just one more term." Rather than hurt their feelings, we give them "one more term." A law limiting service to two terms would take us off that uncomfortable hook.

Another reason I (and the League of Women Voters) were for some limits was that there are many capable, energetic, creative people who want to serve and who would bring new ideas to the table—but there are no openings. This bill would open up some slots for them. It would make room for blacks and women who were not even considered for appointments until recently. The first year the bill never got out of committee. I filed the bill every session, with a growing number of cosponsors, including David Beasley, who reminded me every two years to include him in. Sometimes it would pass the House but never the Senate, held up by Senator Marion Gressette, keeper of the graveyard of unwanted House bills. More recently, the bill didn't even make it through the House, held up by Senator Gressette's nephew John Felder, among others. Eventually, some boards and commissions began to set limits for themselves. But not many. One fear expressed by the opponents was that they, the legislators, would be the next victims of term limits. But there is a difference between term limits for elected officials, who are accountable to the people who elect them, and appointees, who are accountable only to those who appoint them. The reasons for appointment are not necessarily consistent with good policy or the public's interest. Last time I asked, in 1996, no action had yet been taken on this idea. However, with the new cabinet form of government, some of the state boards and commissions have been abolished, so the problem has decreased slightly.

Another bill which I filed every two years without success was the seven-day waiting period for purchasing a handgun. After the assassination attempt on President Reagan, Senator Strom Thurmond vowed to wage a war on crime, saying he would press for adoption of a congressional resolution to encourage states to implement a waiting period for the purchase of handguns. The day I read his statement with his picture attached, I filed my bill, exuberant to have such a politically powerful leader on my side. Maybe this time it would pass.

I addressed the Judiciary Committee, which was considering my bill: "I understand you all have been getting a lot of phone calls. And so have I. Apparently, whenever any type of firearms legislation is introduced, the NRA computers alert members and crank them into action. It is such an efficient lobby that we must continually remind ourselves that the polls consistently show that over seventy percent of the public really want us to find a better way to sell handguns, and those seventy percent are also our constituents, even though they are more silent." (That was almost twenty years ago. In 1996, the polls show the seventy percent had increased to eighty percent who support some type of gun control.)

My bill was not radical. State law already called for purchasers to fill out a form swearing they were not criminals or mentally unstable. But those forms often took months to be examined by the State Law Enforcement Division (SLED), too late to stop the wrong people from walking out into the world with a gun. My bill mandated that the forms be sent by the store to SLED the day a person fills out the application; SLED would process it with its computers and notify the store within seven days that the purchaser was or was not eligible to buy a handgun. This would prevent those who should not have handguns from having them. It would save SLED the problem of looking for someone months later who had a bought a gun illegally. It also provided a "cooling off" period for those who would run into a store in a moment of anger to buy a handgun to do someone in. This was not an insignificant problem in South Carolina. A staggering seventy-seven percent of the murders in 1979 were committed by friends or relatives of the victims, and one-half were murdered by handguns. The murder rate is highest in the Southeast, where there are the weakest handgun laws.

My bill did not apply to rifles or shotguns. It did not create a new bureaucracy but used what was already in place. I reminded the committee that I was not taking away the constitutional right to bear arms. That right did not, cannot, and should not apply to convicted criminals, the mentally incompetent, illegal aliens, dishonorably discharged military, or children. SLED would stop them and no one else from buying handguns. Everyone else would be slightly inconvenienced by waiting seven days, and even then, there was an exception for emergencies. I ended my remarks by quoting a letter to the editor from Noel Seeburg, my conservative Republican lawyer friend, printed in the *Beaufort Gazette:* "Is a seven day wait too long? Compare the 'waiting period' for a car loan, the probate of a will, the issuance of a driver's license, a home mortgage loan, a building permit and many other every day things. They may all vary, but we all wait. Seven day's wait does not seem unreasonable in dealing with deadly weapons." I also brought a letter from the owner of a local sporting goods store saying that he had no problem with my bill as it was written.

Another year I introduced the bill with Francis (Archie) Archibald as my cosponsor. Archie had been in law enforcement and a security officer at the Charleston Naval Base. I just knew these credentials would be more effective than mine. I picked up reluctant endorsements from a few sheriffs (who, because they are elected, were as frightened as my fellow legislators by NRA opposition) and strong endorsements from city policemen, who are often the victims of illegal handguns. There were, as always, a few legislators who testified that in South Carolina "we love our guns" and talked a lot about the Second Amendment and the right to bear arms. I asked Senator Thurmond for an endorsement, but his aide said he never interfered with state legislation. (Many years later, when I wrote to ask him to vote for the seven-day waiting period being considered in the U.S. Senate, his aide replied that gun control should not be a federal issue.) The best I could do was to circulate the newspaper editorial with Thurmond's photo and purported statement that there should be a seven-day waiting period.

The press was solidly in my corner. But this was one instance when it just didn't matter. The NRA was just too powerful, with its hundreds of thousands of members ready at the call to pick up phones and threaten elected officials with defeat at the polls the next go-round if they voted to control guns, or to write letters to the editor defending guns and criticizing any official who voted against their wishes. The NRA generates threats and fear. Several times an NRA representative came to Beaufort scouting for a candidate to run against me. If a candidate is likely to have a tight race or is marginal in some way, NRA money and votes can make the difference, and the candidate knows it. True, the NRA finally lost some battles nationally, when the Brady Bill and restrictions on automatic assault weapons were passed in 1994 and 1995. But who knows how long they will hold? Bills which pass can be reversed. It takes eternal vigilance, because whenever a special interest is involved, it rarely goes away. It just regroups. While opposition to special interests is often underfunded, with a shifting volunteer force that dissipates unless a crisis is at hand.

In 1996 the legislature further weakened our existing handgun law by permitting anyone eligible to buy a gun to carry a concealed weapon, with a few exceptions. Those exceptions were added one by one by amendments introduced by Senator John Land. In a valiant effort, he managed to at least impose some limits to where these concealed weapons could be carried.

During the early years, when I was working on energy and waste problems, my name was proposed to the South Carolina Wildlife Federation as a candidate for the legislator conservationist of the year. I was voted down because of my seven-day waiting period bill, presumably because many of the Wildlife Federation members are hunters and NRA members. But allegiance to the NRA is weakening as its platform becomes more extreme. A year or two later, the opposition to my nomination weakened, and I did receive that award, which I gratefully accepted, not knowing of my first rejection. The federation became my ally in many future ventures involving the environment.

One issue I ran on during my first campaign was the bottle bill, filed unsuccessfully year after year by Ed Simpson, a Republican from Clemson. Several times he asked me to be the lead sponsor, to change the tone a little. But I did no better than he. This bill, which required a five-cent refundable deposit on all cans and bottles containing beer and soft drinks, addressed three of my major concerns—our rapidly diminishing energy resources, our garbage landfills, which were using up more and more land at great cost, and the ever-increasing litter that was trashing America.

It was supported by state and local garden clubs, the S.C. Wildlife Federation, the League of Women Voters, and the Farm Bureau; it was opposed by the beer and soft drink associations, canneries, some unions, bottle manufacturers, and supermarkets. The opposition spent a great deal of money lobbying the legislature, saying that the bill would greatly increase the cost of drinks and would cause unemployment and hardship for all related industries. We supporters cited the U.S. General Accounting Office prediction that with a national bottle bill, oil consumption would be reduced by eighty thousand barrels a day. We would use three million tons less of iron ore (thirty-three percent of which is imported) and one million tons less of bauxite (ninety percent of which is imported), thus improving our balance of trade and reducing our dependence on the South American, African, and Arab countries. And we would save a lot of water, a resource that is becoming precious all over this country. In Oregon, one of the first states to pass similar legislation, some jobs were lost in the manufacturing of bottles, but others were created in recycling and distribution, with a net gain of jobs. Naturally the businesses affected would have dislocations, and that was regrettable, but this is not a new problem in the American free enterprise system. There is no doubt the horse and buggy trade suffered with the advent of the automobile.

My interest in the bottle bill grew partly out of experiences on county council. I was horrified to hear how much we had to pay for land to bury our garbage and how little land was suitable with our high water table. I then learned how much space bottles and cans took up. Then there was the flow of letters to the editor from new residents criticizing our littered highways. I also knew, from experience in Beaufort, about the Sisyphean problem of reducing litter. A retired army general, Frank Osmanski, with a Ph.D. in business administration agreed to take on a litter control program. He organized it as only a general and a Ph.D. in business could, with volunteers from twenty-five organizations, a county litter officer with power to give tickets, and an educational campaign. Litter was picked up but the volume was not reduced, because littering continued at the same pace. Carl Hendricks served on Governor Edwards's Beautification Committee, and he picked up trash Saturday mornings with other volunteers. Both Hendricks and Osmanski initially opposed the bottle bill, thinking a strong community spirit would do the job; but in no time at all they became strong supporters of mandatory deposits.

In the House, that first year I was there, Ed Simpson garnered over seventy sponsors and was on the verge of winning, but he made a fatal error. He came to the podium to speak on behalf of the bill, and he talked and talked and talked. While he was talking, the opponents scrambled around and picked off many of our supporters. We lost—by just a few votes. We never came that close again. The special interests regrouped and never let down their guard from that day forward. One year we offered a bill with many sponsors, calling for a referendum to let the people tell us what they wanted. The opposition managed, by flexing their political muscle and masterfully using the rules of the House, to hold up debate on our bill and take up instead a bill of their own, which created a pilot project using prisoners in three counties to pick up litter, at the cost to the taxpayers of a half-million dollars. This was pushed by the "Piggly-Wiggly Caucus," four House members who owned Piggly Wiggly supermarkets. And they won, with the help of many lobbyists representing the beer industry, the bottling industry, small businesses, and labor unions up in the balcony and crowding the lobby. Each one of these factions had their own group of legislators, their buddies, to whom they contributed and with whom they socialized. Their combined strength overwhelmed us.

I had no problem with prisoners working but questioned that picking up roadside litter should be considered a top priority. Was picking up litter more important than mending potholes, cleaning irrigation ditches, fighting beach erosion, repairing railroad beds, insulating government buildings, or learning a trade? And where were our priorities in spending taxpayers' money? That year, after a huge debate, we just barely managed to find a million dollars to fund fourteen day-care centers in depressed counties and struggled to address Medicaid-Medicare funding for nursing homes. And yet we bowed to special interests' maneuvering by allocating a half-million dollars to pick up litter in three yet-to-be-named counties. Not only did it not make sense, but it was galling to me that one of the forces behind this move was the highly praised Keep America Beautiful. Keep America Beautiful was the creature of the beer and soft drink industries, originally created as a weapon to fight bottle bills across the country. True, their Adopt-a-Highway program has been widely acclaimed and is an improvement over doing nothing. But is picking up litter really better than preventing litter? I didn't think so, although the legislature obviously did. Repeated attempts to pass a bottle bill met with failure as our legislature became more and more responsive to industry and their lobbyists.

My opinion was that the litter problem would not be solved until we attacked the source of litter and provided incentives to change the throwaway mentality, like the deposit law in Oregon, which reduced bottle and can litter by ninety percent and total litter by thirty-nine percent without spending state money or using up landfill space. Studies also showed Oregon's bottle bill conserved as much energy as was used to provide electricity in a town of ten thousand. Not only do those who pay the deposit return most containers to get their deposit back, but those containers which are thrown away are picked up by others who can earn five cents apiece for them. In contrast to the Oregon approach, the state of Washington initiated a litter control program, taxing the bottle and can and paper industries to help pay for cleaning up litter; they collected one million dollars from industry taxes and spent eighteen million cleaning up, also using prisoners. Net cost to taxpayers was seventeen million dollars a year.

I offered another bill related to beer and wine bottles and cans that year, which prohibited having an open cup, bottle, or can of alcohol in a car. The S.C. Department of Highways had long identified alcohol as one of the chief factors in driver error, which contributed to over eighty percent of traffic accidents at that time. A driver who gets behind the wheel after drinking is bad enough, but to continue to drink on the road only compounds the problem. And a large percentage of those drinking drivers were between eighteen and twenty-four years of age. The bill was tabled in committee. Joyce Hearn filed the bill the next year without letting me know, which was unusual and also irritating. She served on a committee studying alcoholism, I believe, and she did get the bill passed, so I forgave her. By that time I was immersed in many other issues. (I had one other experience of having someone else file bills which I had initiated. Those bills provided ways to shorten our sessions. We tried for several years, then David Wilkins filed the bills, possibly thinking he was in a better position to get them passed, as he was then chairman of the Judiciary Committee, or perhaps he was hoping to put it to political advantage. However, I'm sorry to say, he failed too, and that issue is still before the legislature, eight years later, still unresolved.)

I learned many times my first year in the legislature that there was no such thing as an uncontroversial bill. I learned that the League of

Women Voters was wrong; that it was not enough for an idea to just be sensible and right and fair to win. I learned from these bills, and even more so from bills which followed, that when I was working behind the scenes, someone else on the other side was working just as hard, out of my sight. At least on county council in my small town I usually had gotten a whiff of what was going on behind my back, but when I first came to the legislature I was totally blindsided by my busy and successful opponents on some issues. How naïve I was then.

There were several nonlegislative events that highlighted 1978 for me. I was able to save twenty-five to thirty stately oak trees lining both sides of a country road on St. Helena Island, in my district. The state Highway Department had already cut down four huge trees when someone living on the Dulamo Road called me early one morning and asked if I could help stop the massacre. I rushed out and literally stood in front of the bulldozer until the driver agreed to stop, at least until I talked with state highway officials. It seems some highway official had decided to repave the road, and department regulations required a sixty-foot right-of-way, wider shoulders, and deeper ditches. That meant cutting down those wonderful old trees. The road went nowhere, coming to a dead end at a small, yet-to-be developed residential enclave. Why were they doing this? Somehow, three years before, that road was put on a schedule for resurfacing when a county road maintenance supervisor was asked for recommendations for using state and federal funds for road improvement. (How often we rush into projects because government funds are available.) The morning I was called I managed to do two things: I asked the state Highway Department to send officials to Beaufort to look at the trees and the road before another tree was cut, and they did; and I asked the circuit court judge to grant an injunction to stop the destruction of the trees until a hearing was held, and he did. Two days later, the Highway Department agreed to stop the project, and the wonderful old oak trees are still standing. One irony: a resident who lived at the end of the road and who never failed to thank me whenever we met, later led the campaign effort of my first opponent because he was a Republican!

That year I was asked by the state Democratic Party to make a presentation to Walter Mondale, who was the keynote speaker at the state convention. When Mondale had run for president two summers before, for some reason he opened his campaign in Beaufort, at a shrimp boil in our new waterfront park. There he made a huge gaffe—he ate his first boiled shrimp without peeling it. According to a local paper, "He still managed to praise its taste, but found the Low country delicacy even better after bystanders pointed out the shell should be removed." My presentation (but not my idea) was a plexiglass paperweight containing a genuine preserved South Carolina shrimp, along with the seal of the state. I was a little embarrassed for him, and for myself, thinking the idea tacky. However, I was new in politics, and perhaps such good-natured ribbing was healthy. Thankfully, Mondale accepted this memento with good humor.

A more serious task was serving on an eighteen-member transition issues team for Governor-elect Dick Riley. I was honored to be asked, though puzzled as to why. At our first meeting I learned that Riley was very interested in the environment and nuclear waste and was determined to reform educational policy, all issues I had already become identified with.

Serving on his committee provided a wonderful opportunity for me to get to know Governor Riley, and we became allies on many of the issues which took over my legislative life—nuclear waste and energy conservation, education, the arts, even changing the rules of the House which controlled filibusters. If they had not been changed, filibusters would have been the death knell for much of his agenda—and mine.

Pauline Steinberg Hirschfeld

Barnard College Basketball Team, 1908. Pauline Hirschfeld (front row, second from right)

Isador Hirschfeld

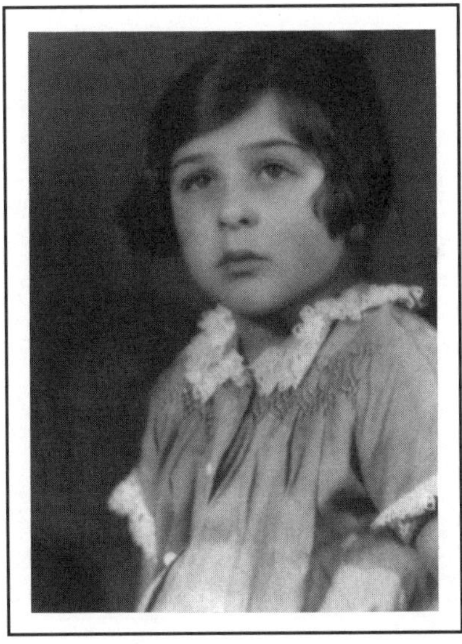
Harriet Hirschfeld at age six

Pauline, Harriet, and Lennie Hirschfeld, ca. 1928

Harriet Hirschfeld's confirmation class, Rodeph Sholem, 1935

Harriet Hirschfeld as a college freshman, 1940

Lennie and Phyllis Hirschfeld

Jennie Hyman Keyserling

William Keyserling

Keyserlings in the family Reo at Frogmore, S.C., 1916

Bethsheba, Leon, Rosalyn, and Herbert Keyserling

Herbert Keyserling, with his father, William, and Harriet, receives the Silver Star, Columbia, S.C., 1944.

Billy, Paul, Beth, and Judy Keyserling, 1960

Herbert and Harriet Keyserling

Reverend Martin Luther King Jr., with Courtney, Elizabeth, and John Siceloff at Penn Center, St. Helena Island, S.C., 1967. Courtesy John Siceloff.

Beaufort County Council, 1974. Clockwise from rear: William Grant, Gary Fordham, Bill McBride, David Jones, Booker T. Washington, Leroy Browne, Harriet Keyserling, Arthur Horne, Grady Thames. Courtesy *Beaufort Gazette*.

Political advertisement from the 1976 campaign for the S.C. House of Representatives

Beaufort County Representatives Harriet Keyserling and Wilton Graves and Senator James Waddell sworn in by T. Legare Rodgers, 1976. Courtesy *Beaufort Gazette*.

"The Krazy Kaucus" political memorabilia, 1977

Harriet Keyserling (third from left) watches Governor Richard Riley sign Holocaust "Day of Remembrance" Resolution, June 14, 1978. Courtesy Isadore Lourie, Columbia, S.C.

Harriet Keyserling with Governor Richard Riley (left) and Lt. Governor Nick Theodore, 1982

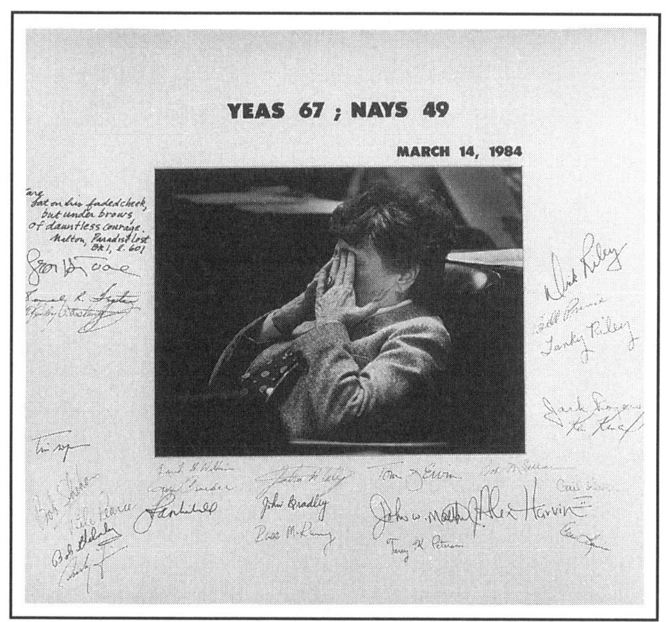

House passage of the Education Improvement bill, March 14, 1984

Governor Richard Riley signing the Accommodations Tax Act, 1984

Harriet Keyserling in debate on the Handgun bill, 1985. Robert Ariail cartoon. Courtesy Robert Ariail, Columbia, S.C.

Harriet Keyserling in debate on the Living Will bill. Robert Ariail cartoon. Courtesy Robert Ariail, Columbia, S.C.

House Rules Committee, 1987–1988

Visiting a Beaufort County public school

Working late at the Statehouse, Columbia

Representatives Mike Fair, Terry Haskins, and Senator Nell Smith discussing sex education on SCETV's "Crosstalk," 1988

Harriet Keyserling accepts from Governor Carroll Campbell the Elizabeth O'Neill Verner Award for Contributions to the Arts, 1989.

Harriet Keyserling with Ted Stern, President of the College of Charleston (center) and Maestro Gian Carlo Menotti

Harriet Keyserling (left) in the dinner party scene from the movie *The Prince of Tides*. Courtesy *Beaufort Gazette*.

Artist Jonathan Green and Harriet Keyserling at the 1993 S.C. Humanities Council Festival. Courtesy South Carolina Arts Commission.

Novelist Pat Conroy with Harriet Keyserling at a reception in his honor, Thomas Cooper Library, USC, 1997

CHAPTER 11

Nuclear Waste

I was introduced to nuclear waste issues in 1979 by a *Charlotte Observer* article, sent to me anonymously. The article reported that the South Carolina Department of Health and Environmental Control (DHEC) was allowing more low-level nuclear waste to be buried by Chem-Nuclear, at Barnwell, than the regulations allowed. I don't know if I was the only one who received that article, but I seemed to be the only one who reacted to it. I suspect a House staffer sent it to me, knowing I would take the bait.

I called in the DHEC people and asked them to explain. They seemed to dance around the question, saying that the limit set had nothing to do with health and safety but was an arbitrary number based on past experience with market supply and demand. Unsatisfied, I introduced a resolution saying that DHEC must abide by its own regulations. Motherhood and apple pie—but it was handily stopped. Five people objected to the resolution, all that was necessary to hold it up, perhaps forever in those days of filibusters. Then Sol Blatt, protesting my interference in the affairs of his district, moved to send it to committee, where it of course died. Everyone shrugged. It was not popular to tamper with the nuclear industry . . . or Sol Blatt.

My low-level nuclear waste involvement broadened over the years to include all kinds of nuclear wastes. A book could, and should, be written just on nuclear waste policy and the power structure in S.C. But for now, here's a brief history—as I see it.

After my unsuccessful efforts with DHEC, I became the protégée of a variety of people—research staff, environmentalists, university professors—who fed me information on this subject. They knew, and I was to learn, that South Carolina stored or buried more nuclear waste than any other state, with the possible exception of the state of Washington. We had eight-five percent of the nation's low-level waste, thirty percent of the nation's high-level defense waste, and were a prime candidate for storage and reprocessing of most of the commercial high-level waste. When I learned how mired in nuclear waste the state was, I asked Speaker Rex Carter to appoint me to the Joint Energy Committee, which studied energy-related subjects, and he did. This provided me with the status, the platform, the allies, and access to a staff to explore my concerns not only with nuclear waste but all the other energy issues I was so interested in—especially conservation and alternative sources of energy. Rex also appointed me to represent the South Carolina House on the Energy Committee of the National Conference of State Legislatures (NCSL), where I eventually became a vice chairman. My involvement with nuclear waste snowballed.

I was invited to serve on an advisory panel for the U.S. Office of Technology Assessment, which was developing information for Congress on the disposal of high-level radioactive commercial wastes. The panel was made up of nuclear industry representatives, environmentalists, scientists, and two elected officials (as it happened, both women) who were to represent the public point of view. The other woman served on a county council in Florida, and her expertise lay in public participation in policy setting. We met several times a year. Our role was to read material supplied us, then discuss and respond to proposals written by the staff, proposals which would eventually turn into a formal report to Congress. This report was to aid congressmen as they worked on nuclear waste legislation and policy. In addition to all the information the staff provided, I seemed to be on everyone's mailing list—the nuclear industry and the environmentalists. As I read, I began to question nuclear policies that were about to impact on South Carolina. I also questioned the lack of any long-range energy planning in state policy. Several government and industry committees existed to study these issues, but there was no connective tissue between them, and nobody seemed to be in charge.

Meanwhile, the committees on which I served offered me helpful resources—knowledgable staff, unlimited position papers, historical background, new research. I became the House nuclear waste expert. A positive aspect of my status as expert in this arena was the credibility it gave me. This made it a little harder for my natural enemies, the Fat and Uglies and a handful of Republicans, to challenge me in committee or on the House floor, at least on this issue, though they continued to try to undermine me on other issues. There was usually someone who recruited four others to object to any bill of mine that came up for consideration, if not to stop it, to at least slow it down. Sometimes I felt it was personal, sometimes they felt strongly about the issue, and other times they were doing the bidding of whatever special interest lobbyist I may have been making uneasy. But on nuclear waste their opposition was more hidden than open. Possibly I intimidated them; or possibly it was respect for the abilities of my Crazy Caucus allies who kept them at bay. Just as I deferred to and depended on members of my caucus on judicial and constitutional matters, they deferred to and depended on me on nuclear matters. When it was time to debate or vote, we were there for each other.

One negative aspect to my work in this area in the legislature was that in many minds I became the symbol of antinuclear activism, although I thought of myself as neither pro- or antinuclear. Actually, I probably was more pro, because I wanted us to become less dependent on foreign oil. I believed, and still believe, that the nuclear plants in operation must continue until we find better, environmentally safe ways to meet our energy needs. So I considered myself a middle-of-the-roader. But I did not think we should be building more plants until we resolved the nuclear waste problem.

For me the basic danger in the nuclear industry was the unknown quality and quantity of radioactive materials when they are emitted into the air we breathe, the water we drink, and the food we eat. We know that tiny specks can cause cancer or can rearrange our genes, causing birth defects in future generations. We know that they cannot be seen, smelled, or heard—and only time can reduce their potency. But scientists are divided on the risks involved in various states of the nuclear cycle, and only time will tell who is right and who is wrong. And then it may be too late. Leaks which may be declared "within safe limits" today may cause trouble years from now for unborn generations. Therefore, the risks of unsolved problems and unknown hazards should be shared by all who enjoy the benefits of nuclear armaments, nuclear power, nuclear research, and nuclear medicine, all of which produce different kinds of radioactive waste. Yes, the citizens of South Carolina were enjoying those benefits, but we bore an inordinate share of the risks, not only in the general operation of nuclear industries but in the varieties of waste they generated. This waste varies in strength, ingredients, and longevity. It is difficult to define the levels exactly. But inexactly, there are three general categories we store or bury in South Carolina. Low-level wastes are in the form of clothes, tools, and parts of machines used in nuclear plants, as well as medical and research wastes. These may be radioactive from a few weeks to four hundred years. The only official definition of low-level waste is "anything that is not high-level." Really! Chem-Nuclear, a private disposal company, buries hundreds of truckloads a week into twenty-foot trenches in Barnwell, on state-owned land. When they first went into operation, they just backed up the trucks and dumped the waste into unlined holes. And there was leakage. Now the hole is lined with plastic, the waste is packaged in containers, and the land is monitored for leaks. When the land fills up, Chem-Nuclear will move out, and the state will have the responsibility of monitoring the site forever after.

High-level defense waste can be potent and dangerous for up to 500,000 years. At the time I began to delve into this issue, South Carolina held about thirty percent of the country's military wastes in the form of twenty-eight million gallons (that number grew to thirty-five million by 1996) of highly radioactive sludge sitting in rusting containers in an earthquake-prone region over the Tuscaloosa Aquifer, which provides the principal reserve of fresh water for parts of South Carolina and Georgia. Most of this waste was produced at the Savannah River Plant (SRP), a residue from producing the ingredients for materials for atom bombs. The original plan was for this waste to be moved out within ten years, but forty years later it is still at SRP—because it can't be moved in its liquid state. At long last, after the United States government spent a billion dollars and after several failed attempts, SRP has begun to solidify this waste so it can be moved. The only problem is there is still no place to move it to.

High-level commercial wastes are primarily in the form of spent fuel rods from nuclear power plants, which are also potent for thousands of years. The used rods sit in water-filled concrete "cooling ponds," waiting to be moved to a permanent disposal site or reprocessed. Fuel rods can be used in the generators for only three years and then they must be replaced, so obviously the ponds at reactor sites are filling up. Reprocessing these rods was prohibited by Presidents Ford and Carter, for nonproliferation reasons, and there is still no site available for their disposal, despite twenty years of everyone acknowledging this desperate need. According to the most optimistic estimates, there won't be a site before the year 2010. The ban on reprocessing brought to a halt the attempt to put into operation the Allied General Nuclear Services (AGNS), which had been built in Aiken for that purpose. As an alternative to reprocessing, and in the absence of the timely construction of a permanent disposal site, one option that has been looked at for years, to tide us over until 2010, is away-from-reactor or monitored retrievable storage for the nation's thirty thousand tons of spent fuel rods. This would mean identifying, locating, and getting the approval of a state or community to store these spent fuel rods until a permanent place is ready. This was one of the most debated sections of the recommendations of the OTA advisory panel on which I served.

How did South Carolina get so enmeshed in the nuclear industry? It began in the 1950s, when the Atomic Energy Commission built a bomb plant—the Savannah River Plant in Aiken—at the urging of our powerful political figures; Sol Blatt, Edgar Brown, and Strom Thurmond all represented that region. If I'd been there then, I probably would have joined them in this effort to bring industry and jobs to a very poor state. Add to that our state's ardent support of all things military. The plant brought an enormous economic boost—thousands of jobs—and the people were proud to be contributing to the cold-war effort. The industry grew here because of the many technical experts who came into the state and the favorable political climate.

Several state actions to reinforce support of the nuclear industry followed the start-up of SRP. In 1967 there was the South Carolina Atomic Energy Act, which called on the State Development Board to specifically pursue, as state policy, nuclear plants, nuclear industry and nuclear waste burial sites. In 1978, Governor James Edwards's energy advisers urged more nuclear plants for the state as the major source of energy. Our political and industry leaders were also lobbying the federal government to store the nation's spent fuel rods in Aiken, in the empty pools at the never-opened AGNS plant. This seemed to me not only unfair but madness in a state with our geology and so little empty space—and most of that fragile. Why should we bear all the risks to health and safety while the other states enjoy the benefits of nuclear technology without sharing the risks? But Senator Bill Knotts of Aiken thought differently. In 1979 he introduced a resolution urging the federal government to decrease impediments to domestic nuclear power and to insure that the AGNS plant be used for storage and reprocessing. This resolution came to an abrupt halt after the Three Mile Island nuclear plant mishap in March 1979. As I have said before, timing is everything is politics. Three Mile Island and then Chernobyl were the timing agents that helped change the climate, helped to moderate our state's nuclear waste policies. Before I arrived in the legislature there were other legislators opposed to our state's nuclear policies—Sam Manning, Butler Derrick, Bill Campbell, and Alex Sanders—but they didn't have a chance in the political environment of that time. I was luckier in my timing.

After discovering just how much waste we were already storing, and how no progress was being made to provide for permanent disposal of nuclear wastes, I was aghast to learn about our state policies to encourage more nuclear plants and more burial sites. I filed a bill to amend the Atomic Energy Act in an attempt to remove the provision calling for the Development Board to encourage new plants and new waste dumps. On the House floor my pitch was that times had changed and the philosophy on how best to increase industrial activity had to change as well. In the light of the problems with nuclear wastes and the increasing costs of building nuclear plants, there was a need to look at other sources of energy and resources, to aim for a balance between different forms of energy. The League of Women Voters, which had brought the Atomic Energy Act to my attention, helped educate the legislature about the subject. My bill passed the House with little fuss, was acted on favorably by a Senate committee the following year, and was then killed on the Senate floor.

But in 1980, newly elected Governor Riley took a strong stand against South Carolina assuming the nuclear risk for every other state; Three Mile Island and Chernobyl brought the risk to everyone's attention as never before. I thought that if we asked our questions and protested vigorously enough, and if the newspapers tuned in, the public would finally say "Fair is fair, and enough is enough." And it did.

Dick Riley put his staff to work first on the low-level waste issue. Although there once were six regional burial sites for this waste, only three remained in the entire country—South Carolina was burying eighty-five percent of the nation's waste, while Washington and Nevada took care of the remaining fifteen percent. But in 1980 those two states threatened to close down; they considered the transporting and packaging of the wastes unsafe. That would leave South Carolina with it all. Riley wanted to cut down on wastes from outside the state, but his problem was the United States Constitution. The interstate commerce clause of the Constitution states that if we accept wastes (of any kind) from one state, we must accept it from all. Only the United States Congress could give us the right to restrict incoming wastes by creating a compact system.

President Carter, recognizing a national problem, created the State Planning Council to recommend a national policy for the storage and burial of nuclear wastes and appointed Governor Riley chairman. The council concluded that high-level radioactive waste must be the responsibility of the federal government, and low-level wastes should be the responsibility of the states. South Carolina, Nevada, and Washington led the way in lobbying Congress to pass the Low-level Nuclear Waste Policy Act of 1980, which gave the states the right—and the responsibility—to take care of low-level waste either alone or in groups called compacts. For the first time, states could keep out the wastes of other states IF they joined a compact. Compacts had to be ratified by Congress. Identical legislation had to be passed by all member states and then approved by Congress. This took great persuasion and a lot of time to achieve, because most states saw this as a threat to their present waste solution, which was good old South Carolina. Governor Riley assigned me to work with legislators from other states in setting up a compact for the Southeast region. I also traveled with him to Washington to meet with senators from key states as a voice—and an ear—for the South Carolina legislature.

In 1982 eight Southern states formed the Southeast Low-level Nuclear Waste Compact. A commission was formed to run the compact, funded primarily by fees paid by the waste producers. Each member state had two commissioners, who were usually governor's aides or directors of environmental state agencies. I served as an alternate commissioner to the compact during the Riley administration and attended most of the meetings. The chairman was Dr. Richard Hodes from Florida, whom I had known when he was a legislator and the president of the National Conference of State Legislatures. He was and still is a strong but patient chairman, but the problem of dealing with eight states, each trying to protect their sovereignty, was a very hot political potato. South Carolina offered, much to the other states' delight, to keep Barnwell open until 1992—if they would agree to take turns in hosting sites for regional waste, each for twenty years. After much jockeying by all the member states, North Carolina was selected, based on criteria debated for months, as the first site to replace Barnwell when it closed in 1992. But in 1992 North Carolina was nowhere near ready to open because of strong political resistance. The situation continued downhill.

The South Carolina legislature, bending to the pressure of Chem-Nuclear and lobbyists of other industries which produced wastes that went to the site, and over the almost dead bodies of some of us, voted to extend the date and keep Barnwell open for another four years, until 1996, at least for the members of the Southeast Compact. Most of the other states breathed a collective sigh of relief, although a few were concerned about the delay and changing timetable, which had been so difficult to set in the first place. That delaying action was, as we warned, a signal to North Carolina that there was no rush for them to move forward with a site. If we could be persuaded to wait four years, then probably we could be persuaded to stay open forever, I'm sure they all told each other. As the director of the Southeast Commission said in the early days of the commission: "The sited states must remain committed to closing their sites. *A 'crisis of disposal capacity' is the only factor that will compel the recalcitrant states and regions to get their site development efforts back on track*" (italics added).

And that is what eventually happened. In 1996 a new governor, David Beasley, and a majority of Republican legislators removed the "crisis of disposal capacity" by keeping the Barnwell site open. They reneged on the commitment to close the site on the day set by the compact legislation of all the states and Congress. They were easily influenced by Chem-Nuclear to not only keep it open for the Southern members but to open up the site to the whole country AND to withdraw from the compact. In withdrawing from the compact, we lost our right to restrict wastes from everywhere and anywhere. Ten years of carefully molded public policy went out the window.

This action was taken in a disturbing way—by amendment to the appropriations bill, tacked on by the Senate at the last minute. There were no public hearings, always required for such a drastic change of direction of a state policy, no third readings, always required for passage of a bill, and the House never voted on it as a stand-alone issue. The public had said, year after year in polls, that it wanted Barnwell closed, but the leadership did not allow a vote. If House members wanted to vote against this action they would have to vote against the whole appropriations bill, which is politically difficult; most legislators have something in the budget they must vote for. They were handcuffed. Beasley gave cover to the many uncomfortable legislators by promising that the additional revenues from Chem-Nuclear would go toward education. We of course felt this was one-sided economics, that there would be untold costs of being the nuclear waste capital of the country.

As long as there are strong economic incentives for special interests, there will always be attempts to reverse environmental progress. At an earlier time, in another state, Tom McCall, formerly the Republican governor of Oregon who personified the environmental movement of the 1960s and 1970s—conserving energy with the first bottle deposit bill, cleaning up polluted rivers, preserving public beaches, land-use planning—watched new political leaders try to reverse his policies. McCall was known as the governor who invited people to visit his wonderful state "but don't come here to live until we're ready." Depressed by seeing his life's work threatened, he fought back. He made a public statement: "Oregon is demure and lovely, and it ought to play a little hard to get. I think you'll all be just as sick as I am if you find she is nothing but a hungry hussy, throwing herself at every stinking smokestack that's offered." That's exactly how my allies and I felt about the policy reversal on Chem-Nuclear, the Southeast Compact and other environmental regulations which have been weakened.

We weren't as graphically eloquent, but we did try to fight back. I agreed to be the lead plaintiff in a suit, filed by a coalition of South Carolina environmental groups, against Governor Beasley and the legislature. We charged that it was unconstitutional to reverse such important state policy by tacking it onto the budget bill. This was bobtailing: withdrawing from the Compact was not related to a line item in the budget and it was time to put an end to this power-driven practice which ignored the voice of the people. (The state chamber of commerce had brought a similar suit against a bobtailing action several years before, but withdrew after exacting a promise from the legislature never to do it again!)

The Supreme Court ruled against us, saying the impact of this action was related to the budget. I was sorry that Jean Toal, who was a leader on the court and understood this issue so well, had recused herself because of some conflict concerning one of the attorneys. I have often wondered if she had been there if the outcome wouldn't have been different.

Meanwhile, Chem-Nuclear, which had been working on building a new site in North Carolina and making millions during that process, is no longer working on the licensing process there, rumor has it because the North Carolina agency in charge of this project was not satisfied with its progress. The question in all our minds is what incentive does North Carolina now have to build a new site when South Carolina is willing to "be the solution to the nations' nuclear waste problem," as Governor Riley used to describe it. A story in the *State* (July 5, 1997) tells us the sad story that seventeen years after Congress created regional compacts, and after hundreds of millions of dollars have been spent on "studying" new sites in different regions of the country, not one of the ten interstate compacts has opened a site, and none of the five states that opted to go it alone with sites have completed plans to build them. The need to build them disappeared with South Carolina's availability. It is a bitter irony that South Carolina government led the way in developing and finding the solution to the problem of low-level wastes, and then ten years later was the leader in destroying that solution.

During those years starting in 1980, when we were working on setting up the Southeastern Compact, I talked with legislators from other states when we met at national meetings and learned what was happening around the country. I became energized to attack other nuclear waste issues which I thought were inequitable for South Carolina, as compared to other states.

I watched the nascent move by the Department of Energy to select the AGNS reprocessing plant in South Carolina as a storage place for the highly radioactive spent fuel rods from commercial nuclear power plants, both American and foreign. The first effort was called away-from-reactor storage, or AFR. (When opposition to this concept brewed, spin doctors changed the name to monitored retrievable storage, or MRS. Different name, same concept.) It did not seem fair to me that South Carolina, with eighty-five percent of low-level wastes and thirty percent of the high-level defense wastes, should also be called upon to store all the country's leftover spent fuel rods. The question of fairness and equity became a passion with me, and I was pleased that the Nuclear Waste Policy Act of 1982 stresses equity and fairness, perhaps because it was stressed in the OTA report that came out of our advisory committee.

Other states began passing strong measures controlling nuclear wastes—no transportation, no storage, no burial of nuclear wastes in their states. I felt their positions were unrealistic and unfair—also detrimental to finding a solution to a national problem. On the other hand, if we in South Carolina were saying nothing while everyone else was saying no, we would be seen as accepting everything. We would be the path of least resistance.

The need for an AFR was a major point of contention on the OTA advisory committee. I and others felt that "temporary storage" would become permanent, with us forever. This opinion was based on the

South Carolina experience. The pressure would be off to find a permanent place. I also knew that there were only three possible sites in the nation, and AGNS would be the prime choice if Congress decided to go this route. Because the South Carolina establishment was lobbying for this dubious honor while the other states were fighting it off.

In 1980, I introduced a concurrent resolution—which does not have the force of law but expresses the sentiment of the legislature to Congress—which said that before the federal government takes over AGNS for storage of the country's wastes, there must be legislative approval of the South Carolina legislature and the governor.

I called my resolution a states' rights issue, or a voice against the federal government preempting our right to safeguard the health and welfare of our citizens, and I found forty cosponsors. It covered only out-of-state wastes, recognizing that we should take care of our own. I argued that IF the country decided we must have away-from-reactor storage then let's choose the best possible place in the country—based on factors of health, safety, technology, and equity. Let's not decide on the basis of least political resistance and such economic reasons as bailing out AGNS. I cited transportation risks, with a continuous stream of trains and trucks carrying the highly radioactive rods into our state. And there was the question of how long was "temporary," when there was still no agreed-upon technology or site for permanent disposal. But above all it was a question of fairness and equity. How could it be equitable for South Carolina, using only five percent of the country's nuclear power, to be burying and storing almost all the country's wastes? The two other candidate states for an AFR were New York and Illinois. Illinois had already passed a law prohibiting establishing an AFR there. If we were silent, it would be assumed we wanted to continue our unquestioning, unending hospitality to the nuclear waste industries. These arguments resonated, as they say in 1996, and made it very difficult for legislators to oppose my resolution, despite the ever-present lobbyists hovering about.

I agreed to a change requested by Sol Blatt which would require only a majority vote of the legislature to approve an AFR, instead of the two-thirds vote I had proposed. It passed the House with no debate, then sat in the Senate Medical Affairs Committee for a few weeks. The senators urged me to talk with industry people, who wanted to change a few words. Not wanting to appear unreasonable to these senators I barely knew, I agreed. We met, and I agreed to change a word they wanted changed. Instead of saying Congress should "exclude" consideration of South Carolina, we said Congress should "abstain" from considering South Carolina. Semantics for me; I'm not sure what it was for them.

As reported in the *State* on March 28, 1980, Senator John Drummond of Greenwood, who moved for approval of the resolution, said, "I know your concern, and I admire you for it." "I think she has fine tuned it and we ought to report it out," agreed Senator Verne Smith of Greenville, who said he would "push" the resolution in the full Senate. No doubt I was helped by several strong editorial endorsements, including the *Greenville News,* which urged the Senate to act. The one I liked best concluded: "That the Keyserling Resolution passed with practically no fanfare is a tribute to the Beaufort Lawmaker who has withstood untold pressure from the pro-nuclear lobby but who in the end prevailed because she listened to all sides and earned the respect of even her opponents." The following year I turned this concurrent resolution into a joint resolution, which has the force of law, if only for a specified time, in this case until 1990 (as compared to a bill which stays on the books unless and until amended or obliterated). It moved relatively quickly through both the House and the Senate. I now am very sorry that I did not try for a bill, which would have stayed on the books forever, instead of a resolution which was no longer in effect after 1990. The AFR question is back with us in 1996, and I doubt that the legislature, as it is presently composed, will even try to stop it.

Shortly after, I put in another resolution, to create a committee to consult with the federal government in the event South Carolina was named a site for an AFR. This was in response to the national Nuclear Waste Policy Act of 1982, which called for consultation and concurrence between states and the federal government. It passed. On our committee was the governor as chairman, the lieutenant governor, two House members, and two senators. I was one of the House members appointed to it. The committee was to meet twice a year and be briefed by the governor's staff and Department of Energy officials. During

Governor Riley's term we met regularly. In 1984 we expanded our duties to include study of any other issue addressed in the national act, including selection of permanent repositories for nuclear waste. As a speaker at the South Carolina Energy Forum, I told a group of industry people, "Now industry may call this [my various Resolutions] politicizing an issue, but the issue had already been politicized by industry. I agree with you that there are technical solutions and answers to what to do with nuclear wastes, but it is a fact of life that political considerations have superceded them." Although I talked emotionally about equity and fairness, I felt that with all the time and studying I had put into the subject, and with all the information provided me by others, I was able to approach the subject on an intellectual level, more with my mind, than my heart. I wanted the industry folks to know that I knew what I was talking about, not just having a political romp.

And political this committee became. When Carroll Campbell became governor, he either found the committee a very low priority or he was opposed to its existence. Instead of chairing it himself, he appointed Lamar Priester, who represented a waste industry, to chair it. Although the law said we must meet at least twice a year, we didn't meet. I challenged Dr. Priester's right to be chairman, contrary to the law, which named the governor chairman. I challenged the fact that he didn't call meetings. He called a few, then they tapered off into nothingness. John McMillan, the governor's aide responsible for environmental issues, paid no attention to our complaints. I gave up.

The next nuclear waste issue revolving around AGNS involved reprocessing spent fuel rods from foreign countries. It was bad enough to talk about storing all America's waste, but now they were talking about waste generated in a long list of foreign countries. When Ronald Reagan became president, he reversed President Carter's policy against reprocessing spent fuel rods, and the debate about activating AGNS breathed life again.

I had no position on the merits and demerits of reprocessing. However, in 1982, the economics of opening the plant were questionable, even to the *Wall Street Journal*, which wrote an editorial against it. The price of natural uranium had gone down, the supply was plentiful, and private capital wasn't available to start AGNS up. David

Stockman convinced the administration that it should not spend the billion or so federal dollars required. When the news seeped out that foreign countries were being courted to invest in the plant and send their rods here, I took a position against such an idea. Reprocessing may get rid of spent fuel rods, but it generated another kind of very radioactive waste, similar to the liquid defense wastes. With no assurance of a solidification process, and no place to put the waste, I could see a situation similar to the defense wastes sitting at SRP for thirty years—when they were to have been gone in ten. There was also the provision in the Nuclear Waste Policy Act calling for storage of commercial foreign nuclear waste in the United States, with AGNS the likely candidate. If we had our own national problem of storage, why add the world's problem to ours? I was never sure whether the purpose was to once again try to save a private investment or to recover fuel from waste. My resolution had sixty-four cosponsors this time. (The number of cosponsors for my nuclear waste bills was increasing in geometric progression.) As a member of the Energy Committee I was able to run it through that committee first and pick up the five House members as cosponsors, most of whom were considered conservative and industry friendly. I carefully listed their names first on the resolution, rather than in the usual alphabetical order, before soliciting more cosponsors.

I argued that public policy should not be set to protect or bail out a particular industry at the expense of the citizenry; rather, this resolution protected the greatest number of people, admittedly at the expense of a particular industry.

The bill passed, but in its final form, the Savannah River Plant (SRP) was excluded from its provisions. This is sadly pertinent as it is SRP and not AGNS which is now the point of contention with respect to storing and reprocessing foreign wastes. Could this have been forward thinking by the friends of SRP?

Another issue which went on and on revolved around the highly radioactive defense wastes and the aging, deteriorating reactors at SRP. This was a particularly sensitive issue for my constituents, because the Savannah River is Beaufort's main source of drinking water, and we are downstream of SRP. We worried about the occasional reports of tritium found in the water and cesium in the fish. This was of course not just a local issue; it became more of a state and national issue as stories from the state and national press began popping up concerning the safety of the plant, past, present, and future. There were reports from congressional committees, the Environmental Protection Agency, and the General Accounting Office that the Department of Energy (DOE) and Dupont, the private contractor that ran SRP (it became SRS when Westinghouse took over its management), was not operating as safely as possible and was not releasing information about spills, accidents, and other hazards. The General Accounting Office concluded that "safety has not been DOE's number one priority in operating what GAO calls 'potentially one of the more dangerous industrial operations in the world.'" William Lawless, an engineer at SRP responsible for research in radioactive waste management programs, resigned after six years, saying higher-ups had persistently sat on, downgraded, or bounced his reports on questionable procedures—especially the pumping out of wells located around the dump area—and on radiation levels up to 200,000 times the EPA standard for drinking water. Dupont and SRS denied these allegations.

This turmoil came to a head when the Department of Energy proposed reactivating the K and L reactors, which had been shut down either for safety reasons or mothballed because the demand for their product, tritium, had slowed. They proposed restarting them without developing an Environmental Impact Statement (EIS) and without installing a cooling tower, which would prevent the release of water hotter than the ninety-degree maximum allowed by the Clean Water Act. This decision caused a furor, and rightfully so. A commercial nuclear plant making such changes would be required by the Nuclear Regulatory Commission to have an EIS. Why should standards for the Department of Energy (DOE) be less stringent than standards for commercial power plants? Risk is risk, and waste is waste, regardless of whether the operation is defense or commercial, and they must be treated with the same seriousness and care. It was not acceptable to say the federal government could not afford the same safety practices required of private industry.

Another glaring problem was that DOE monitored itself. The reports of poor past performance of its nuclear weapon plants was proof that this was a dangerous policy. There should be independent oversight in monitoring operations. It was no longer enough for DOE to say "trust us." Those days were gone forever.

I drew up a concurrent resolution calling on the governor and the attorney general to employ negotiation, discussion, and, if necessary, lawsuits to "protect the health, safety and environmental quality of South Carolina and her citizens." I was joined by Senator Alex Sanders and Lieutenant Governor-elect Mike Daniel at a press conference detailing the need for state action. Although a concurrent resolution does not require committee consideration and has only one reading instead of the three required for bills and joint resolutions, this particular concurrent resolution was tossed to and fro, back and forth between committees in both the House and Senate. It finally passed the House because our rules made it particularly difficult to stop a concurrent resolution other than by voting it down. And obviously few would publicly vote against a resolution calling for the protection and safety of the state. But the Senate opposition did better. They managed to send it back to yet another committee, where it died at the end of the session, without taking a direct vote.

But we won in the end, by another route. The South Carolina Energy Research Foundation and the Natural Resources Defense Council joined forces and brought suit against DOE, and eventually the courts ruled that DOE had to conduct the environmental impact statement and had to build a cooling tower to reduce the heat of the emissions.

Some thought I was trying to close down SRP. Far from it. I want SRP, now SRS, to remain intact and move forward with solidifying and moving those thirty-five million gallons of wastes. And clean up the many other forms of wastes around the plant before they seep into our aquifer or are flushed into our surface water.

Nuclear waste issues, where the stakes are so high and the lobbyists so powerful, keep popping back up. In 1996, away-from-reactor storage is once again on the front burner, as is the arrival of spent fuel rods from other countries. Nothing is forever in the legislature, neither victory or defeat. The *New York Times*, in an 1996 editorial, says it bluntly: "In New York State's Capital, special-interest groups have a secret strength. They endure. Governors come and go. Even incumbent legislators . . . retire eventually. But the special interests remain, submitting the same bills year after year until they triumph by exhaustion." Needless to say, this applies to any state capital and is even more on target in states where the lobbyist/good ol' boy culture is so strong.

Repeated struggles for (or against) an issue year after year had a debilitating effect on me. It is difficult to feel the same passion with the same intensity when the arguments and rationale for your position don't change. And passion and intensity are necessary weapons to win difficult battles. The best tactic for the legislator passionate about an issue is to continually bring in new blood, new passion to take the lead, to replace the inevitable staleness which comes from such prolonged wars—to match the never-tiring, self-replenishing lobbyist brigade. In 1990, there was some new blood on this nuclear waste disposal issue, including some good women legislators. But in 1992, when I retired, they were soon redistricted out of their seats. My son Billy, who ran in my place, joined the remaining defenders against waste. But just as I was in the right place at the right time, they were there at the wrong time. The political climate had so changed that the opportunities for open, responsible debate were gone. There was no cadre of allies, nor a governor on their side, to balance the power of the lobbyists who took control of the nuclear waste debate.

One discomforting element in the SRP or SRS debates was that even with the admitted history of SRP dangers and risks, we who fought to "fix" the problems were seen as being un-American, disloyal, or unconcerned about national defense. We always felt we had to "prove" we were not. My friendship with Francie Close Hart made me especially conscious of my defensiveness.

When I first heard about Francie, a granddaughter of Elliot Springs of Springs Mills, she was a "peacenik," an environmentalist known mostly for opposing nuclear weapons. Her assistant called me one day to make an appointment to discuss a particular resolution I was working on. I hesitated, then asked him to please not mention her name when he was announced at the front desk. When he arrived I explained to him that I was trying hard to maintain my (true) image of being neither antinuclear nor antiwar, and who knew what rumors might start if it was known I was consorting with her group. I did not feel good about this, but felt my position in the House was so tentative that any little tilt could be the difference between credibility and doubt, success and failure. They forgave me. In time Francie became more established in her mode of operation. Her group switched from emotion and protests to scientific facts and legal arguments. Francie set up the Energy Research Foundation, which funded research and lawsuits in high-level nuclear waste matters, especially related to SRP. She also published excellent background information reports on nuclear issues with special attention to SRP, information the layman had little access to, and little understanding of. They were an invaluable resource for me and others.

What most impressed me was that she didn't just spend money, she mastered the subject herself, testifying at hearings and meeting with industry representatives. She often shared with me and anyone else who asked for it legal and technical information which she gathered from national experts in the field of defense wastes. She earned the respect of friends and foes in this arena by her diligence and consistency. In fact, she parallels those special interest lobbyists the *New York Times* described in one way; she was there year after year, monitoring government policies relating to her interest, and I hope finding new banner carriers in the legislature. I am sorry to add, as I edit this chapter in January 1998, that Francie has just notified her board, on which I serve, that she is closing down Energy Research Foundation. But I am sure she will be available, if needed. In another way, however, she is very different from many lobbyists. Her "special interest" is not profit nor glory, but the health and safety of the public.

I have one other memory of the nuclear waste wars. I don't remember which war it was, but there was an occasion when I experienced my first flutter of power. I, like most women in politics, was not motivated by a lust for power. In fact, I scorned those who were, possibly because I never thought I could win it, minority that I was in so many ways. But gradually I did gain a sort of power, which Bob Sheheen described as "power derived from knowledge" rather than power derived from position.

One rainy day, at a time when one of my resolutions was under consideration (probably it was the one involving AGNS and spent fuel rods), I was working in my office when I received a phone call from former Governor McNair, whose law firm represented several nuclear-related industries. He said he wanted to talk with me and asked if I would come around to his office for a cup of coffee. My reaction should have been, given my predisposition for "getting along or going along," to say "Sure." But I didn't. My first reason (or excuse) was that it was difficult to find a parking space near his office, and I didn't want to walk in the rain. My second was that I had to be ready to run to a committee meeting when a bill of mine was to come up for discussion, and I didn't know when that would be. But overriding all of that, I admit here for the first time, was the thought, "He would never have asked a man to run up to his office for a cup of coffee. He would have suggested meeting for lunch or a drink." I have no idea if that was so. There may have been a time crunch, and the discussion had to be then. I don't remember. What I do remember is Governor McNair and his senior law partner coming over to my little office in the rain to talk to me. That was my first whiff of power. Which led me to reevaluate my notions. I came to realize that it was only self-serving power I should scorn, not all power. If it could be used to further public service goals, then it was good and necessary.

CHAPTER 12

Filibusters

In 1977, my first year in the legislature, I wrote a column in the *Beaufort Gazette* about the first prolonged filibuster of the year. I wrote in good humor: "As I listened and watched, I thought what good theatre this was—there was drama, action, humor, suspense and a cast of colorful players." For the next five years I wrote many columns about filibusters, but my good humor disappeared, to be replaced by bitterness and acrimony against those who held us hostage for so many hours of the day and days of the week. Year by year my frustration deepened as I was forced to sit though more and more filibusters, often on insignificant bills. Each year the House calendar filled up with important bills which we never reached because we wasted so much time either waiting out filibusters or giving up and going home. How frustrating it was to watch important bills languish and die, and how angry I was at those who set up the roadblocks and logjams.

In December 1982, I wrote my last column on the subject, and my good humor had returned. We won a huge battle to change the House rules and finally put into place some controls over debate—one of the last states in the union, I believe, to do so.

The filibuster is a weapon used by the opponents of a bill to stop that bill from passing when they don't have enough votes to defeat it. It is usually used by minority groups. In our House the minorities were, at the time I was there, the Republicans, the Black Caucus, and the Fat and Uglies. The strategy of a filibusterer is to stay at the podium and talk, talk, talk to keep the bill from being voted on. While a speaker has the podium, only he can make a motion to vote for passage of a bill, no one else. There can be motions from the floor to table a bill, to continue (kill it for the year), recess, or adjourn, and such motions are made repeatedly—sometimes by the pros, sometimes by the antis—but a motion for passage can only be made from the podium.

At first, during a filibuster the speaker addresses the substance of the bill, then after several hours, there is repetition, irrelevancy, and boredom. According to the rules, the debate has to be germane, related to the subject at hand, but the rule is loosely enforced so that almost any topic can be stretched by a passing remark and in that way made germane. While this is going on, the speaker's supporters work the floor, trying to change votes. Lobbyists stand outside, sending in notes to members, trying to change votes. Constituents call members to the phone, trying to change votes. When a speaker shows signs of tiring, his supporters ask him long questions, partly to give his mind and voice a rest, partly to give him new ideas to talk about, partly to reinforce his arguments—just in case anyone is listening. As time goes by, no one listens. Rather, we take care of other business, write letters, make phone calls, gossip . . . or work the floor.

The only way to cut a filibuster short is by invoking cloture or, as it is called, "moving the previous question." Attempts to do this are sucessful only if the House is, for some reason, outraged. According to our House rules, sixty-eight votes are needed to invoke cloture when a member has the podium. There are rarely more than a hundred House members present, and if you subtract all the minority caucus members, who never vote for cloture, obviously sixty-eight votes are very hard to come by.

There are several good reasons people hesitate to vote for cloture. Many members feel it is discourteous to cut a speaker off, especially a friend, and even an enemy. Secondly, cloture imposes a strict set of time limits; once cloture is invoked, debate is limited not only for the person at the podium but for everyone else who follows. Each amendment is allowed a total of only four minutes of discussion, two minutes for each side. Amendments making substantive change need more than two minutes to be clarified. In fact, many amendments strike out the words of the entire bill and substitute a new bill. How can anyone vote responsibly after only a four-minute discussion of a bill? Those who have not yet been heard or have important amendments to follow are not willing to set limits which will affect them if and when they finally have a chance to speak. Further, many members feel if one person has already spoken for hours, days, or weeks, it just isn't fair for everyone else to have only two minutes. Perhaps most important, once cloture is invoked, no new amendments aimed at a compromise can be offered.

Filibusterers who are articulate, humorous, or passionate in their beliefs are easy to take. Those who flail out at the opposition with disdain or play to the press are hard to take. As are those who just stand there killing time by mumbling or reading out of the legislative manual or statistical charts.

During the major action, lots of skirmishes take place, more like a battlefield than a debate. There is continuous stream of test votes—motions to continue, to recess, to invoke cloture, to adjourn in an attempt to assess the situation at a particular moment—as members usually follow their leader on these votes. After each vote, workers from both sides rush to the front desk to get printouts to see how everyone voted, to measure their strength, to see who is missing. Strategists huddle over the printouts, then separate to work the floors. What may look to the uninitiated like people strolling around are really people begging their allies to hold firm, to stay, not to adjourn, to sit it out. If we adjourn, the filibusterer can rest up, may become exhilarated by his press coverage, and may even gain votes by giving the grassroots back home time to organize. Efforts are made to persuade waverers to change—or to hold firm.

Different members have different roles to play. For instance, my assignment during the Public Service Commission filibuster was to be a row captain. I took polls periodically on how the people in my row planned to vote on various amendments or whether they would sit out the filibuster or vote for cloture. I also watched their votes. When someone defected from our side, I would try to turn him around or find someone else who could. When one or more of our side left the chamber to talk to someone in the lobby, to make a phone call, or to smoke a cigarette, I would try to pull them back in when a vote seemed imminent. We studied printouts of each vote, talked with the governor's aides who were out in the hall, and met with the governor in his office to discuss new compromise amendments. The other side was doing the same. They had conferences with their leaders and the utility lobbyists who hovered close by, working their charms on susceptible members. It was truly amazing to me to see votes change back and forth on an issue that was so black and white. All the while, partisan spectators nervously watched from the balcony.

When Rule 3.2 is invoked, the sergeant-at-arms must find all absent members, wherever they may be, and bring them back. This is one way to be sure our people will be present if a vote is called for. And, if we have to sit there and endure a filibuster, everyone else ought to share that misery. Members sitting in committee rooms (sometimes listening over the intercom) or at nearby restaurants are brought back. The highway patrol searches out those who left town. As the missing return, they are greeted by cheers. Those trying to break a filibuster try to persuade people to stay the night if necessary. There is just so long one person can stand at the podium, and once he leaves that podium, cloture can be invoked by a simple majority rather than the sixty-eight votes. (During our first filibuster, Sylvia Dreyfus asked a seat mate what a filibusterer did when he could no longer contain himself. She was told that there was a receptacle under the podium, and if it was a man, he just used it as he spoke. Sylvia was seen strolling behind the podium and peering in. She found a brass spittoon.)

All the while, small clusters of people huddle together inside and outside the House chambers, looking for a compromise acceptable to the podium holder. For compromise is another way to end a filibuster, but he who holds the podium must agree with it.

A siege mentality creeps over us. Large bags of peanuts from Cromers suddenly appear on desks, the sign we are there to stay. As time goes by, more serious food arrives. Pages run in and out, taking orders for the nearest fast-food place. Occasionally some of us order real food. I remember the night when we were sitting through the Public Service Commission filibuster, we of the Crazy Caucus decided to go gourmet and ordered our favorite dinners (I remember well that mine was almond glazed lamb chops) from the Elite Epicurean, our favorite restaurant. We created a little circle of elegance in the midst of the smells of the french fries, hamburgers, hot dogs, and onions.

In addition to eating, I'm sorry to say there was drinking. A lobbyist or a group of lobbyists would set up a bar in an empty meeting room in the building, unused since the advent of a new office building for House members. As the nights grew longer the noise level escalated, with little clusters of raucous members. One night of the month-long Public Service Commission filibuster, Sam Tenenbaum, a citizen activist, member of the State Development Board, and a strong supporter of the bill—and of Governor Riley, who was pushing the bill—brought a German industrialist to the House to watch the proceedings. They had come from a dinner at the Governor's Mansion, where Sam had taken the governor's place as host because the governor was at the State House waiting out the filibuster. When they arrived at the State House, they saw an open bar, not hidden away in a room but in the lobby of the State House, right in front of a portrait of John C. Calhoun. And they saw drunken legislators wandering around. Sam was not just embarrassed, he was furious. He threatened to call the national employer of the lobbyist who was pouring that night and have him fired. He was talked out of doing this by a promise from higher-ups that the practice of plying good buddies with liquor in the State House would end. Woody Brooks, who dispensed grants money, also dispensed Bloody Marys from time to time in his office. Governor Riley ordered him to stop. The flow of alcohol was reduced, but I'm not sure it dried up until the filibusters themselves were ended, after we changed the rules. Those drinking were usually the Old Guard or the Fat and Uglies. The Crazy Caucus remained cold sober, adding to our initial advantage of mastery of the rules. In fact, Liz Crum, at that time the director of the House Judiciary Committee, tells me she was in charge of plying us with coffee to keep us alert during the Public Service Commission (PSC) action.

The PSC bill, sometimes called the merit selection bill, gave the governor the power to appoint a merit selection panel that would seek out the most qualified persons to serve on the Public Service Commission, as opposed to the status quo, under which legislators elected their buddies, usually other legislators. After six weeks of frustrating filibuster, a vote was finally taken on the Judiciary Committee amendment (which I supported), which was the meat of the bill. As those red and green lights filled up the board, often changing sides during the vote as row captains pressed on members, it was impossible to tell who was ahead; then a great shout went up as the totals appeared. We had won by one vote.

However, it turned out we celebrated too soon, because another amendment appeared, which if passed would wipe out our amendment. Test votes showed the sponsors of the new amendment had the votes to pass it. Palmer Freeman (on our side) managed to get the podium when we were thirteen votes behind, to wrap it up, state our case, and go down gracefully. Ginger Crocker said, "Let's try one more time." She made a procedural motion, and, to our amazement, we won it by six votes. So Palmer stayed at the podium for seven hours, filibustering for our side, until a compromise could be worked out, around three in the morning. With exhortations from leadership of all factions, it was voted in with only a few dissenting votes. Tom Marchant, one of the conference committee members, held us up still further when the committee wouldn't place his name first on the conference committee report. The House met the next day at 10 A.M. to take up another contentious issue—a judicial reform bill that created an appeals court.

The PSC debate became known as the longest in the history of the House, with the most procedural motions and with each vote having only a two- or three-vote swing—which is why it was so important to keep our troops in their seats. The main proponents of the PSC reform were the Crazy Caucus, Governor Riley, and other reform-minded legislators. It was the battle that molded us into a group. It also began the healing process between the supporters of Dick Riley and Brantley Harvey, who had faced each other in the Democratic primary for governor. Bob Sheheen and Jean Toal had been in Harvey's camp, and they joined together with Riley's upstate supporters on the PSC issue. The major opponents were the legislative leaders with close ties to the utilities, some of them on retainer from them for legal work, who wanted to retain their right to appoint PSC commissioners, and the Fat and Uglies, who hoped to inherit their power eventually. Or were doing the bidding of the lobbyists. The chief filibusterers were Tom Marchant, whom someone wickedly described as a "strut standing still," and John Felder, a leader of the Fat and Uglies. PSC reform was the first of many battles between our caucus and theirs.

I remember one night during those six weeks when the Crazy Caucus had dinner at Liz Crum's house and sat around for hours in a depressed state. Were we wasting our time in a legislature that was paralyzed? Was it possible that things could get better—or worse? Should we leave en masse? Our PSC victory was a magic elixir for that temporary insanity, and most of us stayed on to enjoy many more good victories.

The filibuster is a valid instrument in the democratic process as long as it is not abused, a tool to protect minority rights in a society where more and more such an idea is scorned. But there was no question in my mind, at the end of my second year, that it was being abused to the extent that the majority was totally handcuffed. One irony is that the filibuster was originally used by Southern politicians to protect their minority viewpoint as best as they could in the U.S. Congress. Now these Southern white leaders, Democrat and Republican, were finding that weapon used against them by the new minorities.

My personal feelings about filibusters? As long as a speaker is presenting information and sticking to the subject, as long as attempts are being made to find a compromise, as long as the issue is passionately felt by the speaker, I would not vote for cloture. But when I supported a bill being filibustered, I always voted to sit it out, not adjourn. And if that just didn't work, I usually (but not always) voted for cloture, to bring the issue to an end rather than return to it day after day. The filibuster serves as a roadblock for bills which may be rushed through without enough debate. It is, as a political scientist described it, a way to delay impetuous action. And it is an important avenue to take on the road to compromise. For these reasons I think it is important for one chamber, the smaller, more deliberate Senate, to keep alive the ability to filibuster.

One late night, when I was sitting out a filibuster, I went into the small ladies' room in back of the chambers to put my feet up and to listen over the intercom. I woke up hours later to find the chamber emptied out except for the cleanup crews sweeping away the popcorn and other debris. I didn't know until the next day if the bill had been killed or passed. Most of the time we did not stay late into the night. Most of the time, when we saw a filibuster building, we would adjourn for the day after a few hours of polite listening. Or when members at some point become impatient to get on with other bills, especially their bills, a sudden motion to continue (kill) the bill would pop up and quietly pass; the bill was dead for that year, sacrificed, as it were, in order to get on with other business—without the bill's sponsors ever having the opportunity to explain or debate their bill from the podium.

Before the 1982 session began, a political reporter took an informal survey of legislators to find what their priorities were for the session. The following were deemed essential: congressional reapportionment; property tax relief; creation of an appeals court to relieve the three- to four-year wait people had to endure to appeal decisions of lower courts; a constitutional spending limit; blue laws reform. How well did we do with our priorities by the end of the year? We batted zero. As one newspaper said, the six issues were victims of "an appalling legislative paralysis. . . . Both houses were choked by aimless and endless filibusters."

In addition to those six issues, there were others we spent years talking about, which were annually filibustered to death: the accommodations tax, requiring child safety seats in cars, the living will, and a bill to limit filibusters, all issues I favored. There was no doubt about it. Filibusters decreased productivity, increased frustration, and weakened the democratic process. They also encouraged thoughts of flight from the legislature by good legislators.

It was not just those bills I was concerned about. I became obsessed with the vast number of important bills which sat untouched and unreachable on the contested calendar. Different legislatures have different rules, and one has to know the rules and procedures of the South Carolina House at that time to fully comprehend how much damage could be done.

Every bill must have three readings in the House and three readings in the Senate to pass. The "first" reading is when the title of a bill is read aloud by the House reading clerk and the speaker sends it to a standing committee to be studied. If and when it is reported out favorably by the committee, it is placed on the bill calendar to wait its turn to be taken up for "second" reading.

Every morning, as we start at the beginning of the bill calendar and work our way through it, a great variety of things can happen. As a bill's turn comes, any House member may "object." If three members "object," that bill goes on the "contested calendar" and can not be debated or voted on until we finish the "uncontested" calendar or until some objections are removed, leaving fewer than three objections. There is a special time each day for "removal of objections." Thus debate can be delayed for days, weeks, or forever, depending on the length of the calendar and how much time we spend in session. Other possible motions are to "adjourn debate," which postpones debate for a day or more, to "continue" the bill, which kills it for that year, or to return it to committee, or move to "table," which kills it forever. There are rules which set the order of these motions, and conditions under which they may be made.

Most debate takes place during the second reading, as the third reading is more or less perfunctory in the House (but important in the Senate). According to our rules then, the "uncontested" bills were taken up first, and we didn't get to the "contested" section of the calendar until we completed the "uncontested" section. At certain times of the year, that section lists hundreds of bills. So three people can in effect keep the House from ever debating a bill—unless they can be persuaded to remove their objections, or unless the Rules Committee votes to put a bill on "special order" for a specific day. (This is why the Rules Committee is always referred to as the "powerful" Rules Committee.)

When we spent only a few hours a day, three days a week, in session, and part of that time was eaten up by filibusters, it was impossible to reach the contested bills on our calendar. In my first few years, important bills were killed by inaction or by filibusters, which ate up this valuable time and sometimes caused people to adjourn out of frustration.

There were several other excruciating filibusters I remember. Norma Russell, who was running for lieutenant governor, filibustered a one-cent increase of the gasoline tax, on and on and on. Alex Harvin sponsored a bill to allow twin trailer trucks on our highways. He had eighty-three cosponsors. Only about eleven members consistently voted against it. The truckers' association filled the outer halls and covered our desks with fact sheets. Yet it took eight years to pass, as every time one of the opponents came to the podium, someone moved to adjourn. Jean Toal, who strongly opposed twin trailers, took turns at the podium, holding it while others tried to work out a compromise. John Bradley, her ally, made a mock-up of twin trailers and provided the humor. But nimble use of the rules and a little humor couldn't stop forever the heavy lobbying effort, which just never wore down and never gave up. It is surprising to me now how few twin trailers I see on the South Carolina highways, considering the investment the industry made to pass the law to allow them.

Reapportionment, or the redrawing of boundaries of House districts every ten years to maintain government by "one person, one vote," is a prime subject for filibuster. Every district must have the same number of people: that number is reached by dividing the total population of the state by the number of districts (124). Although much of the work is a mechanical process carried out in "the map room," where, for several months, hundreds of rolled-up maps and census tracts are worked over by staff members with calculators and computers. Delegations are given maps and asked to try to draw their own plans. Some do and some do not. The hope is to patch them all together. But most delegation plans are not self-contained. The problem is that some districts grow and some shrink. Those that grow will have people spilling into another's district. Those that shrink may lose a representative, unless they can raid a neighbor's district. I served on the Judiciary Committee in 1980, when it drew the lines. We started with the border counties, the perimeter of the state, just as if we were working a giant jigsaw puzzle, for there were only two directions the population could be moved—sideways and inwards. Problems accelerated as we worked our way to the center of the state. Chairman Bob Sheheen colorfully likened the process to pushing around marshmallows in a bag. The bulges keep changing but have to be contained in that bag.

Finally, the plan was declared finished by the subcommittee—until it was discovered there were 125 districts instead of 124. The chairman of the subcommittee, a big man with a big appetite, made the enormous mistake of leaving the room to get a hamburger. The missing chairman lived in Lexington County and was most at risk because his district was in the very center of the state. He lost his seat while he was out eating hamburgers, when the committee cut up Lexington County to get back to 124 districts. When the plan came out of committee, a filibuster was inevitable. So many political lives were at stake. Each political party fought to maintain a lead. The Black Caucus fought for more seats. There was little effort to kill the filibuster. This was an issue that needed time to discuss up front and compromise behind the scenes. As there was a deadline, there was not the usual goal of killing the bill. Everyone knew we had to pass it in some form.

A bill which took eleven years to pass was the library depository bill, first introduced in 1971 and not passed until 1982. The state librarian, with whom I had worked on the library consortium when I was on Beaufort County Council, asked me to take it on in 1979. This bill required all state agencies, departments, and institutions to furnish fifteen copies of state publications to the state library, which would distribute them to ten public or university libraries strategically located around the state so as to increase public access to these documents. Every state in the nation had some form of depository by that time.

The first year, I managed to get the bill through the House after days of debate, but it stalled in the Senate. The following year I filed it again, and it fared even worse. It never got out of the Ways and Means Committee. The chief opponents were Tom Marchant and some senior Ways and Means Committee members, who said it would cost too much. The state librarian said the only cost would be eight hundred dollars annually, for postage. When a bill is opposed so vigorously there's usually some special interest at stake, and as Tom Marchant was often a spokesman for the state Highway Department I assumed that was his special interest. (My friends said Marchant's special interest was in defeating anything I proposed.) Marchant offered amendments to exempt all or some of the Highway Department papers. His ally on this issue, Norma Russell, said costs to the state would be more than the eight hundred dollars estimate. To prove her point, she asked a staffer to phone every state in the union, including Hawaii and Alaska, to find out how much their systems cost. I daresay the phone bill far exceeded eight hundred dollars by the time this survey was completed, and as she never released any dramatic cost figures, I assume she couldn't prove her point.

In 1982 we tried again, and this time it passed the Senate first. I asked the speaker to refer it to the House Education Committee, which was more friendly to the idea than Ways and Means. Education approved it swiftly. Marchant and his allies, of course, put objections on the bill to place it on the contested calendar. While I was out of the legislature, attending a meeting in California, Marchant and his allies, realizing I was not there to defend it, removed their objections on my bill—which put it up for debate immediately. Ginger Crocker, the Crazy Caucus watchdog, frantically looked for someone to defend the bill and found Jean Toal, who knew little about the issue but managed to talk her way to victory. The bill passed while I was out of town. This solidarity in helping each other's causes (unless there was a deep philosophical difference) was one of the things I loved the most about the Crazy Caucus.

Whenever I went to meetings of the National Conference of State Legislatures, I would ask legislators from many states how their legislatures worked. I learned that most had time limits for a speaker at the podium ranging from five minutes (Illinois) to fifteen (Missouri) to thirty (Georgia). I was amazed to learn how they controlled their time and the flow of legislation. They were amazed that the South Carolina House still tolerated filibusters. Some states spend only two or three months in session, and they go into session every other year. If they could do it, I asked myself, why can't we—instead of our five, six, or seven months every year.

In 1980, I filed a bill to change the rules so as to control filibusters, which Jean Toal, chair of the Rules Committee, and other Crazy Caucus members helped me write. I gathered thirty-two cosponsors. The bill limited a speaker to one hour the first time at the podium and a half-hour the second. The time could be extended, the limit waived, by majority vote. Reapportionment and money bills were excepted. It was a modest proposal, but it was killed 53–47 after a long day of filibustering, despite the support of the speaker and committee chairmen. The opposition was the Black Caucus with its twelve members, the Republican Caucus with its sixteen members, and the Fat and Uglies, with approximately thirty members, which included some of the blacks and Republicans. Although they were disparate groups on many issues, they were cohesive on this, and they fought ferociously to preserve filibusters, their major weapon. Years later, I believe most Republicans and blacks came to understand they were hurt more than helped by filibusters, and they did not support a few attempts made by the Fat and Uglies to turn the clock back.

In 1981, as I sat in my seat day after day waiting out filibusters, I decided to keep a diary to see just how much time we were wasting and how much damage was being done to our agenda. I listed speakers, issues, days, and hours. At the end of the session, this diary showed that of the ninety-five days we were in session, thirty-two (or one-third) had been totally lost to filibusters. At the end of the session, I circulated this information to fellow House members, and in 1981 our support increased from less than a majority to almost two-thirds of the membership. A two-thirds vote is required to change the rules, except at the beginning of a session when the House organizes itself, at which time a majority is sufficient. There was hope. I filed another resolution. But we couldn't quite find the sixty-eight votes to stop the inevitable filibuster. After four days I moved to continue (kill) my own resolution because there were other matters we should have been working on. I couldn't in good conscience waste any more time by being the cause, if only indirectly, of yet another filibuster.

I kept another diary in 1982, and it showed the days of filibusters increasing from one-third to one-half the days in session—33 of the 67 days. During the summer, I visited newspaper editors around the state with copies of my diary in hand. I cited statistics about the number of days in session, bills offered, and bills passed. They were startling. In 1981 we passed only 275 bills of the 1,300 bills introduced, the least number since records of the legislature were kept—this in the third longest legislative year on record. I wrote op-ed pieces and was supported by the leadership when the media called them for comment. The result was a flurry of editorials just before the primary elections. Candidates were pressed to state their positions. The naysayers countered with the old logic that the less legislation passed the better off the state is. My response was, perhaps—but if that is so, then let's pass fewer bills in less time, not more time. Think of the savings to taxpayers if we cut the sessions in half! And think of the selection process whereby

275 bills were passed and 1000 were not, often because three members out of 124 put objections on bills they did not like. That is not democracy.

The serious charge against our side was that we would threaten the rights of minorities by cutting off filibusters, their only protection. My response was that minorities have more to fear from democracy not working, if the democratic process is corrupted. In a speech on the floor I said that I believed that in permitting nonstop filibusters we were thwarting the majority will, which is crucial to democracy. Democratic government just won't work if the majority will is stifled over and over again for sustained lengths of times. When I used the words *majority* and *minority* I was not talking about Democrats and Republicans, blacks or whites, establishment or antiestablishment. I was talking about the small groups that form to oppose particular bills, who keep everyone else from voting, even from debating them. On rare occasions, a few times a year, there were matters of grave concern which were filibustered, and we all accepted their importance—which is why my resolution exempted reapportionment and treated money bills differently. But now we had filibusters as a routine, a new one every day. We also had filibusters to use up time so we wouldn't reach other legislation on the calendar, a kind of second-degree filibuster. Obviously there can be no compromise or resolution when the object of the filibuster is unstated and unreachable. Filibusters cut the legislative process off at the pass, with only one side of debate heard or no debate at all on legislation many legislators had worked for years trying to develop. My impassioned speech was followed by defeat of my resolution in early 1982.

In December 1982, during the orientation meeting for freshmen, several of us rules-change advocates were given the opportunity to educate the new members to the issue, then proselytize. During the three-day organizational session immediately following, when we elect officers and approve the House rules, several members spoke in favor of change, some against, then someone began to filibuster. After several hours we adjourned, disheartened, even though we thought we had the votes. IF we could get to a vote. Early the next morning the Freshman Caucus met and voted to stay all day and all night if that was necesary to change the rules of debate. Some had been impressed with our pitch. Others had run on the issue of curbing filibusters, and this was their chance to do so. They circulated a notice of their intent to all House members, a psychological shot in the arm for "our side."

When we convened at ten, the filibusterer was again at the podium. Someone moved to invoke cloture. Cloture was invoked, following an intricate battle on the rules, and we finally were able to vote on our resolution, which passed 67–49 after a short debate. Many people spoke eloquently in its favor. As reported by the *State,* Sam Foster, a black high school principal, broke ranks with the Black Caucus, saying, "We're losing credibility. The people I'm hearing from are getting tired of our doing nothing." David Wilkins, a Republican, said that in the previous session, when he was a freshman, he wouldn't break with the Republican Caucus because he had to find out for himself if change was needed. Now he knew it was. David Beasley, on the other hand, was quoted as saying it was better to stop legislation than to pass legislation.

It was like the sun coming out from behind the clouds for us. By 7:30 that evening, we adopted the whole new package, including a rules change to reduce the number of votes needed to invoke cloture and to increase the number of objections needed to stop a bill from three to five. We also limited the time spent on the "uncontested" calendar so we could reach the "contested" bills more easily. As we walked out of the chamber, someone said, "You know, for the first time in a long time, I am really looking forward to the new session."

The German philosopher Schopenhauer observed that "Every truth passes through three stages before it gains recognition: In the first stage it is ridiculed, in the second it is opposed, in the third it is regarded as self-evident." So it was with the filibuster fight.

Some of my colleagues have told me that persisting in this fight was my most important contribution to the state. Not that I did it alone, but I had the time and the energy to organize it and the anger to keep pushing. If we had not changed the rules, most of our group would have quit and others would have been discouraged from taking our place. If we had not changed the rules, it is unlikely we could have passed such controversial legislation as the Education Improvement Act, the Nuclear Waste Compact, the living will, the accommodations tax, court reform, or solid waste or energy policy bills. In the next few years, the debates on controversial bills proved that our new rules were fair and did not disempower the minorities as threatened. For instance, during the EIA debate, it was three weeks before there were even attempts to invoke cloture, and the body refused to do that until it was obvious that the intent of "extended" remarks was to keep us from voting forever. Even then, we invoked cloture one section at a time rather than on the entire question. No one was cut off during serious debate while he or she still had something to say. Everyone was heard who wanted to be heard. But we kept moving forward.

For me, the stance of the Freshman Caucus in response to the heavy hitting on filibusters by the press was proof that the public will listen if the message is clear. I often wondered if the defeat that year of John Felder, the filibuster king, was related to this issue. He returned two years later, which may prove that there was no connection, but then, on the other hand, it may prove that the public has a very short political memory.

In 1983, the *Greenville News* named me legislator of the year, citing my work on nuclear waste and filibusters. Their selections, I was told, were made in collaboration with the wire services and the legislative staff. Over the years I have received quite a few legislative awards from groups I had helped in some way—women, libraries, educators, arts and environmental groups—and I was honored and pleased to receive them. But the *Greenville News* citation was in a class by itself, because I was not being rewarded for having done something specific for the rewarder, or for anticipated future assistance. I was being cited by those—staff and press—who understood the issues better than anyone and who had no personal stake in making the selection.

CHAPTER 13

The Five-Percent Reserve Fund Caper

While Public Service Commission reform brought the Crazy Caucus together in 1977, it was the five-percent reserve fund caper in 1978 that was our special team project; it bonded us and was our signature piece.

That year, Governor Edwards, a Republican, and State Treasurer Grady Patterson, a Democrat, led a crusade for a constitutional amendment to require the state to maintain a reserve equal to five percent of the general fund. It could be used only to cover budget deficits and, if used, would have to be replenished within three years. Joining them were Speaker Rex Carter, the chairmen of the House Ways and Means and Senate Finance Committees, and the business community of the state. In other words, the power structure. On the other side, relative newcomers Bob Sheheen, Jean Toal, Nancy Stevenson, and I took a lead in the House to oppose it; Lt. Governor Brantley Harvey, who presided over the Senate, joined us later. The proponents called it the most important piece of legislation that year. We opponents called it the greatest mistake the legislature has made in years. The truth probably lay somewhere in between.

In 1975, the legislature had passed a law mandating that a reserve fund be set aside for the "rainy day" when tax revenues turned out to be less than estimated. I did not have a great problem with the concept of a modest reserve fund set by statutory law, but I had a real problem with putting complicated financial formulas into the constitution, where it could only be changed by a two-thirds vote of the membership of both houses and by public referendum—a long process, difficult to achieve. Such a constitutional amendment, in effect, would be tying the hands of all future legislators, despite the fact that the economic picture is ever-changing and unpredictable. The proponents said we needed to make it difficult to change because, who knows, the legislature may be filled with irresponsible people. I thought they were irresponsible for using such an argument, and arrogant, for they were saying we were wiser and more responsible than those who will be elected after us.

Other arguments they made for the reserve fund were that the difficulty of accurately forecasting government revenues makes a reserve fund necessary, for if the revenue estimates are too high, if the economy slows and tax collections decrease, the state will have the reserve fund to dip into, rather than raise taxes; that the reserve fund will discourage government growth by putting a cap on spending; that inefficiencies in government will be prime targets of the spending cuts; that the fund will protect the state's AAA bond rating.

Opponents of the reserve fund countered with their own arguments. The government levies taxes for the purpose of meeting the needs of the people—for education, health, safety. What is left over is, in effect, a surtax. If we can meet the needs of the people and still have millions and millions in tax revenues left over, why not lower taxes or refund unused dollars, as other states have done? No other state had a constitutional reserve fund such as proposed. We had so many needs in our state. Did it make sense to keep so many millions of dollars sitting in a bank? Such a large fund would be a temptation for the big spenders to raid. The law required the fund be replenished within three years. Although the proponents said this would limit government and keep taxes down, we predicted just the opposite: that in good times the fund would be a huge slush fund for those in control and would therefore increase govenment spending; and in hard times, with several bad economic years in a row, we would have to raise taxes to replenish the fund. Besides, we already had a constitutional mandate for a balanced budget. Wall Street authorities said a state's performance and record decided its bond rating, not a constitutional reserve fund.

We also said that the millions of dollars in the bank would be enough to take the sales tax off food, a proposal continuously turned down by those in charge who said we couldn't afford it. Or we could let the taxpayer put this portion of his hard-earned tax dollars into his own bank. (Our arguments sound like an echo of Bob Dole's 1996 campaign speeches against taxes, yet we were called the liberals!)

Five percent of the 1978 budget would be about sixty million dollars, which is not too large for a rainy day fund. But as the budget continued to increase, as it does each year with inflation and economic growth, five percent would soon amount to eighty million, then a hundred million. In ten years, it could be three hundred million, and up and up. One of several flaws in the proposed legislation was that there was no cap, no limit to the dollar amount to be put into the fund. Another flaw was our erratic record in estimating future revenues.

Walter Heller, chief economist for Lyndon Johnson, talked about placing such limits into the constitution at a conference I attended. He said, "You can never anticipate what shifts in public sentiment may occur. Right now, public sentiment is running strongly against government spending. There's no question about that. But, from 1930s to the 1960s, public opinion ran strongly the other way, and we didn't try to build an accelerator into the Constitution then. The Constitution should not be used to freeze spending at either a high or low level. Setting limits to spending—or saving—in the Constitution is just a total distrust of the democratic process."

The question of changing one's mind was relevant, and evident, even within a span of a few months. Charlie Hodges, a senior member of the House Ways and Means Committee, changed his position after the bill passed and in October said in a news conference, "The reserve is a wolf in sheep's clothing. After reviewing it, I've changed my mind." The *Charleston News and Courier* went the other way. It opposed the reserve fund in early October, then supported it later. The House Black Caucus members voted for the fund on the vital second reading, when a two-thirds vote was needed, but changed its collective mind, too late, after it passed. Their votes made the difference between passing and failing. The South Carolina Chamber of Commerce favored the fund while it was being debated in the legislature and before the referendum, but changed its stance in December, after the referendum had been approved by the voters, urging the legislature not to ratify it in January. All these switching positions surely were a sign that this issue should not be set in concrete in the constitution.

Despite our efforts, the constitutional amendment squeaked through both houses in late July. In the muddled rush, the bill only had one reading in the Senate, instead of the required three, but for some reason this did not seem to be an impediment. The next step in the process would be a public referendum of Proposition 1, as it came to be called in the November elections, and if the public approved it, the legislature would again have to ratify the public vote.

Bob Sheheen called a meeting of five-percent reserve opponents, at which time we decided to launch a political campaign before the November election to educate the public and the press on the issue as we saw it. Bob called a press conference to announce the formation of the South Carolina Taxpayers Coalition. Our board included Bob as president; Jean Toal, vice president; Palmer Freeman, secretary; and me, with no title. We were joined by a dozen other lawmakers, including charter members Henry Floyd, Tommy Hughston, Vic Rawl, Nancy Stevenson, Tom Smith, and Bob Woods, chairman of the Black Caucus. Bob McFadden, the staid chairman of House Judiciary, our lone House leadership member, came up with the slogan "Five won't jive." In our prepared statement to the press—and we got fine coverage—we stated our concern that the reserve fund will "enable state bureaucrats to avoid belt-tightening in government by relying on the reserve fund to bail out agencies which have gone on spending binges." In our name and in our words we preempted the language of those pushing for the bill who called themselves conservative. We felt we were the true conservatives on this issue.

We raised a little money among ourselves to pay for a part-time secretary who helped to arrange press conferences for those of us who were willing to do the circuit and to place ads in newspapers just before election. Three of us spent a day going from city to city to meet with the press and television reporters. We talked to civic clubs, did radio and television interviews, and met with editorial writers. Editorials in the newspapers in the larger cities repeated our arguments and our doubts, expressed doubts themselves, then, at the last minute, reversed what we thought was their position and endorsed the reserve fund. No doubt, heavy lobbying from the Governor's Office and the business community impressed them more than we did when the crunch came. Most of the small town papers, bless them, stayed with us. Bob and Jean offered to debate on ETV the powerful Senator Rembert Dennis, chairman of Senate Finance, and Governor Edwards, but their offer was spurned. We received the endorsement of the South Carolina League of Women Voters and the South Carolina Education Association.

We placed ads in the smaller newspapers. The ad in the hometown paper of Senator Dennis was headlined, in large black letters: "We're sorry, Senator Dennis, but our taxes are high enough." It continued, "We believe that our state government should tax the people only for the revenues needed to fund essential services for the people of South Carolina. A balanced budget and sound management practices are all we need to keep us from those 'rainy days.' No slush fund, Senator. Just good government. Vote NO."

We lost that round also, but the referendum was not a humiliating defeat. The statewide vote in favor of Proposition 1 won by a cliffhanger margin of 18,000 votes out of 452,738 cast (about four percent), as compared to winning percentages ranging from fifty-five to seventy-five percent on four other constitutional amendments on the ballot. In Beaufort we defeated Proposition 1, even though we approved the other four amendments. I am sure that this was because the press, Lt. Governor Harvey, Wilton Graves, and I opposed it. Wilton had to struggle with this one, because his Ways and Means friends pushed him to support the referendum but his constituents pushed him to oppose it. Jimmy Waddell was the lone member of delegation who supported it.

Proposition 1 was defeated in nine other counties, including Kershaw County, home base of Bob Sheheen, and Richland County, home of Jean Toal. The largest counties, Charleston, Greenville and Spartanburg, approved it. In a column in the *State*, William Workman

Jr. concluded, "There seems no prevailing political pattern which would link those 10 counties (where it was defeated): some are rural, some are urban; some are big, some are little; some have voted Republican in the past and present elections, others have remained staunchly Democratic. Perhaps the determining factor was the quantity and quality of arguments presented by spokesmen against the proposition in those particular counties." There is a lesson in this for future referenda sponsors.

The last round of the battle started in January 1979, with the vote on ratification by the legislature of Proposition 1, as approved by the public. There was new ferment bubbling up over the issue. The South Carolina Chamber of Commerce changed its position and now opposed it. County governments, to whom legislators were usually responsive, worried that somehow they would bear the brunt of tight funding in times of economic downturn. The *State*, although endorsing Proposition 1 before November, now pointed out flaws before the ratification debate. Bob, Jean, and I filed a bill questioning where the reserve fund would be invested and the rate of return of those investments. Toal called it a "banker's relief bill," with most of the funds scattered in banks across the state and the remainder in treasury bonds. Sheheen said that while this money was sitting in banks collecting low interest, the state had borrowed, just in the past year, $156 million in revenue bonds for capital improvements, with the taxpayers paying debt service. Newly elected Governor Riley, in his state of the state address, proposed cutting the reserve fund from five to three percent and putting a ceiling of sixty million dollars on the fund, with additional safeguards on how it could be used. The only problem was that once the voters approved Proposition 1, it could not be changed in the ratification process.

With all this new opposition and newly raised questions, the balance began to shift. When the time finally came to vote on it in the House, on Thursday, February 15, we tried to postpone the vote and lost, sixty to forty. An hour later, with a great turnaround, we voted 53–52 to table the ratification resolution. A majority of the freshmen voted with us, responding more to the young leaders, Sheheen and Toal, than to the old guard.

The supporters of the reserve fund said they would attempt to overturn the decision by reconsidering the vote on Tuesday. But there first had to be a motion to reconsider, which must be made on the same or the next legislative day. If the motion to reconsider failed, the matter was "clinched"; the bill could not be brought up again and would die. Worried that they might not get the votes to pass a motion to reconsider on that Thursday, with the votes swinging back and forth so unpredictably, the speaker asked Rep. Jim Kinard of Columbia, who had voted on the prevailing side, to go the legislature to make that motion on Friday, when the legislature is technically in session for the handling of only routine and local matters. Usually no legislators are in attendance; nobody would be there to vote against it.

Instead of leaving town and going home, as we usually do on Thursdays, eleven of us stayed in Columbia and had a planning session over dinner that evening. Bob and Jean concocted a parliamentary ploy to keep Jim from making his reconsideration motion. We arrived at the State House on Friday morning, stealing up the stairs in groups of two and threes so as not to draw the attention of any press or lobbyists who might be wandering around, then assembled at the stroke of 10:00 A.M. on the House floor and convened the legislature. The clerks at the desk stared at us, bewildered, not knowing whether to laugh or cry. As the *State* reported the next day: "The nine House members scrupulously following rules as they interpreted them, proceeded to elect temporary officers in the absence of Speaker Carter and Speaker pro tem Ramon Schwartz, who normally would preside.

"Rep. Robert J. Sheheen, D-Kershaw, was elected temporary speaker by acclamation and Rep. Harriet Keyserling, D-Beaufort, was named chaplain so that the session could be opened with prayer in accordance with the daily order of business set by rules.

"In rapid succession, those present reported later, Rep. Keyserling prayed, Sheheen ordered the House Journal corrections and then recognized Rep. Bill Campbell, D-Richland, who made his successful motion to adjourn. This all took place in four minutes, with the clerks at the desk watching, wide-eyed and uncertain about what to do. 'I stood up to make my motion,' Kinard recalled, 'but I didn't get a chance. Rep. Sheheen recognized Bill Campbell in front of me before I could get his attention.' Kinard submitted his motion in writing to House Clerk Lois Shealy to protect his rights in case the House should later nullify what happened Friday. 'I have no doubts about the validity of what they did,' the legislator said. 'They did it to me today.'

"'We followed the rules exactly,' said Rep. Jean Toal who temporarily presided and called for the election of temporary officers. Mrs. Toal said in the absence of House rules on the issue, the group relied on Mason's Manual, a parliamentary guide, to call for the temporary officers. 'We were just buying time,' Sheheen said. Mrs. Toal rejected suggestions that the action might be considered underhanded. 'I don't think there was anything unfair. Everyone knows the rules. If they had 10 people here, we couldn't have done it.'"

Speaker Carter said, when notified of our action, that he didn't question motives of the Sheheen-Toal group. "I know they're sincere in their efforts to defeat the amendment. My disappointment stems from the fact that I would rather a majority of the House defeat or pass it rather than eight or nine on a local session day without notice. You live and die by the rules. Sometimes they work to your advantage and sometimes to your disadvantage. I don't condemn anyone for taking advantage of them." He said he would research the rules over the weekend and make a ruling on Tuesday on our actions.

We were denounced by the *State*. We were denounced by the *Charleston News and Courier*, which said we had denied the majority of the House an opportunity to vote on reconsideration (not recognizing our point that the speaker had denied us the right to vote by having someone make the motion on a Friday when no legislators were there.) We were denounced by Sol Blatt, who said this was the blackest day in the hallowed halls of the S.C. House of Representatives.

On Tuesday, the speaker ruled that our nine-member session, operating under Mason's rules, was not a valid session because House rules, not Mason's rules, were in effect. A motion to reconsider was made and passed, and Proposition 1 was ratified by a vote of 61–54. Several years later, the five-percent requirement was reduced to three percent. I am told that in 1992 the Budget and Control Board did find a way to use the fund to deal with some crippling budget cuts.

As with all memories, certain parts of an exciting experience fade and others never leave you. What stayed with me were two things: the speaker's tolerance not only of my opposition to him on the bill he wanted so badly but of my part in the Friday session caper, which must have been hugely embarrassing to him. But then again, he won, so it was easier to forgive. I also remember my embarrassing performance as temporary chaplain. I was given this opportunity to give a nondenominational prayer because I sometimes complained that our chaplain's daily prayers were uncomfortable for me to sit through, as we prayed to a God who was not my God. But as I was hastily reading a prayer which was printed in a past legislative journal, and concentrating on trying to control my laughter instead of thinking about what I was saying, I ended with "In Jesus name we pray," and there it was, printed in Friday's journal, as read by Harriet Keyserling, Chaplain. Several years later I told our kindly chaplain, Alton Clark, about this incident, and he said he hadn't thought about the possible discomfort of the Jewish members; from that time forth he gave nondenominational prayers.

CHAPTER 14

The Education Improvement Act

When Governor Riley took office in 1979 he pledged to improve education in South Carolina. He began by forcing the state to focus on how education impacts on problems the state faced—jobs, economic growth, health, and law enforcement. The hard and unpleasant facts were that South Carolina was at that time first in the nation in prison population, first in the nation in infant mortality, near the top in the failure rate of those taking tests for the military services, in school dropouts, and in illiteracy rates, and at the bottom in expenditures per pupil on public elementary and secondary school education. Obviously, these facts were not unrelated then, nor are they now. It also was obvious that it is less expensive to provide our children with improved education than to treat the social ills of crime, unemployment, and poor health conditions, all of which are the result of the lack of a good education. Riley and his education aide, Terry Peterson, started looking for solutions to our overwhelming problems, exacerbated, I believe by our long history of educational deprivation of our black population, as well as many white children in the poor rural areas.

Governor Riley's education emphases during his first term were on raising standards for teachers, on vigorously promoting—along with his wife, Tunky—greater parental involvement in the schools, on expanded early childhood opportunities, and on fully funding the phase-in of the Education Equalization Finance Act, which was enacted the year before he came into office but not funded until he was governor.

In the 1983 session, Governor Riley proposed fifty million dollars of expenditures on a potpourri of educational programs, including stricter standards for students and teachers, and a politically volatile combination of funding sources, including an increase in the sales tax and tinkering with property taxes. Many of the proposals had been initiated by Charlie Williams, state superintendent of education. It soon became evident that each element drew opposition from one group or another, with the business community leading the way. The plan was put together too hurriedly for action, requiring substantial new funding. Efforts to build public support for this effort first were too little, too late. Crosby Lewis and John Talley, strong advocates for public education, felt it was not comprehensive enough, and, if passed, would delay real reform. They voted no, and the bill was killed by one vote in the House.

About this time, national and regional reports began to circulate, filled with the words CRISIS and RISK. U.S. Secretary of Education Terrel Bell circulated his report *A Nation at Risk: The Imperative for Educational Reform,* setting off alarms that the inadequate education of our children was creating the RISK of an inadequate future workforce. Other reports followed, citing a CRISIS in American education as we entered the international, technological world. National pollsters Lou Harris and Gallup indicated the public wanted improvement, even at a higher cost, and would support higher taxes for education, but only if they could be guaranteed accountability. There was national recognition of the erosion of American economic strength and the relationship of student performance to the job market and economic growth of cities, states, and the nation. This created an environment in which everyone was saying "we have to do something!"

If the nation was at risk educationally and economically, there was no question but that South Carolina was most at risk. In 1979, a third of our beginning first graders were not ready to begin learning and were at risk of failure in school. In the ten years before the Riley effort, every Southern state had made a greater, real-dollar per pupil investment in public elementary and secondary education than had South Carolina. We had slipped from forty-fourth in the nation in per pupil spending to fiftieth. Mississippi, the state we used to thank God for, invested over one hundred million dollars in new money in its schools when we would not.

Governor Riley used these reports as the basis for a new, more aggressive, better-organized campaign to build public support for a comprehensive package of educational changes—and the funding for them. He tried to convince leaders of the business community that education is good business, the key to economic growth, and he made a compelling case that spending for education was the best investment state government could make. Major business leaders around the country were also making these arguments, and other states, including our neighbors and competitors for industry, were moving ahead. If we didn't join the crusade, we would be left behind. Riley promised, "We can raise our public schools from the bottom of the list, but it will take the involvement and the investment of the whole State to do it."

And some of our industry leaders listened. They came to grips with the fact that economic development, jobs, and their profits were at stake. They began to understand that if South Carolina was to move forward, the changes in the economy demanded different kinds of jobs, jobs requiring brainpower rather than muscle. The governor convened a dozen of the most influential business leaders in the state in the late spring of 1983. They agreed to help him if they could participate in planning a comprehensive education plan, including substantial funding, tailored for South Carolina.

The governor appointed two blue-ribbon committees to develop such a comprehensive plan of action. The first one included top-level corporate and bank executives and legislative leaders, who were to give broad direction to the effort. Governor Riley personally chaired this committee, with Dr. Charlie Williams as vice chairman. Bill Page, a business executive from Greenville, agreed to chair the second committee, which was composed of educators, legislators, parents, and school board members. These were the nuts-and-bolts people who would turn strategy into action. The committees developed a five-year educational plan with seven major goals.

At the same time the committees were starting their work, two important conferences were being held and were tied to the reports that were gaining recognition throughout the nation. As governor, Riley was able to take ten to fifteen legislative and educational leaders to these meetings—the Education Commission of the States in Denver and the Southern Regional Education Board in Asheville. For several days these leaders were engaged in nothing but education reform discussions. Our state leaders saw firsthand that other states were moving forward. South Carolina could either lead or be left behind.

While these committees were working on a plan over the summer of 1983, other "political" activities were going on. A foundation was created to explain and sell the plan. Eighty thousand dollars of private funds was raised for a campaign to win public opinion. A public opinion poll was commissioned, which showed that sixty to sixty-five percent favored a one-cent sales tax if that's what it would take to improve education—and if they could be assured of results and accountability. (That percentage was to be similar to the final votes in the legislature on the bill.) To build continued support there were statewide television ads, newspaper ads, mailings to individuals, and telephone banks put into motion, so that when the action plan was finalized the communication strategies would be ready for launching in the late fall and early winter, in time for the opening of a new legislative session.

Meanwhile, Governor Riley's staff set up a series of public forums across the state to gain local input and advice as to what actions should be included in the reform plan. This outreach strategy was designed by Riley's top political and education team—Dwight Drake, Bill Prince, and Terry Peterson. The School Board Association and the School Administrators Association joined the teachers' and parents' associations, along with local chambers of commerce, in creating audiences and interest, an unusual display of statewide unity and enthusiasm. Over thirteen thousand people attended forums in seven cities. They gave suggestions, through small group discussions, which were passed on to the blue-ribbon committees. An important consequence of these forums was that thirteen thousand people interested in education were identified, and their names put into a card file which the governor used during the debate in the legislature. This file became a powerful component of the grassroots effort and a key political factor in passing the legislation which evolved from this process.

In the region of the state where the forums were being held in the evening, prominent state leaders visited every county in that region during the day, giving speeches at civic clubs, talking to TV and radio journalists, visiting schools, and speaking at PTA meetings. In some regions, fifteen state leaders were simultaneously engaged in a dialogue about education. Another forty thousand people were reached through this arm of the grassroots campaign.

Out of the almost weekly deliberations of the blue-ribbon committees, advice from the forums, and input from all the other grassroots activities, the education program was launched. The program was named the South Carolina Education Improvement Act (also known as the EIA). It called for increasing academic standards through strong remedial programs; new standards for teacher training, evaluation, and salaries (increasing their pay to the southeastern average); improving leadership and management skills of administrators; incentive programs that encouraged teachers, districts, and schools to improve quality and productivity; new standards of accountability through student testing and comparisons of results in schools and districts; building effective partnerships between schools and parents, the community and business leaders; special programs for four-year-olds at risk, the gifted and talented (including the artistically gifted); advanced-placement programs; and funding for new school buildings.

These goals were not just a wish list. The sixty sections of the bill spelled out what actions must be taken to achieve them, including a penny sales tax increase. The blue-ribbon committees likened the package to a jigsaw puzzle: all parts neatly fit together, and if any pieces were removed, the package would fall apart. This was the argument legislative supporters voiced when efforts were made to cut major programs out of the $210 million package.

To continue to build public support for the package, Governor Riley secured a half-hour of prime time on televison stations throughout the state to explain the need for the Education Improvement Act, including the penny sales tax increase to pay for it. The next day, an ad campaign was started with the theme "A penny for their thoughts." The ads featured a pregnant mother, a blue-collar worker, and a business executive all getting involved in education and organizing others.

When Governor Riley circulated the bill, looking for sponsors, only twenty-one House members agreed to put their names to it. We who did were called the Smurfs, for the group was an unlikely medley of people: two Republicans, John Bradley from Charleston, who was usually the acerbic opposition to anything labeled progressive, and David Wilkins from Greenville, a city where public education had wide support; most of the Black Caucus; and some white Democrats. As Governor Riley noted, "Not one of the twenty-one early supporters were in a leadership position. We had to organize a new leadership." Not a single officer of the House, not the speaker, the speaker pro tem, or one committee chairman, supported the bill. New leadership was especially needed in the Ways and Means Committee, where the early battles were fought, and that turned out to be Crosby Lewis, Sam Foster, Beattie Huff, Bob McLellan, and me—all of us junior members of the committee. (The story was different in the Senate, where leaders Rembert Dennis and Jimmy Waddell, chairman and vice chairman of the Senate Finance Committee, supported the bill, as did Senator Harry Chapman, chairman of the Senate Education Committee. They stepped up early and actually served on the blue-ribbon committees.) It also helped that by the time the bill reached the Senate, it was being swept forward by a great victory in the House and a huge wave of public support.

Few legislators openly admitted to opposing Riley's program. The major conflict, they said, was in funding it. Most said we didn't have a chance if we tried to raise the sales tax in an election year, and they would be no part of it. The House Education Committee voted in favor of a bill, but it included no funding! And so it was sent to the Ways and Means Committee, whose leaders also opposed funding the total program.

Proposing an increase in the sales tax for education was not a novel idea, but dedicating it to a specific school reform program was. The general retail sales tax has traditionally been used to finance and improve elementary and secondary education in South Carolina since the 1950s. Prior to that time, most improvements were accomplished locally by politically organized educators. State legislation concerning education, and in particular funding for education, was not a high priority. "Let local governments take care of it" was the prevailing attitude. In 1948, a national Peabody Commission study of South Carolina education recommended that the state finance a program to consolidate the seventeen hundred school districts, equalize tax imbalances among them, and create a program for renovation and construction of school buildings. This was dismissed by the legislature as too expensive, but a committee, chaired by Representative Fritz Hollings, was created to study the issue of education funding.

In 1951, the Hollings committee called for a three-percent sales tax to aid public education. State leaders were determined to meet the "separate but equal" standard, and Governor James Byrnes was a force in passing the sales tax. He said, "We must provide schools substantially equal for both white and Negro pupils." In fact, this was the only alternative to integration. Debate centered mainly on exemptions requested by merchants' associations and labor groups who claimed the sales tax was unjust. The new law stipulated that revenues be used for school purposes only. It consolidated the 1,700 school districts into 109, built new schools, and provided school bus transportation for rural black students to attend the consolidated schools. In 1961 there was still considerable public support across the South for maintaining dual black and white school systems. Southern states labored to support two school systems, thus diluting the state's overall educational resources. Some observers noted that by the time substantial school integration was achieved in the early 1970s, South Carolina had already fallen behind in funding and educational progress. The state is still suffering from the consequences of this "education deficit," the primary reason we compare so poorly to other states. I agree with the many who believe it will take several generations to overcome these setbacks.

In 1969 Governor Robert McNair, upon consideration of a 1968 Moody Investors Report, proposed a one-cent increase in the sales tax to fund an $800 teacher salary hike (the average pay for white teachers in South Carolina at that time was $6,880, and less for black teachers) and a $20 million kindergarten program. His bill was filibustered, with debate centering on exemptions from the tax and exemptions from the kindergarten program, but it passed, some say illegally, hours after the session was officially ended. But that was never challenged in the courts.

With this history of persistent opposition to tax increases, it was not surprising that Governor Riley's increase in the sales tax was also hotly resisted. What were the alternatives, if the House wanted to do something for education but would not raise the sales tax? Many were offered; the two most seriously discussed came from the Ways and Mean Committee leadership, on the one hand, and a group led by Bob Sheheen and Jean Toal on the other. (Ginger Crocker and I broke ranks with them on this one.)

Although I personally think the sales tax is regressive, and I tried often and unsuccessfully to make it less regressive by exempting food and drugs, I favored it in this instance. I was convinced we had to make major reforms in our education policies. I believed most of my constituents wanted improvement and were horrified that South Carolina ranked at the bottom of the country in test scores, in dollars spent on education per pupil, and in teacher pay. And that they understood the connection between those rankings and the national rankings where we were at the top: infant mortality, illiteracy, prison inmates per capita. I was convinced that the sales tax was the only source of revenue large enough and dependable enough to take us through the proposed five-year program that could change these statistics. And I was relieved that many industry and business leaders at last understood the fact that the best way the state could attract more industry and increase productivity was to produce more workers who can read, write, and think. For in South Carolina, without the support of the business community, we could never win a tax increase. In addition, an economist at Lander College found that if the sales tax is dedicated to students from kindergarten through twelfth grade, with particular support for early childhood programs and those children at risk, the sales tax is not regressive, because young families, often among the poorest, would benefit the most. Of course, Riley's team highlighted these findings.

In considering the bill, the education subcommittee of Ways and Means adopted only a few of the original elements of the plan and scaled down, delayed, or phased in elements to fit a $67 million budget instead of the requested $210 million. Once the subcommittee's report came to the full committee, the committee leaders proposed to use a one-time surplus of $33 million (which would not be available the next year), a $25 million increase in revenue projections (which was, of course, uncertain), and $27 million from an insurance reserve fund for state employees. Not one of these was a dependable, continuous source of funding. Such uncertain funding could well make this a one-year, rather than five-year, plan. They scaled down or cut out programs for remediation and improving teacher skills. But how could we legitimately mandate higher standards for students, or withhold promotions for those not meeting those standards, while taking away the resources for remediation needed to achieve these goals? The public was screaming for "accountability," yet the committee proposals removed the tools to achieve accountability. The jigsaw puzzle would come apart.

When this watered-down version of the EIA came up for consideration by the full Ways and Means Committee, we started the effort to bring the bill back to its original form. Of course, Chairman Tom Mangum and his three vice chairmen united to oppose us. Mangum was adamant in his opposition to the penny increase. He really wanted to bury the bill in his desk drawer and never put it on the committee agenda, but Bob McLellan warned Magnum that if he did this, he would go public with the fact that the chairman was refusing to let the committee even consider a bill which had so much public support. Mangum gave in, but at the same time vowed that though we took it up, it would never get out committee.

Of the twenty-four committee members, there were only four strong advocates for the bill—a lawyer, a black high school principal, a businessman, and a housewife. Once up for discussion, we four Riley soldiers came up with a scheme and somehow managed to execute it. We forced the committee to vote on the elements of the bill, not as a whole, but item by item. And as we voted for each item, a staffer listed the items and their cost on a flip chart. The program list grew longer and longer, and the price list larger and larger.

And while we voted, the audience, many from the home counties of Ways and Means Committee members, sat and watched the chart and watched the hands go up—or not go up. They waited to talk with their representatives when we recessed or adjourned. Or had their friends call them that night. The thirteen thousand people who six months earlier had taken part in the local forums were organized by counties and House and Senate districts. Through phone banks operating in the evenings and the coordinated contact teams of all the education groups, PTAs, and urban chambers of commerce, key votes were quickly publicized, and supporters rallied to call or attend the sessions in person. The grassroots effort was at work. To counter this, the speaker, in a most unusual move, came into the committee room and sat beside Chairman Mangum, as a show of strength during our most volatile sessions, when parliamentary questions were being raised. Also hovering around, but less conspicuously, was Bob Sheheen, author of the third plan, who was opposed to both the chairman's plan and ours.

To allow the public to tune into this debate—we knew from the polling data that popular support was clearly on our side—we organized the hearings and votes on the legislation to have a full discussion of the needs and merits of each section of the bill. The debate and hearings lasted for weeks. Terry Peterson, the governor's aide, was designated by our team as the only person who would testify—and he did, day after day, the longest testimony in recent history, or perhaps ever. The press carried detailed reports.

These were the major items we debated, one by one, to build support for the key components of the package:

1. Should we increase standards for high schools by increasing requirements for diplomas from eighteen to twenty units, with one additional unit of science and math?

2. Should we require the State Board of Education to establish a minimum standard of student conduct and behavior and a system of enforcement?

3. Should we mandate all school districts make kindergarten available for all five-year-olds?

4. Should we authorize public development programs for four-year-old children with predicted readiness deficiencies?

5. Should we require school districts to offer advanced placement courses and college credit for their completion?

6. Should we expand gifted and talented programs?

7. Should we provide more relevant vocational training programs? And follow up on students' job placement and employment needs in the future?

8. Should we require passage of an exit exam for high school diplomas and mandate remedial programs for those failing the exams?

9. Should we require establishment of remedial and compensatory education programs and evaluate them annually?

10. Should we require the state to support all EIA programs?

11. Should we expand alcohol and drug abuse intervention programs?

12. Should we decrease teacher-student ratios?

13. Should we create programs to attract the brightest high school students to teaching and lend them funds to attend college for that purpose?

14. Should we offer conditional teaching certificates to meet critical shortages in specific disciplines or geographic locations?

15. Should we raise teacher salaries to meet the southeastern average?

16. Should we reward teachers who demonstrate superior performance and productivity?

17. Should we improve teacher training by creating centers of excellence and require formal evaluation of teachers no less frequently than every three years? Should we do the same for school administrators?

18. Should we mandate school advisory councils and an annual school report for every school?

19. Should we create a committee to monitor annually the implementation of the EIA?

And most controversial: 20. Should we increase the sales tax by a penny?

Need I say how difficult it was for those members to vote "no" on these items before we reached the crucial sales tax proposed to fund them all? Every item had been called for by the blue-ribbon committees, the press, and the public. How could we improve education without doing these things? So they voted for most of the elements of the program but still flatly opposed the sales tax increase. Although we did not win a vote on the one-cent increase, or the "penny" as Riley called it, our votes got closer and closer in the two weeks we worked on it in committee. Finally, Mangum won through what Howard Schneider of the *State* called "a suspect maneuver." To reduce costs, one of his vice chairmen, Marion Carnell, proposed an amendment to delay teacher pay increases for six months. But the committee had already voted twice to provide the teacher pay increase (thus clinching it and making it irreversible). Carnell's amendment could not be taken up again as a part of the EIA bill. So they had to look for another vehicle for the amendment. That year's appropriations bill was already on the floor of the House, but somehow the committee adjourned debate on the education bill and took up the appropriations bill instead, which had not been recalled to the committee. They then maneuvered to take portions of the EIA, Carnell's amendment, and some other tax adjustments, and roll them into one amendment to the appropriations bill.

But the appropriations bill was technically not in committee: it was pending before the House at the time. We protested, saying this action was out of order: certainly everyone knew that a bill couldn't be in two places at the same time. But the chairman ruled otherwise, with the speaker sitting beside him, nodding. And none of us were savvy enough about the rules to force him to back down. We had several parliamentarians on our side, but unfortunately they were not members of Ways and Means. To compound the irregularity, the Ways and Means leaders then went a step further, and by a simple majority designated the changes as a committee amendment, which carries increased clout. Despite the fact that a two-thirds vote is required by the rules for such a designation. So the essence of the EIA, with the committee changes, suddenly was out of committee and ready to be debated as part of the budget. As reported by Schneider in the *State* on February 19, 1994, "Thursday's meeting resulted in such confusion that at least one lobbyist remarked that he couldn't tell which way the vote needed to go for things to work as he wished." And at times, committee members were just as confused.

We decided to offer the original bill as an alternative amendment to the appropriations bill, and it became known as the Jack Rogers amendment. Jack Rogers was asked by the governor to sponsor the amendment, possibly because he was not a member of Ways and Means and could bring another group into the action. I suggested we try the same ploy on the floor of the House as we used in the Ways and Means Committee, that we divide the question, forcing everyone to vote on each and every section of the program. The speaker indicated that this was permissible under the rules of the House.

By this time, the 124 members of the House were split three ways on the question of funding—Ways and Means leadership, the Sheheen-Toal group, and the Smurfs each had about forty supporters. No group seemed to be able to muster a majority to pass its particular plan. We needed somehow to develop a coalition, to assemble enough votes to break the deadlock.

The State Department of Education and the Governor's Office prepared elaborate notebooks, similar to trial notebooks used by lawyers in the courtroom, at the suggestion of our leader, Crosby Lewis, and ran training sessions for teams of two to three legislators on each section. Our Smurfs knew more about education by the end than almost anyone in the state—or nation. The notebooks, which contained the bill, pro and con arguments, and details of costs and benefits, section by section, were assembled for the floor leaders—McKinley Washington, Tim Rogers, Bob McLellan, Lewis Phillips, Ginger Crocker, John Bradley, David Wilkins, Jack Rogers, John Matthews, and John Talley are those I remember best. I was put in charge of assigning sections of the bill to these floor leaders, who would then be responsible for explaining and answering questions about them at the podium and in the aisles. We also had row captains to maintain discipline and attendance.

Crosby Lewis felt we also needed two key staff people who knew the programs and finances on the floor with us. In a rare move, our team quickly made a motion, after a lunch break when attendance is low, to allow two nonlegislative staffers and non-legislator Bill Page to be on the floor to provide technical help for "both" sides. We won that motion by a couple of votes, and Henry Hollingsworth of the Department of Education and Terry Peterson were granted permission by the House, for the first time in history, to sit in the House chambers, at a small card table overflowing with books and reports, and answer technical questions raised by either side.

One advantage we had was that Ways and Means Committee chairman Tom Mangum was not a strong leader on the floor, and at that time few of his lieutenants were, either, as compared to our side, which had several soldiers skilled in strategy and parliamentary tactics. Mangum could not control the floor debate, which countered the accepted wisdom that you had to have a comittee chairman in your corner to win. The important factor was who had control, not who had the title. The exception was during the appropriations bill debate, but then the whole committee usually stands together and dissension can be very expensive for the disloyal.

The debate ran on for five weeks, starting on February 21 and ending on March 27. The coalition which supported us outside the legislature kept growing. The chambers of commerce of our largest cities joined us. The businessmen who had served on the blue-ribbon committees corralled support from their peers. Bill Page of Greenville led the way, along with Bill Youngblood of Charleston and John Lumpkin of Columbia. According to Terry Peterson, "The absolute key to our success was involving powerful business leaders from the very beginning and giving them a substantive role in helping develop the plan." He pointed out that Riley was able to divide the state business and industrial community on the tax issue, much as he divided the legislature—by selling the package and then convincing those who bought into it of the absolute need for the tax to pay for it. The media provided major support. All the education groups threw in their support, even though the bill meant changes that might pose problems for them in the future. At one point the Black Caucus left us, possibly with the acquiescence of the state teachers' association, when we debated raising teacher standards and incentive pay. But they all came back when faced with the alternative of no bill. The League of Women Voters and other civic groups, all the black churches, and some of the white churches actively lobbied for us. And there were the thousands of people who had attended the public forums, writing letters and making phone calls. Continued polling showed seventy to eighty percent of the public was with us. It was compelling and powerful politics, and the opposition felt it.

The balcony overlooking the House chambers filled up every day with grassroots supporters. The opposition made snide references to "all those teachers in the gallery, why weren't they at home teaching?"; but in fact there were as many parents, civic leaders, and businessmen up there—and always on the front row was the governor's wife, Tunky, our greatest cheerleader despite undergoing chemotherapy at the time.

Often we worked late into the night, both on the floor and off. We regrouped often, during the day in the Governor's Office and in the evenings at the Governor's Mansion. Bob McLellan recently reminded me of the governor's "good luck" boots. When we went to his office, he sat with his feet propped up on the desk, always with the boots on. Governor Mark White of Texas gave Riley those boots to help him during this long debate. He wore no other shoes until the EIA passed.

Sometimes I spent Thursday nights at the mansion when I had given up my hotel room, thinking I was going home but stymied when we adjourned too late to make that two-and-a-half-hour drive back to Beaufort. At such times, Tunky Riley graciously invited me to stay over in one of the elegant guest rooms in the mansion. In the morning, after reading newspaper reports of our actions the previous day much as actors do after an opening night, we continued strategy talks over great breakfasts, served by prison trustees in white jackets in the cheerful, informal dining room overlooking a little garden.

At other times Crosby Lewis invited me to drive to Winnsboro and spend the night at his wonderful historic home in the country, a forty-five-minute drive on quiet roads lined with pine forests (until a hurricane changed the landscape). We had time to talk over the day's events or just enjoy the peace and quiet of the countryside. I learned about electric co-ops, hunting wild turkeys, and South Carolina politics. His charming wife, Cleo, was always waiting patiently, no matter the hour. His home was a joy to visit, having the feel of an English manor, with terraced gardens, a brook, lots of birds and trees, and a luxurious guest house, which I had to myself. He was a treasured friend, greatly missed when he left the legislature.

The S.C. Textile Manufacturers' Association became our most vigorous opponent, but too late in the game. At that time, the textile industry was the most politically powerful sector of industry and generally controlled the state chamber of commerce, which also opposed the EIA. (They said they did not oppose the bill, just the funding.) The Textile Association lobbyists had been told in the early stages of debate not to worry, the bill didn't have a chance. They sniped at us a little behind the scenes but were unprepared when they suddenly realized the House was on the verge of passing the EIA, tax and all. Called together by

Roger Milliken, a textile magnate in Spartanburg, the association drew up a resolution declaring that the industry unanimously opposed the penny tax. But Ann Close, representing the Springs Mills family, the state's largest publicly held textile company, and Walter Elisha, president of Springs Industries, wrote a letter stating that they favored the EIA, funding and all, and that the textile industry was therefore not unanimous in its opposition. Their letter was placed on every legislator's desk alongside the Textile Association's resolution. Also on our desks was an ever-growing pile of pink slips—slips with telephone numbers of constituents who had called and wanted us to call back, slips with names of people waiting out in the lobby to talk to us about the bill.

More evidence of business support was offered by Mike Daniel, the lieutenant governor, and his staff, who helped a group of progressive business leaders produce a videotape stating that if the EIA did not pass they would not expand their businesses in South Carolina.

During the second week of debate, Jean Toal used her considerable parliamentary skills to have Sheheen's amendment taken up before the Rogers amendment. The Sheheen plan would cost about a hundred million; he reduced costs by phasing in remediation programs and teacher pay increases over several years. His proposed money source was forty million dollars cut out of state agency budgets and redirected to education, along with increased taxes on wine, beer, and nuclear and hazardous waste to raise an additional forty million. He also would use twenty million dollars in growth revenues. His problems in drawing enough support for his package were multiple: state agencies all have their in-house allies in the legislature who would fight to the death cuts to those agencies. And legislators had been trying to raise the tax on wine and beer for years without success, because the lobbyists for those industries were just too strong. The governor's political and policy staff quickly convened all the agencies to document why this proposal would hurt them and be inadequate to help education. But above and beyond all that, Bob and the other opponents lost because we successfully sold the whole package with our one-at-a-time votes and in effect backed the legislators into the penny tax, because it was the only way the provisions they voted for could be funded. Bob couldn't round up the votes he needed and still resisted the penny increase on principle. But I always felt that in his heart he was closer to us than to the Ways and Means crowd, that he really wanted education reform to pass, while they didn't.

The debate was long and serious; there were so many amendments, motions, and points of order, and so many close votes. Crosby Lewis recently said, "Practically every day from the beginning of the Ways and Means Committee debate to nearly the end of the House debate I did not know if the bill would pass. There were days that I came to the House convinced in my own mind that we could not survive the day. What I could not measure was the mounting public pressure for the passage of the program."

We finally passed all sections of the original bill except for the building fund. But we still hadn't agreed how to fund them. We remained divided into three factions, but our team was gaining votes. The third week into the debate, on March 11, there was finally a direct vote on the one-cent increase, and it resulted in a tie, with fifty-five votes for and against. On a second try we lost, fifty-eight to fifty-five. We were concerned that this margin could increase, depending on who was absent and who was present when votes were called for. Our group discussed a compromise which might change enough votes so we could win with a safe margin. It would mean a little less revenue, but enough to fully fund the programs, with only the building fund decreased. In truth, the building fund was the one part of the bill that could be decreased without harming the rest of the programs. The price tag for the EIA was estimated at $210 million because that was the projection of what the one-cent increase would generate. The building fund was flexible, to be set after the big ticket items of remediation, teacher pay increases, and special programs were funded.

Over the years I had often talked with Bob Sheheen and Jean Toal about my goal to someday remove the sales tax from food. They always tried to help me with the bills I introduced to do this, but we were stymied when we tried to find a politically viable way to replace the dollars that tax brought to the state's general fund. So, as we looked for ways to find a compromise to break the deadlock on funding the EIA, I floated the idea to them that if we increased the sales tax by a penny for education, we could use part of the new revenue to phase out the sales tax on food over three years, thereby removing the most regressive aspect of the sales tax. They agreed to the concept, and we drafted a compromise amendment to that effect. They brought over to our side enough votes to finally pass this compromise amendment and break the logjam. The House finally fully funded the EIA, after a filibuster attempt by Tom Marchant, by a vote of sixty-seven to forty-nine. I ended up with a severe case of laryngitis and a photo of me in the *State* newspaper with my head in my hands, portraying relaxed exhaustion. I have on my wall the original photo, surrounded by signatures of the major players on our team, including the Rileys.

But I personally didn't feel totally successful. The day after we passed the compromise amendment, several legislators who owned Piggly-Wiggly grocery stores, the Piggly-Wiggly Caucus we called them, managed to garner enough support for an amendment they whipped up overnight to put back the sales tax on food and in its place offer a tax credit equivalent to what an average family of four would spend on the food sales tax. They said it was too difficult to change the computer-driven cash registers. As our list of exemptions was identical to the food stamp list, and as the computers are already set to exempt food stamp items from a sales tax, this was not a legitimate argument to me. It also seemed shortsighted on the part of the Piggly-Wiggly Caucus, for if people didn't pay a tax on food, they could spend more on groceries.

I was furious at those on my side who seemed to have caved in so readily in accepting this change. I never even knew negotiations were going on until the amendment popped up on the screen. I knew that it would be many, many years before we could ever get that close again to removing that tax from food. (In 1996 there is still no relief in sight, although many have tried.) The following year it was discovered that the tax credit did not help the really poor people, for they did not pay income tax and received no credit. Governor Riley proposed that the tax credit money be allocated instead for health-care programs for the indigent. I agreed to support this proposal. My friends, Bob and Jean, were upset with me for "breaking the faith" by allowing our compromise to be rescinded. But I felt our compromise had already been nullified, and Riley's plan would at least benefit the same people we had intended to help by eliminating the sales tax on food.

At 2:00 A.M., March 27, the House finally passed the EIA intact as part of the appropriations bill, rammed through with the help of our newly acquired parliamentarians, Bob and Jean. During the last week of debate, motions and points of order of all sorts were flying fast and furious, and it was comforting to have the rules experts on our side at last. The bill then went to the Senate, from which it came out with few serious changes.

Governor Riley gained national recognition for his work in developing and passing the EIA. He was invited to speak to groups all over the country, and for several years he took some of us Smurfs with him. He appointed several of us commissioners to the Education Commission of the States (ECS). We appeared on panels at ESC meetings to describe exactly what we did and how we did it. ECS is a national organization composed of governors, legislative leaders, and educators that holds conferences and publishes papers on education at all levels. This kind of show-and-tell is one practical way for states to build on the success of others, without reinventing the wheel. It was a wonderful and unusual experience for us all to see South Carolina admired for our innovative and progressive education program.

I was subsequently asked by ECS to chair a S.C. branch of its State Education Policy Seminars program which ECS established to educate policy makers on current education issues. I agreed to be a cochair with Dr. Jim Rex, the chairman of the Education Department at Winthrop. I first met Jim while working on the EIA. He and Phil Lader, then president of Winthrop College, came up with the grand idea of creating a center for teacher recruitment and a teacher cadet program, initially funded by the EIA and still successfully fulfilling its mission. For the seminars, Jim and I brought experts to talk to legislators, policy makers, educators, and businessmen (all the partners of the EIA battle) about the many educational issues the state had to tackle. Jim knew the education issues, and I was supposed to provide the political instincts for identifying the hottest subjects and the most sellable speakers and to build the guests list. These seminars, which we ran for five or six years, kept me happily connected to education, even though in the legislature my attention was pulled in other directions. Later, when Jim moved to the development office of the University of

South Carolina, I worked with him in connecting Beaufort's Penn Center and the university, a project we thought was mutually advantageous for both institutions. The partnership has lately begun to falter, but we both hope a remedy will be found to cure the substantial problems before the partners become too set and inflexible. As I am no longer on the Penn Board and he is no longer with the development office, the problem is in other hands.

Governor Riley remained active and focused on education issues within the Southern Regional Education Board, the Education Commission of the States, and the Governor's Association, working with Governor Bill Clinton of Arkansas and Governor Lamar Alexander of Tennessee. In 1992, Clinton, now president, asked Riley to leave a successful law practice to come to Washington. He accepted and became the hardworking and highly respected secretary of education.

A multitude of committees were created to oversee the implementation of the EIA. Bob Sheheen, who is very good about watchdogging major legislative actions, made sure that he was appointed to the legislative oversight committee and served as long as it existed. I served for a short time on the Department of Education's State EIA Implementation Council, which received reports from regional councils and reviewed proposed guidelines and regulations. Unfortunately, the meetings were held while the legislature was in session, and I had to drop out. Crosby Lewis chaired the legislative oversight committee for four years. "During this time," he told me, "we maintained the integrity of the bill. After a particularly bitter fight with some educators who were trying to water down standards, Dick Riley accused me of being a purist. Maybe that was a compliment?"

Many have criticized the EIA for failing to produce dramatic results. But in fact, it did. No other state made as much progress between 1983 and 1989—the height of the EIA debate and phase-in of all the key programs. Student absenteeism dropped. College attendance went up. Basic skill scores went up. Advanced placement enrollments increased at a rapid pace. A researcher from the Rand Corporation called it the most comprehensive reform in America at the time. In 1986 our success was cited by Education Secretary William J. Bennett and published in newspapers from coast to coast, including the *New York Times* and the *Wall Street Journal*. The Carnegie Foundation spotlighted it, as did the Education Commission of the States. After several years in place, our SAT scores improved more than any other state in the nation. But then, in 1990 test scores hit a plateau, as compared to other states, whose scores kept rising.

I believe there are several reasons for this. Other states developed similar comprehensive reforms in their education programs, and many went even further and invested more heavily than we did. Many states literally copied South Carolina's reforms. Oklahoma used our teacher recruitment center model, and Illinois some of our accountability features. When South Carolina surpassed North Carolina in SAT scores in the late 1980s, North Carolina sent teams into our state to figure out why. Since that explosion of school reform throughout the area in the mid-1980s, there has been a wave of new education ideas throughout the South, but virtually none in South Carolina. I believe that although the Campbell administration, following Riley's tenure, talked about the importance of education, it made two big mistakes: it began to chip away at the special funds for specific EIA programs, directing them to the general education budget instead. And it started no new reforms.

I will never forget the angst I suffered when newly elected Governor Campbell vetoed the line item of the EIA for the artistically gifted and talented programs. The Cultural Affairs Committee, which I chaired at the time, had worked so hard to have these included in, and protected by, the EIA. But Campbell, who had been out of the state for some time as a congressman, wasn't aware of the increased interest in the arts in the schools. He learned painfully, thanks to the ardent parents of artistically gifted and talented children who, once aroused, tirelessly and doggedly fought to hold on to the gains that had been won for their children. Several months after the veto, we received a signal from the Governor's Office that he might reconsider his position if we were to propose funding for the program in the next year's budget. And of course we did.

But this success was the exception. Other programs didn't have such strong, well-organized advocates. Some of the programs of the EIA have been weakened or discontinued. A key component of those states moving forward in education in the 1980s and 1990s (North Carolina, Georgia, Kentucky, and Texas) is the involvement of business/education coalitions. South Carolina repealed our Business-Education Partnership Committee in the EIA. Another important part of successful education reform is accountability. While the rest of the country instituted tools for more accountability, both Campbell and State Superintendent Barbara Nielsen led the charge to eliminate our independent Division of Public Accountability. Once again, in the 1990s, rewarding teachers is a major issue. President Clinton is raising this issue along with Secretary Riley in 1997. But in South Carolina, after Riley left the governorship, the state eliminated the teacher incentive pay portion of the EIA. And if the move, initiated by Governor Beasley, toward school vouchers becomes successful, there will be further competition for public education funds. In 1996 that move was stifled, but it can always reappear.

As I write this chapter, in 1997, the U.S. Department of Education released the national math test scores that show how states have done during the past few years and how they compare one against another. Unfortunately, my story about what has happened since Riley left office and since the EIA was phased in (and now is being done in) is proving correct. By 1990, coming out of the EIA reforms, South Carolina had risen from the bottom in national rankings, passing many of our neighboring states in math achievement. In 1990, we were approaching the national average, which, for a poor state, was dramatic. But here we are, in 1997, one of only two states that did not improve its eighth-grade math scores; in fact, nine states have passed us since 1990. Once again, it is obvious that rhetoric is no substitute for action.

What a shame it is that the EIA, which was born of such labor and commitment, was not kept intact as well as our new filibuster rules. (In the present political climate, perhaps I should knock on wood as I say that, for certainly there are still some in the legislature who would like to reverse that rules change so they can disrupt or control the action to fit their agendas.)

Poverty and illiteracy have not always pulled us down. On the eve of the American Revolution, South Carolina had the fastest growing economy and the highest per capita income of any colony. On the eve of the Civil War, we had the third highest per capita income (excluding slaves) of any state. But by 1929, South Carolina had become the poorest state in the nation. We can thank the New Deal with its emergency programs for starting to pull us up. And we can thank progressive state leaders who struggled to improve education in the attempt to strengthen our economy and create jobs. We have generations of neglect to make up for and a long way to go. It is possible that someday we may return to the top of the list. But only if we can find the way and the will to provide a superior education to every child in the state.

CHAPTER 15

NCSL: Going National

My appointment to a committee of the National Conference of State Legislatures (NCSL) was the equivalent—on the positive side—of a bodybuilder going on steroids. NCSL's mission is to serve the legislators and staffs of the nation's states, commonwealths, and territories. Its members are the states, who fund it and assign legislators to participate in it. It is a bipartisan organization with three objectives: to improve the quality and effectiveness of state legislatures, to foster interstate communication and cooperation, and to ensure states a strong cohesive voice in the federal system.

In 1978 NCSL created a task force on the arts, and all state legislatures were invited to appoint at least one member to it. Bud Ferillo, knowing of my long-standing interest in the arts, suggested to the speaker that he appoint me. These appointments are often competitive. Most legislators love to go to NCSL conferences, which are held in great vacation cities, and those serving on NCSL standing committees are more likely to have their requests to attend the conferences approved by the speaker. But I don't imagine there was a great demand by South Carolina House members to serve on an arts committee; and as I was already on the Energy Committee, perhaps the speaker thought I could do two for the price of one. He appointed me. These two committees served as a springboard for what were to become major parts of my legislative agenda.

From the time of my election I wondered what I could do as a legislator to promote the arts in South Carolina. But as I came to realize just how poor South Carolina was, and how many unmet needs there were, it seemed unlikely I could do much—so I didn't try. Much to my surprise and delight, the NCSL task force on the arts provided a wealth of ideas on how state government could indeed promote and assist the arts without spending a lot of money.

Like all the other NCSL committees, our task force met during NCSL annual meetings, which were always held, for logistical reasons, in large cities. We were a group of many thousands: one thousand to two thousand legislators, their families, another thousand legislative staffers, lobbyists, political organizers, experts who served on panels, speakers at the many luncheons, and, of course, the national press. Two more arts task force meetings were held during the year in smaller cities, in tandem with the Assembly on the Legislature, a branch of NCSL.

At our arts meetings there was lots of "show and tell": members informed the group about innovative programs in their states. There was a strong competitive element between states, which was good. We were energized to go home and put our new ideas to work. Then at the next meetings, we who had been behind could tout our new success stories. At least, that's how those meetings affected me.

And we had such fun while learning. Most or our members were already interested and active in the arts, which set us apart from the mainstream legislators. It was an extremely comfortable group for me, for I had a lot in common with so many of the them. There was a disproportionate number of women and Jews. This did not at all reflect the makeup of state legislatures or NCSL, which was comprised of predominantly male leadership types, especially in those early days of NCSL in the late 1970s and early '80s. What it did reflect, however, is the general makeup of contributors and participants in the arts. Several members and I became close friends; we kept in touch, often calling to ask each other how particular issues were handled in their state. When we weren't discussing arts we were exchanging notes and views on environmental issues, women's issues, education issues, with which we all seemed to be involved, usually on the same side. We exchanged research. We exchanged bills. We even exchanged speeches. I passed on to several women my successful speech on the floor of the House against the proposed human life amendment which was similar to those being filed in every state at that time, and I was gratified to hear that some or all of it was used in other legislatures.

In the early years the arts task force had half-a-person for its staff support, in the interest of economy, but after the committee produced a wonderful book on arts legislation, state by state, and after the senior NCSL staff members attended some of our meetings and saw for themselves the work we were doing, we were made a full-fledged committee and given a full-time director. The director planned our programs with the host city of our meetings, and with the arts councils of whatever state we were in; our agenda included meeting the cultural, government, and business leaders involved in the cultural life of the city, as well as experiencing the arts of that city.

We met several times in Charleston, a favorite city for delegates. I remember well the magical day when we sat in the garden of the Dock Street Theater and listened to a discourse from the charming Gian Carlo Menotti, then artistic director of the Spoleto Festival USA and known to many as the composer of *Amahl and the Night Visitors* (which my children and I watched every Christmas on television when they were young). We heard from city officials about the cultural and economic benefits of the festival; we learned about cultural tourism and how it helped Charleston's revitalization efforts and contributed to the area's economic development. We heard from the Historic Charleston Foundation about preserving the city's beautiful eighteenth- and nineteenth-century homes and the effect these resources have had on the city's tourism efforts. We learned about international tourism and methods to develop that market. All the while, in the background we heard the background music of songbirds and a violinist practicing for the upcoming festival. The red-tiled roofs surrounded us, a backdrop that created the illusion of sitting in a piazza of a small European town.

At all the sessions there was always the opportunity to ask questions, because our group was relatively small and the meetings informal. Interspersed with the "talking" programs were the visits we made to museums, historic buildings, a plantation oyster roast, great restaurants, and concerts. What a pleasant way to learn!

Our task force book, *Arts in the States*, describes some of our experiences: "In Sante Fe we discussed artists' needs with Native American artists and craftsmen. . . . In New York we were treated to an exhilarating studio performance by the Dance Theatre of Harlem, followed by

Director Arthur Mitchell speaking about the difficulties of funding scholarships for disadvantaged youth." We toured the Soho district, talked with artists in their studios, and discussed the issues of live-work space, and the problem of decreasing available space because of gentrification and increasing costs. We visited Lincoln Center, learning about in-service teacher training for arts education. In New York we also learned about the rigors of dancing firsthand by actually taking a lesson at the Eliot Feld Ballet School. Well, to be honest, I didn't—I watched. But Senator Jack Faxon of Michigan did and was inspired the following Christmas to play the role of Herr Drosselmeyer, Clara's godfather, in *The Nutcracker* when it was performed by the Detroit Opera Company.

In New Orleans we listened to jazz and talked with musicians. We visited the New Orleans Center for the Creative Arts, a public arts high school. In Nashville we visited a recording studio and talked with producers and manufacturers about problems in the music industry, and we also visited a wonderful crafts center.

One of the most important lessons I carried home with me was the necessity of stressing the economic benefits that the arts bring to a state when seeking support, legislation or funding for the arts from a legislature and a governor. This argument makes some cultural purists unhappy, but it doesn't take long in politics to learn the worth of pragmatism—as long as it doesn't weaken the ultimate cause. If the economic benefits argument is valid, and we have been able to document that it is, it follows that it is important to bring cultural agencies into the mainstream of government, to interface and coordinate programs related to the arts with politically powerful agencies—those overseeing economic development, tourism, and education—thereby extending their power into the cultural agencies.

In the summer of 1979, after I had completed my first term in the House and my second year on the arts task force, I was one of thirty-four legislators elected to the executive committee of the NCSL. I don't know the exact definition of "serendipity," but it seems like the right word to describe my being selected for this highly sought position. On the same day the nominations for NCSL officers and executive committee members were to be made, the NCSL Arts Task Force was having a luncheon meeting, and I happened to sit at a small table with Senator

Tarky Lombardi, a New York Republican who was on the nominating committee. We had a pleasant chat about the many interests we had in common, and then he left for his committee meeting. As luck would have it, the committee was looking for a woman, a Southerner and a Democrat—gender, region, and politial party have to be balanced in the NCSL—and the executive committee had no one that fit that description. There I had been, sitting at the same table, fitting the bill, fresh in his mind, so Tarky nominated me. The NCSL staff conferred with Bud Ferillo, who told them they were lucky to have me, despite my very junior standing. My speaker then had to approve my serving on the Executive Committee, because it entailed meetings and travel to be paid for by the House, and he did. My name was then placed on the slate of nominees, which guaranteed my election without my having to campaign for it, something I would never have dreamed of doing. I was the first South Carolina legislator to serve on the executive committee. My nemesis, Tom Marchant, tried to get the speaker to appoint him in my place the following year, but failed. After my nonrenewable three-year term was up, Frank Caggiano, the clerk of the South Carolina Senate, was elected as one of the legislative staff members, and so South Carolina maintained a presence for a little while longer.

The executive committee then consisted of thirty-four legislators and seventeen legislative staff persons from across the country, and we were served and guided by a small staff of experts who developed information about the pressing issues of the day—taxes, energy, environment, welfare, and children. They also staffed the standing committees which make recommendations for "action," in the form of resolutions that the entire body (over a thousand) votes on. The "action" includes lobbying Congress and the White House on specific issues which affect state government.

The staff also compiles and stores in computers information on laws and proposed legislation on specific issues in all the states. They were a wonderful resource for background information on bills I was working on. When the S.C. legislature started to reform itself in the early 1970s by creating a research department and building office space for members, NCSL provided help. As a member of the executive committee I had an insider's advantage in getting their experts to visit South

Carolina to help us look at ways to improve our legislative process, shorten our sessions, strengthen our rules. They also helped me with energy issues and obtained federal grants for pilot projects in conservation and alternate energy sources. I amassed a huge library of information on tax and fiscal policies with their help while trying to remove the sales tax on food and trying to enact a "circuit breaker," a policy which would help low-income people who live in areas where property values (and taxes) are skyrocketing, while their incomes remain low.

This was a problem I saw firsthand on Hilton Head, as well as in other parts of Beaufort County. Steven Gold, a staff member of NCSL at that time, was an expert on "circuit breakers," which had alleviated this problem in many states. He sent me enormous amounts of information, including his book on the subject. But despite his help, and despite the interest it peaked in Senator Waddell, who chaired the tax study committee, we couldn't get it through our legislature. There wasn't enough money to repay the counties for the property taxes they would lose under the plan. (I had a solution, but everyone else considered it political suicide. My idea was to remove the homestead exemption, which reduced property taxes on homes of those sixty-five and over, and use the money saved by the state to fund exemptions based on income rather than age. Originally the homestead exemption was put in place because older, nonworking people needed that help. But times had changed with pension plans, IRA's, and investments, and so many people I knew who were sixty-five and over did not need tax relief. Why not tie the exemption to need instead of age? I tried to enlist the AARP: they listened but were unconvinced. I finally gave up on this issue, but I keep passing on my library of information to others who try. Someday the time will be right, and someone will succeed, thanks to NCSL and Steven Gold.)

I served on the NCSL Energy Committee until I left the legislature, including several years as a vice chair. Then there were the various ad-hoc NCSL nuclear waste committees, which were created whenever a particular issue came to the national forefront. These meetings helped me keep up with what was happening across the country.

More serendipity. The day before the NSCL nominating committee met, I had dropped in on a networking meeting of women legislators, some of whom had been searching for ways to elect women to the executive committee. Their ultimate goal was to have more women chairing committees; committee chairmen were appointed by the NCSL president, with input from the tightly knit executive committee, at that time about ninety-five percent white males. The women were discussing strategies to lobby the nominating committee. I was a silent observer. I had not gotten involved in NCSL politics because, I rationalized, I would rather spend my time and energies on issues. In truth, I found it intimidating. Most of the NCSL bigwigs were house speakers, senate presidents, and committee chairmen in their own states. I was not in their league and had no hope or ambitions to be, because that's the way South Carolina is.

I must admit to feeling a little guilty the following day when I was so effortlessly nominated to the executive committee. So many of those women had toiled in the vineyard, cultivating the soil. But not guilty enough to keep from accepting, for there was no way I knew to substitute any of their names for mine, with so little time to maneuver it.

Another meeting of the Women's Network was held after the news was out about the slate of nominations. Since I was to be on the executive committee, I could be the best link between it and the network, and so they proposed I chair the group. (There was one other woman on the executive committee, but she had never attended meetings of the Women's Network. Many said she was a good ol' girl who felt very comfortable with the men and didn't see the need for a support group. Several years later, when she ran for president of NCSL and lost, she joined the network and admitted that we women had to help each other, after all.)

I was hesitant about accepting the chair of the Women's Network because I had really not hooked into women's issues at that time and didn't feel knowledgable enough to lead in this arena. Not that I wasn't interested, but like the arts, I didn't see much hope for any kind of a woman's agenda in the South Carolina legislature with our small, disparate group of women, some of whom opposed the ERA, affirmative action, and reproductive choice. I reluctantly agreed to be a cochair if

Nevada senator Jean Ford, who had much more experience than I, would serve with me. Together, we were able to increase the number of our group by writing to women in all state legislatures about NCSL and suggesting they ask their speakers to send them to our conferences and appoint them to NCSL committees. In the early days, the leadership of many legislatures did not spread the news about NCSL but rather kept these appointments for their friends and followers. But once women legislators received the information, many followed through, and our numbers at the meetings grew. Jean and I produced a few good speakers and workshops to increase legislative skills. The network is now well established, with many lobbyists willing to subsidize speakers and luncheons.

In 1994, Karen McCarthy, a legislator from Missouri, became the first woman to be elected president of NCSL, an unthinkable possibility just a few years before. She left in the middle of her term when an opportunity to run for Congress came along. She seized it and won. She is one of several women legislators I came to know through NCSL who went on to Congress or to statewide offices. Another, Jane Campbell of Ohio, was elected to fill her term. Mary Landrieu, elected to the United States Senate from Louisiana in 1996, was also quite active in NCSL, chairing the Women's Network several years after me. I assume she built up her own network from her NCSL contacts which helped her run and win first the office of state treasurer of Louisiana, then US senator. I know I was on her mailing list and happily contributed to all her campaigns.

I learned about big-time politics while on the NCSL executive committee. We committee members were wined and dined all through the conferences, surrounded by vice presidents of government affairs (lobbyists) for various industries, professions, and businesses, who picked up the tabs for our food, our wine, and our convention speakers (some of whom represented their views, although NCSL tried to be as evenhanded as possible in offering different viewpoints). These same lobbyists also audited committee meetings where their particular issues were being discussed and voted on. Before a meeting would break up, there was often a friendly lobbyist hovering in the back of the room, waiting to explain his or her position if you didn't vote the "right" way. Such discussions were often followed by a motion to reconsider the vote so we could vote again. I felt this especially on the energy committee, where the stakes were high for all special interests. We dealt with water rights, nuclear industry, and hazardous wastes, co-ops versus private utilities—and the lobbying was intense as we voted on resolutions. The committee itself was divided along regional lines as well as political parties, so the meetings often ended in deadlock, which gave the lobbyists more time to work their wonders. I remember the heated battles in the early days when I and several other "environmentalists" voted for energy conservation and tax credits for alternative sources of energy and for anything that would reduce acid rain. Those members from the coal and oil and nuclear states, including the chairman, opposed us and usually won.

About a year into my term on the executive committee I expressed my concern to anyone who would listen about the ever-present, attentive, generous, special interest-lobbyists who were in a position to strongly influence our decisions. After all, the resolutions we voted on and the policies we adopted were sent to Congress and the White House as representing the will of all state legislatures. No one had an answer. Added to these pressures, several conservative organizations, such as the American Legislative Exchange Council, found us to be a forum (with a great mailing list) for the legislation they were promoting. It was depressing to me to see this influence at work without a counterbalance.

Our South Carolina lobbyists soon discovered golden opportunities in consorting with South Carolina legislators at NCSL meetings. I remember the horror of a senator friend from Wisconsin, where they have the strictest of lobbying laws, when a utility lobbyist invited some of us on the energy committee to dinner, or when she witnessed a group of legislators take off for an all-day fishing trip hosted by Chem-Nuclear, the low-level nuclear waste contractor. Sometimes it would be golf. These outings did not surprise me, but I was irked to know they were out there partying at the state's expense while I was rushing from one meeting to another. Eventually, NCSL rules were changed so that no entertainment could take place while meetings were scheduled. And

South Carolina rules were changed so that legislators could not be hosted by lobbyists.

But eventually the counterbalance to these special interests showed up in the form of the Center for Policy Alternatives, a coalition of public-interest groups. Its member organizations represented environmentalists, women's groups ranging from the League of Women Voters to the National Women's Political Caucus, educators, labor, pro-choice advocates, and civil libertarians. They could not begin to compete with the more traditional lobbyists in the wining and dining of legislators, but they provided a network for progressive legislators who sometimes felt adrift in a sea of conservatism. The center began to distribute information on progressive legislation à la the American Legislative Exchange. They also provided a forum for media attention. They developed a list of legislators who supported at least some of their goals. I tried twice as hard to fit their meetings, as compared to others, into an impossibly crowded conference schedule, full of meeting and time conflicts, because I saw their meetings as an antidote to the other pressures swirling around. And because I found it always comforting to meet the other legislators who came from different parts of the country but shared similar concerns. I understand that the Center for Policy Alternatives has since started an action network to parallel the American Legislative Exchange.

And then there were the caucuses—the political parties, the blacks, the Hispanics, the women, the Catholics, and the Jews all had meetings with noted speakers and all were jockeying to put their leaders on the executive committee and in committee chairmanships, or to get resolutions passed which fit their special interests. The conferences as a whole, with the nonstop meetings, luncheons, dinners, family outings, and hospitality rooms, were energizing—and energy depleting. I would come home exhilarated and exhausted.

Aside from the pleasant entertainments and convention souvenirs, I enjoyed an occasional game of tennis, squeezed between late afternoon meetings and dinner. There were a few of us at about the same level (of tennis skill); some of those I played with were Harriet Woods, who became president of the National Women's Political Caucus after being a state senator, lieutenant governor of Missouri, and almost a U.S. senator; and Representative Minette Doderer, a progressive from Iowa who has served since 1969 and chaired many important committees. Occasionally a man joined our game.

One of the really significant perks for members of the executive committee was the opportunity for international travel. I was lucky enough to be invited to join a group going to Israel, a trip arranged by the Israeli government. We were given royal treament, meeting with the president, the prime minister, legislators, cabinet officers, and businessmen. I was the only Jew in our group of eleven legislators and two staffers, and the only one who had been to Israel before. People turned to me for information when no Israeli was around, as the next best source of information, thinking their resident expert would know more than she actually did. As a matter of fact, Representative John Bragg of Tennessee was a Sunday school teacher and a true bible scholar who could always connect our location of the moment with Old Testament history, making me truly ashamed of my sparse knowledge.

It was fun for me to watch the educational process unfold. I remember riding on a bus, toward the end of the trip, when Senator Joe Merlino of New Jersey, in a discussion of a certain Arab-Israeli war said, "We won that one"—*we* meaning Israel. In our group were two senate presidents, two house speakers, two majority leaders—people of importance in their states who probably would bring home a positive message about Israel. I made some good friends on that trip. I learned a lot about Mormons from Senator Miles Ferry of Utah and his wife. I learned about New York politics from Bill Passanante, who represented the Greenwich Village district. I learned about Southern Baptists and the Bible from John Bragg. We were a very congenial group, and it was always fun to get together and remind each other of some lasting memory at later NCSL meetings.

A second trip I took was to Taiwan. Although the experiences and food were fascinating, the group was not as congenial. We were not the guests of the government, but the government made many of the arrangements for traveling. The style of this group was different from the other, and there were some who seemed more interested in shopping than learning. The one lasting memory I have of that trip was Bill Bulger, our leader and the colorful president of the Massachusetts senate, responding to the many toasts of Taiwanese officials at a banquet, with "Gambe" (Here's to your health), followed by a quick shot of sake, one glass after another. Noted for his sweet Irish voice, he was encouraged to sing, and he did, late into the night.

What was especially interesting for me was to compare the similar positions of Israel in the Middle East and Taiwan in the Far East, as they described themselves. Both were tiny islands (figuratively speaking, for Israel) in a sea of hostility, Davids versus Goliaths, both very young new countries, both having to spend a large percentage of their wealth on arms, but both with talented, entrepreneurial citizens and strong economies as compared to other countries their size, despite the ever-present pressures and crises. I would never have thought to compare these countries in this way, but the pitches made by each of their government leaders for American support were striking in their similarities.

I am so grateful to Speaker Rex Carter, who first gave me the opportunity to play an active role in NCSL and the organizations which followed, and to Ramon Schwartz and Bob Sheheen who continued to reappoint me when I asked. These extracurricular activities broadened my horizons and helped me become more knowledgeable about policies I wanted to influence. Self-confidence followed, as did my credibility in the House.

CHAPTER 16

Women and Politics

By virtue of being cochairs of the Women's Network of the National Conference of State Legislatures, Jean Ford and I were asked by Ruth Mandel, director of the Center for the American Woman and Politics (CAWP) of the Eagleton Institute of Politics of Rutgers University to serve on a planning committee for a ten-year anniversary conference for women legislators in 1982.

The Eagleton Institute was established in 1956 when Florence Peshine Eagleton, a founder of New Jersey's League of Women Voters, made a bequest to Rutgers University for the development of responsible leadership in civic and governmental affairs. CAWP was founded in 1971 to promote greater understanding and knowledge about women's changing relationship to politics and government and to enhance women's influence and leadership in public life. Its first major project was a 1972 conference which brought 50 of the nation's 344 women state legislators together for three days to find out who women legislators were: how old they were, their level of education, their marital status, and the discrimination they had faced in running for political office. The conference gave participants the opportunity to discuss openly their experiences with colleagues from around the country.

In 1982, 908 women held offices in state legislatures, and CAWP knew much more about them than the women they brought together in 1972. In 1982, when the tenth anniversary conference for women legislators was planned, the focus of the meetings had shifted. Sessions moved away from demographics and problem identification and concentrated on the power and potential of women's increased numbers in office, particularly as women came together in legislative caucuses.

They also began to discuss the relationship between political women and public policy, focusing initially on whether public policies have a different impact on female and male citizens.

The 1982 conference was held in Falmouth, Massachusetts, and was limited to sixty-five women legislators who had been selected either because they had a women's caucus in their legislature or because they had the potential to form a caucus. Syndicated columnists Ellen Goodman and Neil Peirce participated and later reported on the event. There was an effort to represent all regions of the country and both political parties. I was there as a member of the planning committee, and it was a defining experience for me. Just as the NCSL Arts Task Force led me to have hope, then take action in South Carolina, this conference led me to try to take a leadership role in bringing together the political women of South Carolina.

I had forgotten what an impact this conference had on me until I recently read a report I had written for the conference wrap-up at the request of Ruth Mandel. Here are a few of my more lyrical passages:

"The Programming was a work of art. It laid out what needed to be done, told us how to do it and fired us up to get going. First we were challenged by Congresswoman Martha Griffiths. . . . She commanded us to work and speak out for all the women who put us in office, for they were depending on us and we owe it to them.

"Then we were inspired by Norma Paulus who, after attending the first Women Legislators' Conference in 1972, had gone back to Oregon and pulled the women of her legislature together to accomplish wondrous things. Further inspiration came from her personal success in climbing the political ladder from legislator to Secretary of State, and now candidate for Congress. What a role model!

"Next came instruction. Leaders of caucuses in several states let us know that you, women's legislative caucuses, can and do make a difference."

My exhilaration came from those tough, articulate, spirited, witty young women who told us how they achieved leadership roles. They understood the need for power, sought it, and gained it. As I watched them I realized I would have to make some changes in my standard speech about women in state legislatures. No longer could I say that I was your "typical woman legislator—a middle-aged housewife, League of Women Voters, better in committees than at the podium, not really understanding power—BUT independent, uncompromising, incorruptible." Among that group I was more atypical than typical.

For here was a new generation of women legislators, cast in another mold, with different strengths and fewer weaknesses. They did not seem to be hampered by my hangups, that lack of self-confidence and assertiveness which is so inhibiting to taking action. But perhaps as they gain power, there may be some wear and tear on those female strengths I have touted—independence, holding the public interest above special interests, and personal ambition. That is a question which is debated in women's groups. My biased opinion is that there will be some, not significant, change for the worse. And that will be outweighed by the benefits that power will bring.

In a 1997 column, Ellen Goodman wrote about a book by Deborah Tannen, *Talking 9 to 5*, which analyzes the differences she hears in what men and women say. Her first book, the best-selling *You Just Don't Understand*, describes the comunication gap between men and women in their personal lives. *Talking 9 to 5* brings that perspective to the workplace, including the political arena. Tannen argues that there are no inherent or immutable gender differences; nor is there a single set of speech patterns for all men or all women. She would rather speak of "conventional styles" or "cultures of genders." Tannen, Goodman says, hears men saying "I" and women saying "we." Men focus on status, and women focus on connection. Men are comfortable with confrontation, while women prefer consensus. The "female style" keeps business running smoothly. The "male style" gets you ahead. One makes for a happier ship; the other is the style of the captain. Goodman concludes, "It's not a coincidence that there's no female Rush Limbaugh." If this anthropological study is valid today, I believe it will be many years before these generalities change. Of course, there will always be exceptions—Margaret Thatcher proves that.

If I were to choose one word to describe the sense of the Falmouth conference, it would be *commitment*. The achievement of the conference for me was channeling of this commitment and pointing it toward specific challenges. The first challenge was to be responsible for women's issues—for if we aren't, who will be? And the scope of women's issues needed to be expanded to all public policy, for every policy impacts on a woman's world.

Eleanor Holmes Norton added more weight to that mantle of responsibility by telling us we are responsible for everyone, not just women. As traditional values have changed in family, work, and morality, she said, there is distrust and malaise in the country, and people will be looking for leadership from those they trust (women), those in government closer to home (state legislatures). As we watched these responsibilities expand before our eyes, I thought to myself that it was obvious that we women legislators must band together in some form of caucus, must recruit more women to strengthen our forces, and must build coalitions and networks with like-minded legislators. Including men.

Several columnists gave the conference a time-frame perspective. Eileen Shanahan wrote, "Ten years ago they argued about whether women in their position could go out at night and have a drink with 'the boys.' They talked about how they should dress. They disagreed vigorously over a fundamental question of tactics—whether or not they should take the lead themselves on women's issues or get some man to front for them."

Ruth Mandel noted that ten years later, the women legislators were less preoccupied by such questions: "I guess that some of them go out drinking with the boys and some don't. But each has found her own style that she's comfortable with—a style that works for her. They don't need to debate it anymore." Perhaps, concluded Shanahan, the biggest change in ten years is in the power the women have in their legislatures and the sophistication with which they are using it.

David Broder wrote in the *Washington Post* (June 27, 1982), "June 30 marks the official death of the proposed Equal Rights Amendment to the Constitution, the cause that has consumed most of the energy of women activists (on both sides of the issue) for the past decade." He said that its demise is being treated by some as a sign that the "uppity females" who have been in the forefront of that battle have been given their comeuppance, and now things can go back to normal. There could not be a more mistaken notion. Women have been strengthened by this battle, and their power is bound to increase. He quoted Kathy Wilson, the chair of the National Women's Political Caucus and a participant at the Cape Cod conference, "Ten years ago a group like that would have talked about how to dress for legislative sessions. This year, they were talking about how to get to be Speaker."

My report concluded, "As the conference wound down, each state delegation caucused, then reported on what issues they intended to tackle when they got home. These were not just words and promises—these were pledges in blood." As indicated by the list of issues placed on the front burners, the very meaning of "feminism" had been so stretched and expanded that all of us there, traditional woman or feminist activist, Republican or Democrat, young or old, fit in some way within the framework of feminism which evolved in Falmouth.

The conference was deemed a great success. The only criticism was that it was too small; many women legislators were disappointed they didn't have an opportunity to participate. A 1983 conference was planned, with an open invitation to all 991 women legislators in office. Three-hundred-fifty attended. Several themes ran through the conference: increasing the numbers and influence of women in public office, especially in state legislatures; moving women up into key legislative leadership roles; and examining possible differences between women's and men's response to public policy issues. My role was different this time. I moderated and participated in a panel on energy issues relevant to state legislators, including environmental concerns. Energy was one of the many public issues that are not thought of as "women's issues" but have a real impact on women's lives. In fact, quite a bit of energy-related legislation is sponsored by women legislators all across the country. Perhaps women are at the forefront here because energy and environmental policies have such long-range consequences and women, the instinctual caregivers, reflect more about the future results of today's policies on the world their children and grandchildren will live in.

One dominant theme of the conference was that women leaders must promote women's issues. But then, all issues are women's issues. In a speech to the National Conference of State Legislatures Women's Network, Ruth Mandel noted that women, comprising the majority of the population, cannot be confined to only a couple of special issues.

But there may indeed be a woman's perspective or special way of looking at all issues. Transportation, energy, defense policy, educational policy, and budget allocations do impact women and men differently, because men and women function in different arenas and activities in many parts of their daily lives. She continued, "Indeed there are a number of specific issues which have a particularly large impact on women's lives, and these might legitimately be called 'women's issues' so long as we remember that while they may be women's issues, they should be everyone's concern."

At one time my only reservation about CAWP was that I felt it demonstrated tunnel vision in assigning paramount importance to women legislators who move up to the national congress or run for governor and in showcasing primarily those who do. I felt there were many women who couldn't move up for a variety of reasons, women who were successful, productive state legislators whose presence in those legislatures should not be looked upon just as stepping stones instead of a destination in itself. Naturally, my own experience led me to this conclusion.

I did not want to move anywhere. I liked my small district and had developed a system of communicating with my constituents which fit my personality and abilities and which I couldn't replicate in a district twenty times as large. I did not think I could be elected to Congress, because my congressional district was more conservative than I on issues important to me, ones I was not willing to compromise on. As a matter of fact, I didn't want to be a congresswoman. The arena was too large, the system too complex, and I didn't want to commute between Washington and South Carolina every weekend, at my age. I didn't want to have to raise hundreds of thousands of dollars every two years and be indebted to whatever special interest might contribute to my campaigns. Commuting and raising money were also functions of running for the state legislature, but on a miniscule scale that I could cope with. And furthermore, state government is where more and more of the action is in these days of trying to shrink the federal government. Above and beyond all that, there were the internal conflicts which made running even for the state legislature a scary and threatening exerience for me. If that was a competitive and rugged environment for me, Congress would be much worse for someone with my self-doubts, albeit reduced by time and experience.

As for running for governor, I knew I could not be elected. South Carolina was not ready for any woman governor, much less a Jewish New York progressive Democrat. I say this as a realist and a pragmatist. Careful reading of the press sends me that signal regularly. Even as I write this chapter, the *State* newspaper bears me out. For example, on January 21, 1997, William Ferris, director of the Center for the Study of Southern Culture at the University of Mississippi, is quoted as explaining why South Carolina is the last state to deal with the Confederate battle flag still flying atop its public buildings: "Of all Southern states, South Carolina has been most resistant to change. That is a reflection of the body politic in the state and a conservative electorate. It's the identity of the state." This conservatism does not just apply to flags. On January 22, 1997, another article describes the new legislative session as one consumed with racial issues: court-ordered reapportionment, which might reduce the number of black legislators; the Confederate flag; a bill to abolish racial preferences in hiring and contracting by state government, in effect ending the programs most people refer to as affirmative action. An attorney who successfully challenged the race-based election districts is quoted as saying, "The only difference between this session and any other session is it's [racism] just more overt. That's why, when other states are debating sophisticated technological issues, education issues, bringing their states into the 21st century, we're still debating the 19th century."

My voting record was out of sync with these statewide leanings, and my visibility in the press would make me good fodder for any campaign against me. Perhaps, just perhaps, I could have been elected lieutenant governor, an office not as competitive in South Carolina, and one that Nancy Stevenson had attained, but I wasn't interested in that job—which most use as a stepping stone to places I didn't want or couldn't reach.

Despite all these incontrovertible reasons for my staying in the legislature rather than aiming higher, the CAWP meetings made me feel a little uncomfortable, even inadequate, or perhaps guilty, because

I was not ready and willing to take up their challenge, to be more important, more powerful, to try to move up to where I could really make a difference. But I felt I was making a difference. Why sacrifice the bird in the hand by taking on something I didn't want and probably couldn't get? I felt there were other women who fit into similar scenarios.

On the other hand, CAWP is right that the most successful way for women to be elected to higher office is to start out in the more easily attainable offices at the lower levels and work their way up the ladder. And if we want women in higher office, which we do, then we have to provide a system to feed them in. So, I have now concluded that we were both right. It is important to offer every aid and opportunity to those who want to go to Congress and be governors, and CAWP and other organizations must be supported and encouraged in these efforts. But it is also important to encourage those women who want to remain where they are and help them be effective in their state legislatures, to gain power there. And it's important as well to motivate them to take the lead on those issues which will improve the lives of women; for if they don't, who will?

A study of bills considered by Congress which affect women's rights and lives shows that most have been initiated, sponsored, and fought for by women and the Women's Issues Caucus. Happily this caucus includes many men, for there certainly aren't enough women in Congress to pass anything by themselves.

Which leads me to my uneasiness with the policy of some women's organizations to support any pro-choice woman over any man, no matter how good his voting record was on their issues. I understand and approve of the drive to put more and more women into office, but my personal experience tells me that in the long view this kind of preference is short-sighted policy. I am reminded of an instance when a woman who had no record and a fuzzy position on choice was endorsed for the South Carolina legislature by a feminist group just because she was a woman, over an incumbent man who had been voting right on every women's issue for four years, putting himself at political risk to do so. If he won (which he did), why should he continue to support women's issues, if he knew women would dump him if a woman, any woman, decided to run against him? And why should other men, seeing this happen, be persuaded by women to support their causes? In return for what? Give-and-take is the quintessence of politics, and rarely can one exist long without the other.

Although I was not enticed to "move up the ladder" by the many inspirational speakers at CAWP conferences, I was seduced into thinking I could and should provide some leadership in bringing together political women in South Carolina, despite their differences, to do something, though I wasn't quite sure what that something could be. Governor Madelaine Kunin of Vermont, when addressing the Women's Network of NCSL about the need for women working together, said, "We who are role models for others, also need sustenance ourselves, and to exchange ideas and find where common ground is." That would be a good starting point for us in South Carolina.

Half of the benefit I derived by working with CAWP and NCSL was personal growth—by listening, learning, and broadening my views. The other half was the pleasure of meeting and spending time with the great mix of people at the CAWP conferences—in addition to staff and legislators, there were the speakers, the experts, some of whom became my friends. One newfound friend, a male among all those women, was Alan Rosenthal, then director of the Eagleton Institute, whose special interest was state legislatures. My introduction to Alan was when he quoted me in one of his books. When I first started writing columns for my newspaper, I thought that possibly my newcomer's perceptions of the way things work in state legislatures might be put to use to help other women new to politics. A reporter from the *Los Angeles Times* who had seen a few of these columns complimented me on my "lean prose" and said for the first time she understood the legislative process. This, of course, inflated my ego enough to move me forward on the idea. After learning about CAWP, I wrote to ask if there was an audience for a book with this kind of information. They responded that they would like to use some of my material in their books. I agreed and dropped the idea of my own book.

Once having met him, I always looked forward to seeing Alan, a regular panelist at all the CAWP and NCSL meetings. I liked to hear his opinions about state government, and his particular sense of humor would start me laughing so hard I couldn't talk, a rarity for me—I usually laugh silently. He is somewhere between a dry wit and a stand-up comic. I have a happy memory of wandering through Epcot Center with Alan, after an NCSL meeting, learning and laughing all the way. His book, *Governors and Legislatures: Contending Powers*, defines and explains the normal and natural struggle between state legislatures and governors and turned a light on in my brain as I struggled to understand and deal with tensions between Governor Campbell and the legislature. I wrote him a fan letter. "I do believe you know us better than we know ourselves. Even though much of the book covered what we live with, you caused me to step away from the power struggles, partisanship and games (which I do not particularly enjoy) and take a wider look at the whole picture—especially the "whys." In the last chapter, there is a lot for both legislators and governors to consider as we muddle through each day."

In 1983, when my son Billy was running the Fritz Hollings presidential campaign, I had a mother's pleasure of hearing praise of him from national political columnists and television commentators covering the CAWP conference, who happened to talk with me and associated my name with his. I also ran into other legislators involved with Democratic primaries in other states who had worked with Billy. Those connections were fun for me.

Back in South Carolina, I gathered together a few friends to discuss the best approach to start women networking in a state where the women legislators rarely discussed issues, in fact rarely got together. (Once in a great while Joyce Hearn or Jean Toal, who lived in Columbia, would invite the rest of the women legislators over for a drink or supper. This was a pleasant social evening, but once Hearn and Toal left the House our get-togethers ended.) It was decided that I should initiate a meeting and create an organization, to be called South Carolina Women in Government, for women in state and local elective and appointed positions, plus the one or two women judges in the state. Speaker Ramon Schwartz gave me logistical support, as did several very enthusiastic women in state administrative jobs. We were astonished to discover that there were over five hundred female school board, city and county council members, mayors, and treasurers. We gathered their names from the rolls of the state municipal, county and school board associations and sent them invitations to a luncheon. Over one hundred women came. Governor Riley and his wife, Tunky, also attended, as they did every year they were able to.

That first year Ruth Mandel, director of CAWP (and now director of the Eagleton Institute), accepted our invitation to be the luncheon speaker, but she became ill at the last moment and sent her assistant, Kathy Stanwick, who stressed the importance of groups such as ours. There was much enthusiasm about the meeting. We asked those attending to fill out a form telling us of their reactions and ideas. The reactions were so positive, with many paraphrasing Kunin in answer to the question "Why did you find this meeting valuable?" They praised the "fellowship and the exchange of ideas"; the "opportunity to meet women statewide"; the chance "to gain new ideas, share common concerns in government and just to meet other elected women"; "the sharing with other women our problems as elected women among so many men"; and the "encouragement and inspiration." These responses encouraged me to keep this good thing going.

The following year I asked the other women in the legislature to cohost the meeting, and from then on the invitations went out on generic House stationery (instead of mine), listing all our names as hosts. Each year, we held workshops and found interesting and nonpartisan (for the most part) speakers: Kathy Wilson, the Republican president of the National Women's Political Caucus that year; Sissy Farenthold, the Democratic Texas state legislator who ran unsuccessfully for governor; Maura Brueger, the political director of the nonpartisan Women's Campaign Fund; and Wilhelmina Holliday, the founder of the Women's Museum of Art in Washington, D.C., who was not political at all.

A major flaw in our organization was that I didn't build into it some system of succession. I didn't try hard enough to find someone else who would assume the responsibility for chairing the effort. Many offered to help, but no one wanted to lead. Meetings took time to organize, and House members do not have secretaries unless they chair a committee. As a committee chair, I was fortunate to have secreterial help, but few other women had that resource. When I left the legislature, Candy Waites took over the leadership, but she left the legislature two years later, and South Carolina Women in Government faded away. One of my hopes in starting this group was that women already serving in local office might think about running for the legislature. And occasionally a freshman legislator would tell me on arrival that she had attended one of our meetings, which had started her thinking about the legislature. That was satisfying.

Out of the five-year experience of women legislators cohosting these meetings sprang the Women's Legislative Caucus, which I initiated and cochaired with Carole Wells, the senior woman Republican, during my last year in the House, in 1992. I suggested that we have cochairs, one Democrat and one Republican, to help bring the two disparate groups together. Without bipartisan leadership in the beginning, in our increasingly partisan House, it would not have gotten off the ground. The only issue we could find to agree on to sponsor as a group that year was a bill to mandate the inclusion of mammograms in insurance policies of state employees. The bill was held up by a (woman) lobbyist at Blue Shield, but the next year Blue Shield did adopt our idea as policy. That same year, when several women were running for judgeships (the legislature elects judges), we invited them to come to our meeting, introduce themselves to the women, and make a pitch for their votes. We did not, as a body, endorse any judge-candidates, but I hope they won some votes by meeting with us. In 1997, a black woman ran for circuit court, the first to attempt this. She lost. She was quoted in the paper after the election as being very disappointed by the lack of support by the Women's Caucus. She won the votes of only ten of the twenty-one women and had expected more.

Some of the male legislators were wary of what our caucus planned to do. A few even started a "men's caucus" in response to whatever havoc they thought we were going to create—or perhaps as a way to ridicule us. Fortunately, their plot was unpopular and short lived, for it had the potential of creating even more division and tension between some of the men and some of the women. One day, Candy Waites, who was an artist, was idly looking around the room and noticed how the women, in their colorful suits, stood out in the monochrome field of men's dark suits. She thought we would be noticed even more if we all wore one bright color. She sent around a note to all the women suggesting that on the following Wednesday we all wear purple. And we did. Those men who worried about us worried even more, asking "Now what are you up to?" Someone suggested we have our pictures taken as evidence of our solidarity. Bob Sheheen, who was speaker at the time, hurried to a back room, put on his ceremonial robe, which was purple, and joined us for the picture. I asked Candy later if she chose purple because it signified power. She said no, she just liked purple. Shortly after that event, Bob Sheheen invited all the women to his home in Camden for a Lebanese dinner. All this brought us together symbolically. Although we were still separated by issues and parties, the caucus encouraged a feeling of connectedness and an interest in working together, at least more than before.

Candy Waites took my place the following year as the Democratic cochair of the caucus, and when she and Carole Wells left the legislature, a newcomer from Spartanburg, Republican Rita Allison, took over the leadership. In 1996, the caucus met once a month over breakfast to discuss issues. It orchestrated a symposium with the Department of Health and Environmental Control on women's health issues and continues to meet with DHEC administrators to discuss legislation the department is proposing.

Another issue the women are discussing is how to get more women appointed to state boards and commissions. Barbara Moxon, the most political nonpolitician I know, attends all the caucus meetings and pushes for her special project, S.C. Advocates for Women on Boards and Commissions, a well-developed grassroots coalition which may have sprung from the loins of another coalition, led by Barbara, that advocated very effectively for the comprehensive health education (sex education) bills that Nell Smith and I struggled to pass for two years.

When I was in the legislature, the South Carolina Women's Commission was quite active and helpful to us. The Women's Commission had struggled through many stages since it was created by statute in 1970 as the South Carolina Commission on the Status of Women. According to Lynne Ford in the *Journal of Political Science* (vol. 24, 1996), the commission in its earliest days found itself hostage to a small budget, no staff, and facing organized opposition within and outside of the legislature. In 1973 a lawsuit was filed by Theresa Hicks, a leader in the Right-to-Life movement, and placed on the docket in 1975 challenging the commission's stand on the Equal Rights Amendment and the legitimacy of its *Legal Guide for South Carolina Women*. As an aftermath of the suit, the commission agreed not to speak on behalf of the ERA, and the judge ruled that it had exceeded its statutory authority in disseminating the legal guide. However, in 1978, the legislature expanded the authority of the commission to allow it to make available information on legal rights of women in South Carolina.

I remember well that one year during debate on the appropriations bill on the floor of the House, an amendment popped up to strike the Women's Commission funding from the budget. The amendment was accompanied by snide remarks and snickers and a comment that we maybe we needed a men's commission, etc. This just happened to be the year when a national report rated South Carolina as heading the list of the worst states for women, economically and legally, and I just happened to have that report in my desk. I looked around and saw no one else moving to save the agency, so I jumped up, got the podium, and waved the report around, saying in the most dramatic voice I could muster, "How dare you laugh and joke about removing the one agency in state government that is trying to help women at the very time the whole world learns that our women need help more than any others." Or something to that effect. There was a shocked silence, probably because that is not how I usually behaved at the podium. Without waiting for any questions, I moved to table the amendment, which went down in flames, with only a couple of votes in its favor.

In 1990, the commission recommended legislative changes to improve the legal status of women and to allow the commission to set a women's agenda that included "advocating for public policy that addresses women's needs and distributing educational information on women's rights and encouraging women to become involved in public policy." But when state government was restructured in 1993, the Women's Commission was one of several placed inside Governor Beasley's office. As with all other agencies within his office, no publication can be printed or dispersed, no opinion voiced, no statements made without prior approval of the governor. This is especially inhibiting for a women's commission during the administration of a governor who has made many appointments to conciliate the religious right. Restructuring of state government also resulted in fewer boards and commissions, which makes it more difficult for women to gain access on the remaining seats, as the competition for them is greater. Further, a governor has more control of appointments, so the stance of a sitting governor on women's issues can be an overriding factor. It should be noted that Governor Beasley has appointed four women to his cabinet of thirteen, an improvement over the distribution of women as department heads. But I do not know if these are women who will stand up for women.

The Women's Legislative Caucus has no meeting room, no staff, and no funds, but I am told that incoming legislators now ask about the caucus and indicate an interest in participating. New blood always helps. It will be slow going for the caucus during these divisive, partisan times, but the fact that it exists and meets is encouraging. The caucus has not been, and may never be in South Carolina a vital force in promoting controversial changes in the status of women. If someone had proposed the caucus support the admission of women to the Citadel it never would have flown. Nor choice. Nor affirmative action. But there was cohesion on one issue. In 1997 all eighteen members of the Women's Caucus cosponsored legislation to increase penalties in domestic violence cases.

Despite the differences between women in philosophies and parties, there are a few select issues where the percentage of women voting for or against was higher than the percentage of men. One year, for a week or so, doing my own research-which-might-come-in-handy-one-day, I collected printouts of roll-call votes in which the difference between men and women was noticeable. Unfortunately, those roll-call votes have disappeared in my files and my memory—except for the vote on one bill mandating that a crossing barrier be placed at railroad crossings to keep drivers from crossing the tracks when trains are coming through. Irene Rudnick filed that bill, year after year after year. In that vote I remember almost one hundred percent of the women voted for it, as compared to a small percentage of the men. Certainly that was an instance of special interests and lobbyists versus caregivers.

Generally, the percentage of women voting yes on reproductive choice, environment, day care, and education was higher than the percentage of men, but exceptions to this pattern increased as the women coming into the House became less independent and more conservative and the votes more politicized. The Congressional Women's Issues Caucus has done several studies showing similar patterns on the same issues. A National Women's Political Caucus bulletin reported that of the forty-seven women elected to Congress in 1995, thirty-eight called themselves pro-choice, the ultimate woman's issue, including nine of the seventeen Republican women. Clearly the men in Congress do not vote on choice at that same rate. If they did, the nation wouldn't undergo the annual trauma of antichoice bills in Congress and state legislatures.

One female group effort in South Carolina was Women against Nuclear Waste, an attempt in 1992 by five women legislators to close down Barnwell's low-level radioactive waste site on schedule. We were joined by the S.C. League of Women Voters and women lobbyists for several environmental groups in a press conference featuring women who opposed South Carolina's continuing role as the number-one nuclear dumping ground in the country. We did our own research, developed position papers, and decided on the arguments to be used and who would present them on the floor. If the House members had listened, they would have heard a good case for closing Barnwell, but votes had already been sewn up by the various special interests that gained by keeping Barnwell open. Few listened—and we lost. But we did turn around several women who were being pressured to vote the other way.

In the early 1980s Joanne Hawks of the Department of History and Carolyn Ellis of the School of Law of the University of Mississippi wrote a paper on the women in the Mississippi legislature. They followed it up with a study, perhaps as a means of comparison, of the women in the South Carolina legislature called *Ladies in the Gentlemen's Club: South Carolina Women Legislators, 1928–1994*. I found it interesting to read their observations, which they gleaned from questionnaires and interviews. They captured the essence of women in our legislature over time and the feel of the environment and its effect on the women.

They put in human terms my generalizations about traits and styles of political women.

(Perhaps this is the place to add here a thought that has clung to me all through the writing of this book. When I make generic statements about men and women's feelings, strengths, and weaknesses they should be read as generalizations, with the understanding that there are many, many exceptions. The generalizations come from professional social scientists who have researched in the field and draw conclusions based on their observations. And they come from amateurs like me who are struck by certain patterns we have seen and come to intuitive, and only intuitive, conclusions.)

Ladies in the Gentlemen's Club describes the South Carolina General Assembly as being composed of select and powerful men, its upper chamber characterized by V. O. Key as a "gentlemen's club" which wields enormous influence on state politics. The ratification of the Nineteenth Amendment in 1920 paved the way for women to enter politics; however, it was 1928 before a woman was elected to the General Assembly. By mid-century only one other woman had served. The authors draw portraits of several women "leaders" and highlight the changing motives and styles of women in politics—then and now, in South Carolina as well as in other legislatures across the country.

The first woman in the South Carolina General Assembly was Mary Gordon Ellis, elected in 1928 as the senator from Jasper County. Ellis was a teacher in one-room schoolhouses and a county school superintendent, so education issues were her focus. She was defeated for reelection.

Harriet Johnson of York County served during 1945–46, filling an unexpired term, thus becoming the first woman to sit in the House of Representatives. As noted by Hawks: "Like many women of the time she was sympathetic to the black child's lack of educational and vocational opportunities, probably an outgrowth of her general interest in education. Also typical was her animosity to the Equal Rights Amendment" (the national effort to amend the United States Constitution to insure equal rights for women).

Next was Martha Thomas Fitzgerald of Richland County, who was elected to the House in 1950, the first woman to be elected to a full term. As Hawks and Ellis wrote, "Typical of the initial entry of women into male enclaves was the legislature's ado over how to address Fitzgerald during the session. . . . Her colleagues introduced a resolution calling for the creation of a committee to determine the proper way to address a woman legislator." As reported by one journalist, Fitzgerald learned early that she could do more good by supporting or rejecting proposed state legislation with her vote than by proposing it herself. "I was more interested in accomplishing what I wanted than in getting credit for it," she said.

However, she was apparently more concerned with form. Managing a perfect attendance record became a source of inordinate pride to her. When speaking of her attendance record, she lost her usual shyness and became quite boastful. It was as if there were some things for which women could rightfully take credit, such as attendance records, and other activities about which they could not boast, such as legislative activities. She was extremely proud of her continual sponsorship of a bill to allow women to serve on juries. It is interesting that jury bills of this sort often became the rallying point for women in Southern legislatures, women who otherwise rejected a feminist label. Fitzgerald's tenure in office occurred at a point when a Southern woman in politics was caught between fulfilling the traditional ideal of Southern lady and the nontraditional role of politician. The balance was difficult to maintain, and generally in such cases the woman's effectiveness as a politician suffered, according to Hawks and Ellis.

Carolyn Frederick, a Republican from Greenville, served in the house from 1967 to 1976 and was a transitional figure in the history of women in South Carolina politics. She stood between the early "lady politicians" and the later "professional politicians." Frederick entered politics out of an intense desire to bring two-party politics to South Carolina. She was also motivated to enter politics by frustration. As a member of the American Association of University Women, she had lobbied for education reforms. She quickly learned that politicians would sometimes display sympathy for a piece of legislation yet not exert themselves on behalf of the bill. Frederick was a prototype of women who ran for office because of the unresponsiveness of some male legislators and the ineptitude of others.

Although by Southern standards she was clearly a lady, she made a clean break with her forerunners who tried to balance "ladyhood" with politics. She astutely noted in 1969: "From the time you were a little girl, you were taught to be sweet and to look pretty and to kiss Uncle Herbert and say thank you to Aunt Susie. The first thing that hits you in politics is that you can't please everyone. Whereas the average man will shrug and move on to the next issue, the average woman will mull it over and worry."

Carolyn Frederick was in the vanguard of women legislators who spoke up for women's equality and what she perceived as women's special interests: education, work laws, and juvenile delinquency. She was an early and avid supporter of the Equal Rights Amendment. Her support for the ERA was in sharp contrast to the anti-ERA stance of a younger female legislator during that same period, fellow Republican Sherry Shealy Martschink, the daughter of Senator Ryan Shealy.

She also advocated in the 1960s that women get involved in politics. She believed that a great influx of women into political office could shape South Carolina in a more positive, creative, and compassionate way than was then being accomplished. I am so sorry she was defeated for reelection the year I arrived. I would have loved to have worked with her.

Hawks and Ellis cited Jean Toal, a lawyer, who exemplified a new professionalism of women in the male-dominated legislative arena. Her legal education provided her two important edges: a legal framework as well as valuable contacts. Toal, one of only four women in her law school class, was aware that women had to be a "cut above" the male students to be successful. "Toal's legislative approach was to grapple with the more complex and demanding work and to gain expertise in the intricacies of the House rules. She was generally recognized for her mastery in parliamentary procedure, and because of that ability she was considered capable of sophisticated political maneuvering."

Toal was either floor leader of, or a significant participant in, court-reform legislation, consumer credit, Home Rule, and ethics reform. In addition to chairing the Rules Committee, she was the first woman to sit on the House Judiciary Committee. Toal was also one of the staunchest ERA supporters in the House.

"Harriet Keyserling exemplified a different, albeit effective style. Keyserling devoted most of her adult life to the roles traditionally performed by women. When she entered the General Assembly, she was 55 years old. . . . Like many of the political women of her generation, her political maturation was a product of club work. . . . Once elected she quietly began to study and observe; she quickly gained a reputation for 'doing her homework.' She shied away from a dominant speaking role in the House, but she poured her energies into writing articulate and convincing position papers for the local newspapers. The observation that female politicians are likely to communicate more often and better in writing than in legislative debate was true of Keyserling. . . . In her steady way Keyserling seized several important issues and became the spearhead for them."

The authors compared me, who came late to politics, to Elizabeth Patterson of Spartanburg, who was born to it. Patterson's father, Olin Johnston, was one of South Carolina's more important twentieth-century political figures. According to the authors, Liz had been groomed to be a politician's wife and waited for her husband to run for elective office. When her husband announced finally that he had no interest in leaving his law practice, Patterson herself ran. "To the extent that she expressed legislative interests, she did so vaguely. Her chief interests appeared to be education and mental health. Patterson was essentialy constituent oriented, a characteristic quite probably learned from her father. . . . She shunned the label of 'woman legislator.'" But the legislature did not always accommodate her. Patterson noted that when a study committee assignment was created with the word "woman" or "child" in it, she was automatically put on it.

Then there was Nancy Stevenson, who focused on education, health care, the ERA, child abuse, and housing legislation. She was in the legislature only two terms, leaving to become lieutenant governor.

"Toal, Keyserling, Patterson and Stevenson were all Democrats. While the Republican numbers were small, Carolyn Frederick, Joyce Hearn and Norma Russell showed that diversity nevertheless existed on the Republican side of the aisle." Hearn, who represented a district in Richland County, described herself as a "progressive conservative." Before becoming politically active, Hearn taught school. It was there that she developed an awareness of women's problems when she discovered that women were not paid equally for equal work. Despite this, she was not an active supporter of the ERA. Her legislative interest tended to fall into categories to which women have traditionally related. She was the chief author of a sexual assault law. She also worked on adoption laws, medical research, drug abuse legislation, and judicial merit selection.

According to the authors, "Norma Russell represented a different kind of Republicanism. A former court reporter, she described herself as ultra-conservative . . . an ambitious woman, who was defeated for lieutenant governor in 1982, and was largely ineffective in passing legislation. She was characterized as uncompromising and as a 'spitfire with a quick temper and scorching tongue.' Russell launched a one-woman crusade designed to ferret out abuse, notably sexual favors, in government. Consequently many of her colleagues shied away from either professional or personal contact with her. Her extremism in philosophy and style put distance between her and other female legislators."

Hawks and Ellis concluded that while these seven women exemplified various types, they shared certain similarities. "All were highly motivated, ambitious, and hard-working. All were vocal and influential. They were from one of the most traditional Southern states; the idea of 'ladyhood' was a particularly strong notion in South Carolina. The motivation that impelled them to walk to the beat of a different drummer has a consistent theme. Virtually all the women claim that their basic reason for running was to serve the public. Only a handful tried to build on their legislative experience for higher office."

The authors concluded, "Feminism as such was not something to which they paid much attention. However, the substance of feminism was familiar ground for them, for most belonged to the 'I'm not-a-feminist-but-I-believe-in-equal-pay-for-women' school of thought. No matter what degree of feminism different individuals professed, they all assiduously eschewed the feminist tag. To the extent that this avoidance was conscious, it was done primarily for pragmatic reasons. An avowed feminist in the mid-1970's would have been a pariah in the General Assembly. . . . They perceived, and perhaps rightly so, that in aligning themselves with the feminist camp they would have placed themselves outside the mainstream of legislative politics. Pragmatic concerns such as these delayed the formation of a women's caucus. The dilemma in South Carolina was solved by creating an informal network of women."

This attitude was probably truer in the South, where there were fewer women in legislatures, where women held no leadership positions, and where there were no women's caucuses. In fact, it is still true, according to a paper titled *The Politics of Women State Legislators: A South/Non-South Comparison* by Lynne E. Ford of the College of Charleston and Kathleen Dolan of the University of Wisconsin, Oshkosh, published in the *Southeastern Political Review* (June 1995). It states that in a "traditionalistic" political culture, "those without defined roles to play in politics are not expected, nor encouraged, to be even minimally active as citizens and certainly not as legislators. . . . Southern states were particularly slow in admitting women into public life and, as one scholar observed, 'the myth of the southern lady has served as a golden cord binding women to traditional roles.' . . . Contemporary scholarship continues to find lingering traditional attitudes relegating women to the private sphere and consistent with their position on the pedestal." They conclude: "Finally, the mere fact that there are so few women serving in southern state legislatures itself may prove to be a deterrent to creating the kind of environment that allows women to 'stand for' women on issues related to women, children, and families. . . . When women's numerical presence falls below the token level of 15%, they, like other minorities, are constrained in their legislative goals and behaviors and are therefore less likely to introduce and pursue legislation regarding the interests of women, children, and the family." Chalk this thesis up as another important reason, for those concerned about women and children, to work even harder to elect more women in public office to reach and pass that fifteen percent level!

Between 1984, when the University of Mississippi study was written, and the present, many interesting women came and went, in addition to Candy Waites, Nell Smith, and others I have mentioned in other contexts. Sarah Manly was elected in 1989 and Kathleen Kempe in 1991, both from the upstate. They were ardent supporters of environmental and women's issues. Irene Rudnick of Aiken, a veteran legislator who was first elected in 1973, kept being reelected, except for two brief periods, in her increasingly Republican district, until the lines were changed beyond even her political skills. In 1994, redistricting did them all in. It has been said that women were more often the victims of reapportionment than men, and it certainly seemed true in the South Carolina House. It may be because they had no power to fight for their seats during the committee process of drawing the lines, or they were just judged to be expendable. One exception, Denny Neilsen of Darlington, managed to beat the odds in a district the Judiciary Committee tried very hard to cut up. By vigilantly watching the committee's every move, she succeeded in having a manageable district drawn and won reelection.

Kathleen Kempe put herself at risk by filing an important piece of legislation called the "bad boy" bill. This bill would have mandated that the regulatory agencies review past environmental performances of any industry moving from another state and applying for a license to start up in South Carolina, if that industry produced potentially dangerous emissions, an eminently reasonable idea in a state with a fragile environment and many polluters already here. She couldn't move that bill; even worse, she had very heavy industry opposition in a newly drawn district and was defeated while trying for a second term.

Charlestonian Lucille Whipper was a dignified and articulate spokesman for several causes: women's and children's rights, education, abortion rights, and separation of state and church (despite the fact that her husband was a minister). She was a woman of my generation, a retired college adminstrator and an active member of the Black Caucus. We had a lot in common, including sons. Her son, a lawyer, ran for the legislature from a neighboring district. But unlike Billy, who followed me, her son served with her until she left to spend more time with an ailing husband.

Gilda Cobb-Hunter, of Orangeburg, was a social worker who arrived the session before I left and immediately made a name for herself. She took the lead on bills involving the environment, housing for the poor, women, and children. In no time at all, she became the chair of the Black Caucus. I personally wish that she had been more flexible and long-sighted on reapportionment, because the hard line she took resulted in the loss of many of her allies in the next election, which led to losses on those issues she espoused. But that is my view, not hers.

Jean Harris from Cheraw ran for the House after her husband left the Senate to become a circuit court judge. She defeated George Gregory, a leader of the Fat and Uglies. She was a charming Southern lady who worked very hard for her constituents and her town. We could depend on her support for education, the environment, and women's rights. She was a faithful and productive member of the Cultural Affairs Committee, and I was delighted that when I stepped down as chairman she stepped up and kept the committee healthy and strong until its funding was cut off in 1996. She died tragically of a massive stroke early in 1997, much too young. She was loved and respected by all.

In 1977 there were only ten women in the House, eight Democrats (seven white and one black) and two Republicans. There were no women senators. Twenty years later, the numbers had switched dramatically. There are twenty-one in the General Assembly: seven Democrats in the House (two white and five black) and eleven Republicans. There are three in the Senate: one white Democrat, one black Democrat and one Republican.

In my opinion, most of the Republican women now are more conservative, less interested in women's rights, less identified with specific issues, and more in lockstep with the party than the women featured in the University of Mississippi study. This is certainly true if compared to Carolyn Frederick and Joyce Hearn. There are exceptions: Republicans June Shissias and Holly Cork both refused to automatically follow the leader on every issue and strongly spoke out for women's rights and environmental protections. As a consequence both were openly opposed by the Republican party machine in the 1996 primary elections. June lost in the primary, running against an incumbent senator when she decided she could no longer stay in the House as it was; Holly narrowly won the primary against a candidate from the religious right who had purportedly been recruited by the Republican leadership. This opposition was not too surprising, for Holly did not support David Beasley in his race for governor two years before, and she opposed his policies on abortion, nuclear waste, and kindergarten funding during his first two years in office.

In my last few years in the House, some of the Republican women at least wavered and agonized when they had to choose between the leadership dictates and how they might have preferred to vote . . . though they usually went with the leadership in the final vote. I am told that even wavering and agonizing has decreased, replaced by lockstep obedience with a few exceptions on a few issues. I write this with sorrow, because women historically have been more independent, putting issues before partisanship. And isn't that why we want more women in politics? Of course this phenomenon of blind allegiance is a reflection of the body as a whole, men as well as women, national as well as state. Which is why so many independent-minded legislators at the state and national levels dropped out in 1996. Bill Bradley, who left the United States Senate, sums it up in his recent book when he says that the cantankerous bickering and lack of bipartisanship got to him. One senator doesn't make much difference in the large scheme of things these days, he said.

Pat Schroeder, who left Congress after twenty-four years, says much the same thing, but in even stronger words. No one listens to each other, no one relates to others, no one respects others' views, she said. Bitter partisanship created an atmosphere of "them against us": "I'm right and you're wrong." She concluded that she could do more on the outside than on the inside and decided to leave. These were the very words my son Billy used when he decided not to run for the South Carolina legislature last year.

My serendipitous connection with the NCSL Women's Network and the opportunity to meet people I would never otherwise have known and have experiences I never would have had gave me a better understanding of the place of women in society, but even more important, of myself. I learned that the weaknesses I saw in myself, which had inhibited me in so many ways, were common to women and could be overcome more easily if understood in that way. I learned the importance of ego building and self-confidence.

After finishing the first draft of this book I read Katherine Graham's *Personal History* and found myself saying "Yes," as she first described her lack of self-confidence and insecurities as a young woman and then her thoughts and experiences when, after her husband's death, she entered the world of men and took over his job. She admitted that her feelings of inadequacy were so great that often she didn't speak her views for fear she would be wrong or even boring. That's one fear that I didn't include in my own list of liabilities until, on reading her words, I realized this was part of my pattern also. Her personal reactions to being catapulted into the business world when she became publisher of the *Washington Post* were so similar to mine jumping into the political world, as was the slow process of overcoming these crippling fears. She described them with such depth, openness, and vividness that I have included a sampling of her thoughts to augment and underline the points I have tried to make in this and earlier chapters.

"I seemed to be carrying inadequacy as baggage." How many of us are pulled down by this feeling! "I still felt like a pretender to the throne, very much on trial. I felt I was always taking an exam and would fail if I missed a single answer." How often I asked myself if people saw through my posture of knowing what and how to do things. "What most got in the way of my doing the kind of job I wanted to do was my insecurity. Partly this arose from my particular experience [an unaffectionate mother who turned her children over to a nanny, and an insecure husband who put her down], but to the extent that it stemmed from the narrow way women's roles were defined, it was a trait shared by most women in my generation. We had been brought up to believe that our roles were to be wives and mothers, educated to think that we were put on earth to make men happy and comfortable and to do the same for our children." I hope this is changing. "I adopted the assumption of many of my generation that women were intellectually inferior to men, that we were not capable of governing, leading, managing anything but our homes and our children. Once married, we were confined to running houses, providing a smooth atmosphere, dealing with children, supporting our husbands. Pretty soon this kind of thinking—indeed, this kind of life—took its toll: most of us *became* somehow inferior. We grew less able to keep up with what was happening in the world. In a group we remained largely silent, unable to participate in conversations and discussions. Unfortunately, this incapacity often produced in women—as it did in me—a diffuse way of talking, an inability to be concise, a tendency to ramble, to start at the end and work backwards, to overexplain, to go on for too long, to apologize." It's painful to admit, but the description fits so many of us. And "Women traditionally also have suffered—and many still do—from an exaggerated desire to please, a syndrome so instilled in women of my generation that it inhibited my behavior for many years, and in ways still does. Although at the time I didn't realize what was happening, I was unable to make a decision that might displease those around me. For years, whatever directive I may have issued ended with the phrase 'if it's all right with you.' If I thought I'd done anything to make someone unhappy, I'd agonize. The end result of all this was that many of us, by middle age, arrived at the state we were trying most to avoid: we bored our husbands, who had done their fair share in helping reduce us to this condition, and they wandered off to younger, greener pastures."

Several years after Mrs. Graham became publisher of the *Post,* she was asked to speak at the Women's City Club of Cleveland on the suggested topic "The Status of Women." She responded, "It may be that I am inevitably saddled with this subject as it has, I must confess, come up before. It is one in which I am honestly not interested nor educated but it may well be that I should become so. . . . If you really insist on the status of women I'll try to adjust." She was the only woman in a world of men and had no female peers with whom to talk over the condition of working women. Several years later she began thinking things through with editorial writer and friend Meg Greenfield. They read a "bunch of books" and began to change their views. "There was no single dramatic moment that altered my views about women; rather, I just began to focus on the real issues surrounding the women's movement. However slow I was to learn—no doubt much too slow to suit many women—I finally became increasingly aware and involved. Looking back, I can't understand, except in the context of the times, why I wasn't quicker to recognize the problems." I moved more quickly in recognizing the problem than Mrs. Graham, possibly because I had worked with women before going into politics and possibly because I was elected to my position and had to be responsive to the constituency which helped elect me.

I quoted Mrs. Graham at length because she sums up well the roots—and consequences—of the influences that shape most women, certainly of our generation, without us even knowing it. Her experiences, so similar to mine although our backgrounds and responsibilities were so dissimilar, bears out the fact that these problems for women are universal. The only solution, for women who want to be not only their husband's wife and children's mother but to have their very own identity, is to have an understanding of all the forces at play. It also helps to know that the insecurities and fears we have are not just weaknesses of our own but were placed on us by the psychological straitjackets society wraps around us, bindings which are removable.

I for one am sorry that this knowledge came to me so late in my life, after I had raised my family. I might have recognized and done something about my symptoms of lack of self-esteem and self-confidence, rather than repeat the mistakes of my mother with my own children. They had to work their way out of the problems this caused, just as I did. Fortunately, in their own ways, and in their own time, they have succeeded.

CHAPTER 17

The Arts and State Government

In 1980, after two years of learning experiences on the NCSL Arts Committee, I suggested to Governor Riley that he create a South Carolina Task Force on the Arts. He was enthusiastic about the idea, for he had chaired the Arts Committee of the National Governors Association and understood the potential of such a project. The task force laid the foundation for building an infrastructure for the arts in South Carolina, though I must admit that I didn't consciously think "We must build an infrastructure for the arts" when I suggested the idea. I was really groping around, looking not only for allies in the legislature but also more visibility and clout for the South Carolina Arts Commission within state government.

The task force's mission was to examine what was going on in the arts in our state, to make recommendations to encourage and expand the arts and cultural activities in both the public and private sectors, and to encourage as much cooperation among all players as possible. Riley asked me to chair the effort and assigned Terry Peterson, head of his education division, to help us. We had no staff and no budget. By this time I was serving on lots of committees, and the bills I filed were stacking up, needing my attention. Not knowing how much of my time the task force would take, or how much time I would have to give to it, I suggested a cochair, and Riley appointed Carlanna Hendrick, a dynamic college history professor and chair of the State Library Commission. I couldn't have asked for a better partner.

Governor Riley created the Governor's Task Force on the Arts by executive order, with many supportive "whereases" stating our case and giving us a lot of latitude. "Whereas, the performing, visual and literary arts are an essential element of the quality of life in every state, a means of creative expression for artists, and a source of enjoyment for all . . ."; "Whereas, state government has a continuing interest in the availability of the arts and should encourage coordinated efforts among all levels of government fostering the arts, and can act to ensure an environment conducive to the freedom of artistic expression, enabling the arts to contribute to our cultural, educational and economic well-being"; and so on.

I had a say in selecting the twenty-four members, including three representatives and three House senators. My aim was to educate some key legislators, so as to have a core of support for any recommendations we might make to the legislature. There were slots for all the cultural agencies: S.C. Arts Commission, State Museum, S.C. State Library, S.C. Educational Television, and the Governor's School for the Arts. We also included all the "establishment" agencies which had the potential to include the arts in their programs: the Department of Parks, Recreation and Tourism; the State Development Board; the State Department of Education; the Commission on Higher Education, S.C. Department of Archives and History. Thanks to the direct involvement of the governor, the chairmen of these commissions and the executive directors of the agencies did not designate underlings but personally attended the meetings, which made for quicker decision making. There were also representatives of the governor and lieutenant governor and five public members, one of whom was Tunky Riley, a great worker who never missed a meeting. The list of categories for study included the appropriate level of state support for the arts; the level of demand for the arts; the place of arts in education; minorities and the arts; the role of government versus the private sector in supporting the arts; the need for a legislative committee on the arts; art in public places; the role of individual artists in the state; and rehabilitation of neighborhoods and historic preservation.

I had envisioned an agenda similar to the NCSL Task Force, but there were differences. Although we did meet in several arts-related sites around the state, such as museums and the Governor's School for the Arts, our main focus turned out to be creating dialogue among the state agencies so they would know better what was happening statewide and could interface with each other. The task force found more cultural activity existed than we had expected. But we found little cohesion among the players. Our very existence created a coalition which helped arts advocates, both public and private, to expand and move the arts forward at a surprising rate for our relatively poor state.

In our five-year existence, we built a satisfying list of accomplishments, the most important of which, I believe, was to bring the Arts Commission into the mainstream of South Carolina. We discovered the Arts Commission was doing a splendid job, but it was off in a corner of state government, often unnoticed by all but the most active participants in the state's cultural life. Even I, who had been actively involved for years in the arts in Beaufort knew very little about its programs. Our task force connected with the commission and led them into a strong working relationship with the State Development Board and Department of Parks, Recreation and Tourism, both of which had large budgets, many resources, and great industry connections. This networking resulted in cooperative ventures and a positive climate for the arts to grow and thrive, in both state government and the private sector.

We first developed a position paper on why government should be involved with the arts. We started with the pocketbook arguments, the bottom line, the typical approach of any committee headed by a legislator. We cited economic impact studies, which showed that spending money on the arts makes economic sense, that every dollar spent on the arts has an astounding multiplier effect in generating dollars (and jobs) within a community. For instance, at that time the state contributions to the Spoleto Festival USA in Charleston ranged from \$140,000 to \$180,000 a year, an investment on which it earned great returns. In 1983, it was estimated that Spoleto produced \$35 million in tourist dollars, created 600 new jobs, generated \$1 million in state sales tax revenue, and spawned more and better hotels and inns, more and better restaurants, more and better shops—all of which bring in more sales and income tax revenues to the state. Much of this can be attributed to the tourists and national, even international, press who attend Spoleto and spread the word, not just about the festival but the delights of Charleston itself. The free publicity goes way beyond what the state and local tourism and development boards can spend on advertising. It was easy to prove that Spoleto is an industry which deserved the same help as any other industry.

This fit hand in glove with another economic argument we touted, that the arts attract industry to an area or a state. To lay this out, we convened a meeting in Charleston in 1982, during Spoleto, and Governor Riley presided. Incredibly, as busy as he was, he stayed with us from the beginning to the end, many hours later. The focus was on the importance of a rich cultural environment in recruiting industry and expanding tourism. In our audience were members of the Development Board, the Department of Parks, Recreation and Tourism, the Arts Commission, the Governor's Office, and members of the business community. Marshall Doswell, a vice president of Springs Mills, South Carolina's great corporate benefactor of the arts, told us, "Good companies are composed of good people—good people who don't want to live in a cultural wasteland." Max Heller, then chairman of the State Development Board, agreed: "National priorities for relocating business used to be taxes, transportation and labor. Yes, those items are still on the list, but the quality of life factors—the arts and education—have equal position on the list."

New channels of communication were established that day between the public and private sectors, which led to other efforts down the road. One product of this new collaboration was a brochure produced by several agencies on the quality of life in South Carolina. Governor Riley and Max Heller put their words into action by inviting industrialists to Charleston during later Spoleto festivals. In addition to the usual golf and fishing, they put our culture on display as bait. When Governor McNair told me recently about how he got state agency heads to talk to each other and cooperate twenty years ago by creating interagency groups, I nodded and smiled and said yes, I know how productive that can be.

We trumpeted another reason why politicians should support the arts: because the public wants them to. Though we tend to think the public sees the arts as elitist, the polls show otherwise. We cited questions and answers in recent polls. Would you be willing to pay five dollars or more in tax money to fund the arts? Seventy percent of respondents said yes. Should state government assist arts organizations? Sixty percent said yes. Do you consider the arts a positive experience in a troubled world? Seventy-five percent said yes. Should schoolchildren be exposed to arts and cultural events? Ninety-three percent said yes. Should art courses be included in school budgets? Seventy-five percent said yes.

We made a survey of existing arts and arts facilities in those counties requesting funding for new or expanded arts facilities. The survey showed pleasant surprises, as well as disheartening voids. This information was then used by the governor in assessing requests for funding a cultural center, which resulted in a saving of state funds and a broader utilization of existing facilities. From that experience we proposed a bond bill to create a revolving fund so that state money would be apportioned for cultural facilities and historic preservation by need, rather than as political plums. But the legislature said no.

We also endorsed and then shaped the accommodations tax, also known as the bed tax bill, which had been lingering close to death for seven years as a result of filibusters. In researching what other states did, I found that several used bed tax revenues to support the arts. When Jean Meyers, the original author of the bill, left the legislature in disgust, I picked it up and added a section to allow the use of revenues for arts activities and cultural centers, based on a nugget of information I brought back from an NCSL meeting. The original bill called for all revenues to be spent on tourism promotion, and we easily made the case that the arts attracted and promoted tourism. Spoleto in Charleston, Brookgreen Gardens near Georgetown, the Greenville Museum with its Andrew Wyeth collection, and the McKissick Museum of Folk Art in Columbia all proved our point.

The revenues resulting from the bill that eventually passed could be spent only for specific purposes: publicity to increase tourism; promotion of the arts and cultural events; construction, maintenance, and operation of facilities for civic and cultural activities; law enforcement and fire protection, public restrooms, parks, and parking lots to meet the needs of tourists. The bottom line was that these revenues enabled cities and counties to enhance their environment, both physical and cultural, without residents picking up the whole tab in property taxes for tourism-related expenses.

Opposition to the bill over the years had come from several directions. The hotel industry felt that a two-percent bed tax would put them at a competitive disadvantage with neighboring states. But as the years rolled by, neighboring states levied even higher bed taxes, and that argument disappeared. One center of opposition was Hilton Head, a tourist destination in my county. Shortly after I filed the bill I received a letter from John Curry, who managed tourism-related properties, Angus Cotton, a Hilton Head hotel manager, and John David Rose, who was in both public relations and the resort business. They asked if I would meet with them to discuss the bill and the tax. Although they were opposed to the bill in its original form, Rose said, he knew there were ways to make it more palatable, perhaps even beneficial—if passage was inevitable. As the director of the Utah Travel Council, he saw a once-dying downtown Salt Lake City revive by using room tax revenues to build an arena, a convention hall, and a symphony hall. He said, "A shabby downtown area has been revitalized with a number of new hotels and shopping malls attracted by the new community facilities. Industry of all types has followed." He argued that if the room tax was used in this way in South Carolina he would strongly support it. But if the revenues were used as a supplement to the general fund or to reduce property taxes, he would fight it to the death. I agreed with his position. At last we had allies in the resort sector.

Opposition also came from those who did not trust local government. Local government in South Carolina can not levy any taxes other than the property tax without authorization by the legislature. As county responsibilities grow, counties are in a bind, trying to provide services without raising property taxes. And the legislature fights every attempt by local governments to find alternatives—such as a bed tax. Advocates for the bed tax bill, on the other hand, were the cities and counties where tourism services are costly, and their lobbyists, the municipal and county associations, fought for the right to find and use alternatives to the property tax to cover these costs.

Legislators from the smaller counties which did not have tourists formed another pocket of opposition. They said it would burden their constituents when vacationing in counties with the tax. But it turned out they were willing to look at the tax if somehow they could get a share of those revenues.

The Hilton Head contingent helped in the drafting of suggested changes. They came to public hearings and voiced their concerns and hopes, flying back and forth to Columbia in John Curry's plane. But more important, they lobbied their counterparts around the state, sold them on the changes we agreed to, and reduced the tourist industry's opposition considerably. We agreed to a formula to disburse the funds: only the first twenty-five thousand dollars would go to the general fund of the local government where the tax is generated; twenty-five percent of the remaining balance must go to a special fund to be used for promotion of tourism, and the remaining balance must be used for tourism-related expenditures spelled out in the bill. We agreed to require a two-thirds vote of the legislature to raise the tax beyond two percent in the future. And we included one more boost for the arts: we mandated that every county and municipal government have an accommodation tax advisory committee to decide how the money will be disbursed. And on that committee there must be at least one person representing the arts. A member of our task force, Fred Brinkman, who was the director of Parks, Recreation and Tourism, held workshops across the state for local governments, the public, and arts groups, explaining the law and encouraging arts groups to seize the opportunity to get a share of these funds. As a result of arts advocates sitting at the table when spending decisions are made, millions have been spent on cultural activities and facilities across the state since the bill passed.

All the funds collected are first sent to the state treasurer and placed in a special fund. To appease the smaller and the non-tourist counties, every county in the state was guaranteed a minimum of fifty thousand dollars from that fund; the remainder is sent back to areas where it was generated. This sweetening of the pot for every legislator helped pass the bill, as did our rules change to control filibusters. The bill finally passed, eight years after it was first introduced.

In 1995, Beaufort County collected over three million dollars in bed taxes, while across the state almost twenty-four million was collected—a large percentage of which came from the pockets of out-of-staters. (Of course, traveling South Carolinians pay bed taxes to other states.) My forte has never been bringing home the bacon for my district. But the three million dollars a year (and growing) I hope evens out that shortcoming, though that was not my target in filing the bill.

The years of networking among the members on the task force raised a lot of consciousness and resulted in some new strategies for promoting the arts. The Development Board spotlighted the arts in its national advertising. I remember the first such ad—Gian Carlo Menotti, the artistic director and founder of Spoleto, framed by a backdrop of Charleston, with the message "Another Italian has discovered America." The Department of Parks, Recreation and Tourism adopted a policy to highlight cultural events in their brochures and periodicals, which were widely circulated around the state and at welcome centers. We also proposed the reestablishment of the South Carolina Arts Foundation to help promote and widen support in the private sector for Arts Commission projects such as the State Art Collection program, which the commission established in 1970 to purchase the works of South Carolina artists and provide fellowships.

Legislators attempted legislation they would not have thought of, or dared to do, without the reinforcement which came from task force recommendations. We filed an art in public places bill, also called Percent-for-the Arts bill, whereby .5 percent of construction costs of state buildings would be used to place appropriate South Carolina artworks—paintings, sculpture, murals—in new buildings. Our arguments were that art in public places enhances and enriches spaces that otherwise would be cold and monotonous; that it creates a museum experience in the everyday lives of those who don't even think about going to museums; that buying art is provided for in building budgets, but most agencies buy decorator prints instead of original art. Why not buy South Carolina art and support South Carolina artists? When it looked unlikely that this bill would pass, we asked the State Budget and Control Board to implement a policy to "encourage setting aside a percent of construction costs of new buildings"—and they did, after we visited each member of the Board. At this writing, some agencies have followed this policy; most have not. Mandatory is better than optional for new ideas in this state. But we took what we could get. North Carolina did pass a percent-for-the-arts bill, but it was rescinded in 1995 when some legislators were unhappy about one of the funded projects.

We introduced consumer protection legislation requiring art dealers to provide specific information about prints and lithographs. This eventually passed when the task force became a legislative committee, with staff to work on the complicated details. We proposed that an "Artists at the Governor's Mansion" program be established to provide the thousands of visitors to the mansion the opportunity to see performances, exhibits, and demonstrations by S.C. artists and craftsmen. It was implemented immediately, with great help from Tunky Riley and the Arts Commission. Concerts and performances became part of most official functions at the mansion. It was not unusual to find a potter turning a wheel or a weaver sitting at a loom at the front door of the mansion on visitors' day, or a juggler or acrobat at an outdoor picnic. Sadly, this program all but disappeared when Riley left office.

We proposed the development of a comprehensive, five-year plan by the State Department of Education for evaluating and expanding the basic arts education program. We praised the significant steps which had been taken to include the visual arts and music in our public schools. And we suggested that these basic arts programs be expanded to include drama and dance, with professionally trained teachers in residency programs in all the arts areas. The first steps toward many of the programs we recommended were put into place by the Education Improvement Act .

In 1983, after sitting on a committee studying the feasibility of establishing a state film office, I urged support and assistance for this new endeavor. There were a few years of growing pains, during which I became a sounding board for intermittent complaints from both the director of the Film Office and the state agency wherein the office resided. The problems were eventually taken care of, though there were touch-and-go times. In 1987 Governor Campbell moved the office to the State Development Board, then vetoed its funds, citing a need for reorganization. After a hue and a cry, the office was reestablished. South Carolina is now known in Hollywood as a great state to make films.

I have pleasant firsthand knowledge of the activities of the film industry. Beaufort is one of the towns attracting the industry, due in part to the movie-adoptable books of Pat Conroy, written, and set, in Beaufort, most of which have been made into movies. Not only has Beaufort's tourism benefitted from these movies, but also they have brought fun and excitement to many of the city's citizens, myself included. As a result of my work with the Film Office, its director, Isabel Hill, invited me to meet with Barbra Streisand and company when they came to consider Beaufort as a possible location for her film version of *The Prince of Tides.* As we sat down to dinner, Streisand, having been told I was a friend of Pat Conroy's, asked me if I could think of a reason he would not return her phone calls. She wanted to talk to him to better understand his characters. The next day I was told the group was going to look at another location in another state, and the choice of Beaufort might be influenced by whether or not Barbra could talk with Pat. I called Pat's good friend and former English teacher, Gene Norris, who always knew how to find him. He got the message through to Pat, who contacted Barbra. Pat later said he had not returned her call because he thought those messages were a repeat of a friend's practical joke. I was rewarded for my intervention by being given a part (very small) in *The Prince of Tides,* which I parlayed into another (almost invisible) part in *Forrest Gump.* I missed the Beaufort opening night gala of *The Prince of Tides* and my film debut. I was in Washington, at a nuclear waste meeting.

I also had the pleasure of knowing the lovely Blythe Danner, who had major parts in *The Great Santini* and *The Prince of Tides*. Blythe lived in Beaufort for almost a year during the filming of *The Great Santini*. She put her children in the public schools and made many friends in the community. This was not the norm for movie stars. She must have made a supreme effort to mingle, because movie schedules are hectic, the work is exhausting, and the working hours don't conform to anyone else's life. My friendship with her was cemented when we found we both felt passionately about recycling, the environment, and choice on abortion. Several years ago, I invited her to come to Columbia to be the guest speaker at a dinner honoring business and industry leaders who contributed to the arts. A Beaufort environmental organization, hearing of this, asked her to come to Beaufort the day before to talk about recycling. She accepted both invitations, then agreed to also speak at a pro-choice luncheon in Columbia. Blythe charmed all three audiences. She had planned to leave Columbia early the next morning, but when I mentioned that I was on my way to a committee hearing on my solid waste and recycling bill, she changed her flight and stayed over to listen. After the hearing, where she sat at the back of a crowded room in which she could not hear much, I drove her to the airport.

In 1985, the task force took on a project which eventually put me in the unenviable position of doing battle with the University of South Carolina over state tuition aid for our artistically gifted students to attend the North Carolina School of the Arts (NCSA). The problem was turf protection and was reminiscent of the opposition to the proposal that we build one-library-instead-of-three proposal when I was on Beaufort County Council.

First some background. Years ago, the Southern states, lagging behind the rest of the country in education, decided it was impossible for every state to provide every citizen training in every discipline. They formed the Southern Regional Education Board (SREB) to develop a plan for cooperation between states rather than compete for scarce resources. Under this plan, if one state does not provide a degree program in a particular discipline, its students can attend schools in other states, paying the same tuition as the residents of the state they study in. SREB contracts for these exchanges. As a result, hundreds of South Carolina students are studying in veterinary, optometry, and mortician schools in other states, with South Carolina paying the out-of-state differential. Hundreds of out-of-state students come to South Carolina with similar help from their states. Obviously, when there is a limited number of students in a discipline, it costs the state much less to contract out this way than to build and operate another program, another school. Another motive for state subsidies to South Carolinians attending out-of-state schools, way back during the 1930s and 1940s, according to Walter Edgar's *South Carolina in Modern Age,* was to avoid integration and building graduate schools for black students. Black students were given subsidies to attend schools in other states!

In most states, there is a coordinating body for higher education. In South Carolina, it is the Commission on Higher Education (CHE), which must approve all new programs at public colleges and universities in the state, as well as develop SREB contracts with other states. CHE was created as a weapon against turf protection and needless duplication.

Back to my story. In 1983, a member of the Governor's Task Force on the Arts, Arthur Magill, one of the leading philanthropists to the arts in South Carolina, sent all our members an issue of *Smithsonian Magazine,* which had a story about NCSA. He asked, "Why can't South Carolina have a school like this?" We read the story with envy and paid a visit to this unusual school for professional performing artists. We met with the school administrators as well as Bill Friday, the president of the North Carolina university system, within which NCSA existed. We were impressed not only by the students, who came from forty-one states and many countries, but by the facilities, which cost over thirty million dollars of public and private money. We learned that the North Carolina legislature's annual appropriation to the school had grown from $335,000 the first year to $7 million the past year. It didn't take us long to conclude that with so many other urgent needs in South Carolina, and without private resources such as North Carolina's tobacco family fortunes, we couldn't build a comparable school. We asked the staff of CHE for advice.

They told us that the number of students in South Carolina who wanted to be professional performing artists was limited. And that this was the perfect example of the wisdom of SREB contracts between states. That year there were eleven college-level and four high school students from South Carolina at NCSA, studying music, theater, and dance. If we paid the difference ($2,500) between the in-state and out-of-state tuition, we could provide a first-rate education for all of them for $37,500 a year. North Carolina subsidizes every student (including ours) by $10,000. What a good deal for us! So CHE put $50,000 in their budget to fund this program, believing a few more students would apply if they had help. The governor joined in the request. The legislature agreed to $30,000.

The following year, USC protested this funding. Frank Borkowski, the provost and a leading proponent of a stronger music department at USC, asked to be heard at a commission meeting. CHE listened to his arguments—USC had a splendid arts program and intended to make it even stronger. Sending good students to another school in another state would make this more difficult, demoralizing the USC faculty, he said.

I also asked to be heard. I said that USC did indeed have fine programs in music, theater, and the arts, but they were not the same as the intensive, conservatory-type training given at NCSA, where all students were selected by audition, and all were preparing to be professional, performing artists. I said every university cannot be all things to all people, and they must make choices. I sympathized with USC for worrying about the possibility that the "cream of the crop" of arts students might go somewhere else, but my perspective was different. My concern was not what was best for the university, but what was best for the students in furthering their careers. A survey of the twenty students at NCSA showed that not one had applied to USC; they had applied to Juilliard, Oberlin, and Indiana, all with programs similar to NCSA but different from USC.

CHE went with my arguments and again voted to request funding from the legislature. The Ways and Means Committee went along with their request, but when the appropriations bill came to the House floor, the juggernaut lobbying effort of USC rolled over us. State universities have the best lobbies in town. They have a built-in constituency—alumni legislators as well as legislators with regional campuses in their district. They won. The line item for NCSA was removed. I was disappointed on principle. CHE was created to methodically compare programs and make recommendations so as to avoid duplication and conserve limited resources. When legislators don't follow its recommendations, decisions become political, duplication runs rampant, and turf protection wins over reason. I also foresaw that the university's next step would be to bring larger requests for funding programs similar to those of NCSA. And I was disappointed as an arts advocate. If the state finds it is in its interest to help those who want to be professional veterinarians and optometrists and morticians, why is it not important to help those who want to be professional artists? Surely they will contribute to our tourist economy, our film industry—and even more to our quality of life.

Some task force members spoke out against USC's provincialism, and editorials were written. The *Florence Morning News* (Carlanna Hendrick's home newspaper), among others, criticized USC for its "small-mindedness" in defying CHE. When the budget arrived at the Senate, Senator Waddell, at my pleading, put back twelve thousand dollars but specified it was to be used only for high school students. That year, nine high school students were admitted, as well as sixteen college students who had expected aid. The small pot was divided among the high schoolers.

At the same time this was going on, the Governor's School for the Arts in Greenville, a fine summer school for gifted arts students and their teachers, began pushing for a year-round, state-funded boarding high school for the arts. And the politically powerful Greenville business community was pressing on the governor and legislature to fund it. Was this a new, but different, turf battle? I thought so, and I opposed starting up this new school for the same reasons I had supported an arrangement with NCSA—and because there were too many unanswered questions. How many high school students are there in South Carolina who are committed to becoming professional artists, willing to leave home, willing to put themselves through the grinding schedule, and talented enough to excel? After twenty years of proven excellence, NCSA had 233 students all told, and only 136 of them were North Carolinians. Would we have to import students from other states to make the numbers work? Would students choose us over NCSA, and would we have to subsidize them? Or would the new school fill the slots with gifted and talented who did not plan a professional career but wanted the arts education as an add-on to their academic careers? Was that the best investment for our state? And is it good educational policy to pull out the gifted and talented, who now add so much to their schools and the education of other students? Would magnet schools in every region be better? For the students? For the schools? For the state? If the Governor's School was meant to be comparable to NCSA, how would we fund it?

By 1993 North Carolina had spent over forty millions dollars on buildings and equipment for NCSA and had launched another twenty-five million dollar drive. Its annual state appropriation for operations had risen to twelve million dollars. Added to that were another three million in private funds. Was South Carolina willing to commit to such funds? Can our private sector raise such funds? And if so, will it be at the expense of every other South Carolina cultural cause? (Having served on the board of Spoleto Festival for years I was sensitive to just how difficult it was to raise even a few million dollars when the festival's life was in jeopardy.) And if not, how would the new South Carolina school compare to the NCSA in faculty, facilities, programs? I raised these questions for several years, admittedly feeling awkward doing so, risking my reputation as a leading arts advocate in the legislature. But I was not a lone voice. Educators who worked with the gifted and talented also expressed concerns.

A committee, chaired by Greenville senator Verne Smith, was created by the legislature to study the matter. But in my admittedly biased opinion the questions they asked were shallow, so the conclusions were unconvincing (to me). By this time the Joint Legislative Committee on Cultural Affairs (which replaced the task force—more of this later) was by then chaired by Representative Jean Harris, who succeeded me. She did some preparatory work for this study and was asked to endorse the findings of the senator's committee. It was probably the only arts issue we disagreed on. She went along with their findings. In 1996, Governor Beasley pressed forward and requested funding for the year-round school. The legislature, prodded by several powerful Greenville legislators, found the funds. Ironically, that was the year the governor and some of the same legislators worked to keep the nuclear waste dump in Barnwell open because, they said, we needed those revenues to fund education needs. Now that this school has been established, I worry that tuition aid to our students at NCSA will be discontinued.

Perhaps the advocates for a year-round school for the arts are right and I am wrong. But I don't think so. In 1997, as I write this, the Governor's School for Mathematics and Science in Hartsville, a proven success, is fighting for a $300,000 line item in the state budget, after the House Ways and Means Committee failed to fund it. But the Governor's School for the Arts was given $1 million. Now that's power politics. But when the state budget tightens and priorities shift along with leadership changes, will the school be able to increase its budget

to make it comparable to NCSA, or even sustain its present funding? The experience of the Governor's School for Math and Science leaves me skeptical.

The most dramatic action the task force took was the creation of the Joint Legislative Committee on Cultural Affairs (JLCCA) in 1985. My Crazy Caucus friend Palmer Freeman, a member of the task force, sidled up to me one day as we were considering the appropriations bill on the floor of the House and said, "Let's put money in the budget to create a legislative committee on the arts. What shall we call it?" I was so preoccupied with thinking of a name that I didn't have time to dwell on what an audacious idea this was. This is not the usual procedure. Most amendments appropriating money that pop up on the floor are angrily struck down by Ways and Means Committee members. But we scurried around and talked to some Ways and Means members, and they agreed not to oppose such a move—possibly because I was one of them, and it is a custom to yield to members' requests if not too outrageous, or possibly because our request was very modest. We asked for only one modestly paid staff person. Our amendment went up on the screen, and miraculously it passed, albeit with some members quietly grumbling and most not even realizing what had happened. Its success was probably due to the element of surprise, by its not being in the budget bill before debate began. (There are those whose sport it is to search for and cut out everything they consider wasteful, and this would have been a choice target for them.) After we finished the budget, I rushed over to the Senate to urge the senators on the Arts Task Force to protect this amendment when it came to them. They did, and the Joint Legislative Committee on Cultural Affairs (I wish I'd had more time to think of a better name) was created. I was elected chairman and Senator John Land vice chairman.

The task force had existed by the grace of the governor. Its life span was uncertain, dependent on the next governor, whoever that might be. The Committee on Cultural Affairs, on the other hand, was written into law. This not only institutionalized culture in the legislature—very important in a state where the legislature is the seat of power—but now there were five House members and five Senators actively involved in cultural issues. At least until the legislature decided otherwise.

As all cultural bills were being sent by the speaker to the House Education Committee, following earlier recommendations of the task force, we stipulated in the amendment that at least one member must be a member of the Education Committee and at least one must serve on Ways and Means. For funding is the ultimate make-or-break decision on everything. In this way we put our advocates in place to be part of the first deliberations of all bills we had an interest in, since it is in the committees that bills are changed, shaped, passed, or killed. And once passed out of the comittee, it is the chairman or subcommittee chairman, not the author, who presents the bill on the House floor. There is an advantage to this. There are some in the legislature who are reflexively turned off by arts-related bills, as well as by me and my ilk. By having others explain and move for passage, the support is broadened and the bill has a better chance of passing.

My first responsibility as chairman was to find a director. This was my first experience in hiring, other than secretaries at home who were already my friends. There were several good candidates, which was surprising considering the meager salary we offered. With guidance from the director of research, we zeroed in on Susan Conaty-Buck, a young woman who had been an arts administrator in Massachusetts and in Columbia. She was quick to learn, a good listener, and had all the instincts to make her a successful operative in a political world in which everyone was competing for attention and money. Not only was she suitably deferential, she was also beautiful, both assets in our legislature.

Our committee's official mandate was very similar to that of the task force, with the major thrust to coordinate and increase cooperation among all agencies involved in cultural affairs. As a legislative committee we had more clout and a greater presence than the task force in making recommendations for programs, legislation, and the use of resources of state agencies. Together with the Arts Commission, we formed the base of a cultural infrastructure. We had an advisory committee, representing the core cultural agencies, with whom we met regularly to exchange ideas, share information, and help each other with projects.

We also networked with the State Development Board, constantly reminding them of the edge cultural activities provide in attracting industry and the advantages of showcasing cultural resources in efforts to recruit and retain major industry. To ensure this point of view would be represented in their everyday considerations, we filed a bill to put one member of our committee on the Development Board. For two years we went round and round on this issue, with Governor Campbell's staff and his close friend Dick Greer, who chaired the board, telling us they were working on it. The problem may have been that seats on the board were the most competitive of any state board, political plums not to be given away to just anyone. Or it may have been my lack of rapport with the governor. It never came to pass.

We facilitated a coalition of the Arts Commission, the legislature, and the State Department of Education to bring arts in education to all students in South Carolina, an effort which culminated in the Arts in Basic Curriculum, or ABC program, a model for the country. The effort to bring the arts into the schools actually began in 1977, when the legislature passed the Education Finance Act. That was the first bill I worked on as a freshman legislator, but I can take no credit for the inclusion of the arts. It was State Superintendent of Education Charlie Williams who urged that funding for art and music teachers be included. This laid the groundwork for further programs, the product of a committed Arts Commission, under the direction of Scott Sanders, working with committed and able arts educators, starting at the top and spreading down to administrators and teachers in the field.

All these people not only work hard at their jobs, but they have built as sophisticated and successful a grassroots lobby as any I have seen. Unlike industry lobbying, they have no money to spend on entertaining or hiring professional lobbyists. They do it themselves, joining with local arts councils and interested parents. They are important partners in our cultural infrastructure, and they have a great impact on the legislators. (In 1997 Betty Plumb of Rock Hill, an active volunteer, became the first Executive Director of the S.C. Arts Alliance, which has increased their ability to follow legislation and organize the troops.)

In 1984, the Education Improvement Act put in place funding for the academically and artistically gifted and talented. In 1986, our Committee on Cultural Affairs initiated, again in partnership with the Arts Commission and State Department of Education, a comprehensive survey of what is available in arts education in every public school in the state. In early 1987, the Arts Commission initiated its "Canvas of the People," regional meetings across the state which served as public forums on the arts. Arts in education was at the top of everyone's list at all the meetings. Educators, artists, and arts councils testified to the need to provide a comprehensive arts education for all students if South Carolina was to have stable arts organizations, a climate where artists can make a living, and, most important, well-rounded citizens. Committee on Cultural Affairs members participated in meetings in their own districts—a very good consciousness-raising experience for the legislators. Also in 1987, our committee's survey on arts education was completed. The recommendation of the volunteer advisory committee was that a comprehensive arts education should be provided to every child in South Carolina.

So, in March of 1987, based on the input from the canvas meetings and our committee's survey, the South Carolina Arts Commission applied for and received a planning grant from the National Endowment for the Arts, one of sixteen states to receive such a grant. By coincidence, I had been invited to sit on the NEA panel considering these competitive grant proposals from all the states. Almost all the other panelists were arts educators or artists, and it was interesting to me to hear their perspective on the positive and negative sides of each grant proposal. I was the only state legislator. Of course, when a grant from the state of a panelist was discussed, that panelist left the room. I remember no promotion of their states among the panelists. It may have been there, but I didn't hear it. I do remember a few of the educators being narrowly focused, unable to allow themselves to accept creative proposals because of the regulations and red tape in their bureaucracies.

The staff and other panelists seemed interested in having a legislator's point of view, because so often these grants must be matched with state funding controlled by legislatures. The following year I was invited to serve again, but I wasn't able to. I was asked to suggest another legislator, and I passed on the name of Mary Zhogby from the Alabama legislature, who had been on the NCSL Arts Task Force. She accepted and enjoyed the experience, she told me later.

South Carolina won one of the grants in a very competitive field. With the grant funds in hand, a state steering committee was appointed and began to develop a plan to incorporate arts into the basic curriculum (called the ABC plan). With good political acumen, the Arts Commission appointed a legislator to chair it. "Hoss" Nesbitt, a former school administrator, was both a member of the Committee on Cultural Affairs and the House Education Committee. Working in tandem with the Arts Commission and the State Department of Education, the steering committee spent a year developing a plan, which the NEA ranked number one in the country. The state was awarded a second grant to implement the plan.

In 1989 another blue-ribbon committee was appointed to develop an additional education reform package, the "Target 2000 Education Reform Act," which some called the Son of EIA. Representative Nesbitt prevailed upon them to insert his committee's ABC plan into their package, and in this way, funding for the plan was provided by the legislature. None of this could have happened without the State Department of Education and Arts Commission working together. And legislative support every step of the way was enormously helpful. This close interagency cooperation placed South Carolina, to the surprise of all, in the national forefront in arts education.

The Committee on Cultural Affairs also worked on an assortment of legislation. The first year we filed a few bills, researched others, and built bridges with everyone we could. One early bill we sponsored was the Abandoned Cultural Property Act to set procedures for the many museums that didn't know what to do with the rooms full of unreclaimed art and artifacts contributed or loaned to them. Our bill was similar to those put in place in a number of states during the 1970s and early '80s, giving the museums legal title to objects that had been in their collection for a long time. The problem was that many of these objects had no deed of gift or other document of legal ownership. The Abandoned Cultural Property Act allowed museums to petition publicly that items which had resided in the institution as part of their collections and had been cared for and displayed as property of that particular museum, and which had no known owner to return them to, could be declared abandoned and established as the property of that particular museum. In South Carolina, with its long history of museums (the Charleston Museum is the oldest in the United States), there were numerous items of questionable ownership held by museums. The South Carolina Federation of Museums requested our help on this, and we voted the necessary procedures, which they developed, into law.

At the suggestion of Dr. George Terry of the University of South Carolina's McKissick Museum, which concentrates on folk art, we introduced a bill in 1986 to establish the S.C. Folk Heritage Award, to be sponsored by the General Assembly. This award was modeled after one that was established by several states and the Smithsonian Institute to recognize significant contributions to folk culture and heritage. A number of the earliest recipients of the national award happened to be natives of South Carolina, and it was felt that our state should have a comparable program to recognize these fine contributors to our heritage. There were programs in the state honoring artists, but no recognition of folk artists. The award gave official recognition to individuals or groups who "have learned traditional skills within their communities and practiced these arts and crafts with uncommon excellence over their lifetimes." I was excited by the idea of an award that calls attention to the men and women who preserve and perpetuate the authentic artistic traditions of their ancestors and their communities and who help retain much of the good and worthy traditions specific to South Carolina culture. The awards were only to be given to folk artists living and practicing their craft within South Carolina, and the emphasis was on maintaining or stimulating a craft or cultural heritage to a higher level of artistic achievement and a wider audience. Each year up to four artists would be given awards, plus an optional award for advocacy of folk arts in South Carolina. These awards are presented, with great pomp and ceremony, in the hall of the House at a joint meeting of the General Assembly. It is the best attended of the many joint assemblies we have, because there is always a performance of one winning group—be it banjo players, gospel singers, fiddlers, dancers—and the legislators happily clap and stomp along with them. We also had winners who were quilters, boat builders, potters, weavers, and shrimp net knotters, and their work is exhibited on the first floor of the State House. This award, renamed the Jean Laney Harris Folk Heritage Award in 1997 in honor of the late Jean Harris, brings the arts to life for the legislators. The program is still popular, with legislators competing to nominate their local folk artists for this award. Inspired by our success with this, I recommended consideration of a state crafts store, and although I did little more than serve on an advisory committee and cheer at the few meetings I could attend, others worked very hard, and there is now a thriving Artisans Center in Walterboro which features juried crafts and demonstrations by artisans.

We researched legislation, introduced by other legislators, which in some way impacted on the arts. One tough one was the Obscene Material bill, which changed the standards of what is obscene in relation to artistic, literary, scientific, or political materials. And we helped with a bill which provided immunity from civil suit for directors and trustees on nonprofit organizations. This was seen as particularly helpful to cultural organizations which have many volunteers and limited funds to pay liability insurance. We pushed for funding for the artistically gifted and talented through the budget process, and our members served on the many committees created by the Department of Education, teachers, parents, and advocates to deal with these issues.

How did we get involved in so many issues? Susan Conaty-Buck, our committee director, checked every piece of new legislation for possible impacts on the arts and other issues within our mandate. Research staff from standing committees came to her for advice and help where there were obvious connections. We had a large advisory committee which brought new issues to our meetings or came to us for help. We did a lot of outreach.

We also monitored the budgets of all the core cultural agencies. For several years I chaired the subcommittee of Ways and Means which handled all those budgets. When the appropriations bill left the

House, our director followed it over to the Senate, where she monitored changes and was available to answer questions. She also alerted our members if lobbying was needed. It is a slight comfort to know that although most of the members of our cultural affairs committee are gone, and the Committee on Cultural Affairs is gone, Henry Brown, who was on our committee, is chairman of Ways and Means at this writing. The arts community is counting on him to hold the fort as well as Senator Land, formerly vice chair of the Committee on Cultural Affairs, who is a senior member of the Senate Finance Committee. So far so good. A January 1998 report released by the National Assembly of State Arts Agencies on state rankings in arts appropriations show that South Carolina was eighteenth in the nation and third in the South in the per capita spending on the arts.

In our first year, we published two research reports: a survey of the status of arts education in South Carolina's public schools and a survey of nonprofit cultural organizations, festivals, professional artists, and business participation in cultural funding. In both we collected information and made recommendations for action.

In our second year, we commissioned the Division of Research of the University of South Carolina to do an economic impact study of the cultural industry in South Carolina. Their findings amazed even us true believers. There were over six thousand jobs in the culture industry, with direct expenditures of $127 million. This activity brought in two million dollars in sales tax revenues alone, plus income and other taxes paid by the holders of the jobs. Add to that the indirect spending, estimated by the conservative multiplier of 1.92 to be $244 million. Additionally, over fifty thousand volunteers gave of their time. Culture was an industry with a huge economic impact, and this study was a tool to recruit support for it. The report came out in 1988 just before Governor Campbell's state of the state address, and he used it to elaborate on the importance of the arts in economic development.

We created a Business and the Arts Award to encourage the private sector to support arts organizations and artists in our state. The awards program recognized and honored businesses, small and large, whose dedicated partnership with the arts included such activities as contributing funds, establishing art collections, donating in-kind services and goods, serving on cultural boards, purchasing artworks for public view, and funding scholarships to artists, among others. The awards were presented annually at elegant dinners attended by 250 to 300 people. We had interesting speakers, such as Blythe Danner and Jim Ferguson, the former CEO of General Foods. We had entertainment showcasing talented young people and good press coverage. There was real competition among business and industry people for these awards. This program died in 1995 when a weakened Arts Foundation, which had cosponsored the dinners and handled the funding, dropped out, and the Cultural Affairs Committee's existence became uncertain. Although the program is gone, I hope the ideas and interest it cultivated will continue until someone else picks up the ball. At this time, some local arts councils have instituted similar, but simpler, recognition programs.

Over the next few years the committee ventured into new partnerships and new programs. At the request of the Department of Archives and History, we strengthened the program for protecting public records, and, in another piece of legislation, we encouraged preservation of historic buildings through local option property tax incentives. We worked with the Institute of Archeology and Anthropology on several projects. We were asked to straighten out the financial problems of the historic Old Exchange Building in Charleston—and amazingly, with the help of many people, we did.

The Arts Commission, in partnership with the State Development Board and the S.C. Downtown Development Association, asked us to host a meeting to discuss ways to bring new awareness of the cultural resources in poor rural areas. Out of this grew the Cultural Visions for Rural Communities Task Force. The Cultural Visions project was modeled after the ABC project and because of the success of ABC, the Arts Commission applied to the NEA and received a special grant designed to support development of the arts in underserved areas. The grant enabled the Cultural Visions Task Force to help rural communities discover their own cultural uniqueness, to create a pride of place and a cultural vibrancy critical to industrial recruitment and retention—and which the Board of Tourism recognized as a great tourism attraction. This project, chaired by Ben

Boozer, the director of the S.C. Downtown Development Association, brought together some thirty state agencies, including the Development Board, the Department of Parks, Recreation and Tourism, the Arts Commission, McKissick Museum, the State Museum and S.C. Archives and History. Working with the state agencies are the S.C. Humanities Council and the Downtown Development Association in a unique public and private partnership. It is still in existence, trying to identify and preserve the traditions, rituals, legends, and lifestyles of the rural areas of the state. Most projects are successful, some aren't.

When our director Susan resigned in 1988 to follow her husband to a job in another state, I felt I could never replace her. I was wrong. Len Marini appeared, bringing wonderful and different skills to the position. The committee continued to earn respect and credibility in the legislature and in state government. Through those years I, other committee members, or Susan or Len served on many task forces and committees which we had created or partnered with, and made lots of speeches all over the state about what we were doing. Year after year the National Conference of State Legislatures invited either our legislators or staff to take part in conferences and workshops. I was invited to serve on the Southern Arts Federation Board, which in turn recommended me as a speaker at the Southern Legislative Conference, to tell legislators from other Southern states what we were doing in South Carolina and how we were doing it. Both the Southern Arts Federation and its funding source, the NEA, had designated arts in education as a priority; because South Carolina was seen as a model, they hoped we could stimulate other states to follow our lead.

My favorite story about South Carolina and the arts during this period was told by a staff member of the South Carolina Arts Commission who, while attending a meeting in New York, overheard a stranger in an elevator say, "Have you heard about the arts in South Carolina? They're really way ahead of everyone." At last we were ahead of, not behind the rest of the country in something.

I resigned as chair of the Committee on Cultural Affairs in 1991 to take over the chairmanship of the Joint Legislative Committee on Energy. I didn't know how much longer I would stay in the legislature, and there was one last energy issue I wanted to work on. Cultural Affairs would be in good hands with any of several members who were interested in chairing it. Jean Harris won the chairmanship, and Len Marini stayed on as director—they were a very good team. The sad news is that in 1996 a new governor, a new legislature, and a new agenda defunded the committee, along with most of the other joint committees, including the Energy Committee. Our little group of legislator-defenders of the arts is no longer held together by law and staff. The cultural agencies will have to find other ways to keep the General Assembly informed of their existence and their needs. The South Carolina Arts Commission and a vibrant grassroots constituency that grew during the good years will help fill the void. The void caused by the loss of the energy committee, on the other hand, will be harder to fill, for there are just a few environmental organizations to follow energy issues and advocate for the environment as a counterbalance to the special interest lobbies which dominate energy issues in the legislature.

I put a lot of hard work into nurturing the arts in the state, but received rewards far greater than my efforts. How nice it is to be in another section of the state and have someone, friend or stranger, come up to me and say, "Thank you for what you did for the arts." I received two Governor's Elizabeth O'Neill Verner Awards for contributions to the arts, one for me and one for my committee. When I received the first one in 1980, I said in my two allotted minutes:

"I can't think of any award I would rather have than this one—and I can't think of a place I'd rather receive it than the hall of the legislature. This occasion brings to full circle the relationship of the arts to my life. I did not fully appreciate what people meant when they said on such occasions that they only wished their parents could be there. Now I do.

"When I was growing up in New York City, our family life was full of musicians and music, artists and art. But when I married and moved to little Beaufort, South Carolina, we all assumed that this part of my life was over.

"However, over the years I found kindred spirits, and we worked together to bring music and art and theater and films to Beaufort. And they were the same people, and I see some of them here today, who ran my campaign and helped put me in the legislature where I can work for the arts on a broader scale.

"I wish my parents were here to see that even though I chose a country road over the city streets, I still managed to follow in their footsteps."

CHAPTER 18

Other Elections

As I worked on my various bills, issues, and projects, I appreciated the advantage I had over most other legislators—I had the luxury of free time. While they struggled every two years to raise money, build campaign teams, and go out on the campaign trail, I was given five marvelous "free rides," with no opposition for twelve years. Just as I was an atypical House member, I was also an atypical candidate. So many politicians say they love campaigning more than any other part of politics. They love pressing the flesh, the chase, the debates, the competition. But not I. I was not a toucher, a hugger, a backslapper, and I never learned to be really comfortable in that role of greeting strangers, knocking at doors, and handing out literature at shopping centers.

And I never disciplined myself to file away names in my memory. Because my picture was in the newspapers regularly, as were my columns, people remembered my face and name. I was a public person, called "Harriet" by everyone. But I was never sure if I should know their names, if I had met them before. This was especially difficult when going door to door. Once inside, sitting in the kitchen or living room chatting, I was glad I'd had made the effort, because I always learned something new about a person, a neighborhood, a problem, a success (or failure) of some project I sponsored. For me it was like jumping into the pool and enjoying the swim once I became acclimated to the cold water.

I did enjoy meeting with small groups, talking about issues, and answering questions, and was always relieved when attendees wore name tags. I did not enjoy asking people for endorsements and money. There was always the risk of being refused, which I tried to avoid even when

I should have been feeling secure. But what I enjoyed most of all in not having to campaign was having the luxury of free time. I had time to develop issues, go to conferences, work on projects. I had time to read, play tennis, be with family and friends, take a vacation, make tomato sauce when the tomato crop was in or pickles when the cucumbers arrived. Herbert's patients brought the cucumbers; we picked the tomatoes in a patient's fields as soon as the professional pickers left, and before the fields were plowed up.

I believe my newspaper columns, even though irregular, may have staved off challengers, though I was not so farsighted as to have thought of writing them for that reason. There were other benefits, as well. In order to write them, I had to really clarify the subject matter in my own mind, which made me better informed about the issues. But the columns also educated my public about the issues, the system, and me. Undergirding my entire political career was the conviction, central to the philosophy of the League of Women Voters, that the healthiest democratic society is one where the voters are informed and active participants. I liked the thought that perhaps my educational efforts made a contribution towards healthier government. Those constituents who read my columns could know what the issues were, know where I stood on them, and why. Many saw me as their spokesman—as one of them, not just one of those politicians. Often people came up to me on the street or at the post office and told me that they didn't agree with everything I did or said, but they thought I was hardworking, honest, smart, and looking out for their interests. And then they thanked me for writing the columns, for serving in the legislature. What more could I ask for?

But it was inevitable, as Beaufort became more and more Republican, that the Republican Party leaders would no longer allow me to go unchallenged. They felt their numbers warranted that seat. Carroll Campbell, who was elected governor in 1986, was dedicated to building the Republican Party and increasing the number of Republicans in the legislature. The state Republican Party judged that I was one of the most vulnerable, because of the number of Republicans in my district, but what they didn't know was that included in those numbers were many Republicans in Beaufort who liked me and my positions on issues. In 1987 I heard rumors the local Republican Party was out recruiting a candidate to run against me, and the most likely challenger would be Ron Atkinson, a home builder and chairman of Beaufort County Council. I started to prepare.

By January 1988 I had formed a two-hundred-person steering committee. The names, in very small type, filled the bottom half of my new letterhead—which looked a little silly, but the quality and quantity of supporters who willingly gave me their names was stunning. There was one deficit in being unopposed for twelve years. I had not personally kept up with my growing constituency as House members normally do who are opposed every two years. There were many new people who may have read my columns and press reports but did not know me personally. I hoped that the list of two hundred prominent, respected people from all sectors of the community would be a shield—at least until I had time to get out to meet the new voters—against what I knew would be a bitter, partisan campaign.

My campaign chairman was Patricia Battey, the wife of a partner in the Harvey law firm which had not supported me in my election bid twelve years ago. In fact, her husband, Colden, had sided with my opponent when that election was contested. My treasurer was Jim Neighbors, president of a local bank, and his politics were somewhere between conservative Democrat and Republican. I knew the drumbeat of the state Republican Party would be that all Democrats are big-spending, high-taxing, antibusiness liberals and that the local party would follow suit and try to pin this label on me. I felt my first line of defense was to find conservative businessmen who knew my record and would stand up for me. I also knew my natural base of women, educators, and blacks had to be organized. Susan Graber, my longtime friend who had links with these groups, was my campaign manager.

I held a press conference, declared my intention to run for a seventh term, and introduced my team. It was very early in the season to do this, but the idea was to make a preemptive strike to alert the Democratic Party that I was running and was strong. As I hoped, no opposition on that front appeared, so I did not have the additional worry that sitting legislators often have of trying to campaign in a party primary in June while the legislature, which continues nonstop into June, was in session. My only contest would be in the general election in November, and I would have the summer to campaign.

That legislative year became tense and testy as the Republicans and several conservative groups which were allied with them politicized every issue and every vote. Issues were brought to the forefront, such as prayer in the school, abortion, the Confederate flag, tax cuts, automobile insurance, and environmental regulations, and we Democrats knew that records of all votes, including procedural votes and double-edged amendments were going to be used against us in the next election if we voted the "wrong" way. This is old hat now, but ten years ago it was a new tension we had to learn to deal with and adapt to. Never had it been more important to keep in touch with our constituents.

On the home front, I was being sniped at more openly than before. The Reverend Phil Spry, minister of the Community Bible Church, came to Columbia to testify against my comprehensive health education (including sex education) bill. He introduced himself as chair of the school district's Sex Education Implementation Committee, failing to mention he was a minister of the Bible Church. He had sought and secured appointment to that chairmanship from a school board dominated at that time by members of the religious right. He was an outspoken critic of providing information to students about contraception as a method of preventing unwanted pregnancy and sexually transmitted diseases, and, as any fundamentalist, he saw no middle ground. He told the Senate committee that I did not represent the views of a majority of the Beaufort County residents, but that he did. I responded in a newspaper interview that I was amazed at this claim, for I felt he represented the narrow religious view of a small group of people, while I had represented the whole community for eleven years, and I felt that being the number-one state in the nation in terms of teenage pregnancy required more than a "Just Say No" policy. This was a very important issue with me, and I believe with most of my constituents. The religious right legislators drove Nell Smith and me crazy as they offered amendment after crippling amendment to weaken our bill. In order to get it passed, we ended up with several loopholes, one of which the Beaufort School Board discovered. They found they did not have to use the recommended textbooks and we ended up with a book titled *Sex Respect*—and the notoriety of being one of the only counties in the state where the teenage pregnancy rate went up, not down. What an irony. So it was a bittersweet victory: I won on sex education on the state level, but lost in my hometown. As I mentioned in an earlier chapter, within a few years, that was rectified.

Because the religious right candidates for the Beaufort School Board had captured the Republican nominations (this was in 1986, during the earliest days of stealth candidates) while hiding their religiously directed agendas during the campaign, because we had so many newcomers who voted a straight Republican ticket without knowing much about local candidates or their agendas, and because the Republican primary turned out to be the only election, due to the lack of Democratic candidates in the overwhelmingly Republican districts, I thought this was a good time to separate partisan politics from school board elections, as is done in many other school districts. I filed a bill to make our school board elections nonpartisan, just as our city elections were. Partisan politics was keeping many valuable potential candidates from running, people who were primarily interested in education but had no party allegiances, who were not involved in party politics and didn't want to be. It just seemed sensible to detach the school board from party politics and concentrate on issues. If people wanted to run to cut school taxes, fine. If they wanted to run to cut out sex education, fine. Let's put the issues on the table, above politics and party labels, and let the ball bounce where it may.

Around the time of the debate on nonpartisan elections, a Beaufort resident who had moved here from Connecticut wrote an open letter to me in the *Beaufort Gazette*. After complimenting me on my concern not only for the welfare of my constituents but also for the costs to taxpayers of various spending plans, he suggested a few ideas for legislation. Then he concluded, "I might as well get this long-standing gripe about you off my chest. You have too often complicated my voting procedure when you are on the ballot, because in order to vote for you I cannot take the easy way out and vote the straight Republican ticket with one punch in the voting card. But that is only a symptom of my real complaint, and that is you really should be a Republican! It's a great year to switch parties." I responded (but not in the press) that I appreciated very much his public expression of appreciation for the things I try to do in the legislature and thought he should know that much of my legislation was supported by most Democrats and opposed by most Republicans. I thanked him for his invitation to join his party and declined. Perhaps, I told him, if he liked my agenda, he might want to become Democrat. He declined. I cite this exchange because he was not unique; it was evidence that often people are conflicted in making choices between candidates and parties. Why not remove this conflict when possible, certainly as it relates to school board members and other local officeholders whose duties are unrelated to ninety percent of the planks in party platforms.

In a speech to the Hilton Head League of Women Voters on this subject, I reported on a meeting of fifty women legislators who were invited by the National Women's Political Caucus (a nonpartisan group) to discuss the 1992 elections. "I heard legislators from all over the country telling the same story—candidates popping up out of nowhere, who talked about cutting taxes, improving education and less government, but whose real targets were women and men who supported women's rights. These so-called stealth candidates were recruited, supported and funded by the radical religious-right churches. During the campaign, no one knew much about them or their supporters. They were recruited for the legislature, city and county councils, and especially school boards. I tell you this, not for partisan reasons, but because this is the antithesis of what the League of Women Voters stands for. We stand for an educated electorate, which has full knowledge of the issues and what the candidate's agenda is on these issues."

My bill providing for a nonpartisan Beaufort school board was a "local bill," for which only the local delegation is supposed to vote, even though the vote takes place in the legislature. But Bill Cork, the lone Republican in our local delegation, persuaded a few of his friends from other parts of the state to join the voting and vote against my bill. When my friends saw the non-Beaufort votes on the voting board, they started pushing their "aye" buttons. By flashing their votes on the board, they indicated they could cancel out Bill's votes if he didn't call his friends off. No one on either side felt good about voting on a Beaufort matter. I can't remember whether they all backed off or whether we just outvoted them. I do remember that the bill passed.

My bill gave the local Republican Party leaders another campaign issue against me. I was, of course, criticized as a partisan Democrat by the Republicans, who opposed my bill because they were on their way to controlling every aspect of Beaufort County. But my move had little to do with Republican versus Democratic parties. It had everything to do with my concern that stealth candidates had taken over our schools in elections that no one paid enough attention to, and were putting their religious views in place. My concern was shared by many Republicans, those who came from cities where school boards had always been nonpartisan, and others who were as concerned by the religious right takeover of the board as I. Looking back, I wish I had made the same effort toward establishing nonpartisan county council elections. I believe there is little place for Republican or Democrat party politics on this level of government, and that many people who are unaffiliated would surface as candidates to give the public a broader choice at election time. This would also remove the partisan rhetoric which has little do with county issues and which causes the public to distance itself from government. Good government is served best by more public involvement, not less. I believe it is for all these reasons that the S.C. League of Women Voters has recently come out for nonpartisan county elections.

In 1987, as we were struggling to implement the Education Improvement Act, we were presented with a mass of facts and figures about state and local funding of education. This came at a time when Beaufort County Council was sparring with the school board over the education budget. Beaufort is still one of the counties in which the school board does not have fiscal independence, and the education budget must be approved by county council. This triggered constant struggles—about operating budgets, new programs, new buildings. Knowing how dismal our education statistics were compared to other states, I usually took the school board's side. So in preparation for the next wrangle, I carefully studied the information pouring out of state agencies about education funding in all the counties and found some startling information. I also compared our education funding with funding for county government administration and was even more startled.

I sorted out the statistics and made them public. Beaufort County Council, which was always lambasting the school board for overspending, was ranked first in the state in spending per capita for county government operations, but we ranked forty-second of forty-six counties in spending per capita for education. Further, of the ninety-two school districts in the state, Beaufort County ranked eighty-ninth in "effort"—that is, what people pay in taxes as compared to their "ability." ("Effort" is judged by how much taxes a person in a $100,000 house pays in one county as compared to taxes paid by persons in $100,000 houses in other counties.)

Beaufort County Council members had varying reactions to these facts; some said they would have to study the figures; some said you can't compare apples and oranges, that all counties are different; others defensively insisted loose management was a problem in the school system. But county opposition to school budgets was defused by my figures that year. Ironically, these figures had unintended consequences. They were picked up by a newly formed Taxpayer Coalition and became part of their "cause" to slow down county government by ordinances and referenda. Although they have achieved a bit more discipline in county spending, they went further in their demands than I meant to see happen. My interest was more in deflecting criticism of school board spending, although I must admit that what sparked my interest in collecting this data was a most ostentatious government center that county council had just finished building at an enormous cost, more befitting a large city than a rural county. Some called it the Taj Mahal.

My information gathering turned out to be a useful weapon in my campaign when Ron Atkinson, the chairman of county council and of the subcommittee in charge of building the complex, turned out to be my opponent. When his finance chairman sent out a mailer saying, "For twelve years Mrs. Keyserling has just coasted along, promoting the trendy issues of the 1970s that translate into more government spending, more government regulation of business, and higher taxes," I could respond: "Look who is calling me a big, liberal spender. My opponent, the chairman of county council, the biggest spender of them all."

In fact, my business supporters placed an ad in the local paper headlined "Who really raised your taxes?" Side by side they had our names, with a little box by each name, and the box on Ron Atkinson's side was checked. Under my name, the script read: "In the last four years Harriet Keyserling has voted for only 2 general tax increases: a 1 cent sales tax earmarked for the nationally acclaimed Education Improvement Act and a gas tax for needed roads and bridges." Under Atkinson's name the script read: "While Ron Atkinson was Vice-Chairman and Chairman of County Council your tax millage rate for County operations (not including schools) doubled from 26.6 to 55. Beaufort County's budget is the highest per capita in the State of South Carolina." And beneath both, in big black letters: "We business men and women thought you would like to know." It was signed by eight heavyweight businesspeople. It was an effective response to the label they tried to pin on me.

In May a story came out in newspapers across the state that an organization of businessmen had targeted ten legislators for defeat, and I was one of them. The organization wrote to businessmen in Beaufort suggesting they support my opponent "as a pro-business newcomer with excellent chances of winning with your financial support. Please spread the good word." The organization was called the South Carolina Business and Industry Political Education Committee—or BIPEC. The list of its advisory committee included fifteen of the most powerful businessmen in the state. The committee had an executive director, Jim Carpenter, who said the recommendations were based on "voting records, trends, demographics and public opinion" but refused to disclose what legislation was used to judge voting records or specify what demographics and public opinion polls were used. I said the process was like a star chamber, where you don't know what you've done wrong, you don't know who the accuser is, and nobody claims to have anything to do with it. That year the chairman was Joe Griffith, an acquaintance of my husband's. I went to visit him and John Tecklenberg, a close friend of my son's, also on the committee. Both were Charleston businessmen. They told me the recommendations, made by the director, were sent to regional committees of BIPEC for their review. But Beaufort did not have a regional committee. Hilton Head had a very small one, but no one would tell me who was on it. I later heard that its spokesman was a leader of the local Republican party. Joe and John could tell me little because they knew little.

My impression was that other than setting up the organization and lending their impressive names, members of the advisory committee paid little attention to the process and gave their director free rein. The papers reported that Jim Carpenter made those decisions based on information given him by unnamed lobbyists who covered the State House. The strangest part of the hit list was that there were no common threads among the ten victims. It was as if different influences (lobbyists) selected people they wanted to get rid of for different reasons. I could guess at who wanted to get rid of me: the nuclear waste industry. And perhaps the textile people who had opposed the EIA. And of course those who just wanted a Republican in my seat. But it's hard to defend against ghost opponents and conjecture.

I had no problem with the concept of tracking voting records or how the organization started out. But their action was so secretive and the method by which it was done had no accountability. That bothered me a great deal.

Several days later another business group, the National Business Association, a Greenville-based organization of small businesses, called a press conference and came to the defense of six of the ten of us, saying, "Calling the lawmakers anti-business was totally in error. Nothing could be further from the truth." Bryan McCanless, founder of the association, said his group had a thousand members and characterized us as good friends of business. He continued, "These senators and representatives are pro-small business, pro-fairness, and pro-individual taxpayers. They are just not in favor of allowing small businesses and individual taxpayers in South Carolina being bullied and taken advantage of by these big special interests." Richard Davis, who represented the South Carolina Association of Realtors and was one of BIPEC's officers, said many in his group were unaware how the choices were made and were upset at the publicity.

My Beaufort business supporters were reassured. After all, Beaufort only had small businesses, and they cared more about my response to their needs than to the larger industries. However, the system seemed so corrupt to me that I kept fighting the BIPEC action, speaking with others of its members, who all were silent or very fuzzy on the details. Jim Neighbors and Bill Robinson, a friend of Joe Griffith's, went to Charleston to talk to Joe. In early September, BIPEC publicly announced it had changed its mind; it removed me from its hit list and endorsed my candidacy. It also withdrew its support of Atkinson. In a telephone interview Joe Griffith told the press the committee's reversal was based on the recommendations of Beaufort County businessmen who had been left out of the earlier decision making. He also said that the list had been intended for private use by members only and said he had been surprised last spring when the list was "leaked" by unidentified sources. Jim Carpenter, BIPEC's director, also interviewed, refused to explain his group's decision to drop me from the list. And he refused to answer any questions about how my name made it on the list in the first place. He did say that my race was the only one in which the committee reversed its decision.

With that fire out, the Republicans took another tack. Within days after I announced that I had filed a bill to create a task force to study ways to decrease the volume of solid waste in county landfills and to increase recycling, Edie Rodgers, then president of the Beaufort Area Women's Republican Club, issued a press release demanding that I resign from the task force because of what she called "a conflict of interest." She said I had received campaign contributions from GSX, which operates a hazardous waste site in Sumter, and the McNair law firm, who represented GSX, and therefore, she continued "Mrs. Keyserling cannot serve with objectivity on a committee studying our state's landfill problem." She also said the Republican Club was upset because I said I had been thinking about the problem for twelve years. "We're bothered by the fact that our representative has done nothing about waste dumps during her 12 years in office and she called for the study in May when she heard she was going to have opposition."

Having observed other people's campaigns over the years, I had come to the conclusion that negative attacks, especially the baseless ones, had to be responded to immediately. The public has such a short memory that it tends to accept as fact what it hears last. Following that conclusion, I always tried to respond immediately, as I did to the BIPEC hit list, to let the public know the last thing they heard was flawed and probably self-serving. (The other side of this coin is silence—just let accusations slide by and become forgotten, rather than build them up into a continuing story. But I think the Dukakis experience proved that such silence doesn't work in the present negative campaign mode and that the Clinton tactic of immediate response does.)

I immediately wrote a letter to the editor: "It is obvious that Mrs. Rodgers is either woefully uninformed about waste problems, is ignorant about my activities in that field, is naïve about the political process—or is intentionally misleading the public for purely partisan reasons." (When told my task force was studying only solid waste, Mrs. Rodgers had answered, "I don't think you can separate it at all. It's all waste disposal.") I went on to explain there were three major types of waste, all treated differently. Solid waste was our everyday garbage placed in county landfills; hazardous waste was chemicals, oils, metals which are toxic and are buried in Sumter, the only licensed site in the state; and commercial radioactive nuclear wastes, which are buried only in Barnwell or stored at nuclear plant sites. Each category has different regulations, different licensing, and different disposal methods.

I also said it was hard to believe that Mrs. Rodgers, an active garden club member, did not know I sponsored for years a bill, supported by the state association of garden clubs, calling for a mandatory deposit on bottles and cans similar to bills in other states which encourage recycling and reduce landfill volume by eight to ten percent. And that I had also tried for years to persuade Beaufort County and Parris Island Marine Base officials to look seriously at how other military bases were burning garbage to provide steam for energy, which would reduce the amount of garbage. And solid waste. Or that I helped Hilton Head obtain funds for a pilot recycling project to reduce garbage. I concluded: "Changing a throwaway society takes time. Mrs. Rodgers is naïve to think it can be done by wishing it so. It takes steady, hard work over the years. And that is what I have been doing." (I didn't bother to explain that the McNair contribution was in kind, representing a party given by my personal friend, Liz Crum, now with that firm, who had been the Judiciary Committee counsel in the heyday of the Crazy Caucus. Or that despite the GSX contribution, I cannot remember a single vote with which I supported GSX in any way, ever.)

The *Beaufort Gazette* came to my defense: "The [Republican] committee is entitled to its opinion, but it is off base. . . . Landfill waste and the hazardous waste which GSX handles in Pinewood aren't the same. . . . Challenging Mrs. Keyserling, too, on her environmental record leaves the Beaufort Area Republicans Club in a vulnerable position. Rep. Keyserling has one of the best records in the state on environmental issues." This was followed by a letter from a total stranger which was more complimentary than anything I could have ghostwritten. Some phrases were: "She can be described as a strong, quiet person, one who talks only when something needs to be said, but says it over, and over, and over until she gets action. Her legislative programs are sometimes called the work of a liberal. Whether they are liberal or conservative, they tend to follow the pattern defined by Walter Lippmann when he spoke on conservative liberalism: that is a person who is willing to bring about change for progress and betterment, but in doing so clings to the best in the old and tried. . . ." And so on. This, from a stranger, was a mighty gift.

In 1990, Edie Rodgers, who served on Beaufort City Council, ran for mayor and lost. At the time she called her opponent's win a "Keyserling" victory, because my son, Billy, had advised the winner in campaign tactics. When I left the legislature in 1992, Billy ran for my seat and beat George O'Kelley, my first opponent in 1976. In 1994 Edie Rodgers ran against Billy in a district which had been drastically changed by reapportionment. The balance had shifted from about sixty to eighty-five percent Republican. Despite this, Billy won, as an Independent. Two years later, in 1996, when he decided not to offer, Edie jumped in and is now the House member representing Beaufort. During her campaign, she supported Governor Beasley in his campaign to keep the Chem-Nuclear/Barnwell low-level nuclear waste dump open, and she supported his pulling out of the Southeast Low-level Nuclear Waste Compact which I had worked so hard to put into place. One of her first votes in the legislature was against raising the state fees levied against Chem-Nuclear. According to the state ethics committee which lists contributions, she received a campaign contribution of two hundred dollars from Chem-Nuclear.

By the end of her first year, although she represented a county which had recently passed a $130 million school building program, she voted against fully funding kindergarten for all five-year-olds. In a county which has recently paid over a half a million dollars for a growth management plan, she voted for a takings bill which would put great difficulties in place for zoning or long-range planning, and on the same bill she voted to allow Chem-Nuclear to sue the state for loss of profits when and if the legislature ever decides it is time to close down the low-level nuclear waste site. In a postsession report, the S.C. Sierra Club gave her a low rating, stating that she had voted "wrong" on thirteen of the seventeen bills affecting the environment that they followed. As I sit back and watch (which is not easy), I wonder whether she will be able to move Beaufort's viewpoint toward hers on these issues by explanations and rationalizations, or whether Beaufort will leap over the fence of partisan politics, as it did with me, and protest her voting record at the polls.

I have digressed. Back to my 1988 campaign. Once through with the business of defending myself, I moved into a more positive position. Hundreds of letters in support of my candidacy went out to targeted audiences: education leaders wrote to parents and teachers, arts leaders wrote to supporters of the arts, a retired Army general wrote to retired officers and a retired noncommissioned Marine officer wrote to all the retired noncommissioned Marines, leaders in the black community contacted black residents, and those concerned about choice and abortion rights wrote their friends. There were coffees for me to meet new residents, a few fundraisers, and a lot of speaking engagements. I went the rounds of country stores and black churches. There was a fundraiser in Columbia with former governors and important businessmen as cohosts and one in Charleston. As an incumbent, I had the advantage of having a record I could cite, instead of just making promises.

Of course, my record also fostered opposition. There were those who were strongly antichoice who coalesced around Atkinson, who opposed all abortions except in the case of rape. There were those who were loyal National Rifle Association members who hated my seven-day waiting period for handguns, even to the extent of tring to recruit a candidate against me. My vote for the penny sales tax for education, and a penny gasoline tax, drew some opposition. And I was an active Democrat in a Republican stronghold.

Ron Atkinson put up large billboards saying "Ron Atkinson—One of Us." No one was quite sure what that meant, and it was amusing how people read meaning into it according to their own identities. The Jewish community felt he was pointing out he was a Christian, not a Jew, the women thought he was saying he was a man, not a woman, the blacks thought he was saying he was white, not black. Whatever, he may have lost more votes than he gained with those signs. My friend Nell Smith was confronted by the same slogan in Easley during her campaign. She felt it was more a badge of the Christian fundamentalist group, which was very strong in her area and which had opposed her on some of her bills, such as regulating church day-care facilities, sex education, and prayer in the schools. I later heard that the slogan was used by many Republican candidates but did not hear who initiated them or why.

Bill Cork from Hilton Head put an advertisement insert in the local paper "exposing" my record and claiming he had to put in the flyer at his expense because the paper would not print his remarks. Tommy Hartnett, our former Republican congressman from Charleston, sent a mailing touting "7 good reasons to vote for Atkinson." (Actually, the text offered seven good reason not to vote for Harriet Keyserling.) One reason was that one year I was named South Carolina ACLU Legislator of the Year, and "the ACLU was for legalization of pornography, legalization of narcotics, removing 'Under God' from the Pledge of Allegiance, rights of homosexuals to marry and taxing of churches. Harriet Keyserling is too liberal to represent our views." He, as well as Cork, cited my low rating by BIPEC to reinforce their case.

The usually nonpartisan editor of the *Beaufort Gazette* wrote an op-ed piece in response to Hartnett's letter. He wrote: "Hartnett fails to tell you that this wife and mother of four also has been named Legislator of the Year by the S.C. Wildlife Federation, the S.C. School Board Association, the S.C. Business and Professional Women and a litany of other organizations. Or that she received the Rotary Bowl from a group of conservative Beaufort business leaders." The article continued to take on the other six reasons and concluded: "She is a lot more in tune with the people of her district and the people of South Carolina on issues of taxation, the environment, the elderly and the needy than these men give her credit."

Meanwhile, Carroll Campbell, the sitting governor, sent a mailing to all Republicans on his official stationery citing the reasons he needed Ron Atkinson to help him lower car insurance, hold the line on taxes, get tough on drunk drivers. "Unlike your incumbent Representative, Ron Atkinson will work with me, not against me." The NRA also sent out a mailing, calling me the Howard Metzenbaum/Ted Kennedy of the South Carolina legislature.

To counteract all these charges by Republican leaders in my Republican district, I ran a full-page ad listing over five hundred leading Beaufort citizens, Democrats and Republicans, endorsing me. My heavies beat their heavies, which proves that the hometown endorsements count the most. I won that election by sixty percent, much to the surprise of the Republican Party. In contrast, the same voters gave Dukakis only forty-four percent to Bush's fifty-six percent. Also surprising was that I had one thousand more votes than George Bush. Also interesting were the results of my polling just before the election. I led Atkinson fifty to thirty percent among men, sixty-two to twenty-seven percent among working women, and only forty to twenty-nine percent among women homemakers. The differences may be related to the fact that these numbers were not broken down by race.

My win was the result of many groups of people who gave their time, energy, and money to my campaign. The women who ran the office and did the legwork; the black community, which enthusiastically went to the polls; and my family, who did all the jobs that needed to be done. Billy told me what to do, then did it for me; Paul was in charge of all those important signs that have to pop up all over town overnight; and Herbert came to all the parties, took me to visit black churches, stores, and homes of his patients, then on election day, stood at a busy intersection, waving my banner at the cars passing by.

My friend Nell Smith was having a very tough race in Easley, and she barely squeaked through. She was accused of "carrying on," leading a licentious life in Columbia. Possibly there were people with dirty minds who couldn't conceive of an attractive widow not "carrying on," but more likely they chose character defamation as a way to beat her. We laughed about it after the fact, remarking that there were some legislators who fit that picture, but to describe Nell in those terms was so patently absurd it wasn't worth talking about. At least they spared me those tactics in Beaufort, I said. Little did I know until just recently that there was an equally ludicrous story circulated about me during that election. Billy recently told me that one of our old Beaufort friends, whose family had been Herbert's patients for fifty years, was heard to say at a gathering, "Did you know that Harriet Keyserling pays volunteer firemen to sleep with her?" I saw that "friend" soon after I heard the story and marched up to him and asked if he did, indeed, say that. He was speechless for a long minute, his face turned dark (blood rushing to his brain?), and he finally said, "No. I didn't say that. But I know who did. I was there when he said it." When I asked who that was, he said, "He's dead." And that's all I could get out of him. It was a rude awakening for me, and I'm glad I hadn't heard that story while I was still in office. I might have wreaked some vengeance.

At this time, there was very little Democratic Party organization, but there was a small group called the Friends of the Democratic Party which provided a nucleus for help. The party itself was fundless. Its primary source of revenue was from filing fees from Democratic candidates, but that source withered, as there were so few Democratic candidates filing. Instead of the party contributing to my campaign, I contributed to the party, so it could have a headquarters for state and national candidates and its few local candidates.

The Friends group was started when Helen Harvey, Patricia Battey, Alice Seeburg, and I met over lunch in the early 1980s to brainstorm about how to pull Democrats together. The Republicans had the Republican Women's Club, which raised money, had luncheons, and provided social occasions for the many newcomers, some of whom joined as a way to meet people as much as for reasons of ideology.

The Democrats didn't have that. If newcomers happened to be Democrats, there was nothing to join. There was an executive committee of the party, but those members were elected at their biannual precinct meetings, and county officers were elected at the biannual conventions. Except at election time, there was no activity. Alice Seeburg was a newcomer to the state who wanted to be connected to other Democrats and wanted to see some action. Her husband was a Republican, but he was very accepting of her political activism, and even tended bar at the Friends' parties. This Democratic wife/Republican husband combination seems to be happening more and more, but it is interesting that the allegiances are rarely reversed, in terms of gender. Patricia Battey had recently married Colden Battey and moved from Charleston, where she had been very active politically.

We decided to start a Democratic Women's Club, but a few men heard about it and protested, saying they didn't want to be excluded. We were happy to have them and also wanted to attract those who weren't active Democrats but were friendly to some candidates or on some issues. We struggled to define our identity and finally selected the name Friends of the Democratic Party. We decided we would have a party, or as Alice called it, a Party party. Between us we drew up a list of possible and probable members and sent out invitations. We included all the Democratic Party officials. We had the first party at the Yacht and Sailing Club, and we had a good, enthusiastic crowd. We even raised a little money.

And then a problem arose. My old friend George McMillan, the man who talked me into running for county council and later wrote a glowing story about me for *McCall's* magazine, attacked us. George was a professional Southern liberal who decided we were trying to exclude the blacks and bypass the Democratic Party. He criticized us for having our first get-together at a sailing club which had no black members at the time. Never mind that we were a last resort in resuscitating the party or that we had invited every black leader we knew. Or that all of us were for inclusiveness. Never mind that we had raised money for the party for the first time in years. George circulated his theory among the black leaders, stirred the pot, and caused ill will and dissension.

Some who knew George well said the problem was that we hadn't brought him into the initial meetings. But then, our intention was to start a women's club. He was right, philosophically, in our poor choice of location for our parties, which was suggested by Alice, a newcomer to Beaufort, who innocently suggested the club because she knew of no other public places in Beaufort to choose from. We agreed to change the venue in the future, moving to private homes. But George couldn't leave it alone, and he drove a wedge between the diminishing number of white and black people who cared about the health of the Beaufort Democratic Party. I doubt this was his intention, but that's what happened. We kept the Friends going for a while, attracting newcomers, building our membership, hosting candidates for state office. But we always had to fight the mistrust of a few black leaders who would not join forces with us. Some of the nonleaders, especially the women, did attend our gatherings, while they lasted.

In 1990, two years after my win, Austin Beveridge ran against me. Beveridge, a former pilot, was a six-year resident of Fripp Island, a barrier island at the tip of St. Helena Island and a Republican stronghold. I don't know if he was recruited by the Republicans or made the decision because he was so upset with the legislature for regulating beachfront property in an attempt to save the shoreline. His property was affected by the setback lines mandated for building and rebuilding on the beach. We differed on other issues, as well: I voted for a referendum to allow voters to decide whether they wanted a local option sales tax; he opposed it. He said the one-percent sales tax I had voted for to put the education reform package in place was wasted money, that the SAT scores were abysmal; I agreed they were abysmal, but not as abysmal as they would have been without the EIA. He was for school vouchers, giving parents the right to choose public or private school with the government paying for either; I was not.

Another conservative organization, the South Carolina Policy Council, sprang up to rate legislators, and I was ranked very low, indicating I was too liberal. We were "graded" on a mélange of issues in addition to everything related to taxes or fees: abortion, bingo, residential home care under the Department of Social Services, support for art in public buildings, homosexuality and other issues related to sex education, the death penalty for drug "kingpins." Sometimes procedural votes were used instead of straight down-the-line votes, which could be misleading by design. There was no allowance for anyone changing one's mind, as I sometimes did after hearing the debate. The council selected which vote would be ranked, and that was the one that counted. In the 1990 "scorecard" most of the lawyers were ranked low, because of their position on insurance. The bottom forty-one were all Democrats, except for David Wilkins (now the Republican speaker), who had the same low ranking as mine, a nineteen. There were lots of zeros. Also in the bottom forty-one was Governor David Beasley, then a House Democrat.

Some of the Democrats with low rankings did a little research and identified all but one of the founders of the Policy Council listed on the stationery as contributors to Governor Campbell; ninety percent of those on its board were his known supporters; the others had been Republican candidates. The litany of issues were far right of the mainstream Republican issues. Some of us believed those issues were selected after they decided what candidates they wanted to get rid of. Knowing how they would vote, the questions were in effect rigged to get the results they wanted. The other interesting aspect for me was that Eberle, the execute vice president of the council, often wrote letters to the Beaufort paper opposing my position on nuclear waste.

I was also one of five Democrats targeted by the state Republican Party because I had opposed Governor Campbell's automobile insurance bill. As the vote was seventy-seven to thirty-seven, and the bill passed, it was hard to know what exactly we five did to warrant this special targeting as compared to the thirty-two others who voted as we did. The general conclusion was that we five (three of us women) had opposed Campbell on other issues like nuclear waste or oil overcharge fees, and he and/or the Republican Party selected a politically sexy issue like auto insurance to come down on us. Auto insurance is still a controversial issue, and the rates will continue to be high until we remove South Carolina from the top of the list of highway accidents and deaths. Frankly, automobile insurance was a subject which caused my eyes to glaze over. I was certainly no leader in that fight. It was one of those subjects I depended on others for guidance. Campbell, on the other hand, received over $250,000 from insurance companies in campaign contributions for his run for governor in 1986 according to an AP story in the *Savannah Morning News* of June 30, 1989. Now, in 1997, he is being paid over a million dollars a year to represent the insurance lobby in Washington. I don't remember the particulars of the bill, as there was a different one every year, but I can only assume that if we were on different sides, then I was more likely to have represented the public interest, and he, the insurance company interests.

After Edie Rodgers described the outcome of her defeat for mayor as a "Keyserling" victory, other letters to the editor followed during my campaign, intertwining me and Billy on any subject one or the other of us was involved with, as if Billy and I were some kind of cabal, a team out to take over the county. Billy had recently returned to live in Beaufort, after twenty-six years away, to set up his own public relations firm. He represented some controversial clients, including a boat manufacturer who wanted to build a plant on a Bluffton river and the Municipal Association, which was pushing for the local option tax. Every time his name was mentioned, my name was mentioned, as if to transfer his negatives to me. My response to these letters as I neared the next election was that I was delighted that he wanted to come home and that I was delighted that Beaufort was at last able to provide a living for the native sons who wanted to return, and that we were two individuals with different agendas which sometimes merge because we share the same values.

I ran on my record, with a slogan "Leadership Matters" headlining my ideas and record on education, the environment, reform, and vision. Beveridge ran as a conservative against an "extreme liberal." As in 1988, I ran an endorsement ad filled with over five hundred names of local leaders, black and white, Democrat and Republican, men and women. My husband, who likes puns, came up with a cartoon and the slogan: "Beaufort Votes November 6th for an Untried Beverage or an

Old Faithful Geyserling" with an illustration of a bottle and a geyser. Cute, but we didn't use it.

I won the election big. This time I won all the precincts except Fripp Island, and even there I did far better than ever before. I received 68.2% of the vote. Also on the Democratic ticket, Theo Mitchell received 35% to Campbell's 64.5%, and Democrat Charlie Williams, the incumbent state superintendent of schools received 36.4% to Republican newcomer Barbara Nielsen's 63.6%. It was very pleasant to get more votes than the Republican statewide candidates, especially Campbell, who I was told again wrote letters of support for my opponent. These figures showed that many Beaufort Republicans were willing to vote for a person they knew and respected, even a Democrat. Also in my favor was that many Beaufort Republicans are moderate and are concerned about the domination of their party by the radical religious right.

In 1992 it was assumed that if I didn't run, no Democrat could win. However, Billy did—by several hundred votes. The following year the new reapportionment cut up his district and removed all the population centers of black voters, even cutting a swath right through the city of Beaufort, thereby reducing the Democratic strength even further. He ran as an independent because he felt disillusioned by both parties. In fact, he had wanted to run as an independent the first time around, but we strongly advised him not to, believing he needed the support of a core group. But the second time he was right. He was known by then; he had followers. But when he quit in 1996, it was virtually impossible for another non-Republican to win. However, in 1997 the courts ruled that this district had been too gerrymandered, and it has been changed once again, a little closer to the district I represented.

In 1997, the Beaufort Democratic Party is still struggling, and the leaders still have not linked up with the Friends, which as a result has became dormant. All the incumbent Democrats in county offices have switched parties, and it is almost impossible to recruit a viable white Democratic candidate. Except for Dot Gnann, once chairman of the school board and presently a member of county council of long standing, who has held on easily to her seat. The voters like her and see her as a hardworking public servant, not a political partisan. As a result of the court ruling on the reapportionment of Beaufort, a new election was set and Sammy Svalina, a young lawyer and newcomer to politics, jumped in as a Democrat to run against Edie Rodgers, who had been in office just a year. He talked about the issues—nuclear waste, the "takings" bill as it related to the county planning effort and the environment, early childhood education—and lost by just a few hundred votes. It would not surprise me if he didn't try again next year. Soon after that election, a young woman architect, Jane Frederick, decided she would challenge U.S. Congressman Floyd Spence and has announced her candidacy, as a Democrat. Perhaps her race will prompt another attempt to resuscitate a Democratic Club in Beaufort. This time, I think it will work.

On the other side of the Broad River, the Democrats on Hilton Head are active and growing in strength, in an area which is about ninety percent Republican. They meet regularly, have good programs, and in 1996 even ran a candidate for the legislature for the first time in years. Although a fine candidate, she only collected thirty percent of the vote. They are trying to recruit candidates for local office with the hope that if their candidates become known on the local level, they may have a better chance of breaking down partisan barriers for the next step up. And if that doesn't work, they can become a bloc vote in tight races for an independent or even a Republican. Perhaps as they make some inroads, we might also.

There may be readers who feel I am too partisan in my criticism of Republicans. If they consider the whole picture I am trying to paint, they will see that I also zeroed in on the Old Guard, all Democrats, and any other person or group which tried to perpetuate the status quo (where it needed to be changed) and protect special interests, as opposed to the public interest. My criticism is of their policies, not their party affiliation.

CHAPTER 19

Energy Policies

The Energy Bill started in my head when I first ran for the legislature in 1976, just a few years after the 1973 oil embargo. And it stayed there throughout my political career, either smoldering or boiling, either lurking in the interior of my mind or catapulted into action by an event, a mood. I, as most of America, was angered at being held hostage by the oil sheiks; we were alarmed about the effect of this on our foreign policy and the economic dangers of the boycott: inflation, as the price of energy went up, and a negative change in the balance of trade. We had to find ways to change course from the profligate way we used oil.

So I arrived at the legislature with the desire to "do something" about conservation and recycling, which was my solution to the problem. I left the legislature sixteen years later after developing and putting into law state policies for recycling and for energy efficiency and conservation—with many steps forward and backwards, successes and failures on the way. It took that long because major policy changes take a long time—and because for me, at least, it was necessary to build credibility and gain the trust of other legislators and the establishment, both public and private. Trust is essential when dealing with technical bills that few can fully understand.

In my first year I cosponsored a bottle bill, which was modeled after the Oregon law, with five-cent deposits on returnable soft drink and beer bottles. Year after year we tried—and failed. In fact, it has failed in every southern state, even in pseudo-southern Florida. It has been passed by many legislatures in the Northeast and several in the Midwest. These regional differences on bottle bills would make an interesting political science research project.

It was in my second year that I became so involved with the problems of nuclear waste, an issue in which controversy intensified when Three Mile Island and Chernobyl broke into the news, changing abstract concerns to real-life threats—and offering a window of opportunity to anyone itching to tackle the problem. Learning from this experience that timing is everything when trying to crack the armor of resistance to change, I scrambled into action when political troubles in the Middle East threatened our oil supplies once again, with bills for recycling oil and tax credits for producers of renewable energy.

In the early years, I crusaded nonstop, taking advantage of every ounce of authority derived from my titles of chairman of the Energy Conservation Subcommittee of the S.C. Joint Legislative Energy Committee and vice chairman of the Energy Committee of the National Conference of State Legislatures (NCSL). In 1977 I joined the fight to improve the Public Service Commission because it was the key to conservation by the electric utilities. In 1980 I addressed the South Carolina Association of Counties, saying, "I believe that energy is just about the most important problem in our country—and the more I read, the more fervent I am about getting to work on conserving energy. I only wish I had the skills of Billy Graham so I could be an energy-conservation evangelist."

Also in 1980 I created and presided over a Statewide Used Oil Recycling Task Force made up of government and industry people. We generated the basic information used ten years later in the Solid Waste Management Act, which set up a successful system for recycling oil with the help of the Santee Cooper Authority, which collects and partially fuels some of its plants with the oil. In 1980, I brought the NCSL experts to town to talk about what other states were doing with geothermal heating, water-source heat pumps, and hydropower. In the summer of 1980 I joined a large group of businessmen and friends invited by Governor Riley to visit Israel. During that wonderful trip I left the group to meet with Israeli government energy officials as well as a manufacturer of solar water heaters, hoping to find an inexpensive, easy way to install solar heaters for South Carolina homes. I found the product but never did find buyers when I returned home.

In 1981, I brought technical assistance from NCSL to review for our Joint Energy Committee two reports by the Governor's Office on developing and maintaining an information system for a state energy plan, but there was no follow-through. I then brought experts from North Carolina to hold a workshop on cogeneration and other conservation methods. The committee listened, but little action followed.

Also in 1981, at a DOE hearing in Atlanta, I tore into a briefing paper for the Third National Energy Plan created by the Reagan administration and presumably former Governor Edwards, who was then U.S. Secretary of Energy. "Conservation and government incentives for new sources of energy and renewable sources of energy are downplayed to an extent I find hard to believe—both in the statements and proposed budget. The statement on Page 2 that 'the level of U.S. imports of petroleum per se has only an indirect bearing on U.S. security and well-being' is contrary to everything we have heard since 1973—not only concerning national security and foreign policy, but just the economics of what the cost of imported oil does to our national economy.

"How can it be said our domestic scene is not affected if we import from 7–9 million barrels a day in 1985 at a cost of $45 a barrel in 1980 dollars, which means over $131 billion a year going out of our country and out of our economy? A matter of such consequence must be addressed by the federal government, and cannot be solved as you suggest 'by the American people themselves—not by the government.' $131 billion dollars going out of the country is inflationary; why shouldn't the government be in charge of this in the same way the Federal Reserve Board regulates interest rates to control inflation and the economy.

"The philosophy that 'Federal public spending should not be used to subsidize domestic energy production and conservation' runs counter to our country's history wherein new technologies have been subsidized in all major industry. If the oil and gas and nuclear industries have been subsidized to the tune of billions (as reported in a recent Battelle report), why blow the whistle on solar and hydro and geothermal at a time when we need them the most? Not to mention conservation, which is the cleanest, quickest and cheapest substitute for the traditional forms of energy." (Could I have subconsciously said that as a counterpoint to those same words of Jim Edwards about nuclear power?)

In 1982 I appeared before the State Reorganization Commission on "sunset" hearings of the Public Service Commission. "It is cheaper to decrease demand for electricity than build more power plants. I am here to advocate that the S.C. Public Service Commission, like its counterparts in other states, enforce the Public Utility Regulatory Policies Act of 1978 by mandating the participation of our utilities in alternate energy production, cogeneration and small hydro facilities when available. In addition, the PSC must be given the responsibility and authority to encourage, facilitate, even mandate that all electric utilities in South Carolina invest in conservation rather than in large construction programs which incur heavy debt, poor cash flow, and the risks of uncertain demand." I continued on, describing the benefits of conservation, concluding: "Ninety-five percent of Fortune 500 companies now have corporate energy managers, programs and budget because they realize that companies which use energy most efficiently will gain the competitive advantage in the global marketplace."

In 1983 I moderated a panel on energy in San Diego for women legislators. "It is said that women intuitively understand the need for world peace and the need to find peaceful methods of dealing with each other if we are to survive into the 21st century. In the same vein, I believe that women intuitively understand the long-term importance of conserving our natural resources and protecting our environment. I realize there are dangers in such generalizations about women, but I believe that such intuitive feelings led me to maneuver to get appointed to our state's Joint Legislative Committee on Energy when it was created. I knew very little about energy problems other than the effects of the '73 oil embargo, but my instincts were to DO SOMETHING to conserve energy to make us less vulnerable; and to DO SOMETHING to protect the environment—a little Quixotic given the fact that South Carolina is the nuclear dumping ground of the country." In addition to this specialized crusade, when I spoke at meetings on other subjects—women, nuclear waste, the arts—I always found a way to inject my thoughts about energy conservation, if only briefly.

Looking back, it may have been this intuitive drive that overpowered my normal avoidance of conflict and reluctance to be assertive when I finally decided to run for the chairmanship of the Energy Committee, an action which was not only assertive, it was aggressive and caused major conflict. Or maybe it was the natural and inevitable culmination of my sustained drive to DO SOMETHING over the years. More about this later.

In 1982 I cosponsored a building energy efficiency bill which passed. With the help of environmental groups and the struggling solar industry we succeeded in creating tax credits for producers of alternate and renewable energy sources. It was also helpful that President Carter had established a national policy with which we dovetailed. But it had a short life. Several years later, when a budget conference committee needed a half-million dollars to fund some program they wanted, and when they noticed a half-million dollars in the budget for energy tax credits, they cut out the line item for tax credits and used the money for whatever it was they wanted. I heard about that too late, after the budget had passed. With those credits gone, the struggling solar industry in South Carolina all but disappeared.

In 1983 my resolution, which came out of the Oil Recycling Task Force, to "encourage" the use of recycled motor oil by state agencies for heating oil, also passed. Not only would it save virgin oil, but it was to help keep used oil from going into landfills or being tossed in the bushes, thereby polluting the groundwater. But "encouragement" does not move inertia. The program barely got off the ground. It slowly fizzled out. That was disheartening, but the ideas kept humming around in my head, waiting for another right time.

My next window of opportunity to create change arrived when a barge, full of New York garbage, was reported to be floating around the South Carolina coast, looking for a home for its cargo. I filed a resolution calling for a blue-ribbon committee to study ways to curtail and control solid waste. It sailed through both houses. What was it about the barge that changed the legislative environment? Probably the visuals on television of the barge and mountains of garbage—and the mounting political power of the "not in my backyard" syndrome. We already were the center of nuclear waste and hazardous waste. Was it now to be garbage?

A theme that the reader may detect running through this book, though I may have not stated it often enough, is that our legislature, like most, is more reactive than proactive. It reacts to crises instead of planning ahead with long-range goals. One reason is that the Establishment, whether it be government or the private sector, resists change, unless and until the public demands change. Solid waste management, if addressed in a comprehensive way, demands a lot of change from both the public and private sector. Just think of what is in the waste stream—bottles, cans, plastic, paper, aluminum, tires, batteries, white goods (such as refrigerators and stoves), construction wastes—each represented by a lobbyist prepared to fight new rules, regulations, and laws. And each used by all of us habit-controlled people in our daily lives. State and local governments also resist new policies and regulations. My only hope was that the public would become aroused and make it difficult for special interest lobbyists and their legislator friends to oppose the changes that were needed. And it was.

Solid waste management was a way to satisfy my old urge to do something to reduce the need for new landfills and also to recycle. While on county council I was shocked to find out how hard it was to find new landfill space in areas such as ours and how much it cost to bury garbage. In Beaufort, with high water tables, thousands of acres of wetlands, and escalating land values, we ran out of space and had to contract with our economically depressed neighbor, Jasper County, to bury our garbage there—at a high cost because we had few chips to bargain with. And how long would Jasper allow this? It irked me also to be throwing away, burying all those valuable resources, never to be used again. Studying the literature put out by bottle bill advocates and other recyclers, I knew there were vast savings in energy from reusing or recyling much of what was in the waste stream.

In a state where hazardous waste was a major concern, leaking municipal landfills brought yet another hazardous waste problem to the public's attention. Imminent EPA regulations requiring heavy and expensive plastic liners for landfills were energizing the business sector to look for alternatives to that increasingly expensive option. All these arguments helped, but that floating barge was the primary catalyst for change.

Usually, the person who creates a task force gets to chair it, but I was told that Senator Moore, then chair of the Energy Committee, really wanted to, so I deferred to him—which in the end turned out to be fortuitous. I agreed to be vice chairman. We convened a blue-ribbon committee to consider the solid waste problem, with members reflecting the many interests that would be impacted by our recommendations. There were representatives of the paper and tire industries, who also represented the state chamber of commerce; there were representatives of city and county government, which is ultimately responsible for solid waste management; there were legislators who would have to push through a bill implementing the task force recommendations; and the public interest was represented by Steve Hamm, the commissioner for consumer affairs. There are advantages, when working on major policy changes, in having a broad spectrum of input. It is also helps those who will be affected by those changes to thoroughly understand the urgency of the problems and want to be part of the solution.

We studied laws in other states and opted for the comprehensive approach, one large all-encompassing bill, rather than a package of bills. It was to be the whole package or nothing, for so many programs dovetailed. The first major question we had to settle was, "Do we mandate recycling and waste reduction or just suggest goals and voluntary action?" If we mandate what products must be recycled, how much can we expect to recycle, and by whom? And how much waste was it possible to reduce? The consensus was to mandate: that local governments adopt programs to recycle and reduce the amount of waste going into their landfills. And we set goals for counties to recycle twenty-five percent of the solid waste stream and reduce by thirty percent the quantity of waste put in landfills, all within six years of the enactment of legislation. I would have preferred mandates rather than goals for specific recyclables, but I lost on that one. Probably the bill would never have passed without that compromise.

We recommended that the Department of Health and Environmental Control (DHEC) prepare a state plan and give technical and monetary assistance to the counties to develop their plans. We recommended a Recycling Market Development Advisory Council within the

State Development Board (which is now our Department of Commerce) to locate and develop markets for recycled materials and bring in industries to recycle. For me, this was one of the most important sections of the bill because it's illogical, even unfair, to mandate recycling if there is no market for the recycled goods.

We recommended a policy for state and local governments to purchase recycled products, thereby providing markets and setting an example to the private sector. We followed the lead of other states and banned specific wastes from landfills—tires, oil, yard wastes, white goods, and batteries—and placed a surcharge on new purchases to pay for the handling and recycling of the old. We struggled to come up with a ladder of preferred ways to reduce waste, as state policy. Each item on the list had unyielding advocates and opponents. The list we finally settled on, in order of preference, was waste reduction at the source, recycling, composting, incinerating for energy, incineration for volume reduction, and lastly, landfill disposal. We tried to address the issue of out-of-state wastes, a matter on which we were handcuffed by the U.S. Constitution. I even managed to put in a provision that if our recycling goals for soft drink and beer containers weren't met, a one-cent deposit would be instituted—but that disappeared some where along the way, deftly managed by the beer and soft drink lobby, who allowed me the pleasure of winning that in committee, knowing full well they would get rid of it before the bill passed.

To pay the costs of all this, we suggested a five-dollar tipping fee to be collected at waste disposal facilities; three dollars would go to the counties, and two dollars to a trust fund for grants and technical aid. There would be rewards for recycling industries, with grants and tax incentives. This also was fiercely debated in committee. We also recommended that oil overcharge funds from the Governor's Office supplement the tipping fee. These were funds the federal government exacted from oil companies which had charged more than the government permitted when price controls were in effect in the 1970s. These funds were then distributed back to the states for conservation programs.

We put all these ideas into a bill, which I introduced in the House and Moore in the Senate. It passed the Senate, but in the waning days of the session, it was killed in the House by a threatened filibuster by John Felder. It took a while to figure out who put him up to it. During our many hearings, there was little stated opposition; rather, more people came to praise than to criticize. When suggestions were made we tried to accommodate. Past experience would have us assume some industry affected by the bill was trying to kill it. But some of the most able lobbyists represented industries who benefitted from the bill and were on our side.

Our opposition turned out to be the S.C. Association of Counties, which didn't like the tipping fee, sensing a loss of control and fearing the costs to the counties. But they never straightforwardly told us they opposed it; their two representatives on the task force did not vote against it in committee. When I learned about their role in our defeat, I raged and stamped around, scowling at their lobbyists. I was angered more by their sneak attack than their opposition, to which they had every right.

During the summer, county officials developed a counterproposal and drew up a bill which was unacceptable to both me and Moore. We met with them and tried to work out differences. I went on the road, talking to groups and newspapers. I said I felt the counties were shortsighted in opposing the bill on the basis of cost. Yes, there could be new up-front costs, but there would be long-term savings and the avoided costs of buying more land, building more landfills, and cleaning up more leaking poisons. A thirty-percent reduction of garbage meant thirty-percent reduction in use of landfills. Yes, we called for tighter—and costly—protections against leaking, but there would be new strict regulations coming from the EPA, with or without our bill. And our bill provided a source of revenue to help them with this, which the EPA did not. We saw the five-dollars-per-ton tipping fee as a user fee, with those using the landfills paying for the service, just as they pay for water and sewer services. The press was supportive of these arguments.

In an effort to compromise, we dropped the tipping fee but held tight to the other major sections of the bill. Sensing the public mood, the Association of Counties publicly endorsed the bill but still tried to water it down. They persuaded the Ways and Means Committee to adopt a formula which had the effect of reducing the recycling goals. But on the floor, Mike Baxley of Darlington replaced their formula with an amendment to return to the original goals, saying, "If we don't pass this amendment . . . we are gutting the bill." His amendment won by a vote of seventy-seven to twenty-five, a big victory for the enviromentalists, a rare loss for the counties. (Mike was a strong and dependable advocate for the environment. He also brought a tin of wonderful cookies, which his mother baked, every Tuesday. As I sat near him, I usually got more than my fair share to go with my overdose of morning coffee.)

When Mike's amendment passed, John Felder, spokesman for the counties on the floor, said "I've been had by the city folks again. This isn't going to get you into environmental heaven." The *State*, in an editorial urging the legislature to resolve the minor differences, said, "Once that has been done, the General Assembly can point to at least one major achievement for 1991." The final vote on the 107-page bill was one hundred in favor and none against.

I am told that the law is working, that the recycling of tires, waste oil, and municipal recyclables is increasing, and that the new director of the Recycling Market Development Advisory Council program, which was slow in gearing up, is now aggressively pursuing new markets and new recyclers. In 1995 the council began sponsoring an annual Southeast recycling investment forum to help potential investors learn more about innovative recycling and reuse opportunities for plastics, tires, oil, yard waste, gypsum wallboard, and commercial recyclables. It also provided opportunities for recycling entrepreneurs to meet investors and economic development officials. In 1995, South Carolinians recycled two-and-a-half times as many tons of materials as in 1994. The Southern States Waste Management Coalition recently published *Economic Benefits of Recycling in the Southern States,* which reported that 137,586 people are employed by the recycling industry, adding $18.5 billion in value to the recyclables processed or re-manufactured. In South Carolina, 10,900 people are employed in recycling, adding value of $958 million to recovered materials.

Two weeks before the passage of this bill I almost sabotaged my own efforts. In a successful coup, as the press put it, I wrested the chairmanship of the Joint Legislative Committee on Energy away from Senator Tom Moore. This was not an impulsive act. For thirteen years

I had served on the committee, hoping that it would do what it was charged to do—develop a comprehensive conservation program for the state. An early chairman, Senator Alan Carter, started the wheels in motion and produced a lot of paper, but somehow the effort came to an abrupt halt for some political reason I never fully understood. T. W. Edwards, the second chairman, worked on individual issues, but still no plan was produced. Moore was elected when Edwards was defeated at the polls, but the committee was preoccupied with controversies over oil overcharge funds. In 1991, when the committee director resigned, I begged Moore to take that opportunity to find a bright, young, aggressive professional with technical training. But he hired the secretary of the Senate Invitations Committee instead, which was a signal to me that we would not be capable of doing what I thought the committee should be doing. I did not want to depend on DHEC and industry lobbyists for my technical information. That would be reverting to the old days, when there was no technical staff to help us. We needed someone who was as detached from any special interest as possible in our political world. And I knew from my experience as chair of the Cultural Affairs Committee that a talented and energetic director would make the difference between keeping the status quo or moving new initiatives forward. At that point I realized the only way to achieve my goals was to be chairman and find that research director.

I asked Bob Sheheen, who was then speaker, to fill the empty House slots with members who would be as motivated as I was to get things done. He did. The committee had five House members and five senators. If I could get all the House members to vote for me and make sure they all got to the meeting on the day we elected officers, and if I could find one senator who would break with tradition and vote for a House member, that would put me in. The other dividing line was party. The three Democratic House members were enthusiastic, but I was not sure about B. L. Hendricks, a Democrat recently turned Republican, who might be influenced against me by Campbell. However, when I asked him for his vote, he commited to me, saying he liked my stance on energy matters, he thought I had worked hard, and deserved to be chairman. Although Moore was also a Democrat, I thought he was on better terms with Governor Campbell than I, which would not have been difficult. Campbell and I disagreed on nuclear waste policy, and we had a serious conflict about the oil overcharge funds from which the governor could propose grants, but over which the Energy Committee had veto power. I opposed some of the oil overcharge grants he made, sensing they were awarded more for political reasons than for merit. It was really hard to tell, because his aides did not let us see the numerical ratings of the many applications that came to them. My instincts about some of their proposals were validated by newspaper stories of the failure of a few funded projects and by a critical audit by the U.S. Department of Energy. I assumed there was the possibility that Campbell might push the Republican members to vote against me.

I thought Senator Phil Leventis would vote for me because he agreed more often with me on energy and hazardous waste issues than with Moore. But before I could talk with him, he left for the Persian Gulf with the South Carolina Air National Guard as a fighter pilot in Operation Desert Storm. I tried to reach him through his wife and his secretary. His wife was out of town, his secretary couldn't reach him. I tried to call him in Saudi Arabia to ask for his vote and proxy, but I couldn't make contact in time for the meeting. I had planned to tell Moore when he arrived at the meeting that I had all the House votes, giving him enough time to withdraw (but not enough time to turn my votes), but he arrived late. He rushed in, called for the vote, and was stunned—and furious—when he counted. Another senator had failed to show up, so Leventis's absence wasn't the sole cause of Moore losing. All five House members were present. Expressing indignation at the turn of events, no senator would accept the vice chairmanship.

Reports came to me that some senators took to the floor to denounce me, saying the vote was in very poor taste and upsetting to good working relationships between the House and Senate. And that some lobbyists were nervous. Tom Moore said it was unheard of for a House member to kick a senator out as chairman of a joint committee. Traditionally, senators either always chaired joint committees or at least they rotated the chairmanship among themselves and House members. He said he would call for another election, presumably when he had all his senators in place.

A *State* newspaper editorial titled "Power over Protocol" read:

"Heaven forbid that a House member should outrank a senator. Several senators were bent out of shape recently when Rep. Harriet Keyserling, D-Beaufort, bounced Sen. Tom Moore, D-Aiken, as chairman of a joint legislative committee on energy. The senators said they were suckered because House members called for a vote while two senators on the commitee were absent. OK, so the House did gang up on the Senate. So what? Sometimes, power politics must take precedence over protocol. The energy panel has been relatively laid back since it was created 13 years ago and charged with developing a comprehensive conservation program for the state. With an activist like Ms. Keyserling in the chair, the panel should be more aggressive in pursuing that commitment. That we applaud."

I'm happy to say that Tom did not retaliate by stopping the solid waste bill. But then, that would have been awkward for him to do. He chaired the blue-ribbon committee, and it was the Senate bill, his bill, that was being considered in the House at that time. When Phil Leventis returned from the wars, I told him what had happened and asked if he would vote for me in a second election. After some thought, he came back to me and told me he would. He also told Moore, to save him further embarrassment, and the election was not scheduled. Phil did this with some discomfort, I'm sure, in not going along with the custom of senators voting for senators. But he has never been afraid to act on his convictions, and he must have been convinced that I would devote more time and more energy than anyone else to work on energy conservation—which was one of his concerns as well. He agreed to fill the empty slot of vice chairman.

Tom Moore stayed on the committee and was helpful in passing the South Carolina Energy Conservation and Efficiency bill. Phil is still in the Senate, fighting lonely battles to protect the environment. Tom Moore went on to chair the important Children's Committee, replacing Nell Smith, who left the legislature the same year I did.

After my election as chair of the Energy Committee, I resigned the chairmanship of the Cultural Affairs Committee and started looking for a director for Energy. Again I was lucky to have John Clark arrive at my doorstep. John, with a doctorate in government and years of experience in Governor Riley's energy office, was perfect for the job I wanted done. I went through an unpleasantness when I replaced the director I inherited, but I was satisfied precedent was on my side. The former director went on to a position with the solid waste management program at the Department of Health and Environmental Control.

Just as the barge full of garbage looking for a home was the catalyst for pushing the state into solid waste management, the Persian Gulf War was the catalyst for revisiting energy conservation. I asked John to get together facts about South Carolina energy use, so we would have a better idea of what needed to be done—as well as have ammunition to help us move forward. The information he gathered was startling. South Carolina was spending over seven billion dollars per year on energy, ninety-eight percent of the natural resources for this energy was imported into the state. We produced less energy than any other state—we had no coal, oil, natural gas, or uranium. Our only in-state energy source was nuclear plants. Importing so much energy took more than six billion dollars out of our economy every year, tragic for a state which is capital poor to start with. We used our energy more inefficiently than most states, in a country which itself is inefficient by half compared to Japan and the industrialized countries of Europe. Which put us at a competitive disadvantage economically with just about everyone. The state had done little to encourage the development of renewable energy or alternative power. For instance, although we have lots of sunshine, we were forty-first in solar energy. While we in South Carolina have more cars and drive more miles than the national average, the state is last in public transportation. Our use of alternative, clean fuels for transportation was minimal, and there was no required maintenance on vehicle emission control. We ranked poorly in the extent to which energy use affects our air quality. This not only endangers our health, our wildlife, our crops, and our forests, it could prevent new industry from coming into the state in the future.

It was time for another blue-ribbon committee. I went to my friend Bill Verity, who was formerly chairman of Armco Steel and served as U.S. secretary of commerce during the Reagan administration. Bill had moved to Beaufort to retire but was a very active citizen, freely giving of his time and knowledge to the community. I gave him our newly found facts and asked if he would chair a committee to help shape an energy policy for the state, and he agreed to do this. I believe that his acceptance was the key to our success. He brought a sense of business conservatism which we needed to counterbalance my activist image. He also was a friend and supporter of Governor Campbell. But most important, he understood the problem and the need for action. He was a pleasant but firm chairman, respected by all the participants. He made every meeting, and I enjoyed the long drives up to Columbia with him discussing politics, issues, and our children.

Three months after I took over the chairmanship of the Energy Committee, Bill and I held a press conference and announced the formation of our blue-ribbon committee, which we called the Energy Policy Panel. We appointed twenty-four top-drawer people who represented industry, government, and environmentalists to serve on it. We also set up three technical working committees of eighty private and public sector experts to develop and sort out ideas and information for the panel to consider. And they did work—at over sixty meetings, for five months—without pay or even reimbursement of expenses. The panel and working groups brought credibility because they were so inclusive. Everyone involved in, or affected by, the changes we were to propose had input.

The panel's findings were as alarming as our initial survey: the state had no comprehensive energy policy, responsibility for the state's energy programs was unclear and divided among several different offices; the few existing programs had no long-range goals or plan and instead spent large sums of money on short term fixes and experiments; research efforts and public education on energy use was spotty, underfunded, and disconnected. The panel set goals to maximize energy conservation and efficiency, to encourage the development and use of indigenous, renewable energy resources, and to demand that government itself become more energy efficient, thereby setting an example and saving millions of taxpayer dollars.

After five months of sharing knowledge, of give-and-take, the panel unanimously adopted a long list of recommendations for meeting these goals. Most of them were incorporated into the South Carolina Energy Conservation and Efficiency bill, which I filed in

February with fifty-four House cosponsors, and which Senator Leventis filed in the Senate.

The bill tackled conservation on many fronts. It mandated long-range planning by the electric utilities, with incentives for energy conservation to ensure new plants are built only when necessary; energy conservation goals for state agencies, with procurement code changes enabling agencies to purchase energy-efficient lighting, insulation, heating, and cooling units and smaller, more fuel-efficient state vehicles; conservation construction standards for residential building and sales tax incentives for energy-efficient mobile homes (which constitute forty percent of new homes in our state!); creation of a study committee to identify and encourage use of alternative fuels for transportation; an assortment of transportation recommendations, from public and regional transportation, to high-occupancy vehicle and bicycle lanes. At the very core of all these recommendations is a permanent, professionally staffed State Energy Office to put all this in place.

My bill took a while to get out of Ways and Means Committee, with John Felder doing his best to slow it down in committee and on the floor. There was no official opposition from the Governor's Office, but rumor had it that they were quietly trying to undermine us. Jerry Beasley, the lobbyist for the Textile Manufacturers' Association, seemed to be agitating against it, but several members of the association said they favored the bill, that Jerry wasn't representing their views. One rumor had it that he was fronting for a textile manufacturer who was stirring it up for Campbell.

Meanwhile, the Senate bill was being held up by Senator Shealy, who was suspicious of it, and Senator Leatherman, who, it turned out, was building houses which would have to conform to it. John spent a lot of time with senators trying to find compromise language. And finally the bill passed and came over to the House. This time, the speaker sent it to the Agriculture and Natural Resources Committee, which studied it and made some changes in response to the special problems of a few industries. When there were firestorms—for instance, the home builders protesting double-paned windows—John and some of the technical people on our advisory committee would huddle with the complaining parties and work out language more acceptable to them. When the manufactured housing people protested the stricter energy standards, we appeased them with tax credits. We also had to patiently maneuver to find an acceptable balance between the rights of the private sector power companies and the electric co-ops. Our anti-anything-new-because-it-might-cost-more members, Jarvis Klapman and Herb Kirsh, tried to slow down the bill when it reached the floor.

But on the whole, John felt there was more nitpicking than determined opposition, caused by a general sense of unease at so many changes people didn't quite understand. No one, other than Jerry Beasley and his assistant, spoke openly against the whole bill. When the bill was passed by the House—during the turmoil of the last day of the session—it was rushed over to the Senate for concurrence. I walked over with it to make sure it was put on the desk and officially received. It was now or never, as far as I was concerned. John and Phil Leventis had to start negotiating again with Senator Leatherman and others. Unbelievably, it passed, with Phil pushing and pulling it through. It could be my swan song, my last legislative contribution to the state of South Carolina. Mission accomplished. Wasn't this the right time to leave?

But we still had to wait, with bated breath, to see if Governor Campbell would veto it. He did not like the creation of an independent energy office, letting it be known that he felt it was duplication of his Energy Office. Our response was that his office concentrated only on dispensing federal funds for heating for low-income people and oil overcharge grants for conservation projects. The panel's initial findings cited these functions as patchwork, not planning. We said the new office would not be duplication, it would be policy setting, and it was necessary to oversee the carrying out of the provisions of the Energy Conservation and Efficiency Act. I was well aware that Campbell resented my Energy Committee's oversight of those millions of oil overcharge dollars and was irked by our specifying, the year before, that five million of the seventy-five million dollars allotted to South Carolina be used to implement the solid waste management program.

During the struggles over an energy office, Fred Carter, director of the Budget and Control Board, offered constructive compromise suggestions. If the Energy Office was folded into the Budget and Control Board, he said, the governor would still have control, because he chairs the board. And if we provided that the new office would require no new personnel or funds, that would squelch the idea that it would be a costly new bureaucracy. The governor allowed the bill to pass without the veto, possibly because of Fred's rationale or possibly because Bill Verity urged him to. But the last day of the fiscal year, he vetoed the line item which funded the Joint Legislative Committee on Energy. John Clark and our secretary Phyllis Zander, both of whom had been in state government for many years, lost their jobs with one day's notice.

The governor's stated reason was that since there was a state Energy Office there was no need for a legislative committee. This was the first time in anyone's memory that the executive branch of government had made such a move against the legislative branch. The creation of joint committees was a legislative prerogative. The governor may have thought that if the committee had not funds, it would die and there would be no committee to interfere with his overcharge moneys. But we asked the attorney general for a ruling, and he interpreted the law to say a legislative committee could be discontinued only by a legislative action. And that could only be done by the legislature, which by then was out of session. Speaker Bob Sheheen found some House funds (even though he was no great fan of joint committees) and the Senate found some Senate funds which were patched together to pay John. A job was found for Phyllis (who was an exceptional secretary) to tide her over for the short time until her retirement. I resigned the chairmanship in anticipation of leaving the legislature. Phil Leventis was chairing other committees, so he supported Robert Barber, who was elected chairman (when Barber left, Phil took on the chairmanship).

The following year, when I was no longer there, Governor Campbell moved the people and the money from his energy office over to the State Energy Office. John Clark is now located there and tells me the program is going very well. I was invited to serve on an advisory committee to the Energy Office, and I am so pleased with what I see—high-quality professionalism and the absence of partisan politics in carrying out the provisions of our bill. The goals set for schools and state agencies to reduce energy use by ten percent in five years were more than met in one year. Through education, technical help, and an energy-bank partnership, the energy use per square foot was reduced by 13.5% in one year, saving the taxpayers $17.4 million. Several programs have been recognized nationally for innovativeness and effectiveness.

But as with any bill which affects any special interest, there is no such thing as a permanent conclusion. Early in the 1997 session, a bill was introduced in the House and rushed through a subcommittee at the behest of the electric utilities to do away with the integrated resources planning mandates for the utilities and the Public Service Commission, as provided by the Energy Act. However, when some of us were alerted to this, we sent the information we had developed on integrated resource planning to the authors of the proposed changes and begged them to slow their bill down until all sides were heard. They did, and the bill was amended in a way that left the heart of the Energy Act intact. The Senate followed their lead.

During those frantic two years of total immersion in solid waste and energy I offered other bills, just how many and how varied I had forgotten until I recently looked over my computerized "Sponsor's report" produced by Legislative Services. I didn't remember because I was so taken up by the energy bill that everything else was a blur. One was a health-care power of attorney, which was an addition to my original living will bill (passed); another a consumer protection bill regulating new small businesses selling and cashing checks (failed); judicial reform to change the method of selecting judges (failed); fixing an accounting problem for professional and occupational licensing agencies (passed); a resolution memorializing Congress to transfer savings in the military account to the domestic budget to meet the social and economic needs of the country (passed the House but not the Senate); an amendment to the Solid Waste Act to add a tax credit for recycling equipment (failed); a bill to require a health insurer to include coverage for mammograms and pap smears (failed)—and local bills for Beaufort County. Those that passed succeeded because others helped me work them through the system—either the committee that considered them or my cosponsors. Some that failed were filed the following year and passed. The energy bill consumed me—my attention, my time, my energy. This reinforced a lesson I myself had preached but didn't follow that year. To make change in an institution resistant to change you have to give your total commitment. I should not have taken on all those bills when my priority was energy, which required what passion I had left after fourteen years in the legislature. I filed most of the others because I was asked to, was gratified to be asked, and felt if I didn't do them, no one else would. That was my newly enlarged ego getting in the way of my usual pragmatism, a mistake many legislators make. My first few years, I filed so many bills that it was impossible to follow their progress or lack of progress through the committee system. Over the years, I learned to be more selective, to concentrate on a few important issues which I could effectively watchdog and lobby for. If you can't give it your all, it's best to forget it, for there will always be energetic opposition from some sector, and it is much easier for them to stop legislation than for me to get it passed.

During the energy bill wars I missed the armor-plated support of the Crazy Caucus (almost all but Bob Sheheen were gone by then), which had strengthened my spine, and its esprit de corps, which kept the adrenalin flowing and provided humor to cut through the tension. The fun was gone. I found myself sitting in my seat, looking around the hall and muttering to myself, "I hate it. I hate them." I hated the way some people treated each other. We didn't listen to each other, and we didn't respect each other. The civility was gone and was replaced by a tense, acrimonious, confrontational atmostphere. This wasn't my style of politics, and it took a toll on me physically. I suddenly found myself with an ulcer and high blood pressure. It was time to leave.

CHAPTER 20

Back to Beaufort

When I told Herbert that I thought it was time for me to leave the legislature, he warned me not to make such a big decision without a great deal of thought, certainly not when I was exhausted. He wondered if I would be bored with a life without pressure, excitement, and my name in the news. I told him I really wasn't rushing into this decision. I'd been thinking about it for over a year and had been trying to recruit another woman to take my place, one who would vote my way on the issues that mattered most to me. But with no luck, and seemingly no hope of finding one, I gave up on that. I asked Billy if he was interested in running for the seat, knowing that his political philosophy was close to mine and thinking that he would vote "right" on women's issues as often as the elusive woman I couldn't find. He was interested, but he hesitated, because it would mean a big change in his life. Part of his public relations business was managing campaigns for candidates and issues, and he felt he could no longer do this if elected. But the other side of him wanted to run. After working in Washington for congressmen and senators, he liked the idea of representing his own views, instead of those of others.

When I finally made my decision, he made his. He ran. His campaign was a tough one. His opponent was my first opponent, George O'Kelley, a popular lawyer in town. Billy was disappointed to find that my supporters were not necessarily his supporters. But he had his own friends and followers, he ran a good campaign, and he pulled it off. There was some talk by the opposition of a Keyserling dynasty, which may have caused some reluctance among my supporters to back Billy. There were also those who really didn't know him and weren't going to accept him just because he was my son, and we could understand that. When he ran the second time around, two years later, most of my supporters moved to his side. He had proved himself.

With all that taken care of, I discovered that there could indeed be a full and satisfying life after the legislature. Because of Herbert's warnings that I might be bored, I accepted every invitation that came my way to join committees and boards. The press, which seems to have a list of public figures they target for "comments" when particular issues crop up, had called on me over the years for opinions and background on quite a few issues—nuclear waste, the environment, women, the arts. A reporter told me recently that they also called me a lot because I was less guarded than most politicians, which could make for a spicier story. So people involved in those issues thought of me when they were looking for new board members or help on an advisory committee. I received lots of invitations, and my calendar filled up fast. No time for boredom. But after about a year, I realized I had overreacted to this concern about time on my hands, and I started to peel off committees. A few asked me to stay, leave my name on the letterhead, and miss meetings if I must. I declined. Missing meetings filled me with guilt.

At this writing I am down to a comfortable four or five selective causes. I still serve on the Spoleto Festival board after many years, my role being an unofficial, unpaid government affairs adviser. I am also a member of the board of the South Carolina Coastal Conservation League (SCCCL), which has a particular concern for preserving the coastal environment; the Beaufort Arts Council; the Palmetto Project, whose goal is to bring some sanity to the volcanic, highly politicized racial divisions in our state; an advisory committee to the State Energy Office; and an advisory committee to the recently formed Jewish Studies program at the College of Charleston. I am not involved in politics directly, other than lending moral or monetary support to candidates I admire.

On an impulse, I put out the word that I would be available as a consultant for environmental issues in which I had expertise. In 1995 I was asked to be the S.C. coordinator to work with a national coalition of environmental groups that sprang up as a response to the Republican agenda items that threatened environmental protections. Using my contacts with progressive business and political leaders, and in partnership with SCCCL, I developed a very effective South Carolina network, which helped convince Senator Hollings that the public was behind him. We gave him enough cover to stick with us. His was one of several important swing votes in the U.S. Senate which turned the tide against this special interest legislation.

Recently I accepted an invitation to serve on the Task Force to Study the Status of Women in State Government, a committee formed by the State Budget and Control Board to find ways to break the dense glass ceiling in state government. Years ago I drew up a resolution creating a similar task force, but was persuaded by the state personnel director that this problem was being addressed and "please don't make waves at this delicate time." I bowed to her plea, which I later regretted, for little improvement followed. I didn't try again because I saw little hope of getting another resolution through in an increasingly conservative legislature. But this new effort might just work. The Budget and Control Board has such clout, its director Fred Carter has such determination, and the impressive task force members have such credibility, that I'm sure that creative suggestions for increasing the numbers of women in top management positions will come out of the project, and I am pleased to be a part of the effort.

I look back with satisfaction at some of the projects I started or gave a boost to through the power of my office or through connections developed during my years in the legislature, projects which have added to the quality of life in Beaufort. Some might call this pork, but I don't. They were projects that were initiated and supported by the community and needed small boosts from state agencies whose missions were to provide these boosts.

When I retired I had a pile of chips to call in, and I called them. This was especially true in the arts, as a result of the networking I had done with state cultural agencies—and because I had supported their projects and guarded their budgets while chairing the Ways and Means Subcommittee that oversaw them. I had enjoyed working personally with all the agency heads, and they, in turn, knew I was their advocate, even though I might ask hard questions from time to time in committee meetings.

Just as I went full circle in energy conservation as a legislator, I went full circle in the arts. In my life prior to the legislature I had taken many small steps to build up cultural activities in Beaufort. In my last few years in the legislature, and as I returned to "civilian" life, I found myself able to take giant steps. I became good at putting people together with other people and causes, thanks to my matchmaker instincts—and the power and connections I had accrued.

When I was still on the Ways and Means Committee, I was able to push, on the House side, (Waddell's clout took care of the Senate) for an appropriation to match local and university funds to turn an aging public school building into an addition for the University of South Carolina-Beaufort. This school was just across the street from the university, which was bursting at the seams. The reconditioned building, though not quite the dream I dreamt of—a cultural arts center with artists' studios and music and drama classrooms for the public—now houses, in addition to academic classrooms, the Beaufort Arts Council and a great auditorium for concerts and theater, as well as an art gallery with rotating exhibits. It is now called the Performing Arts Center. I hope that when the university has a larger campus, this building will become a true community arts center and the classrooms will be turned over to the arts.

After it was completed word leaked out that the refurbished building was to be named for Senator James Waddell. A firestorm broke out. The Republicans protested because it was close to election time, saying that this was a political bone thrown to Waddell. The arts activists were furious because they felt if it was named for a person, that person should have been me. They knew that I had pressed hard on the local university administration in the early stages of the funding process to ensure the building would be an arts center. Waddell did not even attend arts events in Beaufort, they said, and was not a patron, so his name was inappropriate as a symbol. The firestorm caused the university to change direction and name it for no one. But Waddell, who no longer lives in Beaufort, will be remembered. There is still WJWJ (James Waddell Jr.), the public television station named for him, the Waddell

Mariculture Center near Hilton Head, and Waddell Road near his former home.

I mention this incident not to cite a slight to me but as an observation about the naming of public buildings, roads, and bridges for living elected officials. I have always been opposed to this, and I'm sorry I didn't initiate a bill to prohibit this political custom, although it probably wouldn't have passed. It seems to me to be a kind of pay-off by government agencies to their patrons for past and future favors. I am increasingly irritated by seeing one after another highways and streets named for legislators. Possibly my thoughts are influenced by the Jewish custom of not naming children after a living person, because that person might do something to disgrace the name before he or she dies. In fact, a bridge was named in Beaufort County for someone who did indeed get into trouble, and the bridge was renamed, after bitter debate.

I can understand and have no problem with the naming of buildings in institutions which are in large part funded by the generosity of a private donor; this is a legitimate tool of fund-raising. If a legislator has fought for years for a cause, like mental health or educational television, I can understand that his name should be linked with a permanent symbol of that cause, such as a hospital or even a TV station. But if a state legislator manages to extract some public money out of the pot of state funds for a local road or project, by virtue of his or her position on a committee which dispenses funds, and has that project named for him, that bothers me. In the case of the Performing Arts Center, it was rumored that it was the Columbia office of the university which proposed the Waddell name, because he was chairman of the Senate Finance Committee and a friend of the university.

Another concern about "namings" is that only men seem to be honored in this way. One reason could be that so few women have risen to the positions of power that stimulate such namings. Offhand (this has not been researched), I can think of no highway and only two buildings named for women: the Breed Leadership Center at the private Columbia College, named for successful businesswoman Johnnie Cordell Breed, who contributed substantially to the leadership program for women, and the Will Lou Grey Opportunity School for children in trouble, named for Will Lou Grey, who pioneered the idea. What an irony that both women have men's names.

I had several times helped start up an arts council in Beaufort to coordinate the scattered groups which competed for time and money, to have a community calendar to avoid conflicts, and to build a corps of supporters with a wider vision. But each effort disintegrated after a few years. In 1990, after the University of South Carolina-Beaufort Performing Arts Center was completed, I invited Scott Sanders, the director of the South Carolina Arts Commission, to meet with the many arts groups in town to advise them and community leaders as to the best way to start up and sustain a council. In a press release announcing Scott's visit, I said that the university administration had indicated a great interest in providing space to an arts council and being a partner to its efforts to coordinate and increase cultural activities in the community. This meeeting would be an excellent opportunity for artists and art supporters to collaborate, to express their needs and their suggestions, and to get advice from the director of our state arts commission.

A large and enthusiastic crowd showed up. We had follow-up meetings to discuss specifics. I talked my friend Betty Ann Mead, a relative newcomer to Beaufort who had been involved with the arts in Boston, into helping. That was probably my most important single contribution to the effort. Betty Ann, a native of Kentucky, a graduate of Emory and wife of a proper Bostonian, moved to Beaufort from Massachusetts. She is a dedicated gardener, an avid reader, and a dynamo. She put the new arts council on the road to success, thanks to her boundless energy, enthusiasm, and creativity. She and Dan Huff, a local teacher and musician, took on the task of writing bylaws. A board evolved out of the core group of attendees at the many meetings, a group which represented the many faces of Beaufort—several artists; a drama teacher at USC–B; a retired banker; the arts administrator of the school arts programs; Adrian King, formerly with the National Endowment for the Arts but at that time in Beaufort as a reporter for the *Charleston News and Courier*; the director of the County Recreation Department; the cultural director of Penn Center—to cite a few as examples of our diversity. We elected Betty Ann Mead as chairman, artist Sandy Williams as vice chair, and banker Bob Kerr as treasurer.

Scott Sanders had indicated to us that the S.C. Arts Commission gave grants to help budding arts councils. Agnes Garvin, a grants writer for the county, wrote a proposal to the Arts Commission for a grant to hire a paid director, and I wrote a supporting letter urging them to be generous, because this time I knew we could succeed. I reminded them that we had always depended solely on volunteer workers and that may have been why our efforts had collapsed in the past. Now we should try another way, with a paid, professional director. We got the grant.

Ken May, who worked for the Arts Commission, later said that their grant to us was the best grant money they ever spent. We hired Jan Newcomb as our director, and seven years later, our Beaufort Arts Council now has 650 members, a staff of two, and is by any measure a success which will continue to grow as Beaufort grows. Evidence of our success was that Jan was hired away from us last year by the state arts commission. Another reason for our growth, of course, are the many newcomers who moved from cities where they had enjoyed the cultural amenities, and want to continue to do so. Marian Draine, a regional coordinator from the state arts commission, comes regularly to Beaufort from Columbia to meet with our many local artists and presenters, to learn personally of their needs and wants. She also attends all our major arts events, a welcome and supportive presence.

When the city of Beaufort decided to rehabilitate the charming but delapidated Beaufort Museum, I was asked to serve on an advisory committee. Some members who were on the committee before I arrived were rushing forward with ideas about organizing and displaying the collection and found professional help. But money was a problem, and I suggested we take advantage of the free services offered by the State Museum. I called the director of the State Museum for guidance, and he sent the director of collections and interpretation to look us over and give us advice on the best way to proceed. This was not a special request: aid to small museums was part of the State Museum's mission. It was my knowing of this policy that was the key to getting help, and their knowing me may have speeded up the process. When the roof of this historic building needed fixing, a phone call to the director of the South Carolina Department of Archives and History also helped.

In 1986, when I chaired the Joint Legislative Committee on Cultural Affairs, I was invited to sit on the board of Spoleto Festival USA. In the early 1990s the festival found itself in a financial shambles after several years of conflict involving Maestro Gian Carlo Menotti. After the first brouhaha, several of the more generous board members resigned when the general manager, Nigel Redden, quit at the insistence of Menotti. The following year Menotti left, causing an exodus of his supporters. More money problems surfaced under a new management team. But Spoleto had become such an important part of the South Carolina scene, culturally and economically, that it had to be saved. I helped choreograph a meeting between the board's most influential members and state government leaders to educate the political leaders on the economic contributions Spoleto makes to the state and to discuss some kind of emergency aid. The state agreed to give Spoleto a loan. The loan is now being paid back, and other substantial debts have been reduced under the energetic leadership of banker Joel Smith, the board's present chairman, and the previous chairman Homer Burrous, who kept Spoleto alive through several tense years with unflagging good humor.

One of the perks of being on the board was the opportunity to meet the artists. It was fun to get to know Charles Wadsworth, who attended most of our meetings. Many credit Charles for the chamber music revival in this country. He founded and directed the Chamber Music Society of Lincoln Center and the chamber series in both Spoleto, Italy, and the Spoleto Festival USA in Charleston. Because of his skill in finding wonderful young musicians and selecting programs which not only please the audience but challenge them, and because of his folksy and charming introductions onstage of the music and the musicians, Charles Wadsworth is a star and his series a drawing card of Spoleto. (Just think about that: chamber music a drawing card in South Carolina!) When the Beaufort concert series was having a problem with programming I called Charles for advice. The net result of that conversation was three Wadsworth chamber concerts in Beaufort last year and five this year. His series is now solid and institutionalized at the university. We love him, and he loves Beaufort. Our audience has become so educated we no longer applaud between movements. After each concert, there is always someone in the audience heard to say, "Can you believe we are in Beaufort, South Carolina?" Other cities are now vying for Wadsworth concerts; Camden has taken the lead with a concert in last year's season, Hilton Head will have several this year, and Savannah is standing in line, waiting.

Randy Akers, director of the South Carolina Humanities Council, was a part of the cultural network which advised the Committee on Cultural Affairs. Before long, I was invited to sit on the council board. The Humanities Council, with counterparts in almost every state, is connected with and funded by the National Endowment for the Humanities and is dedicated to preserving cultural resources and providing access to the humanities for the people of South Carolina. In 1992, the board decided to put on a statewide humanities festival, and Beaufort was chosen to be the first site. There was some competition from other cities, but Beaufort was selected for several good reasons: a strong arts council, attractive inns and restaurants, a university, and our many cultural resources, including the unique African-American community of St. Helena Island, which would be featured. The arts council played a major role on the program planning committee, and we decided that one resource we should share with our visitors was the Hallelujah Singers. Certainly they were an example of a cultural resource to be recognized and preserved.

The Hallelujah Singers is a group of black women and a few men who sing spirituals and work songs going back to the time of slavery. The group was the creation of Marlene McGee Smalls, who had started a school of music and dance for children, with a focus on African-American art forms. After a struggle to cover expenses, she asked her students' parents if they would help raise funds by presenting a concert of African-American music. Marlene, a professional musician who moved here from Dayton, Ohio, coached the volunteers, many of whom sang in church choirs. There were wonderful natural voices in the group, some full and strong and some thin and reedy with unusual timbre.

They whipped up colorful plantation and African costumes, added some patter in the Gullah dialect to describe the customs and music of slave days, and put on a stunning performance in a small historic building, the first school for freed slaves in Beaufort. They were a sensation. They moved their concerts to a larger black church in the historic district, expanding their numbers and increasing their professionalism. The night they sang at the Humanities Council festival in Beaufort, a representative of the National Endowment for the Humanities (NEH) was in the audience, and was swept off her feet. Soon after, an invitation came to the group to perform at the NEH annual breakfast meeting in Washington, in a congressional office building, with an audience of council members from across the country and many congressmen. They received an emotional standing ovation and were featured in later Humanities Council publications.

Since that appearance they have been invited to perform in many states whose council members had heard them in Washington. They parlayed this triumph into an appearance in the movie *Forrest Gump* and provide part of that film's soundtrack. With that on their vita, we persuaded the Spoleto Festival to present them in the grand finale concert at Middleton Gardens, which usually is devoted to celebrated jazz artists. There were some critics who felt they were not professional enough for a Spoleto billing, but others loved their performance, clapping and stomping along with the singers. They are scheduled to perform at Spoleto again in 1998. In the past few years the Hallelujah Singers have become regulars at Hilton Head and other resorts which attract tourists and newcomers looking for local color. In 1997 they cut a professionally recorded CD which they celebrated with a full house in the Beaufort Performing Arts Center. My son Paul and his partner at the Beaufort educational television station spent three years photographing and recording the group and have produced a film about their music and traditions which is scheduled to be shown on PBS stations across the country. How exciting it was to watch the flowering of this small group, and its step-by-step progression from a small room in a small town to the national spotlight of PBS. And how pleasing it was to play even a small role in this amazing success story. An added joy was to feel that not only was I carrying on my parents' tradition of helping talented musicians, but so was the next generation, Paul, Billy and Judy, who contributed their advice and skills when asked by Marlene.

Another Beaufort board I served on was Penn Center, whose history I described earlier. Once Penn had financial security from a substantial endowment built primarily by Philadelphia and Boston contributors. But Penn came on hard times, beginning in the early 1970s; the endowment was dissipated, and most of the fifteen buildings on the campus fell into disrepair. When it was placed on the National Trust for Historic Preservation's most endangered historic sites list in 1990 and as the interest grew in preservation of the sea island culture, I worked to generate support for state funds to repair the buildings and help shore up a flagging program.

To get state funding on the scale we were looking for, we first had to find a state agency willing to be responsible for oversite of the funds and to give direction to the project. The University of South Carolina, whose branch in Beaufort was already partnered with Penn in an early childhood program, agreed to be that agency. Fred Sheheen, the director of the S.C. Commission on Higher Education which oversees all programs for all higher education institutions, recommended this partnership, with funds for this project to be put into a line item of the bond bill, within the university's section. As I was on the Ways and Means Committee, I was in a position to fight for this line item, and indeed I had to fight. That same year, Hilton Head was pressing for a large state contribution for its new cultural center, and Senator Waddell, who served Hilton Head as well as Beaufort, agreed to put in four million dollars for Hilton Head. He then said he could do no more for the Beaufort area. When the bill came over to the Ways and Means Committee without funds for Penn, I took one million of the four million dollars and placed it in the university's section for Penn. It was tough to go against one's senior delegation member, one who had helped me in other budget battles, but this project was too important to be subordinated by personal relationships. I felt it was now or never for Penn; these historic buildings could collapse without immediate help, and the local community had no hope of raising the needed funds.

The $1 million was reduced to $900,000 when every item in the bond bill was reduced by ten percent. But that $900,000 was a great boost in restoring an old building for a new museum and the development of a permanent collection for the museum. Billy, who helped Penn with their capital campaign, developed a comprehensive long-range plan and mission statement. He spent months building an advocacy team comprised of all the top state officials, including the governor, the congressional delegation, and the state and congressional black caucuses. He and George Terry, then director of the University's McKissick Museum, parlayed the $900,000 into $3 million to rebuild the buildings and create an endowment to support the cultural programs. The funds came from the United States Department of the Interior with the help of Senator Fritz Hollings and from the National Endowment for the Humanities, with the help of the university. It may have helped that Billy had worked for Fritz for quite a few years, and I with the NEH on other matters.

Although the campus has been enormously improved by both the infusion of funds and technical assistance from the university, the project has not been without problems. In the agreement, the university was to be connected to Penn by a partnership board. But the board rarely met, certainly not enough to establish the trust and bonds envisioned. Tensions cropped up between the institutions. Penn needed the technical help the university had to offer but resisted being overseen by the university; the university wanted to assist but felt pushed away when trying to monitor specific programs for which the funds were earmarked and for which the university was responsible. And I felt caught in the middle—responsible for bringing the funds and the university to Penn and worried about proposed deviations from the agreement, but still a Penn board member. So far they have both clung to the connection, with neither side giving up what they perceive as their obligations to their own constituencies. I am no longer on the Penn board, and I am relieved to have others do the worrying about this problem.

I am told by those more experienced than I that such tensions over control are common within minority institutions where the minority is very protective of its identity and its power and becomes almost paranoid in its fear of being taken over or controlled by others. (No doubt historical evidence would show these fears justified in some cases.) Time, patience, and real effort must be expended to build trust and knead out these tensions. But until then, racism on both sides creeps in. And so it was with Penn. While I was on the board, several white members who could have been very productive left the board before their terms were up. I remember particularly two women who were disturbed by what they saw as a departure from the mission of integration that had drawn them and uncomfortable with the tension at the meetings. One was the daughter of a former South Carolina governor, another a great-grandniece of one of the founders. Several black members also expressed anxiety. But certainly the cause of Penn is a good one, and the reasons for the university involvement were valid. Both institutions have something to gain from success and much to lose from failure.

In 1992, Beaufort County Council decided that it was time to look at the unfettered way the county was growing. Overcrowded highways and schools and growing demands for water and sewer were continuously surfacing. The public was getting restless. We had a planning commission, but it was kept busy with short-term crises and had no time for long-term planning. The Target 2010 Committee was appointed to address the problem, and I was asked to chair the growth management subcommittee. I accepted. The thirty-odd people on my committee worked for a year and produced a quite professional report, with recommendations. Unfortunately, the report sat on a shelf for a year, while all around us subdivisions kept popping up. That was in itself depressing, but what really irritated me was to discover that while we were trying to find ways to control growth, the county was negotiating without our knowledge with Sun City developers to build a Sun City between Beaufort and Hilton Head, with over five thousand new houses, thereby increasing the county population by more than ten percent, just counting the occupants. This did not include all the newcomers who would flock in to build the houses and provide services.

A year after our report was delivered, the county created yet another committee to study the various Target 2010 reports. I was offered an invitation to participate, but I declined. But others accepted, and work is still going on. Although everyone says we must manage our growth, when you get down to the specifics of "where" and "how," progress slows down. And as we wait, more subdivisions are being approved. Some skeptics feel that by the time some plan is adopted there will be no undeveloped land left to manage. I guess the basic question is whether county council will have the political will to put a recommended plan in place and write ordinances that will make it effective. In 1996, the legislature mandated that every county develop a comprehensive growth plan. Beaufort was the first to get started, and developers across the state are watching us with apprehension. As an antidote to whatever comes, the developers and allied industries are pushing the legislature to pass a "takings" bill which would deter zoning and land-use planning. Which could make the whole question of growth management moot. How ironic . . . and how sad: one year mandating such planning, the next year trying to curb it. The House passed the "takings" bill in 1997. Let's hope the Senate has the sense to stop it.

Despite the full plate of projects and causes, I managed to keep intact my family life and my female role as wife, mother, and finally grandmother. My husband, until 1997, was still practicing medicine nonstop, except for the two-week vacations we finally began to take. And I have more time for friends.

My idea of a really good evening has always been to go to a small dinner party or give one of my own, which was the way my parents entertained. But in the early days in Beaufort, young children, a small house, and a husband I could never count on to be home made that difficult. The chosen form of entertaining in Beaufort was the large cocktail party. Herbert didn't drink, and I didn't enjoy conversations which were interrupted before they ever got going.

But eventually, we outgrew these disincentives to dinner parties. We moved into a larger house with a great expanse of living room, dining room, and "playroom" all running together. The children grew older. And I learned to cope if Herbert didn't show up. And then there was wonderful Maybelle Mack, who made entertaining so much easier. I, like my mother, am not a good cook. But I liked cookbooks and collected recipes. Maybelle could take any recipe and make it even better than it was.

By the 1960s and 1970s I had a small cluster of young friends with whom I could comfortably talk politics and who read the same papers and books I did. But their numbers changed as they moved on to other places, other careers. I kept looking for replacements, especially those with common interests or similar backgrounds. These eagerly awaited strangers eventually started arriving in the late 1970s, as the influx into Beaufort changed from a trickle to a flood. The irony was that by the time they came I had less time to get to know them and to take advantage of their presence. There were too many functions to attend and not enough time to spruce up the house. I was away three days a week in Columbia. But it is nice to know there are now so many interesting, attractive, and obviously wise newcomers who have chosen to live in Beaufort, a far more cosmopolitan town now than when I first came here fifty-odd years ago. And that they will be here when I finish this book and have time to get to know them.

While evenings with friends were nourishment for my psyche and exercise for my brain, tennis was the preferred exercise for my body. Herbert and I started taking tennis seriously over thirty years ago, after Herbert found that even nine holes of golf took too long for a general practitioner with no partner to back him up. One day, Ed Burger, a young Navy doctor stationed at the Marine Corps Air Station, and his wife Sarah mentioned that they were tennis players. I had played some tennis in New York's Central Park and at college; Herbert grew up with a tennis court in his backyard but hadn't played in years. Sarah challenged us to mixed doubles with them, and we hesitantly accepted. They were young athletes who rode bicycles around town with their children strapped to their backs. Much to our surprise and theirs, we won. This was so exciting we decided to build a tennis court at our new home in the woods.

For several years we had the only decent tennis court in town, and the few tennis players in Beaufort used to congregate at our court every weekend. There were no other women who played once the Burgers left, so I played with the men. They tolerated me, usually pairing me with the strongest player, Don Hanna. My game improved under Don's tutelage. Eventually more tennis players (including women) moved to Beaufort, and courts were built by the city and then by the private clubs which followed development. Loie and Charlie Towers, avid players from Long Island, moved to town and found us. We were pretty evenly matched, and we played mixed doubles every Thursday for seventeen years, until this year, when Charlie's ankles and my knees gave out. (Herbert and Loie are still going strong.) I would jump into my car when the legislature adjourned Thursday at noon, drive for two-and-a-half hours, change clothes and be ready for tennis. How wonderful to be out in the fresh air, shutting politics out of my mind (when I could). Herbert and I began to play mixed doubles, and Loie and I women's doubles, in local tournaments, then in the annual state tournament. Loie and I finally won (once) the fifty-five-year-old women's doubles in the state tournament. I had a strong forehand, the result of playing with men, but Loie was steady, and it was her steadiness that made the difference.

I always felt at a disadvantage in tournaments, because I could only play once or twice a week and was always rushing and thinking about what I had to do tomorrow. I rarely played competitively and so was never in shape. I also had to adjust to the heat after sitting in the overly air-conditioned legislature. All the others who played the circuit seemed to play tennis every day, were strong and tanned, lean, consistent, and heat-resistant. As we got older and reached the age group in which the competition started thinning out, Herbert and I reached the state finals several times. But I was not steady enough for us to beat the champions, John Fowler and Chris Covington, who stayed in first place for years in whatever age group they moved to. Herbert still loved to go to the tournaments, which he considered the best form of vacation. His only problem was in finding partners. Aging takes a toll on doubles teams, but he managed to have first-place wins several times in later years with pick-up partners, because he had great anticipation and strong legs from walking miles everyday in the hospital corridors. Loie and Charlie started spending long summers in Vermont and were not available as partners. Herbert's partners also dropped out. My knees became impossible. Three years ago we finally exchanged the annual state tournament for travels in Europe.

I remember the year that I traumatized my knees for the first time, which probably hastened their decline. Loie and I were invited to represent South Carolina's team in the fifty-five-year-old women's division in a Southeast regional tournament held in Charleston (although we were over sixty). It started on a Thursday. I did my usual rush out of Columbia at noon, drove to Charleston, jumped into tennis clothes, and played for the first time in two weeks. It was budget time at the State House, and that meant long days and weeks at work. There was no time to warm up. This was not a relaxed social game. It was very competitive. We had several long matches, straining and stretching ourselves to the limit. And we won. But my unexercised knees took a beating from which they never fully recovered. Tennis was a great hobby, and I was so looking forward to playing on a level playing field with my opponents after retirement. But now that I have time to play tennis as others do, with time to practice and warm up, my knees won't let me. Perhaps we will go back to golf now that Herbert is retired. Until then, I will take more time to sit on my old dock on the creek and watch the fish jump, the crabs scuttle, and the blue herons take off. And enjoy my grandchildren.

Tennis added something else besides good exercise and fun to my life. It brought me some unexpected political allies, such as the retired Marine and Army general who wrote letters for me during my campaigns. We didn't talk politics much, and we didn't agree on some issues, but they knew me as a fair fighter. Several of the women players volunteered in my campaign or attended my functions. Many were Republicans. I know their allegiance to me was very irritating to the Republican Party, which just didn't understand the bonding that takes place on a tennis court.

After I retired, the Beaufort Chamber of Commerce and the arts council thanked me for my service with a wonderful "tribute" at the Performing Arts Center. People actually paid to attend, with proceeds going to the arts council and toward a portrait of me which now hangs in the county courthouse. What a lovely evening. Bud Ferillo came down from Columbia to be a wonderful master of ceremonies, telling about my life in the legislature, much like a roast but classier. I didn't often talk in Beaufort about the details of my life in Columbia. If I had described my victories and my powerful friends, I would have seemed a braggart. If I had complained about the hard work, failures, and enemies, I would have seemed a whiner. So a lot of what the people of Beaufort heard that evening was new to them. My Crazy Caucus friends, Speaker Bob Sheheen and Justice Jean Toal, talked about my contributions to our team so sweetly my eyes started welling up. Bob said he was probably the only Lebanese House speaker in the country with a "Jewish mother." His voice quavered. More tears.

Nell Smith came from Easley and spoke about our various battles together, as well as the companionship we provided each other during those times when it was an especially lonely place for women. (When Bud introduced Nell he called us the "Thelma and Louise" of the legislature.) Governor Riley, who had just been appointed secretary of education, couldn't come but sent his aide, Terry Peterson, to read his message. Scott Sanders, the arts commission director, had just moved to Washington to take a high-level position at the National Endowment for the Arts, but she came and talked about our years of working together. Robbie Wright, the black school principal, talked of the projects we worked on together, such as the bust of Robert Smalls. Nancy Thomas reminisced about starting the League of Women Voters. And Larry Mark, president of the Beaufort Chamber of Commerce, spoke about my being his teacher in Sunday school as well as my contributions to the city and county. The Hallelujah Singers opened the ceremony with some wonderful, spirited songs. Marlene McGee Smalls brought the house down with sentimental words (more tears) and a soaring rendition of "My Way."

It was a very emotional evening. I felt very proud and very happy that my community and friends poured out these words with such afffection, which seemed to me, at least, so much more sincere than I had heard at other retirement parties. But I suppose every honoree feels that way. I'd heard so much praise, and seen so many plaques, given to people who had done not very much that awards and honors had become devalued for me. But not this tribute. This was real, from the heart. Again, I suppose every honoree feels that way.

I was especially proud of the portrait which was unveiled that evening. I remembered the words of Madelaine Kunin describing the effect of the "pictures on the wall" which shaped the mental image of what a governor or a senator looked like—a middle-aged, white male in a dark suit. And I was touched that the idea started with Billy, who asked the Clerk of Court Henry Jackson if it wouldn't be fitting to have my portrait hanging in the courthouse after eighteen years of service to Beaufort County. I would be the first woman to be so honored in a Beaufort County office building. Henry said he thought that was an excellent idea, but the portrait would have to fit well with the other portraits of two legislators and one congressman already there. The artist went to look at the other portraits. She came back and said, "Billy, there is no way I can make Harriet look like those men in black suits." She didn't, but they accepted her portrait of me sitting relaxed in a red jacket, leaning forward in my chair, twiddling my eyeglasses in a typical pose. Quite a contrast to the three male legislators standing stiffly in their frames, in their dark suits. I will be noticed, and, I hope this portrait will change the image of a legislator in the minds of those sitting in the courtroom. The sweetest touch was that the artist was Sue Graber, my longtime friend.

Another unexpected tribute was a series of billboards that suddenly popped up around town with my picture and large, bold words "Thank you Harriet for your fine years of public service." They were a gift to me from the billboard company which was especially surprising since I had pushed for so long to eliminate highway billboards. Perhaps they were trying to show me the good side of billboards. Whatever prompted them,and no matter my lack of enthusiasm for billboards, I was touched by this public praise.

Lest anyone think my head was completely swollen from all this "appreciation" I can honestly say "Not completely." I realized I hadn't been totally cured of my old self-deprecation when I read, and immediately identified with, the words of Sir Isaiah Berlin, a noted and much-honored British philosopher. His words were: "I have been overestimated all my life. I will not pretend that this has been a source of grave distress. As someone once said to me, it is much nicer to receive more than one's due, and I can not deny it. All the same, I cannot deceive myself."

Four years later, when Herbert retired from his medical practice, his turn came to receive community thanks. The Beaufort Hospital gave him a wonderful retirement party to celebrate fifty years of practice and his dedicated service to the hospital and the community. Several young doctors spoke about his work and his readiness to treat everyone, with or without pay. They cited his loyalty to the Beaufort-Jasper Comprehensive Health Services, on whose board he has served since it opened its doors over twenty-five years ago, when it was created by Senator Hollings in response to stories of poverty and the lack of health care for the poor in our area. Lou Roempke, an old-timer, told affectionate and humorous stories about him. The most touching tribute was from Dr. Elijah Washington, an obstetrician and a Beaufort native whose mother was a cook for friends of ours. He carried to the podium a worn doctor's black bag and told the audience that when he graduated from medical school Herbert gave him that black bag, that Herbert was his mentor and had set an example for him of what a dedicated doctor should be. It was announced that a new ward would be named for Herbert, presided over by his portrait. The ceremony was set in a park, on a high bluff overlooking the Beaufort River, next to the hospital. The sun shone brightly, but even when the wind came roaring off the river, all but the very elderly stayed through the whole program. The newspapers dedicated several pages, before and after, to Herbert and his contributions to the people of Beaufort. It was a very fitting way to end a long and dedicated career. It was time that the spotlight had finally moved to him.

Writing this book has been an interesting, all-consuming experience. I bought several autobiographies, looking for ideas on how best to tell my story, but most are still waiting to be read. I was too impatient to get on with writing to take the time to read them. One I did read because once opened I couldn't put it down was the autobiography of Helen Suzman, who served valiantly in the South African Parliament for over forty years, under almost unbelievable pressures. Her story gave me great pause—and a new and humbling perspective about my own political life. Mrs. Suzman was one of a very few whites opposed to apartheid, and the lone member of the Liberal Party to sit in the Parliament for many years. In debate on the floor she was not only castigated for her political views, she endured anti-Semitic slurs as well. Swimming against the tide is a relative challenge, in time and place, and my political life in South Carolina in the recent past was a piece of cake compared to hers in South Africa in those bitter years.

Because I have such a poor memory, and because I rarely had looked back into my files full of papers, collected for over twenty years as a substitute for memory, when I finally started to dig into them to trigger my memory, I was jolted over and over again by reminders of events in my life I had completely forgotten. Friends also reminded me of their favorite stories and urged me to include them in this book.

One Billy recently reminded me of, with great glee, was the day when I was to address the Junior League in Greenville about women's issues. As was the custom for legislators when giving a work-related speech far from home, I asked the Aeronautics Commission if they could fly me to Greenville, which was over a four-hour drive one way by car. They made arrangements for me to be picked up at the Marine Corps Air Station. When I arrived at the air station, I didn't see a state pilot or plane I knew. I walked out on the strip, and seeing only a young woman standing next to a very small plane, I asked her if she had seen anything of the pilot or plane I was waiting for. She told me she was the pilot, and this was the plane. I really hate to admit it, but I had a sinking feeling. Wasn't she too young and inexperienced to be flying? Was that plane safe? Even worse, I knew why I was uneasy, and I was ashamed of myself. I climbed in, without letting on to my anxiety, I hope. I had a safe and pleasant trip and made my speech about equal opportunity for women, with the afternoon's experience giving me a new insight into the built-in problems of preconceptions. I learned later that my pilot had been with the commission awhile and had an excellent reputation. Why she was rarely assigned to legislators and why she was flying that small plane, I could only guess.

An incident I was reminded of by my files was the time I was a panelist in the early days of the now famous Renaissence Weekend started by Phil and Linda Lader at Hilton Head. I was assigned to a panel discussing the Reagan welfare programs, I guess as a counterpoint to David Gergen, who was also on the panel. I had gathered lots of facts and figures on this subject in preparation for my visit as part of a delegation from the National Conference of State Legislatures to the Reagan White House. As I didn't have an opportunity to speak there, I was going to make up for that here, and lay out all my information about the negative effects of the New Federalism. Gergen was very gentlemanly and low-key. He stated his case, then sat back quietly, as one was supposed to do, while I persistently tried to drive home my points. I was probably as irritating (and as effective) as a flea on an elephant, and I all but said, "Why can't you understand?" I know I overplayed my role there. I was surprised to be invited back.

In leafing through my correspondence files I was amused to see how punchy my letters were in answering slurs and attacks on me, which were actually pretty rare. I was sharp and bold, usually ending with a twist of a knife in my critic's back. This was so different from how I saw myself or how I behaved face to face—perhaps they were the deterrent that kept others from writing nasty letters to the editor about me. They evoked more sidewalk praise than the more serious articles I wrote. A few critical letters seemed to be written for political reasons, to discredit me rather than discuss whatever issue was manufactured for that purpose. And so if I stuck to the issue, it was easier for me to discredit the writers, for their knowledge of the issue was shallow and mine was deep. Occasionally there was a letter by an NRA member violently opposing my seven-day waiting period for guns, or an opponent from the religious right against my sex education stance. How sensitive I was to criticism, even when I understood its inevitability.

I have been relieved to find out that in retirement I don't miss the title or the perks that go with the title of a legislator. The only time I feel a pang is when people take a long time to return my telephone calls. But that may be just how things are today, nothing personal. Everyone, including myself, is slow in responding to everything. What was most important to me as a legislator were the issues, the friendships, the victorious battles, the feeling that I had contributed towards the improvement of some people's day-to-day lives. And I believe these are the goals and priorities of many other women who have been down the same path. What I do grieve about is the reversal of some of the steps forward we made and the political environment which brought on these reversals. I say this, fully understanding that no laws are permanent—and that others feel they are improving the world by undoing what we reformers did.

Which laws stand and which fall at a particular time depends on the political climate and the public will. And that will depends in turn upon the public's knowledge. I agree so strongly with the credo of the League of Women Voters that to have a healthy democracy citizens must have the information they need to participate in the political process. And they must understand how public policies will affect them. And how to make their voices heard. As Abraham Lincoln said, "Public sentiment is everything: with public sentiment, nothing can fail; without it, nothing can succeed."

Halfway through this book I realized with a start how warlike my vocabulary was as I described my experiences in politics. That was amusing to me, for I thought of myself as peaceful, with a dislike for confrontation. No more. Everything seemed to be a fight, a battle, a war, a crusade, a preemptive strike; weapons abound, as do enemies, attacks, defenses, tactics, strategies, siege mentality, power. Well, that's the way it was for me. And when there was a squad or a platoon or company on my side, it was invigorating. When there wasn't, it was debilitating—especially when I cared passionately about the outcome. Caring passionately was another change wrought in me by eighteen years in politics. As my ego gradually built up, it allowed me to feel passionate about causes and people. In my other life I would not let myself feel so strongly about politics or anything else, because I didn't see myself as able to do anything about them. Why risk unsatisfied passion, my subconscious must have signaled me. But when I finally found myself in a position of knowing I could make a difference, the passion came bubbling up, like adrenalin during stress. Which is fortunate, because without the intensity and drive created by passion, I could not have won any of those battles and I would not have challenged others, even when I knew they were wrong and I was right. My passion turned reticence into assertiveness, another weapon needed for making change. This, of course, has a downside. I now may seem to others too stubborn, too smug in my opinons, too dismissive of others—especially those others with whom I disagree!

But my husband and my children seem to like my new persona, and so do I. I like the fact that I can openly disagree with others and not worry that I may discomfort them or that they might not like me if

I challenge them. I am no longer inhibited by a fear of unsettling someone or feeling disapproved of. I like my new freedom to speak my mind. I feel released from my old shackles of insecurity and timidity. I have learned an important lesson—that a traditional woman, whose own desires and pursuits are always secondary to those of a man, may lead a marginal life. I am grateful that I escaped that fate by becoming a person unto myself and that my husband and children applaud that change.

I also changed my view of power, which I had always thought of in the negative terms of abuse and self-aggrandizement. As with passion, I didn't seek power because, first of all, I saw it as just an ego trip, and secondly, I never saw myself able (or qualified?) to achieve it. All that changed when it came my way. I realized that without power, either direct or indirect, I was less likely to reach my goals. I found how sweet it was when I became chair of a committee. I could set the agenda and make sure we would always reach the items I wanted taken up. I could set meeting times, to make sure I could always be there. I could provide incentives to other members to join me on whatever crusade I happened to be on at the time. My power also attracted respect on side issues, giving my views more weight and public attention. And wasn't that why I was in politics? To push my causes? The media respected power, and that was very important for my causes. It is still gratifying when friends call me to ask my opinion about a candidate or referendum issue. Their votes added to my vote give my candidate or my position a better chance. So I appreciate the good side of power; I enjoy power. I also understand that those with power have an obligation to use it for the common good. There are many wise people who have defined power, its uses and abuses. The quote I can identify best with is from Theodore Roosevelt: "Power undirected by high purpose spells calamity; and high purpose by itself is useless if the power to put it into effect is lacking."

I want more women to have power, to build their egos, to become passionate, to get involved in making this a better state and a healthier nation. For the odds are, that when women gain power, they will use it for the common good. As it happened for me, it can happen for them.

Index

Index